Ableton Live 9 Power!
The Comprehensive Guide

Jon Margulies

Cengage Learning PTR

CENGAGE
Learning®

Professional • Technical • Reference

Australia • Brazil • Japan • Korea • Mexico • Singapore • Spain • United Kingdom • United States

Ableton Live 9 Power!:
The Comprehensive Guide
Jon Margulies

Publisher and General Manager,
Cengage Learning PTR: Stacy L. Hiquet

Associate Director of Marketing:
Sarah Panella

Manager of Editorial Services:
Heather Talbot

Senior Marketing Manager:
Mark Hughes

Acquisitions Editor: Orren Merton

Project and Copy Editor: Marta Justak

Technical Reviewer: Brian Jackson

Interior Layout Tech: MPS Limited

Cover Designer: Mike Tanamachi

Indexer: Larry Sweazy

Proofreader: Megan Belanger

For product information and technology assistance, contact us at
Cengage Learning Customer & Sales Support, 1-800-354-9706

For permission to use material from this text or product,
submit all requests online at **cengage.com/permissions**

Further permissions questions can be emailed to
permissionrequest@cengage.com

Library of Congress Control Number: 2013932037

ISBN-13: 978-1-285-45540-2

ISBN-10: 1-285-45540-1

Cengage Learning PTR

20 Channel Center Street

Boston, MA 02210

USA

Cengage Learning is a leading provider of customized learning solutions with office locations around the globe, including Singapore, the United Kingdom, Australia, Mexico, Brazil, and Japan. Locate your local office at: **international. cengage.com/region**

Cengage Learning products are represented in Canada by Nelson Education, Ltd.

For your lifelong learning solutions, visit **cengageptr.com**

Visit our corporate website at **cengage.com**

Printed in the United States of America
2 3 4 5 6 7 15 14

Acknowledgments

Many thanks to everyone whom I've had the pleasure of working with on this book: Marta Justak for editing me and making sure I make sense, Brian Jackson for really knowing his stuff and being a great technical editor, and Orren Merton for giving me the chance to do this book and overseeing the project. I'd also like to extend my gratitude to the fine folks at Ableton for all their support, particularly Dennis DeSantis who was always available to answer questions and kick around tricky concepts.

About the Author

Jon Margulies is a producer and performing artist who has been called the "Mr. Miyagi" of Ableton Live. A lifelong professional musician and computer wizard, Margulies has performed as "Hobotech" at festivals such as Coachella, SXSW, Winter Music Conference, and Burning Man. He is the author of *Ableton Live 7 Power!* and *Ableton Live 8 Power!*, and the co-author of *Your Ableton Live Studio*. Visit hobo-tech.com for Jon's latest Ableton Live tips and music downloads.

Contents

Chapter 4 Making Music in Live

Chapter 5 Clips

Chapter 9 Live's Audio Effects   197

Chapter 10 Live's MIDI Effects

Chapter 11 Remote Control

Introduction

Ableton Live 9 Power!: The Comprehensive Guide is an all-inclusive guide to making music with Ableton's revolutionary live performance and studio software. Written for all Live users, from beginners to seasoned pros, this book explores each fundamental feature in Live, although it does presume a basic familiarity with music making and digital audio. This book is intended to supplement and expand on the information included in the Live manual and built-in lessons, so don't forget to take advantage of these great resources. Finally, this book also includes downloadable materials, which can be found at www.hobo-tech.com/livepower.

What You'll Find in This Book

You'll find the following areas covered in this book:

▷ Composing, arranging, and mixing music with Live.
▷ Using Live's built-in instruments and effects, and working with plug-ins.
▷ Performing with Live on stage.
▷ Essential information on Live's add-ons including Max For Live and the Push hardware controller

And much more!

Who This Book Is For

This book is for anyone who wants a solid foundation in using Ableton Live. While it contains all of the basic information needed by beginners, it also delves into deeper topics, providing real-world tips and examples for power users.

How This Book Is Organized

This book starts out with an overview of the most important concepts of Live, explaining essential aspects of the interface and outlining Live's unique workflow. The following chapters provide a detailed and highly practical reference guide to topics such as clips, tracks, devices, and hardware control. The final chapters of the book are devoted to important concepts for performance and useful advanced techniques.

Companion Website Downloads

You may download the companion website files from www.hobo-tech.com/livepower or www.cengageptr.com/downloads.

Live 9

E VERY SO OFTEN, a new piece of technology or software application makes an indelible mark on the way things are done. Ableton's Live has instigated a revolution in the audio software world by transforming computers into playable musical instruments, without sacrificing the power that digital audio workstations are known for. You'll find all the features you'd expect, such as multitrack audio and MIDI recording, nonlinear editing, quantization, pitch shifting, freezing, delay compensation, and more. This comes as the culmination of years of software development infused with DJ and electronic music-making instincts.

Live is also widely used for DJing, live performance, sound installations, and just about any on-stage or non-studio use you can imagine. Unlike other software programs that are based on a traditional DJ paradigm, Live allows artists to create a highly customized performance environment, limited only by imagination. And with the introduction of Max For Live in version 8, Live has an ever expanding community of programmers creating add-on devices to extend the program's functionality.

What Is Live?

Live is a program written for musicians by musicians. Initially, Robert Henke and Gerhard Behles (paired in the Berlin-based electronica group Monolake) were looking for a better way to create their own music through the use of a computer. Both were experienced sound designers and had spent time working for Native Instruments, one of the industry's chief authorities on software synthesizers and sound design software. At the time, the industry lacked a user-friendly software application conducive to creating music as a musician would—both intuitively and spontaneously.

In 2000, they formed Ableton and released Live 1.0, an audio-only program oriented around live performance (hence the name!). What made Live so unique from day one was the Session View, a customizable grid, which is used to organize and play musical elements (such as drum loops, guitar riffs, and synthesizer parts).

While most other music sequencers are organized around a timeline, which is used to lay out musical elements in a left-to-right fashion, Live's Session view allows musical elements to be composed on the fly and mixed-and-matched at will—a highly fluid and interactive process that was traditionally the domain of hardware synths, loopers, and drum machines (see Figure 1.1). Live combines this workflow with the power of modern software, giving you the best of both worlds.

MIDI: Musical Instrument Digital Interface

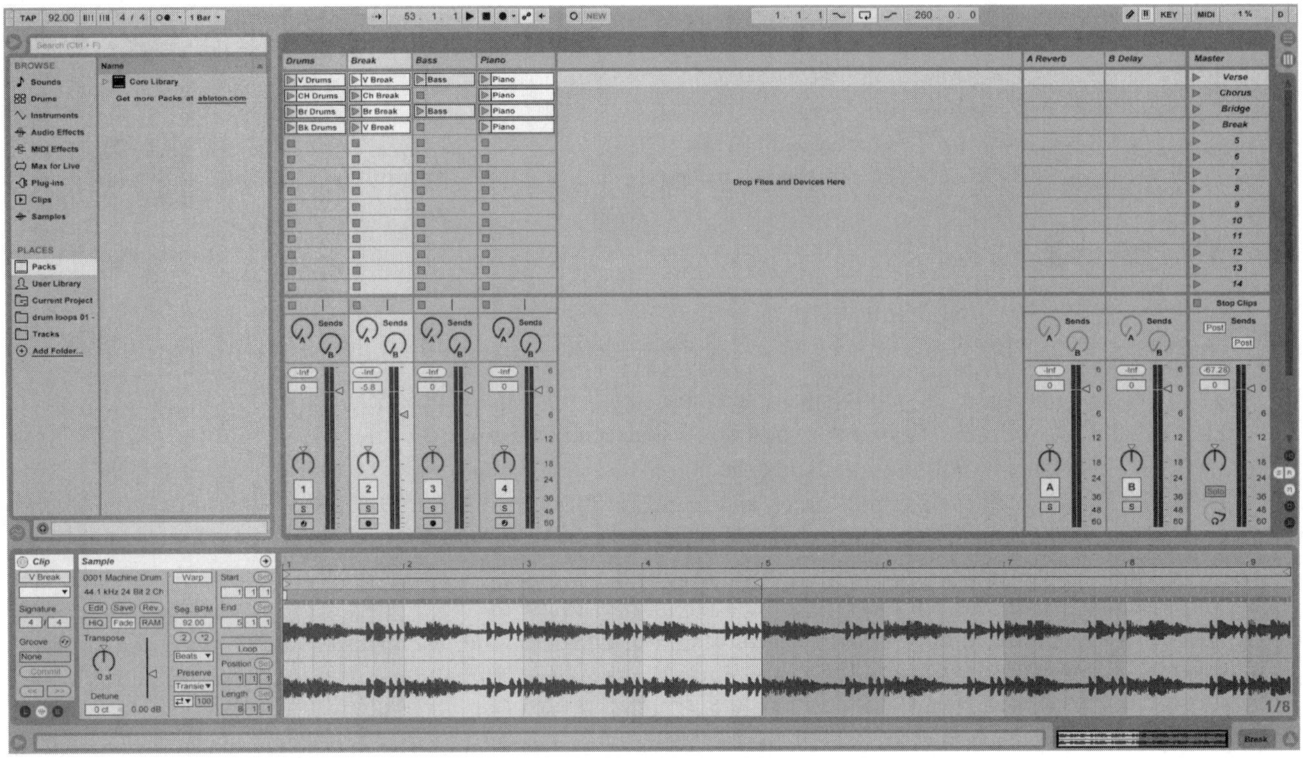

Figure 1.1 Here is a quick peek at the Session View grid in Live 9. The rows make up musical sections called scenes, and the columns function as virtual mixer channels.
Source: Ableton

Another area Live specializes in is stretching audio to any desired tempo or pitch. Want to use that 90BPM drum loop in the 105BPM song that you're working on? Not a problem. Want to transpose the key and change the tempo of some Ozark mountain fiddle music to sync it up with a dance floor banger (as this author has been known to do)? It takes a little skill with Live's Warp feature, but once you get the hang of it, you'll be amazed at how easy it is to combine a wide variety of musical elements with varying keys and tempos.

Not strictly an improvisation and performance tool, Live sports a traditional timeline like that found in other digital audio workstations (or DAWs) such as Digidesign's Pro Tools, Apple's Logic, MOTU's Digital Performer, Cakewalk's SONAR, and Steinberg's Cubase (and Nuendo). Live's timeline (called the *Arrangement*) can be used to capture your improvisations for final polishing, editing, and mixing. To get an idea of what we're talking about, look at Figure 1.2, which features a screenshot of Live's Arrangement View.

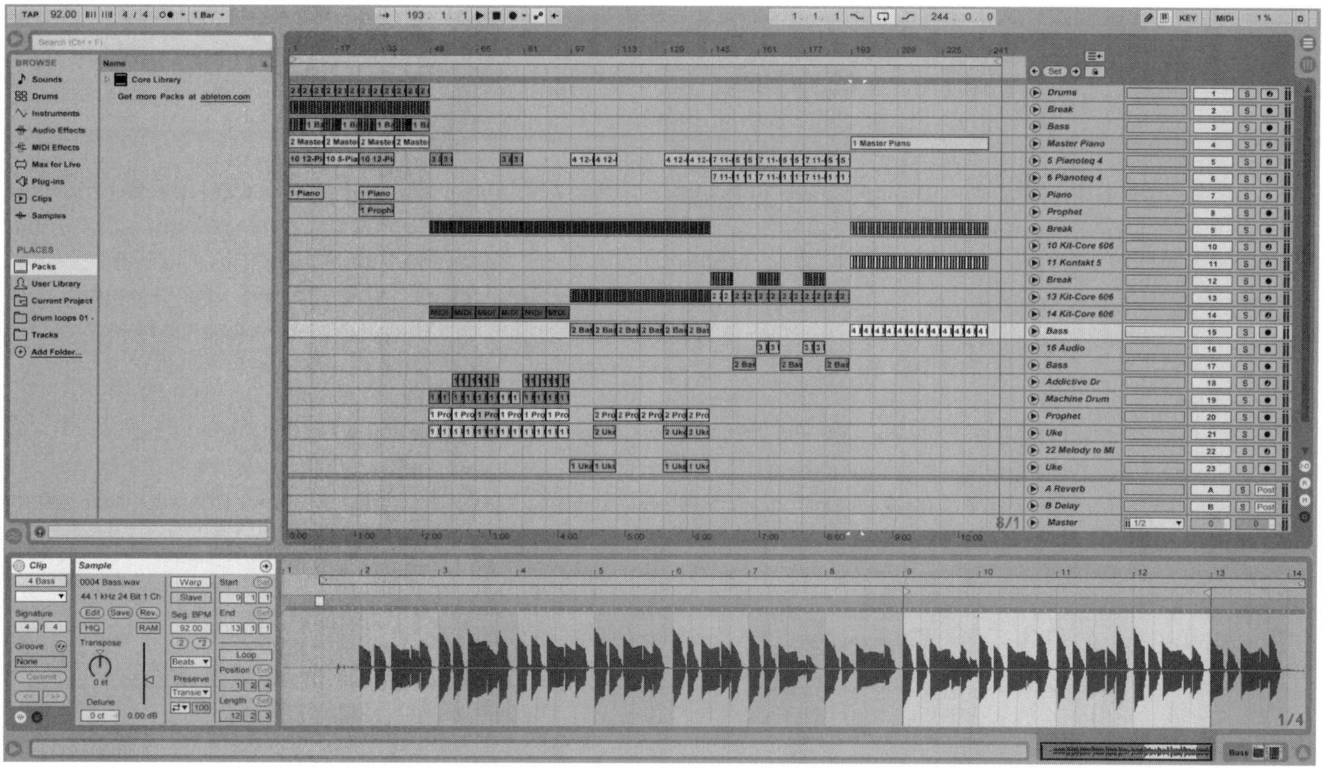

Figure 1.2 If you've used other digital audio workstations, Live's Arrangement View should look familiar.
Source: Ableton

Over the years since its inception, Live has evolved into a fully featured music production suite with powerful MIDI editing, VST/Audio Units and ReWire support, and (with the advent of Live 9) futuristic features such as Audio-to-MIDI and Push, a hardware controller for Live that promises the ability to create most of a song without ever having to grab your mouse or computer keyboard.

What Sets Live Apart?

The digital audio world has exploded since Live's first days. Even the average computer is extremely powerful, and all the major software companies have studied their competitors' features and expanded their products in ways that make formerly incomprehensible innovations commonplace. There has never been a better time to get into the game; for a beginner, it's almost impossible to go wrong.

That said, there are still many things that make Live a unique program. Although this list is far from complete, these few items from Live 9's feature set show a few ways in which Live stands apart from the rest.

> ▷ Ableton is one of the original innovators in the area of real-time time stretching and pitch shifting. While most DAWs now have time and pitch manipulation features, Live's flexibility and ease of use remains unparalleled. With a few mouse clicks, you can adjust pitch and time for synchronization tasks or insane sound mangling.
> ▷ To achieve even more flexibility and elasticity, the Slice to New MIDI Track command can cut a loop into multiple samples and generate a MIDI file to play them back in order, much in the way Propellerhead's ReCycle and Dr. Rex would. (Speaking of which, Live natively supports REX files as well!)

▷ Live is very easy to use with MIDI controller hardware. Whether you're using a device designed for Live (such as Push, APC 40, or Launchpad), or a generic MIDI controller of some sort, it's simple to get your hands off the mouse and onto pads, knobs, and the like. Even if you don't have a controller, Live's flexible mapping feature allows you to control just about anything with a single keystroke on your computer keyboard.

▷ Live lets you build customized groupings of effects and virtual instruments called *Racks*. With powerful routing options, you can create layers, splits, and complex effects like never before. Drum Racks take this concept to another level, allowing you to build drum banks with combinations of audio samples, synthesized sounds, and effects.

▷ Max For Live (included in Live Suite and available as an add-on for Live Standard) allows Live to be infinitely extended. These extensions range from effects (such as convolution reverb) to step sequencers, parameter randomizers, video tools, and interface tools such as Already Played, which will change the color of a clip once it's played to make it easier for DJs to keep track of their sets. Max For Live devices are fully programmable, so if you've got the skills, you can modify any device to taste or create your own from scratch.

▷ Live 9 introduces a new set of Audio to MIDI features that can analyze audio of drums, melody, or harmony and produce a new MIDI track ready for you to tweak and process to your heart's content. Want to sing a melody and then have a synth play the melody? Now you can.

Goals of This Book

Like Live, *Ableton Live 9 Power!* was written by a performing musician. I've spent plenty of time performing with Live and have been recording and remixing in Live for years. Live is built to be musical, and this book will aspire to be the same. It is my hope that you will have many long hours of enjoyment using Live while creating some interesting new music. Although this book is designed to be a "power user" book, don't be deterred if you are new to Live, new to music, or new to computer-based production. This book will serve as a basic guide for interfacing with Live and an advanced tips and tricks collection for taking advantage of Ableton's industry-rocking technology.

If you are already familiar with Live, this book should feel like a souped-up reference manual with some powerful tips and musical ideas for you to incorporate into your Live vocabulary. This book should help you optimize Live's settings for speed and sound, which should translate into maximum musical output. *Ableton Live 9 Power!* covers some sticky but rewarding topics, such as Live's MIDI implementation, editing Live's mix automation, and using virtual EQs and compressors for professional audio results.

The Online Files

To get you going as quickly as possible, you can find online files containing custom-built Live Sets to illustrate the topics in this book as you read about them. After all, what fun is it to read about music? It's much more fun to *hear* music.

Download and install the Live Pack hosted at www.hobo-tech.com/livepower onto your computer. Once you've done this, you'll be able to get to the files by clicking on Packs in the Browser and unfolding the Live 9 Power! pack.

Getting Live Up and Running

2

B EFORE YOU DIVE IN AND START PRODUCING HITS, it is important to take a moment to verify that your computer system is up to speed and that you've installed Live properly. This chapter will provide a few recommendations to help you through the installation process, along with some tips for fine-tuning your Ableton Live studio. I'll cover both Mac and PC setup and talk about several methods for optimizing your system. Also, remember that Ableton's technical support (www.ableton.com/en/help/contact-support/) is an excellent way to get to the bottom of anything not covered in this book, as is Ableton's online user forum (found at http://forum.ableton.com/), which is usually rich with tips, tricks, and advice.

System Requirements

Listed in the pages that follow are Ableton's posted system requirements, followed by my recommendations. The minimum system requirements can be a very different matter from a *desirable* system configuration. This is true with most software applications, and Live is no exception. Ableton Live is a power hungry program, and ideally your system should be put together with the most power you can afford. Don't worry though: not only is power very affordable these days, but there are strategies for making epic sounds with a less than epic computer. (See the "Latency Settings" later in this chapter and "Freeze and Flatten" in Chapter 7, "Using Effects and Instruments," for more information.)

If you're just starting out as a music producer, you'll be able to get away with using a computer with fairly modest specifications until you get deeper into the production process, at which point you may need to upgrade due to audio dropouts and system instability. If you're an experienced producer with a big arsenal of plug-ins, you may be surprised at how quickly Live eats your computer's CPU power and RAM. (Or you may not—it all depends on the program you're coming over from.)

All of the following recommendations are minimums. Ableton provides the minimum to run Live at all, while my recommendations are the minimum to run Live *in style*.

Ableton Live's System Requirements for Macintosh

▷ Multicore processor
▷ 2GB or more RAM
▷ 1024 × 768 display
▷ Mac OS × 10.5 or later
▷ Between 6GB and 55GB of disk space depending on Live Version

Ableton Live 9 Power! 's Mac Recommendations

▷ Modern quadcore processor
▷ 8GB RAM
▷ Mac OS × 10.6 or later
▷ Audio interface (soundcard)
▷ A hard disk big enough that you can keep 10% of it empty

Ableton Live's System Requirements for PC

▷ Multicore processor
▷ 2GB RAM
▷ Windows XP, Vista, Windows 7 or 8
▷ Windows-compatible soundcard (preferably with ASIO driver)
▷ Between 6GB and 55GB of disk space depending on Live Version

Ableton Live 9 Power! 's PC Recommendations

▷ Modern quadcore processor
▷ 8GB RAM
▷ Windows 7 or 8
▷ ASIO-compliant audio interface (soundcard)
▷ QuickTime 7 or later
▷ A hard disk big enough that you can keep 10% of it empty

Installing, Running, and Updating Live 9

If you are brand new to Live and haven't yet picked up a copy or have never installed audio software before, then this section is for you. Here are a few general tips about getting your hands on Live 9.

Live can be purchased as a download or in a boxed retail version. The download version is sold only through the Ableton shop (www.ableton.com/en/shop/). The only difference between the two is that the boxed version includes printed manuals, so if you don't care about these, go ahead and buy the download. The DVDs in the box do offer the convenience of not having to download the content packs, but the software itself is usually out of date by the time it gets to you, and you end up having to download the latest version anyway. The truth is that printed manuals are often a bit out of date as well, since features are regularly being improved and completed.

Live 9 comes in three versions: Intro, Standard, and Suite.

▷ **Intro:** A stripped-down version of Live that supports 16 tracks, 8 scenes, 19 audio effects, all seven MIDI effects, and four sample packs of audio content.
▷ **Standard:** Includes unlimited tracks and scenes, 31 audio effects, all seven MIDI effects, and 14 sample packs of audio content.
▷ **Suite:** Includes all six add-on instruments (Analog, Collision, Electric, Operator, Sampler, Tension), Max For Live (and a handful of useful Max For Live devices), all 34 audio effects, and 25 sample packs.
▷ For a detailed comparison of the three flavors of Ableton Live, please refer to www.ableton.com/en/live/ feature-comparison/.

Live Installation Tips (Mac OS X)

Installing Live 9 on Mac OS X is a breeze. After downloading, open the disk image (.dmg file) and drag Live 9 to the Applications folder on your hard disk. For quicker access to Live, you may want to install a shortcut onto the OS X dock. To do this, simply open your Applications folder and drag the program icon to the dock. An instant shortcut is made. To remove the item from the dock, drag it to the Trash or to the desktop, and watch it go "poof" and disappear.

Live Installation Tips (Windows)

Installing Live onto a Windows machine is much like installing any other Windows-based application. After you open Setup and follow the instructions, Live's installer will ask you where you would like to place the Ableton folder and its files. I recommend using the installer's default setting, which will place Live in your computer's Program Files folder.

Also, pay special attention to where your VST plug-in folder exists. It is common practice to keep all VST plug-ins stored in one common location so that every VST-compatible application will be able to use them. For instance, if you have Steinberg's Cubase SX installed on your computer, you can instruct Live to look for plug-ins in the Steinberg shared VST folder, which is commonly located at Program Files > Steinberg > Vstplugins. You can set Live to use the same plug-in folder.

MAC USERS TAKE NOTE: OS X has a built-in location for storing all of your plug-ins (Library > Audio > Plug-ins). I find that it's handy to drag this folder to the Places area in a Finder window for easy access. Some plug-ins come with installation programs that place the files here automatically while others may require you to copy them yourself. Inside this folder, you'll find separate folders for each type of plug-in that OS X supports. Live can only use VSTs (which go in the VST or VST3 folder) or Audio Units (which go in the Components folder), just to make things confusing.

The first time you launch Live, you'll be offered the opportunity to register Live or run it in Demo mode. Authorizing will open your Web browser and take you to ableton.com where you'll have to log in to or create a user account. If you've bought the download version from ableton.com, your Live 9 serial number will already be entered in your account, and the authorization process should begin immediately.

Ableton enables you to install Live on two computers. If you replace one of your computers, it's possible that authorizing your new computer will fail because you've used up your "unlocks." Not to worry—just email customer support to explain the situation, and they'll take care of you.

Updating Live

Like any good piece of modern software, Live is constantly under development, with bugs being fixed and functionality added and improved. More than some software companies, Ableton releases updates quite regularly so it's very easy to fall behind. This is not something you should lose any sleep over; not only is it very easy to update, but there's nothing wrong with taking an "if it ain't broke don't fix it" attitude toward the software on your computer. However, before you tear your hair out trying to figure out why something isn't working on your system, it's a good idea to make sure you're running the latest version.

The easiest way to stay up-to-date is to turn on Live's Get Software Updates feature (see Licenses/Management in the "Setting Preferences in Live" section of this chapter), which automatically downloads new versions as needed. This is done in the background and is usually quite fast since all that is downloaded are small patches to the program, rather than an entire new version.

For those of you who like to handle it manually, you'll find Check for Updates in the Help menu handy. This will take you to a Web page to download the latest version. The advantage of this method is that the download page contains additional information and links, such as new features and available downloads. You can always find out what version you're running by opening the About Live screen (from the Live menu on a Mac, or the Help menu on a PC).

Basic Computer Specifications

Since everyone uses Live differently, it's tricky to give a one-size-fits-all recommendation for computer specs. There are users who use almost nothing but Live's built-in devices, keep their track count low, and release great music using nothing but a four-year-old laptop. Others use power hungry plug-ins extensively and make densely layered music with loads of tracks, challenging even a top-of-the-line system. Therefore, it's important to understand some of the details of how hardware affects performance, and how you can get the best machine for your budget.

Processor Speed

The biggest performance bottleneck for most digital audio computers is the processor speed. Live is a program that prioritizes elegance and ease of use, rather than extreme CPU efficiency. That said, there are many tasks that Live can handle even when running on a very humble computer. For example, playing back many tracks of audio takes very little CPU power, unless you're using a lot of effects. Sets which rely heavily on MIDI tracks and virtual instruments are often very demanding on the CPU, unless you're mostly using built-in devices like Simpler and Operator, which are very CPU efficient. Keep an eye on the CPU meter in the upper right-hand corner to get a practical feel for all this.

Obviously, a more powerful CPU will provide you with the most ease and flexibility. But this doesn't mean you have to break the bank buying the absolute newest and fastest. Buying a step down from the top can save you quite a bit of money, which you can put toward a quality soundcard and a good pair of speakers or headphones. Your music will be better for it.

Hard Drives

Get the biggest hard disks you can afford. You *will* fill up every single drive you buy, and faster than you think. (And don't forget extra backup drives!) 7200 RPM drives are ideal for audio, but not absolutely essential, depending on how you use your system. If you're buying a desktop computer, these are by far and away the most common type of drive, so this isn't a special consideration.

Laptops are often equipped with 5400 RPM drives, which are fine for most performance applications and many production situations as well. A slower drive can become a problem when Sets grow large and complex with many audio tracks and samples playing back simultaneously. When this happens, you'll hear audio dropouts and the "D" (Disk Overload) icon in the upper right-hand corner will begin to flash.

For the highest performance possible, it's great to have multiple hard drives. For example, you could have one for operating system and applications, a second for sample libraries, and a third for your musical projects. This way, each drive has less work to do and can keep up more easily.

RAM

As your Live Sets grow and become more complex, they use more RAM (memory). It's important not to run out of memory while running Live because when you do, it crashes. There's no built-in way to monitor memory usage (as there is with CPU power and disk usage), so you'll have to run Activity Monitor in OS X or Task Manager in Windows to see where your system memory is going.

If your system has a relatively small amount of RAM, it's important to quit other applications while running Live. Whether you're prone to running out of RAM depends on how you use your system. Some plug-ins are memory hungry; for example, using Max For Live and ReWire both demand more memory because they involve running additional applications.

Live is now available in both 64-bit and 32-bit versions. The only difference between these two versions is how much RAM they can utilize. A 32-bit application can't use more than 4GB of RAM, while 64-bit applications have an astronomically high RAM limitation. At the time of this writing, the 64-bit version of Live does not support video, Max For Live, or The Bridge (integration with Serato Scratch Live), although Ableton is working to correct this. Also, be aware that 32-bit plug-ins will not work in the 64-bit version of Live unless you use a third-party plug-in bridge to accomplish this.

In the near future, all these issues will be resolved, and we'll live happily ever after in a 64-bit world, but for now, most of us survive just fine in 32-bit. This means 8GB of RAM is plenty for most users. Assuming you don't need to be running many different applications at once, this leaves 4GB to handle the OS, while leaving 4GB for Live. If you find that you're crashing Live by going over the 4GB RAM limit, then you'll have to switch to 64-bit and make sure your computer has plenty of RAM in it.

Audio Interface Specs

Almost invariably, the audio capabilities that come standard with your PC or Mac are lacking. Without a specialized audio interface, sometimes called a *soundcard*, you'll find yourself hitting limitations in terms of routing flexibility, connectivity, and sound quality. Choosing an interface can be tricky since there are so many choices on the market. Here are a couple of items to consider when purchasing an interface.

Connection Type

The most common types of audio interfaces connect to your computer via either USB or FireWire. Desktop computers can use PCI and PCIe cards, which fit into slots inside your computer and offer the best performance of any format available. Apple computers are equipped with a high-speed Thunderbolt connector, for which audio interfaces are just beginning to emerge on the market.

Unless you're designing a *very* high-performance audio system designed to record many tracks of audio simultaneously, USB and FireWire are just fine. In fact, the old FireWire 400 speed and USB 2.0 are more than adequate for most audio systems, so don't let someone tell you that you've got to have FireWire 800 or USB 3.0 to survive. Those of you who need a faster connection—you know who you are.

Inputs and Outputs

Most soundcards have a minimum of two input channels, a right and left input, which can be used separately or together as a stereo pair. More inputs are a must if you're planning on recording multichannel sources, such as a live band. But since many musicians overdub one track at a time when recording, two inputs often work just fine.

The advantage to multiple outputs is increased integration with the world outside your computer. For example, multiple outputs give you the ability to send drums to outputs 1 and 2, while sending the vocals to output 3. Then you can send these outputs to different channels on a hardware mixer to apply EQ and outboard effects. If you just have a single stereo output on your soundcard, all mixing has to be done inside the computer. Is this something you should necessarily be worried about? Not at all! If you are just getting started, or you are not sure what all of this is about, then chances are there's no need for you to concern yourself too much about having lots of outputs.

The exception to this rule is if you plan on performing with Live, in which case you will want to have a minimum of four outputs (two stereo pairs), which allows you to use one pair as your main output and the other for cueing (prelistening) to tracks or clips in your headphones, just like a DJ.

After you've decided whether you need 2, 4, 6, 8, or more channels, you may also want to consider what types of connecters the interface uses. For example, if you're always connecting to DJ mixers, it may be more convenient to have RCA outputs on your interface, rather than 1/4-inch or XLR. Ultimately, though, this shouldn't be a deal-breaker, since you can always connect with the proper cables or adapters.

What Do You Need to Know About ASIO Drivers?

ASIO (Audio Stream Input/Output) was first invented by German software-slinger Steinberg (www.steinberg.de or www.cubase.net). Originally, ASIO drivers were created to help musicians and producers using Cubase to record multitrack audio digitally with a minimal amount of time lag within their digital system. This time lag can be a real buzzkill, and it is called *latency*. Latency occurs because the sound you are recording is forced to travel through your operating system, your system bus, and host application to end up on your hard drive. Like bad plumbing, the signal may be coming down the pipe, but there are unnecessary clogs and corners that must be navigated along the way. The gist is that your computer is performing calculations (remember, it's all numbers for the computer), and though they are blazingly fast, it takes a moment for the processor to finish, and the result is latency.

Live 9 supports ASIO on PCs. (ASIO is unnecessary on Mac OS X, thanks to Core Audio.) You'll be happy to know that most popular consumer- and professional-grade audio cards support the format, too. It has become an industry standard and can cut latency down to barely detectable levels. Properly installed, ASIO drivers will make Live as responsive as a hardware instrument with less than eight milliseconds of audio delay—practically unnoticeable. ASIO helps Live users hear the instantaneous results of MIDI commands, audio input/output, mouse moves, and keyboard commands. Someday, we'll all look back and laugh that latency was ever an issue, but for now, count your blessings that there is ASIO. See the "Setting Preferences in Live" section later in this chapter for more on the infamous "L-word."

ASIO FOR ALL: If you're stuck using the internal soundcard of your PC or have an audio card that doesn't support ASIO, there still may be hope for you. Michael Tippach has programmed a freeware driver called "ASIO4ALL," which is available at www.asio4all.com. If you use it, you will have solved your latency problem, but you'll still want to consider a new audio interface because the converters in a pro interface will sound much better than those used in standard soundcards.

Choosing a MIDI Controller

Whether you're using Live to perform or produce, you're going to want some sort of MIDI controller as part of your setup. There is a lot you can do with only your computer keyboard and a mouse, but at some point, you'll want to play a melody, bang out a beat, or crank a knob to apply some effects.

The most important thing in picking a controller is to understand your needs, but this can be tricky if you are totally new to production. If that's the case, the best thing I can recommend is to get something affordable and push it to its limits—it's the one guaranteed method for discovering what your needs are!

Here are some factors to consider:

▷ **Grid:** Some controllers are designed specifically for use with Live (such as the Novation LaunchPad and Akai APC 40), and they feature a grid of buttons for launching clips in the Session View. When connected, a colored rectangle appears in the Session View to indicate which area of the clip grid is available to the controller. On the controller, each grid button that corresponds to a clip lights up, while buttons corresponding to empty clip slots remain dark. These are fun in the studio, and a must-have for many live performers. Ableton's new Push is designed around a button grid, which can launch clips, and do much more as well.

▷ **Keys:** Even if you don't play the piano, you'll probably want to have at least two octaves of piano keys to play with. Some keyboards come with extra controls (faders, knobs, etc.), and may be all you need. Simple keyboard controllers may need to be supplemented with another controller for knobs and buttons. There's nothing wrong with the latter approach. In fact, it can be quite convenient to have several small controllers. After all, you might not need one of them for gigs, and you'll save space in your gig bag over a larger, fully featured controller.

▷ **Drum Pads:** Some people can't live without them. If you like to bang out your beats, drum pads can make it much more fun. That said, I know folks who have no problem playing great beats on a piano keyboard or simply drawing in every note with the mouse. Drum pads vary in feel and sensitivity, so make sure to get ones you like.

▷ **Knobs:** Some knobs have a nice smooth feel and have a limited range, just like a knob on an old synth. Others turn endlessly and click as you turn them. (These are usually referred to as *encoders*.) The former are much better for musical tasks (such as filter sweeps). A bad feeling or awkwardly placed knob is no fun to use, so try before you buy.

▷ **Faders (and Crossfader):** For many of us, volume controls just make more sense on faders rather than knobs. For precision studio work, a nice big fader with a long *throw* (range of motion) is handy, but not essential. Motorized faders are great in the studio, but probably not necessary on stage. In the world of MIDI, a crossfader is just a sideways fader. Whether or not you need one depends entirely on your style. Live's crossfader can be controlled by any MIDI input, so you can get the functionality of a crossfader from a variety of nontraditional controls.

▷ **Buttons:** Some light up, and some don't. Some have a nice chunky feel, while others are downright wispy. For use in the studio, turning the metronome on and off, or controlling Live's transport, these issues probably aren't very important. But during a gig, having nice buttons that light up when you click them can make all the difference.

▷ **Joysticks and Touchpads:** These are often referred to as X-Y controllers since they can be moved along two axes. From a MIDI standpoint, a joystick or touchpad is seen as two separate controllers: one for the horizontal axis and one for the vertical. As you move one of these controllers, two different control messages are simultaneously transmitted.

Control Surfaces

Another factor to consider when picking a control surface is whether or not it is a supported *Control Surface* for Live. In Live's MIDI preferences (see "The MIDI/Sync Tab" later in this chapter), there is a menu that will show you a list of controllers that can be plugged into Live and use remote controlling immediately without any mapping.

Because there are so many different styles of controllers, this technology varies widely from device to device. To see how it's implemented for various controllers, open up Help View from the Help menu, and then scroll all the way down to the bottom and click on All Built-in Lessons. In here, you'll find the Control Surface Reference, which documents the behavior of all supported controllers.

It's also possible for third parties to allow any MIDI controller to behave as a control surface in Live, but this involves the installation of a script file on your computer. The details of this go beyond what we can cover in this book, so make sure to follow the manufacturer's directions for any controller that promises custom control surface support. Visit hobo-tech.com/tag/control-surface for more information on custom control surface configuration.

Setting Preferences in Live

Preferences are more than merely your personal whims about how you would like Live's interface to be colored or where your files are automatically saved. From the Preferences screen, you will be able to control default loop traits, audio and MIDI interface settings, and audio latency settings. If you're brand new to Live, you may just want to skim this section for now. Some of this stuff will make a lot more sense once you've spent some time using the program.

To open the Preferences dialog box on a PC, select Options > Preferences; on a Mac, select Live > Preferences. When you first open the preferences, you will see a small pop-up window with a number of tabs marked on the side: Look/Feel, Audio, MIDI/Sync, File/Folder, Record/Warp/Launch, CPU, and Licenses/Maintenance. We'll have a look at each of these in turn.

Look/Feel

On the Look/Feel tab (see Figure 2.1), you'll find a number of settings having to do with Live's appearance and the way it presents information to you. Let's look at all the settings.

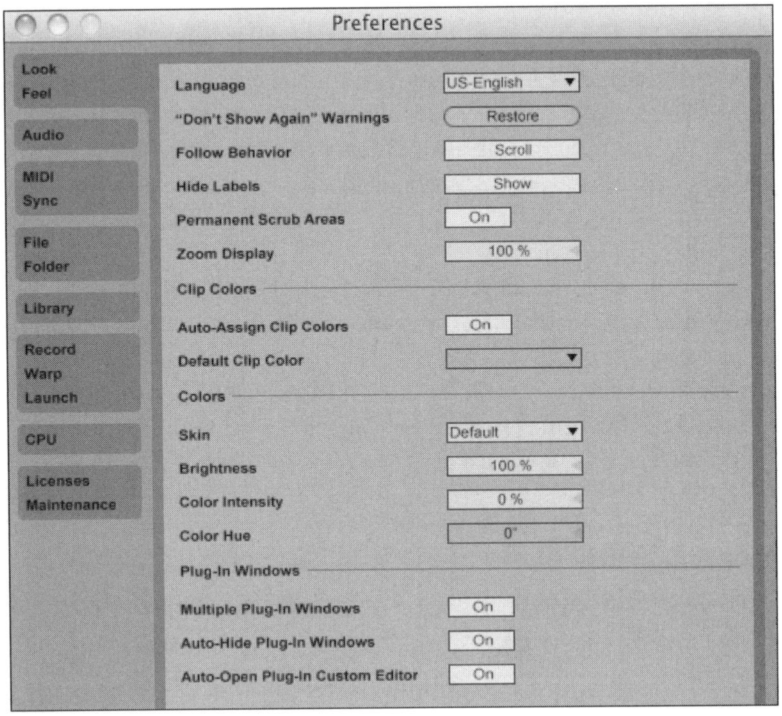

Figure 2.1 The Look/Feel tab in Live's Preferences.

Source: Ableton

The Language setting chooses the language to use for Live's menus and messages. The internal help menus, interface text, and informational messages can be set to read in French, Spanish, German, and English.

The "Don't Show Again" Warnings setting deals with the various warnings that come up when you first perform certain actions in Live. Typically, these warnings will only be seen the first time you perform a particular action, and then you won't see them again. If you want to bring back all these messages and restore Live to the state it was in when you first installed it, click Restore here.

The third option, Follow Behavior, determines the graphical style used when following the song position in the Arrange and Clip Views. When set to Scroll, the playback cursor will stay in place while the window moves smoothly under it. When set to Page, the window will stay stationary while the cursor moves. When the playback cursor reaches the right edge of the screen, the window jumps ahead so the cursor appears again on the left. The Scroll option is much harder on your CPU, so if you are experiencing dropouts or sluggish response, set this option to Page.

The next option here, Hide Labels, helps give you a little more screen real estate once you've memorized all of Live's components and don't need the labels anymore. When set to Show, the Live interface will look normal. When set to Hide, all of the little labels on the interface (such as Track Delay and Audio To) will disappear.

Permanent Scrub Areas turns on or off the scrub area at the top of the Arrangement View or the lower half of the waveform display in the Clip View. With this preference turned on, your mouse will automatically turn into a speaker icon in either of these locations and can be used to jump to any location. With it turned off, you'll have to hold down the Shift key to see the Scrub tool.

Zoom Display is used to scale the entire Live interface larger or smaller. During gigs, I set my display to 120% so it's easier to see what I'm doing.

Clip Colors

With Auto-Assign Colors turned on, Live will randomly choose a color for each new clip you create. (A clip's color can be changed at any time in the Clip View, which will be covered in Chapter 5, "Clips.") If Auto-Assign Colors is off, the Default Clip Color determines which color Live will assign to all new clips. Of course, color will not affect the sound and is strictly a matter of preference.

Colors

The Skin setting sets Live's overall color scheme. To find the scheme you like best, simply click the drop-down menu and use the up and down arrows on your keyboard to scroll through the options. The three controls below are used to customize the skin you select. Brightness adjusts the overall lightness of the skin. Color Intensity and Color Hue work in conjunction with each other. With Color Intensity set to a non-zero value, you can adjust Color Hue to pick a specific color tint.

Plug-In Windows

The three options in the next section of the Look/Feel preference tab determine how Live will display a plug-in's custom display window.

When Multiple Plug-In Windows is activated, you can open more than one plug-in window at a time. When this is off, open plug-in windows will be closed any time a new one is opened. Keeping this option off can help minimize screen clutter. With this preference turned off, you can still open multiple plug-in windows manually by holding down the Ctrl (Cmd) key when opening a new plug-in window.

The second option, Auto-Hide Plug-In Windows, will make plug-in windows appear only for those plug-ins loaded on a selected track. For example, if you have a MIDI track loaded with an instance of Native Instrument's Battery and another track with Rob Papen's Predator, Battery will be hidden when the Predator track is selected and vice versa. This can also help minimize screen clutter and thus is especially useful for laptop users.

The third option here is the Auto-Open Plug-In Custom Editor box. When active, the plug-in window will be opened immediately after the plug-in is loaded onto a track. This makes perfect sense since you'll usually need to make some modification to the plug-in after you load it.

Audio

The next tab in Live's preferences, the Audio tab (see Figure 2.2), is used to select an audio interface and makes adjustments to its performance.

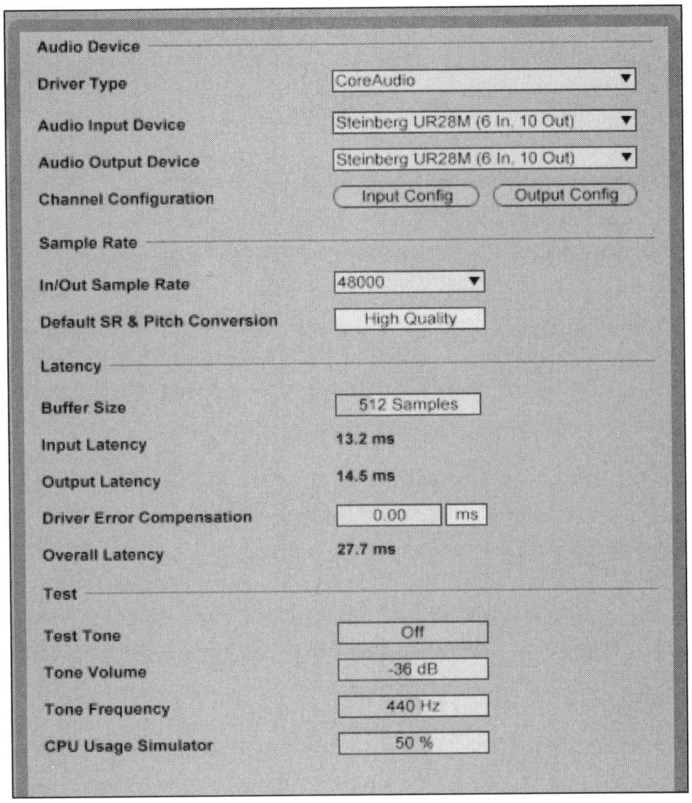

Figure 2.2 Live's Audio Preferences tab. If you're using a PC, this window looks a little different, but the basic functionality is the same.
Source: Ableton

Audio Device

The first section of the Audio tab is labeled Audio Device. The first setting you can choose here is the Driver Type you want to use for your audio interface. On the PC, options will include MME/DirectX and ASIO, and in Mac OS X, you will see just one choice, Core Audio. After you select the driver type you want to use, you will have a selection of audio devices to choose from in the subsequent drop-down menus. As noted previously, you will always get better performance with ASIO drivers, so you should always choose ASIO on a PC if this option is available.

Next after Driver Type is the Audio Device setting, where you actually choose the specific soundcard you want to use. In Windows, you will see only a single menu here; in Mac OS X, you will see separate settings for Audio Input Device and Audio Output Device. Theoretically, you could choose different devices for input and output; in practice, however, you will probably get the best performance by using a single audio interface at a time, so you'll probably want to choose the same device for both input and output. (If you are not recording, you don't need to choose an input device at all.)

Note that you may not find the audio device you want to use when using certain driver types. For example, the built-in audio cards on laptop computers don't support ASIO, so you'll only find these cards listed when MME/DirectX is selected for Driver Type.

The Channel Configuration settings include two buttons: Input Config and Output Config. Clicking one of these opens another small pop-up window that activates various inputs and outputs on your soundcard for use in Live. Only those inputs and outputs that you activate here will appear in Live's other menus and selectors. If you don't need to use all of the inputs and outputs, you may want to leave them inactive here, as doing so will save you a bit of computing power. Please note that Live will always seek out the audio interface last saved in the preferences each time the program launches. If Live cannot find the soundcard—if, for instance, you have unplugged it or swapped it out—Live will still launch, but with no audio enabled. In this instance, the CPU meter will be red and display the word OFF. You won't be able to play any sound in Live until you go to the Audio Preferences and select a new audio device.

Sample Rate

The In/Out Sample Rate setting in the Audio Preferences tab will determine the recording quality of both Live's output and recorded input. The most common sample rate is 44,100Hz, or 44.1kHz, which is the sample rate for CDs and most consumer digital audio. The sample rate for digital video is 48k. Some producers work at higher sample rates, in the interest of sound quality, and *downsample* the audio in the mastering process. There is much debate on this topic, the details of which go beyond the scope of this book. Bear in mind that higher sample rates means larger file sizes and greater CPU demand.

There is also another setting here labeled Default SR & Pitch Conversion. When set to High Quality, Live will set the Hi Q switch to its On position for all newly created clips. This causes Live to use a cleaner algorithm when converting sample rates and transposing clips. Unless you're really strapped for CPU power, leave this in the Hi Quality position. You can always turn it off for individual clips, which you may want to experiment with when using transposition for sound design purposes.

Latency Settings

The next section of the Audio tab adjusts a number of settings relating to the buffer size and latency of your soundcard. You may need to experiment with these settings a bit to get the best possible performance on your particular computer system. Before we get to the experimentation, though, let's make sure we understand the problem.

First, recognize that there is both output latency and input latency. There is a minimum amount of latency that must occur as signal passes through your A/D converters into your computer, just as there is also a certain amount of time that it takes for your computer to send audio to your soundcard and through the D/A converters. While this is a very short period of time, things are complicated somewhat by the fact that we need our audio to play back without interruption, while at the same time our CPU is being interrupted constantly, handling myriad other tasks while our audio is playing back. This is where buffers come into play.

If you've ever used a portable CD player, or an iPod with a hard disk in it, you've deal with digital audio buffers before. On these devices, there is a slight lag between when you press play and when you start to hear the song. That's because before you hear anything, a certain amount of audio is loaded into the device's memory (the buffer), and then the audio is played back from the memory rather than directly from the hard drive. This ensures that if you knock the player around and cause the disk to skip, audio will continue to play back from the buffer while the device finds its way back to the place where it skipped. As long as the device can keep filling the buffer with data before it's all been played back, you'll never hear any problems, no matter how hard you whack it!

The same concept applies to your computer. If something causes your CPU usage to spike momentarily, and you don't have a big enough buffer, audio mayhem will ensue! So, how big to set your Buffer Size? It depends.

A very small buffer gives you low latency and makes your system very responsive, but it demands a lot of your CPU. A large buffer is easier on the CPU and ensures smooth performance, but increases latency. Therefore, you may have to experiment with your system to get the settings right, and you may have to change them depending on what you're doing.

For example, on stage you want to make sure you've got a big enough buffer to avoid audio dropouts or artifacts without generating so much latency that you can't perform comfortably. In the studio, you might keep the buffer low during the early parts of the production process, increasing as your song becomes more complex and more CPU power is needed.

You may or may not be able to adjust your soundcard's buffer size from this Preferences menu. While in Mac OS X, you can usually just click and drag up or down to adjust the buffer size. In Windows, you will probably need to open your soundcard's own proprietary driver interface or control panel, which can be launched with the Hardware Setup button.

Next, we see the Input Latency and Output Latency values. Output latency is the amount of lag time between when you trigger a sound or action and when you hear it. If you're cranking a knob and can hear Live lagging behind you, that's output latency at work. Input latency arises because audio is buffered on the way into the computer, so Live receives this audio a little later than it should. Fortunately, Live can automatically compensate for this when recording.

ROUND IT OFF: While some soundcard drivers will adjust the buffer in increments of one sample, Ableton recommends that you set your buffer to one of the binary "round numbers" that we see so often on our computers: 64, 128, 256, 512, 1024, and so on.

Audio interfaces are designed to report their latencies to Live so it can offset its operations properly. However, in practice, the reported amount is sometimes not completely accurate, and you'll find that your audio recordings are slightly out of sync. To correct this, you must manually enter the unreported latency into the Driver Error Compensation box. Follow the step-by-step instructions in the Driver Error Compensation lesson from the Help View to determine and correct unreported latency.

Test

The Test section of the Audio Preferences generates a test-tone sine wave so you can test your system. You can also adjust the volume and frequency of the test tone using the other parameters in this section. Here are the steps for testing your system:

1. Turn on the test tone.
2. Set the CPU Usage Simulator to its maximum value (80%).
3. Decrease the buffer size until you start to hear crackling or dropouts in the test tone.
4. Increase the buffer size until these artifacts go away.

This test will yield a buffer size that will guarantee smooth audio performance in almost all situations. This will be a good value to use for live performance where stability is paramount. For situations where you need lower latency, you can test with a lower simulated CPU usage, or as long as you are working in the studio, just lower the buffer size as low as you want it and increase it if you have problems.

MIDI/Sync

This brings us to the third Preferences tab, the MIDI/Sync tab, shown in Figure 2.3. This is where you enable or disable MIDI devices, and specify how they are used in Live.

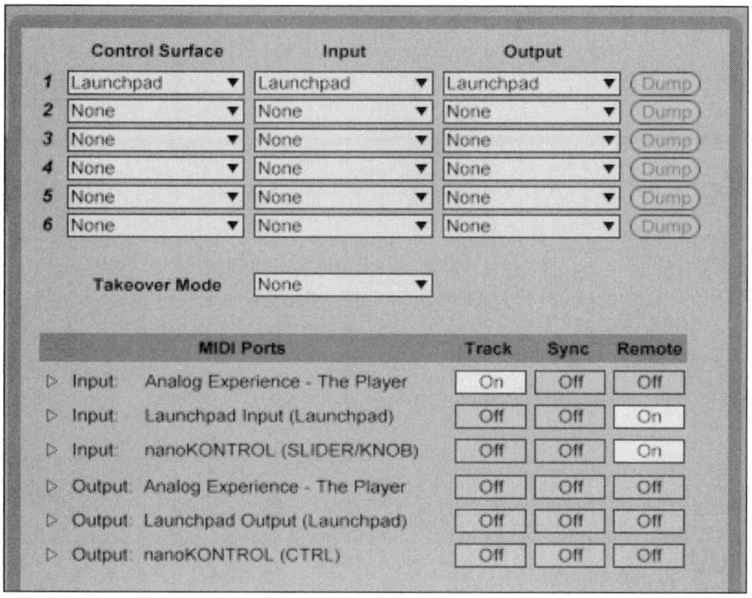

Figure 2.3 The MIDI/Sync tab found in Live's Preferences box.
Source: Ableton

The first part of this tab contains options for setting up natively supported control surfaces in Live. If you are using an interface that Live supports, you can use one of the drop-down choosers in the first column (labeled *Control Surface*) to select it from a list. Once selected, Live will have all the necessary information to support the device. In many cases, the Input and Output ports will be selected automatically, but if you need to select them manually, they are usually the ports with names similar to the control surface.

Depending on which controller you are using, Live may need to do a "preset dump" to the device after you have selected it, in order to initialize it with the correct control values. In this case, the Dump button at right will become active (not grayed out), and you will need to click it once to do the dump.

The second part of this window shows a list of the MIDI Input and Output devices available on your computer. There are columns for the names of each MIDI port found by Live, plus columns named Track, Sync, and Remote. In order for a MIDI device to communicate with Live, it has to be enabled as a Track Input or Output, as a Sync source, or as a MIDI Remote Control.

Enabling Track for a MIDI Input device means that you can use it as an input to a MIDI track. This would be enabled for something like a keyboard that you use for playing notes on a virtual instrument. Enabling Track for a MIDI Output allows Live to send MIDI data from a MIDI track to an external piece of hardware, such as a synthesizer.

The Sync option enables the port as a MIDI Sync source or destination. This will have to be turned on for at least one port for any of the Sync functions to work. When using Sync input, the EXT switch will appear in the Control Bar and can be used to force Live to slave to an external tempo source.

The last column, Remote, is especially nifty. By enabling a remote input, you can map any of Live's on-screen controls to a physical controller. Remote output is used for sending MIDI feedback to MIDI controllers with motorized MIDI knobs and faders, or those with light-up encoders, and so forth. If you have a control surface with these types of controls, moving an on-screen control with the mouse will cause the MIDI controller to reflect that change.

Takeover Mode helps with handling control surfaces and MIDI remote devices that do not receive MIDI feedback. With these devices, moving a control with the mouse causes the physical controller to become mismatched with its associated on-screen control. When set to None, the controls on-screen will jump to whatever value the MIDI controller is sending immediately. This is very simple, but can result in sudden volume changes and other unnerving parameter jumps. Pick-up mode requires that you move the MIDI control to the value of the on-screen control, while Value Scaling moves the on-screen control in the direction that the MIDI control is moved, until the upper or lower limit is reached, at which point normal MIDI control resumes.

File/Folder

The File/Folder tab (see Figure 2.4) is used to specify various external file locations, manage plug-ins, and handle Live's cache for decoded MP3 files.

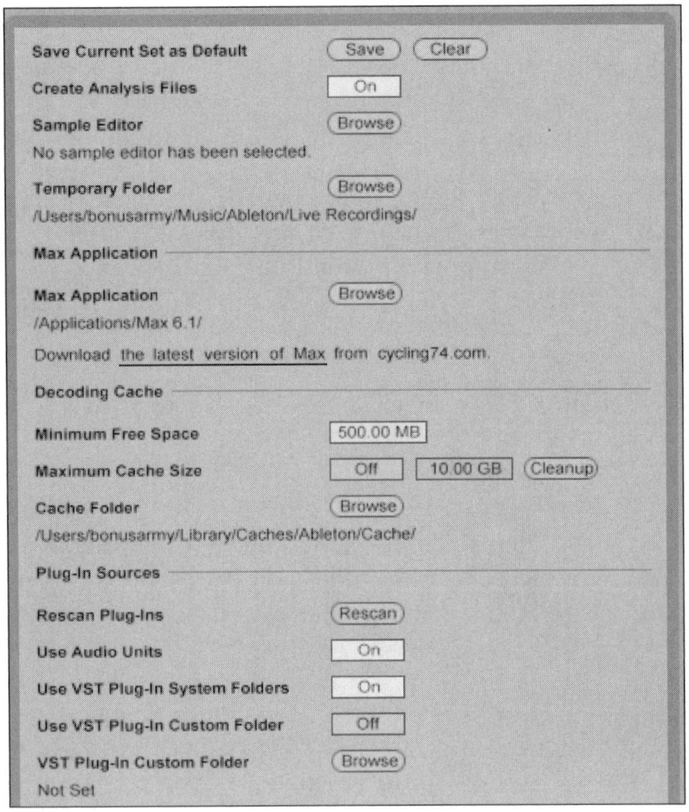

Figure 2.4 The File/Folder tab.
Source: Ableton

The first setting here, Save Current Set as Default, is used to save the current Live Set as the template Set that will be loaded each time Live is launched. This can be helpful for preconfiguring commonly used settings, such as MIDI assignments, input and output routings, and common effect patchwork (such as EQs on every channel). Note that you can save only one template in this Preferences tab. For additional templates, you can create additional Sets and store them in the Templates folder of your User Library. (More on this in Chapter 13, "Live 9 Power.")

The Create Analysis Files option lets you determine whether Live will save audio analysis data for quick loading in the future. The first time an audio file is used in Live, the program will create a waveform display and perform additional analysis on the file. When this option is enabled, Live will store this information in a file on your computer's hard disk. The file has the same name and location as the sample it is associated with and uses .asd as its extension. The next time the audio file is used in a Live Set, you won't have to wait for the graphical display to be rendered again because the file analysis has been saved.

The Sample Editor setting is for defining the location of your favorite wave editor, such as Sonic Foundry's Sound Forge, Steinberg's Wavelab, DSP Quattro, or the excellent freeware program, Audacity. Your preferred editor will launch when you press the Edit button in an audio clip.

Temporary Folder sets a location to temporarily store any files Live needs to create in the course of its operation. Again, in most cases, you won't need to change this from its default setting. This is the folder into which Live places all new recordings made before a Set is saved for the first time.

The Max application section allows you to tell Ableton Live where to find the installation of Cycling 74's Max program, which is required to use Max for Live devices. After you've installed Max, use the Browse button to navigate to the install location (typically in Applications or Program Files).

Decoding Cache

In order for Live to play MP3-format files, they must first be decoded/decompressed into standard WAV files. These resulting files are stored in the Cache. The parameters in this section determine how Live will handle the creation and cleanup of the decoded files.

The first option, Minimum Free Space, is the amount of free space that you always want available on the hard drive. If you set this to 500MB, Live will stop increasing the size of the cache once there is only 500MB available, which can be extremely important if you only have one hard drive on your entire computer system (frequently the case for laptop users). This setting will ensure that a minimum amount of space is available on the drive for swapping files and other housekeeping tasks. Alternately, Maximum Cache Size can be used if you would rather set a hard limit for the Decoding Cache. For example, you might want to make sure that the cache never gets bigger than 10GB, regardless of how much drive space you have left.

You'll notice that if you add an MP3 to your Set and Live decodes it, Live will not have to decode the file again if you drag the same MP3 into a Set at a later time. This feature works this way because the decoded file is still in the cache. If the decoded file gets deleted, you'll have to wait again for the previously decoded MP3 to be decoded again. The larger your cache is, the less this will happen.

Plug-In Sources

To use plug-ins in Live, you'll need to have at least one of these options turned on. In OS X, Use Audio Units and Use VST System Folders allow Ableton's use of plug-ins in their respective formats. PCs can't use Audio Units, and don't have a VST system folder, so you'll have to specify the folder on your hard drive that contains the VSTs you want to use. On a Mac, you can also specify a custom location for VSTs that can be used instead of, or in conjunction with, the System folder.

Library

The first option in the Library tab is Collect Samples on Export (see Figure 2.5). This affects Live's behavior when clips are dragged from the Session or Arrange views into the Browser in order to create new Sets or Live clips. If it's set to Yes, Live will always copy any necessary samples into the new location, along with the new Sets or Live clips you are creating. If it's set to Never, the new Sets or clips will refer to the original locations of the samples they use.

I recommend setting this preference to Ask, which invokes a dialog asking you if you want to export files. This gives you additional control, and allows you to learn by doing.

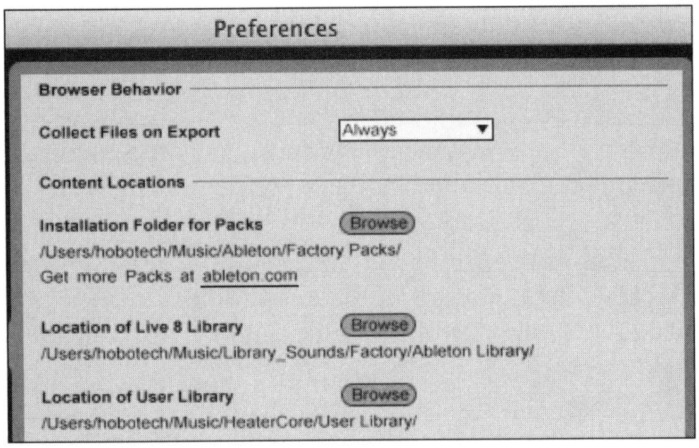

Figure 2.5 The Library tab.

Source: Ableton

Content Locations

Installation Folder for Packs enables you to select where Ableton will install any new Live Packs that you install. Live Packs can contain many different types of content including presets, samples, clips, and Sets. They can be downloaded from ableton.com and from some third-party vendors such as Loopmasters. Once you've installed a Live Pack, it's content will be accessible from the Browser, as explained in Chapter 3, "Live Interface Basics."

If you're upgrading from Live 8, you'll want to set Location of Live 8 Library to the location of your old Library. Live 9 installs a brand new Library, so you'll need to do this in order to access your custom presets or other Live 8 content. The Live 8 Library will appear in the Places area of the Browser.

The last option here is the location of your User Library. This can be any location on your hard drive. The User Library is where any custom presets you save will be stored, so it's highly recommended that you place it in a location that gets backed up regularly.

The Record/Warp/Launch Tab

As you might guess, this tab contains settings dealing with Live's recording, warping, and clip launch functions (see Figure 2.6).

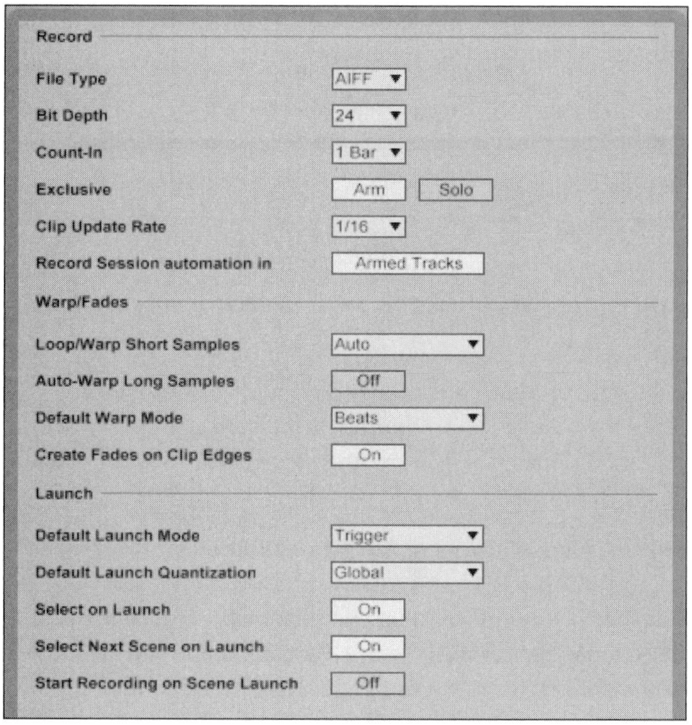

Figure 2.6 The Record/Warp/Launch tab.
Source: Ableton

Record

The Record section makes various default settings relating to how Live records audio.

Any time you record new audio, whether through resampling or from an input on your soundcard, it will use the Record parameters you set here. First, you can record in WAV or AIFF format. Sonically, these file types are identical. Historically, WAVs are associated with PC and AIFF with Mac, but nowadays the difference is largely irrelevant and both types can be used on both platforms.

More important is the Bit Depth, which should usually be set to 24. At 24-bit, you can capture highly detailed recordings at lower levels. If you have to record at 16-bit for some reason, you need to be more conscious about getting a higher level into the computer while being cautious not to overload the inputs ("go into the red").

The next option in this section is Count In. When set to None, Live will begin to record immediately when the transport is engaged. If you select a value here, such as 1 Bar, Live will provide one bar of count-in time (the metronome will sound, but Live will not be running) before it begins to record. This feature is useful if you're recording yourself and you need some time to get to your instrument after you've engaged recording.

The Exclusive buttons are used to determine whether or not more than one track's Solo or Arm switch can be engaged simultaneously. For example, when Solo Exclusive is on, only one track may be soloed at a time. If you click the Solo button of another track, the previous track's solo status will turn off. The same is true for Arm Exclusive. Only one track can be record enabled when this button is active. You can override the Exclusive setting for either Solo or Arm by holding down Cmd/Ctrl while clicking these switches in the Mixer.

The Clip Update Rate is the frequency with which Live recalculates changes made to a clip during playback. For instance, if you transpose a clip in Live while the Clip Update Rate is set to 1/32 note, you will hear nearly instant changes to the pitch of the loop in the clip. Conversely, choosing a Clip Update Rate of 1/4 note or the even slower rate of Bar (meaning one update per measure) will result in changes occurring more slowly.

Record Session Automation specifies how the Session View behaves when the Automation Arm switch is turned on. When set to Armed Tracks, automation in the session view will only be recorded into tracks that are armed for recording. If this option is set to All Tracks, all your knob movements and other automation will be recorded, regardless of whether the tracks are armed or not.

Warp/Fades

This section includes various settings relating to Live's Warp engine, which controls the time flow of clips, keeping everything in sync.

The Loop/Warp Short Samples menu determines the default state of a new audio clip, be it a loop or a one-shot sound. The Auto setting will cause Live to try and determine the nature of an imported sample on the fly and set its loop and warp settings accordingly. Live typically does well at automatically determining settings for short samples, and when it makes mistakes, they are easy to correct.

The next option relates to Live's Auto-Warp feature. When the Auto-Warp Long Samples option is on, Live will attempt to determine the tempo of the imported audio file and will place Warp Markers into the audio clip automatically. This will only happen on long samples—files that Live assumes to be complete songs. Auto-Warp works better with some kinds of material than others (for example, dance music with clear tempo and transients), so what you do with Live will determine whether or not you want this setting enabled. With long samples, Live sometimes makes mistakes that are difficult to correct, so turning this feature off can be desirable. You can still use Auto Warp, but you'll invoke it manually, as explained in Chapters 5, "Clips," and 12, "Playing Live...Live."

Default Warp Mode specifies which of Live's warping algorithms will be applied to new clips. There are six Warp modes (beats, tones, texture, re-pitch, complex, and complex pro), all of which produce different results when modifying the tempo or the pitch of a clip. The Warp modes are explained in detail in Chapter 5. Until you've mastered these, it's just fine to leave this setting on Beats or Tones.

Finally, the Create Fades on Clip Edges preference can be turned on or off. In its On position, the Fade switch will be turned on for all new Session View clips (which creates a fixed 4ms fade at the start and end) and will create an editable fade whenever an Arrangement View clip is created or split. Fades are typically desirable because they prevent the ugly digital popping that can occur when editing or looping audio. For more about fades, see Chapter 4, "Making Music in Live."

Launch

When triggering a clip to play, Live gives us some options called *Launch modes*. The full rundown on these modes can be found in Chapter 4. For now, I recommend leaving the mode on Trigger or Toggle.

The next setting, Default Launch Quantization, determines the default point at which new clips will be launched in relation to the time grid. Unless you've got an advanced understanding of this subject, you should leave this set to Global, which means the clip's quantization will automatically follow the global quantization value in the Control Bar. Launch quantization is discussed in detail in Chapters 3 and 4.

Select Next Scene on Launch is a setting designed primarily for live performance. Any time a scene is launched by keyboard or remote control, Live will automatically advance the scene selector to the one below it. If you've already laid out the sections of your song in a top-to-bottom arrangement in the Session View, you can progress through the song with just one button.

Start Recording on Scene Launch determines if clips will begin recording when launched by a scene. Having this option off will allow you to launch Scenes without recording, even if some tracks are armed. Having this option turned on can be useful for recording several clips simultaneously, or starting recording in one track and clip playback in another at the same time.

The CPU Tab

The CPU section of Preferences has only three settings, which the average user will never touch (see Figure 2.7).

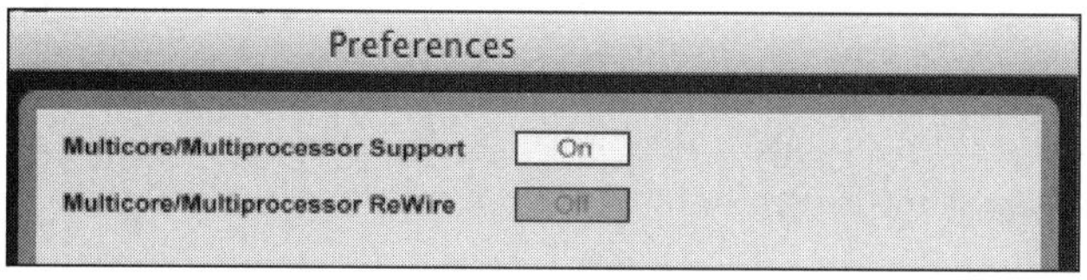

Figure 2.7 The CPU tab.
Source: Ableton

Multicore/Multiprocessor Support should generally be left on because all modern computers are based around a multicore or multiprocessor architecture. When off, Live will be forced to run on a single processor, which may be useful for troubleshooting or serve as a way to throttle Ableton Live if you are running other CPU-intensive applications alongside Live. But in almost all cases, you should allow Ableton to make full use of all your machine's CPU cores.

There is also another option to enable Multicore/Multiprocessor support when you are using Live in ReWire mode. Try turning this off if you're having problems using Live as a ReWire slave with another program.

Licenses/Maintenance

Typically authorization is done the first time you run Live, but if you need to do it after the fact, you can use the "Authorize at ableton.com" or "Authorize offline" buttons on this screen (see Figure 2.8). Offline authorization is only necessary for computers that are never connected to the Internet. If you select this option, Live will give you a code that you will enter by logging into your ableton.com account and selecting "Authorize offline." You can then download a file that can be copied to the offline computer and opened to authorize Live.

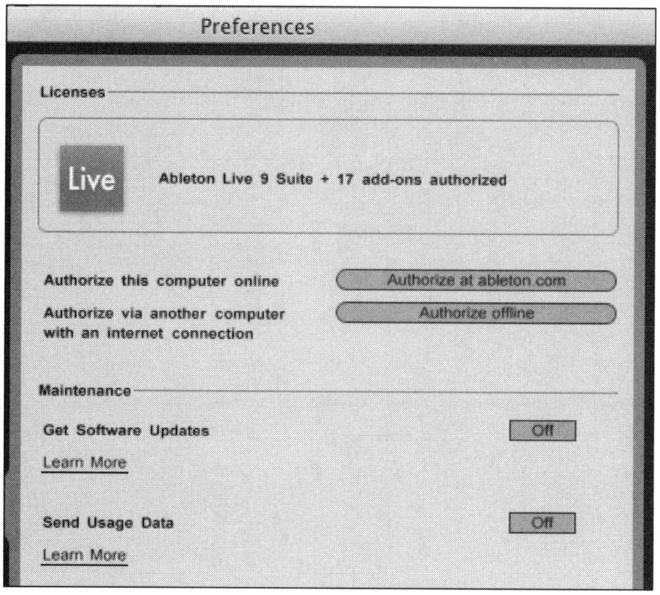

Figure 2.8 The Licenses/Maintenance tab.
Source: Ableton

Maintenance

As mentioned previously in the "Updating Live" section, you can turn on Get Software Updates to make Live automatically keep itself up to date. Updates are downloaded while Live is running and take effect the next time the software is launched. At the time of this writing, this feature is not 100% reliable, so you may still want to manually check for updates from time to time.

Send Usage Data is a feature that anonymously shares configuration and usage information with Ableton. The data is uploaded when you launch Live, and is used to fix bugs and develop improvements based on common usage habits.

IMPORTANT NOTE: START TRANSPORT WITH RECORD: As this book was on its way to the printer, Ableton added an important new preference to the Record/Warp/Launch tab: Start Transport with Record. This preference affects the behavior of both of Live's Record buttons. When set On (the default), recording behaves as described in the rest of this book.

When Start Transport with Record is set Off, clicking Arrangement Record or Session Record will prepare Live for recording without starting playback. To begin recording, you must then press Play. (This behavior will be familiar to users of prior versions of Live.) Additionally, Session Record will not initiate clip recording as described in the "Session Record Button" section of Chapter 4.

Live Interface Basics

ONE OF ABLETON'S DEFINING ACHIEVEMENTS IS LIVE'S SIMPLE, elegant interface. Only two views are needed to accomplish everything in Live: Session View and Arrangement View. Session View is geared for use in live performance, for loop experimentation, and as a quick multitrack sketchpad, while Arrangement View facilitates detailed editing and song arranging.

In this chapter, we'll be covering the basics of getting around Live. I'll also mention a few things that you may not use until you're deeper into the program, but nevertheless need to be discussed at the outset.

Before We Begin...

To get started, it's important to know that a Live file is called a *Set*. When you first open Live, you're presented with an empty Set containing four tracks (two audio and two MIDI). To the Set you'll add prefabricated elements, such as samples or Live Clips, and create new parts by recording audio or programming MIDI parts with virtual instruments. Don't worry if you don't know what all of this means. That's what the book is about!

To switch between Session and Arrangement Views, press Tab. You can also use the horizontal and vertical line icons in the upper-right of your screen. But seriously—use Tab. Try it now.

Showing and Hiding

As you work with this book, you may notice that the figures don't always match what you see on your screen. This is because Live allows various interface elements to be shown or hidden. At the far right of Live's screen, you'll see a set of show/hide buttons. Try clicking on them, and you'll see various sets of controls appear and disappear. The ones pictured in Figure 3.1 are for various aspects of the mixer, but that's not important yet. Just be aware that these turn up in various parts of the program. Whenever you see them, click them on and off to see what happens.

Figure 3.1 Buttons like these appear in various places in Live to show or hide interface elements.
Source: Ableton

In the corners of the screen (except for the upper-right), you'll see a different type of show/hide buttons containing a triangle (see Figure 3.2). These are used to show or hide the Browser, Info View, and Track/Clip View, all discussed later in this chapter. This type of button also appears elsewhere throughout the interface to reveal additional controls and features. Make sure to try these out as you come across them.

Figure 3.2 Some views are shown or hidden using these triangular fold/unfold buttons.
Source: Ableton

Finally, you'll find all of Live's optional views can be shown or hidden from the View menu. Open this menu, and learn the keyboard shortcuts that are displayed next to the various commands. You'll be glad you did.

Working with Knobs, Sliders, and Boxes

Live has several different controls for adjusting values, which all have a lot in common, even though they look different (see Figure 3.3). Sliders are adjusted by dragging vertically, just as you'd expect. What might not be obvious is that knobs and numeric boxes are dragged in the same vertical fashion. These controls can also be adjusted by single-clicking and then using the up-and-down arrow keys. Finally, numeric boxes can be adjusted by simply typing in a value, which is often faster than dragging the mouse.

Any control can be returned to its default value by single-clicking it and then pressing Delete. Additionally, some knobs have a triangle, which can be clicked to reset to default (see the Transpose knob in Figure 3.3 for an example).

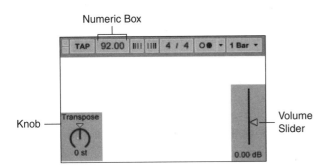

Figure 3.3 All three of these control types can be adjusted by dragging vertically.
Source: Ableton

Common Editing Commands

Under the Edit menu, you'll see Live's editing commands. Some of these are specialized commands we'll be discussing later, while others are common commands you'll want to learn right away because they are used throughout the program. For example, Duplicate can be used to make a copy of just about anything you can select with the mouse: clips, tracks, scenes, and devices. Rename works the same way. It's good to get in the habit of naming things (especially tracks and clips) before your Sets get too big and confusing. When using Rename, press Enter to confirm the name, Esc to cancel, or Tab to confirm the name and jump to the next object. As you'd expect, Live supports Cut, Copy, and Paste for moving and duplicating clips, tracks, and devices as well.

There are many editing commands that can be applied to multiple objects simultaneously. For example, it's possible to duplicate several clips in one step or to adjust the volume of several tracks simultaneously. To select multiple objects, hold down Ctrl (Cmd) while clicking on them. Alternately, Shift-click can be used to select a range. In other words, to select tracks 1 through 8, click on the title bar of track 1 and then Shift-click on the title bar of track 8.

Context Menus

Context menus contain a list of commands relevant to a particular object. They are a very useful part of Live's interface and are something you should plan on becoming very familiar with. For example, the context menu for a track contains commands to create additional tracks, as well as commands to delete or duplicate the selected track.

Context menus are typically invoked by right-clicking with the mouse. If you're on a Mac, you may need to configure your OS X Keyboard and Mouse preferences to enable the right mouse button, or you can Control-click with the left mouse button instead. If you're using a MacBook, you can also configure the trackpad to register a right-click when you click with two fingers.

The Info View

The Info View is a retractable display in the lower-left corner of Live that provides information about whatever control your mouse is hovering over (see Figure 3.4). The information displayed here is brief but very handy, and even if it doesn't answer every question, it will at least tell you the name of the thing you're looking at, which is a great help if you want to look it up in this book or (gasp!) in the Live manual.

I strongly recommend you keep the Info view open while learning Live. The "?" key can be used to quickly hide it to protect your reputation when a friend looks over your shoulder.

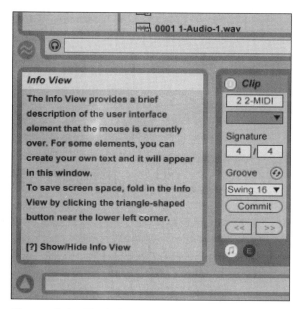

Figure 3.4 The Info View can be hidden or expanded to give you quick bits of pertinent Live wisdom.
Source: Ableton

The Help View

This view can be opened by selecting Help View from the View menu (see Figure 3.5). This view differs from the manual in that it provides step-by step tutorials organized by task, such as recording or programming beats. Exploring these topics is highly recommended for new users or experienced users moving into a new area of the program. Make sure to scroll to the bottom of the Help View and click the link that reads "Show all built-in lessons" to see all of the included content.

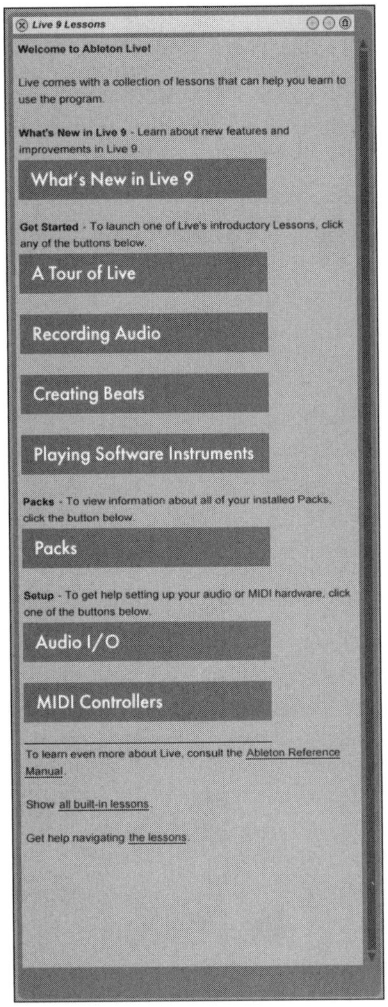

Figure 3.5 The Help View offers useful lessons and reference guides.
Source: Ableton

Session View

Live's Session View (sometimes referred to as the *Session* for short) is far more than just a tool for live performance. It's the launch point for many compositions, where ideas are sketched out and quickly captured without worrying about how and where they'll be used in the final production. The next phase of the process is handled in the Arrangement View, but there's no need to worry about that right now. Just focus on having fun in the Session View.

> **SPACE OUT:** The spacebar starts and stops audio in Live, as it does in most other audio software applications.

Clip Slot Grid

The Session View's defining characteristic is the grid that covers most of the screen. Live's clip slot grid is a palette upon which to create, organize, and experiment with the sonic colors that will eventually become your masterpiece. Just as a painter will mix colors before starting to paint, today's music producers will often gather and create appealing sounds in the clip slot grid before giving form to a song.

Each cell in the grid shown in the Session View—Ableton calls them *clip slots*—can contain a clip (see Figure 3.6). A clip is a piece of audio or MIDI that can be launched via the mouse, computer keyboard, or MIDI controller. Try dragging a few loops out of the Live 9 Power! Live Pack and dropping them in clip slots. Then launch them by clicking their triangular "play" buttons. (For more information about loading clips into slots, read "The Browser" later in this chapter.)

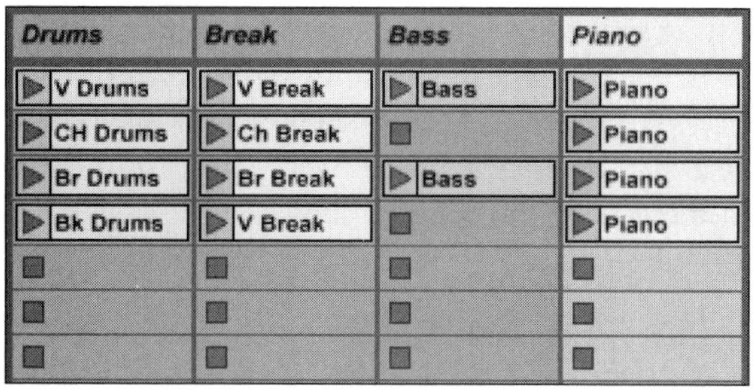

Drums	Break	Bass	Piano
▷ V Drums	▷ V Break	▷ Bass	▷ Piano
▷ CH Drums	▷ Ch Break	▢	▷ Piano
▷ Br Drums	▷ Br Break	▷ Bass	▷ Piano
▷ Bk Drums	▷ V Break	▢	▷ Piano
▢	▢	▢	▢
▢	▢	▢	▢
▢	▢	▢	▢

Figure 3.6 The clip slot grid with a few clips loaded in some slots. Each clip has its own launch button.
Source: Ableton

Every empty slot contains a square stop button. (The bottom of the clip slot grid also contains a permanent row of stop buttons that will remain visible even if you've filled every slot in the grid above.) Clicking the square in one of these slots will cause any clip playing on the track above it to stop. Also, there is another box labeled Stop Clips in the Master track at the right. This button, as its name implies, will stop all clips—both audio and MIDI—when triggered.

There's another way to stop a clip—by launching a different clip in the same column or *track*. In other words, Live only allows one clip at a time to play back in any given track. This means that any time you have two clips you want to play simultaneously, they must be in separate tracks. That's why Figure 3.6 is organized as shown, with the drum parts in one track, the bass parts in another, and so on.

Tracks and Scenes

The columns of the grid are referred to as *tracks*, while the rows are called *scenes*. The type of track determines what type of clips it contains: Audio tracks can only contain audio clips, while MIDI tracks are strictly for MIDI clips. There are also types of tracks that can't contain clips at all, but we'll get to those in Chapter 6, "Tracks and Signal Routing." We'll also be getting further into the workings of scenes later, but for now just know that scenes are a handy way to organize musical ideas. For example, when you've got a drum, bass, and keyboard part that work well together, drag around the clips in the grid so the ones you like are all in the same scene.

The Scene Launcher

At the far right of the screen, you'll see a special track called *Master*. Each slot in this track has a Scene Launch button, which is used to launch every clip in the scene simultaneously (see Figure 3.7). When you launch a scene in this way, it's as if you clicked in every single clip slot—even the empty ones containing stop buttons. Therefore, launching a scene also stops playback in any tracks that don't have a clip in that particular scene. Spend a little time playing with this, and you'll get a sense of how powerful this feature is for quickly arranging musical ideas.

Figure 3.7 Click the triangle to launch all the clips in the scene (row).
Source: Ableton

The Mixer

Live's mixer (see Figure 3.8a) is made up of several sections, which can be shown or hidden independently using the View menu, or the buttons shown in Figure 3.1. One of these sections is called *Mixer* and contains basic mixing controls such as volume. When I refer to the Mixer (with a capital "M"), I'm referring to this component, while other references to the mixer are considering the conceptual whole. Live has several different types of tracks (covered in detail in Chapter 6), some of which have unique mixer features, but most of them share the controls shown in Figure 3.8b.

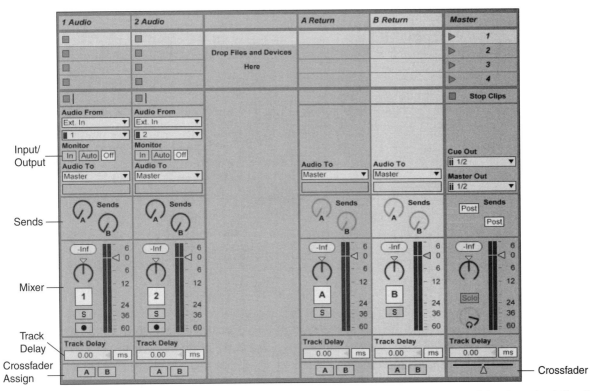

Figure 3.8a Here's the mixer with every section shown. Each of these sections is explained on the following pages.
Source: Ableton

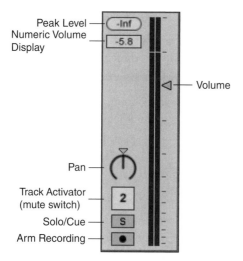

Figure 3.8b A fully expanded mixer channel.
Source: Ableton

Like many features of the Session View, the mixer is also available in the Arrangement View. However, the Session View is more intuitive to use for many tasks and offers a few additional features. I'll use the term Session Mixer when it's necessary to differentiate the two.

Let's take a look at each section now.

Mixer

▷ **Volume:** Drag to adjust the volume of a track, or type in a decibel value into the numeric display if you're in the expanded view.

▷ **Pan:** Drag to move the signal left or right in the stereo field.

▷ **Track Activator:** In most mixers, this is referred to as the "mute" switch. When turned off, the track is silenced.

▷ **Solo:** Activating Solo mutes all other tracks. If you want to Solo more than one track at a time, Cmd+click (Ctrl+click) the Solo switch, or change the Exclusive preference on the Record/Warp/Launch tab of the Preferences dialog. This button can be switched to act as a Cue switch, as explained in Chapter 6.

▷ **Arm:** Allows new clips to be recorded. If you want to Arm more than one track at a time, use Cmd+click (Ctrl+click) or change the Exclusive preference on the Record/Warp/Launch tab of the Preferences dialog. The Arm button can also be used to enable Session Automation recording, which is discussed in Chapter 4, "Making Music in Live."

If you click and drag the top edge of the Session Mixer upward, you can resize it better to see levels when mixing (see Figure 3.8b). When resized, the Peak Level display appears, indicating the maximum level reached during playback. Click on Peak Level to reset it.

Sends

Sends are used to route audio into Return tracks, which are covered in Chapter 6. For example, if you turn up Send A on a drum track, the audio from that drum track will now come out of Return A as well. This feature is typically used for effects processing, in particular to add time-based effects, such as reverb and delay.

Input/Output

The Input/Output section is used for recording and for various advanced routing techniques. The Audio From section is used to specify the source that a track will receive signal from (Input), while Audio To determines where the signal from the track goes (Output). Audio From consists of two menus: Input Type and Input Channel.

In audio tracks, Input Type determines the source that the track will record or monitor, while Input Channel is used to specify a specific input from the selected source. For example, if you want to record a guitar that's plugged into Input 2 of your soundcard, you'd select Ext. Input from the top menu and 2 from the second.

For MIDI tracks, the Input Type is used to select which MIDI device you'll use to record a performance. By default, this is set to All Ins (meaning All Inputs), which typically works just fine unless you have a very complex setup with a lot of MIDI gear. You can then use Input Channel to limit input to a specific MIDI channel, or leave it on the default, which receives all channels.

Audio To consists of Output Type and Output Channel. Just like the Inputs, these can be used to route audio to external outputs on your soundcard or MIDI to external hardware. It's also possible to route signals to other tracks within the set, but I'll explain the how and why of that technique in Chapter 6.

You may notice that the Output Channel menu is disabled by default. This is because Live's two default track settings are Master and No Output, neither of which has channel settings. If you pick a different Output Type, the second menu will activate.

The Monitor section controls whether or not the signal from the Audio From can be heard through Live's mixer. It has three modes:

▷ **In:** The input source is passed through to the mixer at all times.
▷ **Auto:** The input source is passed through to the mixer if the track is armed for recording, *and* there is no clip playing back in the track.
▷ **Off:** The input source is never passed through to the mixer.

If you're an experienced engineer, these modes should be quite familiar. If not, don't worry. Just leave your tracks set to Auto (the default). I'll be explaining different routing configurations as necessary throughout the book, and you can refer back here if you don't remember what the different modes mean.

Crossfader

Live also features a DJ-style crossfader. For many years, analog crossfaders have been used by DJs to enable the mixing of two tracks together, with one simple gesture. Scratch DJs have taken crossfader technique to incredible levels, transforming the mixer into a musical instrument.

Live's crossfader consists of two components: the crossfader itself (located at the bottom of the master track), and the Crossfader Assign switches at the bottom of every other track. To use it, you will have to assign tracks to either the A (left) or B (right) side of the crossfader. As you move the crossfader to the right, you increase the volume of all channels set to B, while decreasing the volume of all channels set to A. The reverse holds true when you move it to the left. Unassigned tracks are disregarded by the crossfader and play back regardless of its position.

Opening the crossfader's context menu reveals the transition modes, which determine the volume curve used when transitioning between A and B. Constant, Dipped, and Intermediate are curves that slowly change the volume across the entire range of the crossfader. With all three of these modes, there's a gain reduction to both sides in the center position (Dipped reduces gain the most, Constant the least) to compensate for the volume overload you can get from mixing together two powerful sources (like dance tracks). Fast Cut, Slow Cut, and Slow Fade have both sources at maximum amplitude before the center position is reached. Slow Fade provides the largest amount of transition between the two, with Fast Cut providing almost none.

Track Delay

Track Delay isn't a mixer control in the traditional sense, but it provides a very valuable service in the world of digital audio. It allows the output of a channel to be delayed or advanced by small amounts of time (measured in milliseconds or samples) to compensate for sluggish hardware, plug-ins that generate excessive latency, or as a creative tool. (Theoretically, Live can automatically compensate for all plug-in latency, but this depends on the plug-in accurately reporting its latency to Live, which not all plug-ins do.)

Positive values make the track play back later, while negative values make it play earlier. For example, you might be sending MIDI to an external synthesizer and hear that it's responding late and messing up the groove. Set track delay to –50ms to bring it into sync. Or maybe you've got a hi-hat clip that you think would sound better if it lagged a little behind the beat. Set its Track Delay to 10ms to add a little vibe.

Note that in order to hear the effects of Track Delay, Delay Compensation must be activated under the Options menu. To make the Track Delay setting visible at the bottom of each track, select the Track Delay option under the View menu.

Arrangement View

Beginners may think of it as merely Live's "other" window, but Arrangement View (sometimes called the *Arrangement* for short) is incredibly important. It's the place where final decisions about composing and arranging are made, and where songs are completed. If Session View is the spontaneous right-brain-tickling creative screen, Arrangement View is the analytic left-brain-stimulating, "finishing touches" side of Live.

You may notice that Live's Arrangement View closely resembles other multitrack applications (see Figure 3.9). These programs, such as Cubase, Logic, and Pro Tools, are based on horizontal, left-to-right audio arrangers (also called *timelines*). If you like this method of working, you will be right at home making music in the Arrangement.

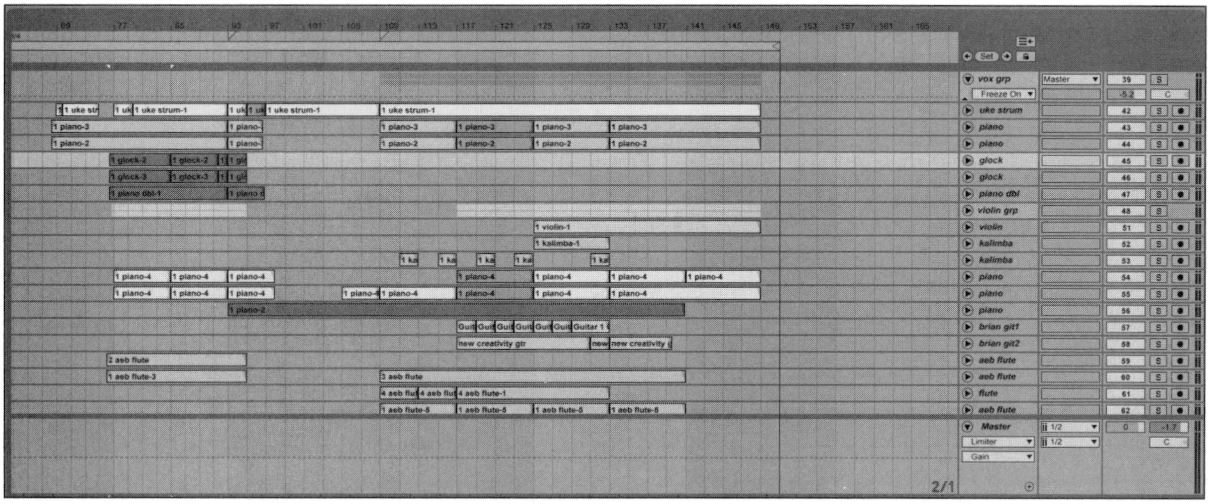

Figure 3.9 Live's Arrangement View is where songs are finished. Each horizontal line in Arrangement View represents a track that corresponds to a vertical channel in the Session Mixer.
Source: Ableton

For those who didn't read the figure caption, here it is again: Each track in Session View corresponds precisely to its track counterpart in Arrangement View. If you have eight tracks in Session View, you will have eight tracks in Arrangement View. You can add a track in either view, and it will appear in the other.

Clips can be added to this view by dragging and dropping (just like you would in Session View), or by using a method called *Arrangement Record*, which allows an arrangement to be created interactively by launching clips and tweaking controls, such as track volumes and effect parameters. While this is a fairly deep topic, the basics are quite simple. Try this out:

1. Click on Arrangement Record, the solid circular "record" button at the top of the screen (next to Play and Stop).
2. Launch some clips in the Session View and adjust some track volumes.
3. Press the spacebar to stop and press Tab to switch to the Arrangement View.
4. You'll see every clip you launched laid out left to right in the timeline, and the movement of every volume you adjusted represented as a red line called *automation*.

When you start playback while looking at your new arrangement, Live may not do exactly what you expect. Instead of playing back the arrangement you just recorded, Live ignores it and resumes playing the same clips that were playing back when you stopped recording. Confused? Excellent. Everyone is at this point!

To hear the arrangement, you'll have to click on Back to Arrangement, as seen in Figure 3.10. Once you do, you'll immediately start to hear the Arrangement View clips play back, and you'll also notice that they pop into full color instead of being dimmed out as they were before. So what's going on here? Read on and I'll explain.

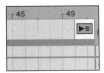

Figure 3.10 The button in the top-right corner of this figure is called Back to Arrangement. This all important control allows you to hear the contents of the Arrangement View.
Source: Ableton

Relation to the Session View

Although the Arrangement and Session Views may seem very different, they are closely related. The main difference is the way in which they handle clips. Arrangement View deals with them in a linear fashion: clips play in the order they show up in the timeline, from left to right. Session View is a non-linear beast: clips are launched interactively to play in any order you want. Both views allow you to place multiple clips in a track, but in any given track, *only one clip can play back at a time.*

In the Session View, this is seen in a behavior described earlier—launching a clip stops playback of any currently playing clip in the same track. In the Arrangement View this behavior can be demonstrated by dragging a clip and dropping it on top of an existing clip. The clip you dropped *replaces* what was there before. They can't "overlap" and both play simultaneously.

The same rule applies to clips in the Session and Arrangement Views. As mentioned previously, the two views are just different ways of looking at the same set of tracks. Therefore, any given track can either have a clip playing back from the Session View or the Arrangement View, never both simultaneously. In order to hear clips play back from the Arrangement View, you need to *explicitly give control to Arrangement View*; otherwise, the clips in the Session View will win out.

This takes some getting used to, and like all good rules, there are a couple of exceptions. But not to worry! Read on and practice using the program. It will all make sense eventually, I promise.

While playing back an arrangement, you're free to return to the Session View to launch clips. When you do this, two things will happen in the Arrangement to show you that clips from the Session have taken over: the clips in the Arrangement will be dimmed (grayed out), and a triangular "play" button will appear at the far right of the track (see Figure 3.11).

Figure 3.11 The top track has been overridden by a clip in the Session.
Source: Ableton

To hear what's going on in the Arrangement again, you have two choices. Click Back to Arrangement (as described above) to restore the Arrangement for *all tracks*, or click the triangular button on the right to restore an *individual track*.

This relationship between the two views means that you can arrange a song in the Arrangement View, but return to the Session View at any point for further experimentation. For example, maybe you're not crazy about a percussion track in a song you're working on. Just head back to the Session View to launch a few percussion loops while listening to your arrangement. If you find something you like, hit Arrangement Record to replace the part. When you're done, use the methods described previously to return control to the Arrangement.

The Arrangement Mixer

The Arrangement View's mixer controls are located on the right side of the screen, as seen in Figure 3.12. Also notice that there's a triangular "unfold" switch, which is used to enlarge the track so that all of the mixer controls are visible, and a detailed view of the clips in that track can be seen as well.

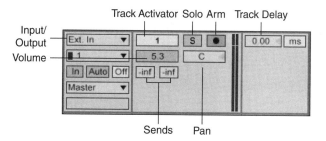

Figure 3.12 All the mixer controls can be accessed from Arrangement View.
Source: Ableton

Every mixer control seen in the Session is also available in the Arrangement. The only difference is visual: The controls have been turned on their sides and are represented by values instead of graphical controls. Also, unlike Session View, the sends are displayed as part of the Mixer section.

Clip View and Track View

The bottom of your screen is shared between two views: The Clip View which allows detailed manipulation of audio and MIDI, and the Track View, which is for working with devices such as effects and instruments.

To access the Clip View, double-click on a clip. In the Session, you can double-click anywhere but on the launch button, while in the Arrangement, you can click anywhere except for the waveform/MIDI display that's visible when the track is unfolded.

The Track view is accessed by double-clicking on the top area of a track where its name is shown (called the *title bar*). You can easily switch between these views using the Shift-Tab keyboard shortcut. Both views can be hidden or shown by pressing Cmd+Option+L, or via the Detail section of the View menu.

The best way to understand how these two views work together is to think of the Track View as happening "after" the Clip View. For example, let's say you have a bass loop playing back in a track. The Clip View is where you would change the loop itself, modifying its key, timing, and loop points. The sound then flows into the Track View and is processed by any effects you've added. In the case of MIDI clips, there's no audio flowing out of the clip; instead, it's MIDI data, which is like a set of instructions (for example, what notes to play when). These notes flow into whatever instrument is hosted in the Track View, which, in turn, produces sound and sends it into the Mixer.

The Clip View

When the Clip View is open, it shows the details of whatever clip is currently selected in the Session or Arrangement (see Figure 3.13). In the lower-left corner, there are switches used to show and hide the different sections: Launch, Sample (for audio clips), Notes (for MIDI clips), and Envelopes. When you're in the Arrangement, the Launch box isn't shown since its settings are only relevant in the Session.

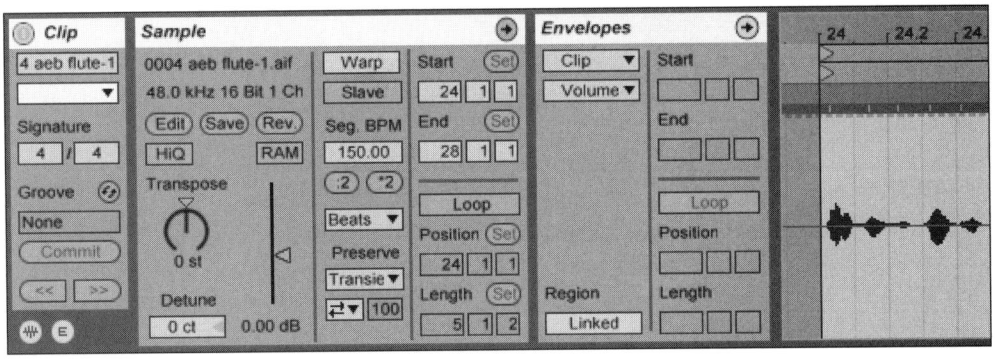

Figure 3.13 Here's the Clip View for an audio clip.
Source: Ableton

The parameters in the Clip View are a big subject that we'll be covering over the next three chapters. At first, all that's important to know is that this is where you refine, tweak, and mangle individual clips. Launch an audio clip, and then explore this view and experiment a little bit.

Crank the Transpose knob, and you'll hear the pitch change immediately. Next to Transpose, there's a volume slider, which can be used to adjust the volume for this clip only (unlike the volume control in the Mixer, which will change the volume for any clip playing back in that track). Press the button marked Rev. to make the audio play backwards.

The Track View

The Track View is home to devices: Audio Effects, MIDI Effects, Instruments, and Plug-Ins (see Figure 3.14). Until you add some devices, the Track View will be empty, except for a caption that tells you what sort of devices the track will accept. Audio tracks can only accept Audio Effects, while MIDI tracks can use any type of device. Signal flows from left to right in the Track View, passing from one device to the next.

To see the Track View in action, click on the Audio Effects view in the Browser and drag an effect device into a track. All clips played in this track will now be processed by this effect. We'll be discussing effects and instruments in greater detail in Chapters 8, "Live's Instruments," and 9, "Live's Audio Effects," but for now all that's important is to have fun and experiment.

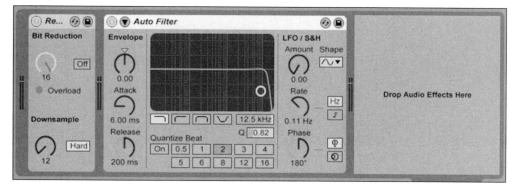

Figure 3.14 Here's the Track View with a couple of effect devices loaded in.
Source: Ableton

The Browser

Before you start having fun with Session and Arrangement views, it's important to familiarize yourself with Live's content portal, the Browser. The Browser window (see Figure 3.15) provides the means to access all of the elements you will add to a Live Set such as samples, MIDI files, Live's built-in devices (Instruments, MIDI Effects and Audio Effects) and third-party plug ins. The Browser is available in both the Session and Arrangement Views, and can be hidden to save space when you're not using it.

Figure 3.15 The Browser is for accessing all of the content and devices you'll use in Live.

Source: Ableton

Basic navigation of the Browser should be familiar to anyone with a working knowledge of Windows Explorer or the Finder on a Mac. Any item containing additional content (such as a folder) has a triangle to its left, which can be clicked to "unfold" the item and display the contents within. The left and right arrow keys can be used for folding and unfolding as well.

The Browser can also perform functions similar to the Explorer or Finder. You can drag and drop files and folders from one location into another, as well as rename and delete files. Right-clicking on a Live Set or other file in the Browser will bring up a contextual menu with options for creating folders and other common tasks.

Categories and Places

The left area of the Browser is divided into two sections: Categories and Places. Below these headings, you'll see a list of icons that I'll refer to as *views*. Categories is a fixed set of views for exploring different types of content, while Places contains views for exploring content by location rather than type. Let's take a look at Places first.

Places

Places is customizable, but by default it only contains the following views:

▷ **Packs:** Live Packs contain content for Live such as presets and samples. This view allows you to view all of the packs you've installed and browse their contents. As you load up your computer with Packs, you'll find this an incredibly handy way to explore.

▷ **User Library:** New to Live 9, this area conveniently separates your personal content from that installed by Live or add-on Live Packs. Whenever you save your own device presets, Live stores them in the User Library.

For presets that have associated sample files (such as Simpler presets), the sample files are copied here as well. This area is also home to items such as Defaults and Slicing Presets.

▷ **Current Project:** This view displays everything contained within the project folder of the currently open Set. Typically, this is samples and Sets, but other files of your choosing can be stored here as well. (For more information on Project Folders, please see "Saving Your Work" later in this chapter.)

▷ **Live 8 Library:** For users upgrading from Live 8, this view will display the old Library. If you have a Live 8 Library but it does not appear here, visit the Library tab of the Preferences screen to locate it.

You can also add any folder from your hard drive to Places by using the Add Folder option at the bottom. For example, you might want to add sample libraries or your DJ music folders. Folders added here will be scanned and added to Live's database, which can take a while if the folders are large. This feature enables fast searching, and also allows content to be shown in the appropriate Browse areas.

Categories

The Categories area displays both factory and user installed content, by category:

▷ **Sounds:** This view shows Live's factory Instrument and Instrument Rack presets organized by type of sound. See Chapters 7, "Using Effects and Instruments," and 8, "Live's Instruments," for more information on Instruments and Racks.

▷ **Drums:** Here you'll find Drum Rack presets, as well as a folder called "Drum Hits." This folder contains both drum samples (with .WAV and .AIF extensions) and individual drum presets (with .ADG extensions) for adding to your Drum Racks.

▷ **Instruments, Audio Effects, MIDI Effects:** This view displays Live's built-in devices, which are described in detail in Chapters 8, 9, and 10. Devices can be unfolded to show folders containing their presets. Instrument presets saved into the User Library will appear under their associated device in a folder called "User."

▷ **Max for Live:** In this view, you'll see that Max for Live devices are categorized by Instrument, Audio Effect, and MIDI Effect, just like Live's built-in devices. The truth is that these devices can go beyond any of these categories and extend Live in all sorts of wild and wonderful ways.

▷ **Plug-ins:** This is where you access your third-party software effects and plug-ins. You can use a wide variety of third-party plug-ins with Live, in either VST (PC/Mac) or AU (Mac only) formats. Plug-ins can be either instruments or effects, but aren't automatically separated into categories. To tell them apart, you'll notice that instrument plug-ins have a small piano keyboard in their icon, while effects do not. Like built-in devices, plug-ins can be unfolded to reveal presets, but typically all you'll see are presets you've created yourself, since most plug-ins manage factory presets internally.

▷ **Clips:** Live Clips are musical parts saved in a special format that allows them to also contain devices and automation (which can't be saved with standard audio or MIDI files). Bear in mind that while Live Clips can be audio or MIDI, there's no way to tell them apart in the browser, so you'll just have to jump in and try them out.

▷ **Samples:** Here you'll see every audio file in the Live Library, the User Library, and any folders you've added to Places. This is typically a pretty gigantic list of files, so it's mostly used in conjunction with the search function described next.

Searching for Files

Even with all of the handy views offered by the Browser, you'll still find the Search function quite handy. To get started, just type something into the search box at the top of the Browser. As soon as you begin to type, you'll see a new view called *All Results* appear in the Browser (see Figure 3.16). As you'd expect, this view displays every file containing the search term, regardless of its type.

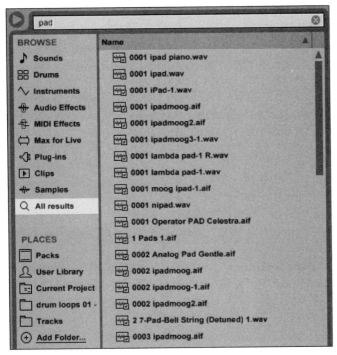

Figure 3.16 Searching the word "pad" and selecting All results on the left shows you every file from every place that has "pad" in its name.

Source: Ableton

The real power of the Browser is revealed by clicking on the other views, which will display a filtered list of content matching your search term. For the search shown in Figure 3.16, clicking on Sounds will reveal a list of folders containing presets with "pad" in the name. The same holds true for Places. By combining search terms with filtering by type (Browse) or location (Places), you should be able to find anything you need without much suffering.

Preview Tab

The Preview Tab is located at the bottom of the Browser. Previewing can be toggled off and on by clicking the headphones icon shown in Figure 3.17. When turned on, the icon turns blue, and you'll be able to hear the sounds you're browsing right away. Audio files (such as you'd find in the Samples view) will play back automatically when selected, and an image of the waveform will appear to the right of the headphones. In the case of Live Clips, this same area will display the words, Click to Preview. You can follow this instruction, or use the right arrow key to begin playback.

Figure 3.17 The Browser's Preview allows you to listen to audio or MIDI clips at either the current project tempo or their original tempo.

Source: Ableton

QUICK PREVIEW: The right arrow key can be used to preview individual files when the Preview switch is disengaged.

Every instrument preset (found under Sounds or Instruments) installed with Live 9 has a preview snippet built in. When previewing, you'll hear a two-second sample of the instrument playing middle C. For Drum Rack presets, you'll hear a loop of a beat being played with that particular kit. Presets from older versions of Live, or those created by third parties, may not have preview snippets. When you come across these, you'll have to add them to your set and try them out in order to hear them.

If you use preview during playback, Live will begin the preview at the beginning of the next bar and attempt to play the preview at the current Master Tempo. With factory content and loop libraries, this feature should work perfectly, but for longer files and content where Live can't determine necessary Warping info, it may not. If you want to preview a lot of content quickly, it's better to stop the sequencer first.

> **CUEING THE MIX:** You can adjust the volume of loops heard via Live's preview feature by rotating the Preview/Cue volume knob in the Master track. In Session View, this control appears as a knob with headphones next to it.

In Use

Items from the Browser are added into Sets by dragging and dropping them into tracks. You can also double-click, but I strongly recommend using drag and drop until you're quite familiar with getting around the program. Double-click doesn't always do what you'd expect, and it can be a bit confusing.

Obviously, there are quite a few different things in the Browser, and you'll need to know more about the details of each one before understanding the how and why of using them in a Set. Everything you need to know will be explained in the coming chapters.

The Control Bar

Running across the top of the screen is the Control Bar, which handles all common transport functions (start/stop, playback position, loop, tempo), along with important system information and helpful tools, such as tap tempo and a metronome. In this section, we'll move from left to right, examining every function.

Tempo, Time Signature, and Quantization

The left side of the Control Bar deals with all things timing related (see Figure 3.18). The buttons are (from left to right): External Sync Switch, External Sync Indicators, Tap Tempo, Tempo, Tempo Nudge, Time Signature, Metronome, and Quantization.

Figure 3.18 This subsection of the Control Bar is devoted to time.
Source: Ableton

You won't see the external controls unless you've already set up an external sync source or destination in the MIDI/ Sync Preferences tab (see Chapter 2, "Getting Live Up and Running"). You'll need to do this if you want Live's tempo to be set by an external device, or if you want Live to control the tempo of a drum machine, synth, or sequencer. The External Sync switch engages or disengages Live's MIDI synchronization to an outside source, while the monitoring lights announce that the MIDI sync signal is being sent or received.

The Tap Tempo button is a handy song-starting feature in Live. For a quick test drive of one of Tap Tempo's features, click the button four times, and your project will begin at that tempo. This is a great feature if you need to sync up with your drummer or manually synchronize to another device, such as a turntable or CD player.

Next up are Live's project Tempo and Time Signature settings, which are found just to the right of the Tap Tempo button. Live can handle tempos ranging from 20 to 999 BPM (beats per minute), time signatures with numerators ranging from 1 to 99, and denominator choices of 1, 2, 4, 8, and 16—an absurdly huge range of possibilities.

Moving to the right of Time Signature, you come to Tempo Nudge Down, followed by Tempo Nudge Up. These controls are used to change Live's master tempo momentarily in order to bring it into sync with another source, much the way a DJ beat matches two tracks by physically dragging the record back or speeding it up slightly before letting go of it. Tapping these controls will yield very slight tempo changes (less than 1 BPM), while holding them down can be used to slow the tempo to a third of its original value or speed it up by as much as two-thirds. Releasing either control immediately returns Live to its original tempo.

When the Metronome button is engaged, you will hear a click (metronome) that can serve as a guide for new recordings and help with loop editing. The volume of the click can be adjusted by using the Preview/Cue volume knob in Live's Master track (the same knob you use for adjusting the preview volume when browsing for samples). Notice that there's a small arrow to the right of the metronome. Clicking it reveals a drop-down menu for Count-In settings, which are explained in the Preferences section of Chapter 2.

Quantization

Finally, we come to the Quantization menu, which is used to set Live's *global quantization* for launching clips. You may be familiar with the concept of quantization if you've worked with sequencers or drum machines before. In music, quantization means eliminating or reducing imprecision by forcing rhythms to conform to a predefined set of values. For example, you might play a drum part on a set of pads and then quantize it to correct any hits that were played early or late.

The quantization dealt with in this menu is for *launch quantization*, which is a little different than the common example shown previously. You may have noticed while experimenting in the Session View that clips don't start playback immediately when you click on them. Instead, they wait until the beginning of the next bar and play back in sync with the other currently playing clips. In other words, the launching of the clip is being quantized to 1 Bar, the default value in the Quantization menu.

Exploring this menu, you'll see that you can quantize to a whole range of values, including None, which allows clips to play back immediately. I strongly recommend that you experiment with different values to get a feel for this feature, and that you return quantization to 1 Bar when you're done. It will make life much easier as you're learning the program. Also, bear in mind that there's lots more information on launch quantization in the "Clips" section of Chapter 4.

SO FINE: To make fine adjustments to the Tempo (the values to the right of the decimal point) and small adjustments to other controls such as volume, hold down the Ctrl(Cmd) key while dragging.

Transport Controls

Most starting and stopping in Live is best handled with the spacebar (tap it once to start, tap it again to stop); however, the second area of Live's Control Bar has Start and Stop buttons (see Figure 3.19). You will also find the Arrangement Record, Automation Arm, and a few other advanced controls that will be covered in Chapter 4.

Figure 3.19 Here is the transport section of Live's Control Bar. This is mission control for playback, recording, and automation.
Source: Ableton

The next section of the Control Bar contains basic transport controls, along with several controls that deal with recording clips and automation. Recording and automation are complex topics that will be dealt with in upcoming chapters, so I'll just be giving basic definitions on these controls for now.

▷ **Follow:** When turned on, Live's display will follow the song position (in the Arrangement) or the clip position (in the Clip View) to keep the currently playing part visible. It works in conjunction with the Follow Behavior preference in the Look/Feel tab of Preferences.

▷ **Arrangement Position:** This box provides a continuous readout—in measures, beats, and subdivisions—of where you are in the song, whether you're listening or recording. You can manually enter a start time value into this box or drag up and down with the mouse to change the setting.

▷ **Play & Stop:** These buttons start and stop playback, you can also toggle between play and stop using the spacebar.

▷ **Arrangement Record:** This button is used to initiate recording clips and automation into the Arrangement.

▷ **MIDI Overdub:** When recording MIDI into the Arrangement, this button can be enabled to allow notes to be added to existing MIDI clips. When disabled, MIDI clips are overwritten during recording.

▷ **Automation Arm:** This enables the recording of Session Automation and allows overdubbing of automation into the Arrangement View. This is a somewhat complex topic and will be covered in detail in Chapter 4.

▷ **Re-Enable Automation:** Just as it's possible to override Arrangement clips by launching clips from the session, it's also possible to override automation by manually changing an automated parameter. Whenever automation has been overridden, this button will light up. Clicking on it will restore automation for all clips and tracks.

▷ **Session Record (Session View only):** This is a multi-function button that works in close conjunction with the Push controller, but is used without Push as well. It is used to record new clips, as well as to overdub MIDI and automation. These topics are covered in the "Recording" section of Chapter 4.

▷ **Prepare Scene for New Recording (Session View only):** This button was also created with Push in mind, but it can be used without it. It's only enabled when a non-empty scene is selected, and at least one track is armed for recording. Clicking it immediately gives you a clean slate: you're moved to an empty scene, and any playing clips in armed tracks are stopped immediately.

Punch In/Out and Arrangement Loop

This section of Live's Control Bar, shown in Figure 3.20, is used in conjunction with the Arrangement View. The first box displays a number indicating the loop's starting point, while the last box shows the length. In other words, Figure 3.20 shows us that the loop starts at the beginning of bar 111 and is 28 bars long. This is also displayed graphically in the Arrangement by a brace that appears over the looped bars. In the center of this section is the Loop switch. When depressed, the loop is activated, and the Arrangement will indefinitely repeat the portion of the timeline defined by the position and length values just mentioned.

The bent lines on both sides of the Loop switch are called *punch points*. These can be used to automatically enable recording temporarily, so you don't have to worry about recording over sections you want to keep. We will cover recording in detail in Chapter 4, so don't worry if this description seems a little brief.

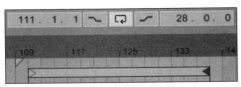

Figure 3.20 Live's Loop Start and Loop End controls also double as the punch-in and punch-out locations. The brace seen below can also be moved or resized to adjust these values.

Source: Ableton

Draw Mode, Computer MIDI Keyboard, Key and MIDI Map, System Performance, and MIDI I/O

The first item in this area of the Control Bar is used for turning Draw Mode on and off (see Figure 3.21). This is colloquially referred to as the *pencil tool* (but you won't find that term anywhere in the Live manual). Used for drawing automation and MIDI, this mode is toggled on and off with a quick press of the B key, or temporarily invoked by clicking and holding B. The piano keyboard icon turns MIDI input from the alphanumeric computer keyboard on and off; this is a feature that allows you to use your computer's keyboard as a MIDI input device, which can be handy when working on a laptop on the go. The Key (Key Map Mode Switch) and MIDI (MIDI Map Mode switch) buttons are your entrance points to controlling Live without using your mouse. This feature is called *remote control* and is discussed next.

Figure 3.21 Pictured above is the fourth segment of Live's Control Bar. From here, you can monitor your hardware (CPU load and MIDI input/output) and set up your Key and MIDI controls.

Source: Ableton

Knowing how much gas is left in the tank—or whether you're running on fumes—is important in the computer world. Here to help, Live's CPU Load Meter continuously shows the amount of strain on your system for audio processing. If this bar approaches 100 percent, you may begin to experience performance degradation or audio dropouts. The Hard Disk Overload Indicator (the letter "D") just to the right of the CPU meter will flicker red if your computer is not able to get data from the hard drive quickly enough. This will also result in dropouts and usually occurs because your hard drive is too slow for the number of audio clips you are trying to play back simultaneously.

The two small indicators at the far right light up when a MIDI signal is present. The top indicator shows MIDI input, while the bottom one shows output. There also are two similar indicators between the MIDI Map mode and Key Map mode buttons. These illuminate when remote control messages are sent in or out of Live.

MIDI and Computer Keyboard Remote Control

Just about everything in Live, from launching clips to tweaking device parameters, can be *remotely controlled* from a MIDI controller or the computer keyboard. What follows is a brief introduction to a topic that is covered in detail in Chapter 11, "Remote Control."

If you're using Ableton's Push, or one of the many controllers for which Live has control surface support, Live creates *instant mappings*, which means that some of Live's controls are automatically mapped to the controller. However, regardless of the controller you use, Live makes it easy to create your own customized mappings.

To assign a key on your computer keyboard, first click the Key Map Mode switch (refer to Figure 3.21), or press Ctrl (Cmd)+K. An orange overlay will appear over any control that can be mapped. Click on the control you want to map and press a key on your keyboard to map it. Then press the Key Map Mode switch again to restore Live to normal operation, and you're done! Be aware that when Computer MIDI Keyboard is enabled, much of the computer keyboard will not function for remote control.

Before you can use a MIDI controller for remote control, you must visit the MIDI/Sync tab of the Preferences screen and set Remote to On, as explained in Chapter 2. After you've done that, click the MIDI Map Mode switch in the Control Bar (shown in Figure 3.21 above), or press Ctrl (Cmd)+M. The blue overlay that appears indicates the controls that can have a MIDI message assigned to them. Click on the control you want to map and move the MIDI control you want to map it to.

WITH THE PUSH OF A KNOB: Live will allow you to assign MIDI knobs and sliders to on-screen buttons. In this case, the button in Live will turn on when your MIDI control passes its midpoint (64 on a scale of 0 to 127). It will switch off when you move the control back under 64.

You can also assign a MIDI button or computer key to an on-screen slider or knob. In this case, pressing the button or key will make the slider or knob toggle between its lowest and highest settings.

Key and MIDI mappings are saved with the Set, so every song can have a different control scheme. If you find yourself always making common assignments, you can assign them and save them as part of your default set (see "File/Folder" in Chapter 2).

Overview

Just below the Control Bar is the Overview. (If you don't see it, select Overview from the View menu, as shown in Figure 3.22.) The Overview, which resembles a very small timeline, is there purely for navigation and reference purposes to show you where you are in the Arrangement. So long as you have clips in the Arrangement View, it offers a bird's-eye view of your entire composition, displaying tiny colored lines representing the clips.

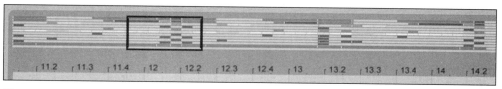

Figure 3.22 Live's Overview is a view from above.
Source: Ableton

In the Session View, the mouse transforms into a launcher when placed over the Overview. Clicking will cause Live to jump to that point in the Arrangement.

In the Arrangement, the Overview contains a black rectangle to indicate the portion of the Arrangement that is currently visible. Dragging the edges of this box causes the display to zoom in or out, making more or less of the timeline visible.

You can also use the Overview for navigating. Place the mouse pointer over the portion of the Overview bar you want to move to, and a magnifying-glass icon will appear; click once, and you will be moved to the corresponding location in the arrangement. To zoom in and out, hover over the Overview bar, depress the mouse button (left on PC), and move the mouse up and down to zoom in and out, respectively. Clicking and moving the mouse left or right will scroll the visible area of the timeline.

File Management

Learning how to do effective file management seems incredibly boring at first, but yields great benefits later when you are enjoying the creative process of making music, rather than tearing your hair out searching for lost samples and digging through multiple versions of songs, trying to figure out the right one. Here's my advice: Adopt good practices at the outset, rather than make a mess and have to clean it up later.

Sets and Projects

The first time you save a Set, Live 9 will automatically create a project folder called *<Set name> + Project* to hold all the files associated with the Set. Before you get too deep into using Live, choose a location on your hard drive to save all of your Live projects. Whenever you start a new song, save it into this folder. For example, let's say you create a folder called *Live Projects*. Every new song you start gets saved into this folder, so eventually you will have a folder full of projects, as seen in Figure 3.23.

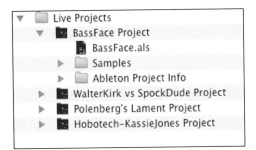

Figure 3.23 A neatly organized projects folder. Each new song has its own project. Inside the project folder is the Set (.als) file.
Source: Ableton

What you want to make sure you *don't* do is save all of your new Sets into an *already existing* project folder, as seen in Figure 3.24. This becomes a nightmare when any sort of project sharing or advanced file management is necessary later.

Figure 3.24 A project folder with a bunch of random unrelated Set files inside it. This will eventually drive you crazy.
Source: Ableton

This is not to say that you never want to save multiple sets into the same project folder. In fact, this is often a desirable thing to do when saving *multiple versions of the same song* using the Save As command, as seen in Figure 3.25.

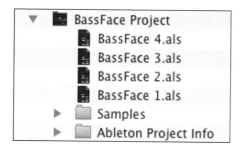

Figure 3.25 A project folder with several versions of the same song in it. These might be Sets with different purposes (such as radio edits or alternate mixes) or simply a way of ensuring that you can get back to an old version in case you change something and want to go back.
Source: Ableton

Saving multiple versions is an essential part of any experienced producer's process. How often you save a new copy is up to you. The important thing is to leave a *breadcrumb trail*—a record of what changed when. Having done this, you can recover previous settings in case they are accidentally lost, or you can simply decide you don't like the direction you've gone and go back and try again.

Saving the Live Set

Live offers four ways to save project files: Save Live Set, Save Live Set As, Save a Copy, and Collect All and Save. If you are familiar with common computer documents, such as word processor applications, Save and Save As work in exactly the way you'd expect. Save, which can be done by pressing Ctrl/Cmd+S, saves the document (in this case a Live song file called a *Set*) in its present state, under its present filename. This is the most common way you will save while you are working on a new song, especially when you like the results.

Save Live Set As (Ctrl/Cmd+Shift key+S) is the command for saving the current song file in its current state under a *different* name and is usually done only when you want to begin a new song or modify an existing song without changing the original version. To do this, select File > Save Live Set As, select the location where you would like to place the file, and type the song's newest name.

If you are modifying a song but would like to preserve a copy of it in its current state, use File > Save a Copy. This command is the same as Save As in that it allows you to save the file under a new name, but instead of opening the newly named copy, the Save a Copy command will keep the version you are currently working on open, while simply saving the new copy to disk.

Collect All and Save

The most comprehensive save method is Collect All and Save. Live allows you to add files to a Set from anywhere on your hard drive(s). This is very convenient, as you may have sample libraries where you keep content that may be used across many different projects. However, over time, hard drives get reorganized or left at home (or in the studio), and you're faced with the inconvenience of opening a Set and discovering there are samples missing. Collect All and Save eliminates this problem by copying all files used by the Set into the Project folder.

NO PLUG-INS: Even though Collect All and Save works wonders for keeping all your files together, keep in mind that any external plug-ins (VST and AU) used in a Set cannot be saved within the project. This means that if you transport your song to a different computer, all of the plug-ins used on your song must be present on that computer as well. Unless you know you'll have all the necessary plug-ins on the system you are moving to, it's a good idea to Freeze plug-in dependent tracks before moving your session (see Chapter 7, "Using Effects and Instruments").

Making Music in Live

I N THIS CHAPTER, we'll be covering the core concepts and basic workflow of Live. This is a big chapter with a lot of information, but if you spend the time to take it all in, you'll find the rest of the book much easier to manage. Also bear in mind that this chapter builds heavily on Chapter 3, "Live Interface Basics," so unlike some of the other content in this book, these two are really meant to be read in order. The rest of the chapters are spent digging into the details of various components (audio clips, MIDI clips, devices) and advanced techniques (such as the Groove Engine and Follow Actions).

I'll also be introducing many important commands. While Live has a very manageable set of commands compared to other programs, there are still quite a few to learn. With a few exceptions, I'll be directing you to Live's main menu bar and its many context menus when new commands are introduced. The menus display keyboard shortcuts next to the commands, and I strongly recommend taking a moment to learn them as you go.

> **UNDONE:** There's a good reason that most programs have the Undo command as the first option in the Edit menu. The only way to learn a program is to get in there and experiment, knowing you can back out of any mistakes you make. It may sound funny to say, but Ableton Live has one of the best Undo features in the business. Unlike some other programs, almost everything you do can be undone. (Exceptions include the Solo and Arm switches, some file operations in the Browser, and certain parameter changes in complex plug-in devices.) Be aware that the Undo queue is emptied when you save a Set or quit Live.

While the fundamental concepts behind Live are equally important to all users, the actual music making process differs quite a bit from person to person. Like most things, discovering your method is a matter of practice and experimentation. We'll be looking at some standard approaches here, so it's well worth your time to familiarize yourself with them; however, in most cases there's no one "right" way to do things, so don't be afraid to find your own way.

The basic procedure goes like this:

▷ **Create individual musical parts**: Record bass parts, guitar riffs, keyboard lines, drum grooves, and MIDI instruments, or import samples and MIDI sequences. These are called *clips*.
▷ **Create song sections**: Arrange clips that go together horizontally in the Session View to make *scenes*. Each scene represents a section of your song, such as intro, verse, and chorus.
▷ **Record an Arrangement**: Launch clips and scenes in the Session while using Arrangement Record to capture your song into the Arrangement View.
▷ **Finalize the song**: Edit the Arrangement, add effects to the mix, layer additional parts, finalize the automation, and export the song to disk.

Clips and Tracks

Clips are the musical building blocks of Live. They come in two varieties: audio and MIDI. Audio clips produce sound from audio files on disk, while MIDI clips contain MIDI data for playing either virtual or hardware instruments.

Clips in the Session View are played or *launched* by clicking the triangular Clip Launch Button at the left side of the clip. Clips in the Arrangement View are played as the playback cursor (the thin vertical line that moves from left to right when Live is running) passes over them.

In the clip slot grid, audio and MIDI clips look exactly the same, and there's no way to tell them apart. However, in the Clip View the difference is immediately apparent, as seen in Figures 4.1a and 4.1b. It's also easy to tell audio and MIDI apart in the Arrangement, as seen in Figure 4.2.

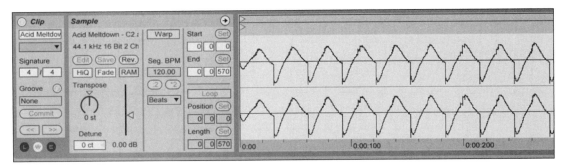

Figure 4.1a Audio clips display a waveform.
Source: Ableton

Figure 4.1b MIDI clips display sequences of MIDI notes.
Source: Ableton

Figure 4.2 Clips in the Arrangement View can be resized to change how long they will play. Note that it's easy to tell the MIDI track (notes are displayed) from the audio tracks (waveform is displayed).
Source: Ableton

As briefly explained in Chapter 3, clips are contained within tracks. Before going further into the details of working with clips, let's take a closer look at tracks.

Creating Tracks

Tracks are created using the commands in the Create menu (Insert Audio Track, Insert MIDI Track, and Insert Return Track). These commands can also be accessed in the context menu that appears when you right-click in the title bar of any existing track. To remove a track, click on its title bar and press Delete.

Tracks can also be created by dropping items from the Browser into the Drop Area (the empty part of the Session and Arrangement views labeled "Drop Files and Devices Here"). For example, you could drop an audio file here to automatically create an audio track or drop an instrument to create a MIDI track.

This method of track creation is particularly handy when dragging in Live Clips. Live Clips can be audio or MIDI, and at the time of this writing, there's no way to tell them apart. Drag them into the Drop Area, and Live will automatically create the right type of track.

Audio Tracks and MIDI Tracks

Audio tracks can contain audio clips and audio effects. All an audio track requires to produce sound is an audio clip—effects are completely optional (and completely fun). MIDI tracks can contain MIDI clips, instruments, and MIDI effects. A MIDI track is a little more complicated than an audio track, in that a MIDI clip alone isn't enough to produce sound—an instrument is required as well.

Figure 4.3 shows an empty MIDI track, which looks a bit different than the tracks next to it. A MIDI track without a virtual instrument inserted does not output audio; thus, there are no Volume, Pan, or Send knobs in the mixer. You still have the Track Activator, Solo/Cue, and Arm buttons, which function the same way as their audio track counterparts.

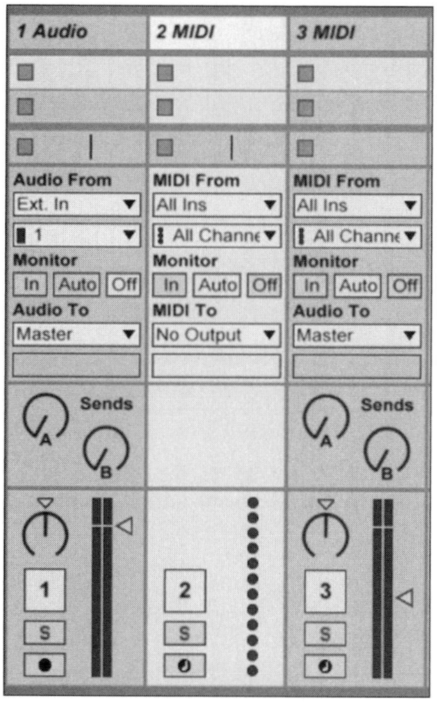

Figure 4.3 An audio track, an empty MIDI track, and a MIDI track with an instrument device loaded. Notice that there's a note in the Arm button of the MIDI tracks, which makes it possible to tell them apart from audio tracks, even when an instrument is loaded.

Source: Ableton

When a virtual instrument is loaded onto the track (see Chapter 7, "Using Effects and Instruments"), the full set of mixer controls will appear. Drag an instrument from the Sounds or Drums view of the Browser into an empty MIDI track if you want to see this transformation in action. A MIDI track with an instrument inserted is essentially a hybrid MIDI/audio track. It passes MIDI input from MIDI clips (or a MIDI controller) into an instrument, which produces audio in response. The audio is then optionally processed with effects and passed into the mixer.

A MIDI track without an instrument can be used to send data to external hardware (such as sound modules). Notice that the lower menu in the empty MIDI track shown in Figure 4.3 is labeled Midi To. To sequence external hardware, select the port and channel the hardware is connected to, and you're all set. (You can also use the External Instrument device for this purpose, as explained in Chapter 8, "Live's Instruments.")

Understanding Clips

Clips are created by dragging files into the Session or Arrangement, or by recording new audio and MIDI performances into Live. MIDI clips can also be created by double-clicking in an empty clip slot or by selecting Insert MIDI Clip from the Create menu.

Audio clips *refer* to audio files. They do not *contain* them. A clip merely contains the information necessary for Live to play an audio file from disk. However, audio clips have all sorts of special properties, such as the ability to flexibly adjust the pitch and tempo of the audio. Not only that, but you can also create many different clips from the same audio file without needing multiple copies of the audio on your hard disk. A single audio file can be referenced from as many clips as you want, each having its own parameters: loop points, transposition, Warp markers, automation, and so on.

This ability to duplicate, chop, and mangle clips all day without affecting the underlying audio file is sometimes referred to as *nondestructive editing*, and it is one of the things that makes Live (and every other modern DAW) so powerful. However, this fact also warrants a few words of caution.

Should a referenced audio file become altered by another application, such as a wave editor, each clip that used that file will now play with the same alteration. If you delete the file that is referenced by a clip, the clip and any other clips that used that file won't play anymore! This is why it can be very important to use Collect All and Save (see Chapter 3) to copy audio files into your project folder, in order to help protect them from being modified by other projects or programs.

Unlike audio clips, all of the data in MIDI clips is stored within the Set (.als) file. MIDI clips can be created by dragging in standard MIDI files, but it's most common to create them yourself by recording a performance using a MIDI controller (such as drum pads or a keyboard), or by drawing in notes manually using the MIDI editor.

Adding Files from the Browser

Adding new clips is a matter of dragging an audio file, standard MIDI file, or Live Clip from the Browser into a clip slot or a track in the Arrangement View. Files can also be added directly from Windows Explorer or the OS X Finder. Since tracks can only hold one type of clip, audio or MIDI, make sure that you drag audio files into audio tracks and MIDI files into MIDI tracks, or drag them into the Drop Area to create new tracks automatically.

You can also grab multiple files (Shift-click to select a range of files or Ctrl (Cmd)+click to select multiple nonadjacent files) and add them as a group. By default, the clips will all be created on the same track. To have Live drop the files into separate tracks, press and hold Ctrl (Cmd) before dropping the files. You'll see the clips change their arrangement, and you can then choose their final destination.

Live can work with just about any audio you've got—any audio file (in WAV, AIFF, SDII, MP3, Ogg Vorbis, Ogg FLAC, or FLAC format) on your computer is fair game in Live. (If you're planning on using compressed audio files like MP3 or FLAC, make sure to read up on the Decoding Cache in Chapter 2, "Getting Live Up and Running.")

A great way to get to know Live is by using audio loops, such as those included in the Live 9 Power! Live Pack. Loops are also available from companies such as Big Fish Audio and Loopmasters, as well as in Live's core library. Don't underestimate the power of what can be done with prerecorded loops. As you become expert at manipulating clip properties, editing clips in the Arrangement, using effects, and other features such as the Slice to New MIDI Track, you'll discover that loops are just raw material from which a large variety of useful and original sounds can be created.

Standard MIDI files have a file extension of .MID. They are included with some third-party content libraries and can be exported from other programs, such as Reason and Logic, for use in Live.

You can also explore the Clips view of the Browser to find clips to use in Live. These are files saved in the Live Clip format. Live Clips can be audio or MIDI, and can contain devices as well. For example, a MIDI Live Clip can contain not just a MIDI sequence, but an instrument as well. So it's like a preset that contains a sound *and* a musical part.

One caveat to know when working with Live Clips is that their devices only get loaded if the track you drag it into *does not already contain any devices.* In other words, if the track has even one device in it, you'll only get the audio or MIDI. If this sounds like a lot right now, don't worry. Live Clips will make much more sense once you've got a handle on the various elements they contain.

Organization and Navigation

Like most modern music programs, Live gives you the power to create a lot of content very quickly. The downside of being able to move quickly is the potential for stress and confusion that piles up as you add piles of loops and record new parts. Don't skimp on organization. Trust me, your music will be better for it.

The first step in clarifying your workspace is to use the Rename command frequently, as explained in Chapter 3. The next step is to use color. You can right-click on clips, tracks, and scenes to bring up a color chooser and apply colors in any way that makes sense to you. For example, you might want to make all your drum tracks and clips shades of red and your basses blue.

It's also important to move clips, tracks, and scenes to meaningful locations. It may sound obvious, but don't underestimate how much easier it is to work on a Set where all of the drum tracks are next to each other, as opposed to scattered around. This logic applies to clips and scenes as well. Tracks and scenes can be moved by clicking and dragging the titles, while clips can be moved by dragging their colored areas.

If you hold down Alt (Option) while dragging an object, you'll create a copy instead of just moving it. For example, you might create multiple copies of a clip and set different loop points, or make a copy of an entire track and apply radically different effects to create a layered sound.

MULTISELECT: Many commands and actions can be applied to multiple objects simultaneously. Command (Ctrl)+click to select nonadjacent objects, or Shift-click to select a range. In the Session View, groups of clips can also be selected by dragging an area around the clips with the mouse. The trick is that you must click and drag from an *empty* clip slot and then move the mouse across the clips you want to select. For example, you might want to select multiple clips and apply the same color or move several tracks simultaneously.

You can also adjust the Mixer for multiple tracks simultaneously. For example, to reduce the volume for several tracks by the same amount, select multiple tracks and then adjust the volume of any of them. The faders of every selected track will move by the same amount.

Finally, it's often overlooked as to how easy it is to navigate just about every part of Live using the arrow keys. After you've selected a Session View clip by clicking on it, you can move up, down, left, or right to select other clips using the arrow keys. If you use the Up arrow to move above the top-most clip, you'll now have selected the track and can move to other tracks with the Left and Right arrows. The arrow keys can also be used in conjunction with Shift to select multiple objects.

Recording

Unless you're strictly using Live to DJ or work with pre-existing material, you'll need to create some clips of your own. The basic process for recording new audio and MIDI clips is very similar, so we'll be taking a general look at recording first. Obviously, there are some big differences between audio and MIDI, and these will be discussed next.

Regardless of whether you're recording into the Session or Arrangement Views, the first two steps of recording are the same: select a valid input source and arm the track for recording (see Figure 4.4). Input/Output and Arm are both introduced in the Mixer section of Chapter 3.

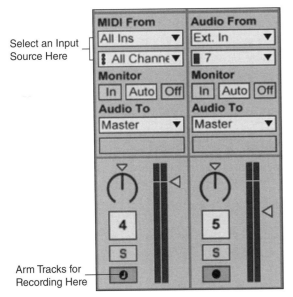

Figure 4.4 An audio and a MIDI track, both ready for recording.
Source: Ableton

If you're making an audio recording, make sure that the inputs you want to record from are enabled in the Input Configuration screen. If you're making a MIDI recording, make sure that your MIDI controller's input has Track set to On in the MIDI/Sync tab of Live's Preferences. (Review the Audio and MIDI/Sync tabs in the "Setting Preferences in Live" section of Chapter 2, "Getting Live Up and Running," for more information.)

Arming a track is simple: just click the Arm button so it lights up. Be aware that if no input is selected, or the selected input has become invalid (for example, your audio interface has been disconnected), the Arm switch may not appear or will be disabled. You're free to arm multiple tracks and record many clips simultaneously if you want.

MULTIRECORDING: Can't seem to arm more than one track at a time? Hold down the Ctrl(Cmd) key and then click the Arm buttons. To allow multiple tracks to be armed without doing this, change the Exclusive setting in Preferences (see Chapter 2).

Recording in Session View

Once a track is armed for recording, all of the square Stop buttons in the track's clip slots will turn to circular Record buttons (see Figure 4.5). Click one of them to start recording a new clip, and then bang on your MIDI controller, yodel into your microphone, or slap the bass. You stop recording by clicking a Clip Stop Button or by clicking on the Clip Launch Button of the clip you're recording. This second method is really handy because the new clip will immediately start looping, and the music keeps flowing!

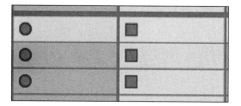

Figure 4.5 The track on the left is armed, so the clip slots now contain circular Clip Record buttons.
Source: Ableton

NO LOOP?: If you click a Clip Launch button to stop a recording and the clip doesn't start looping, this means the Default Launch mode has been changed in Live's Record/Warp/Launch Preferences. Set it to Trigger, and you'll be all set. There's a full discussion of Launch Modes in Chapter 5, "Clips."

Recording loops in the Session View is made easy by the fact that Live uses launch quantization to start and stop recordings. Assuming that the Quantization Menu in the Control Bar is set to its default value of 1 Bar, all recordings will start and stop at the beginning of a bar, and you'll always end up with loop lengths that make sense.

Doing multiple takes is as easy as clicking additional Clip Record buttons in the track. Every time a new recording starts, the previous one ends. You can then go back and listen to each take individually to find the best one. Or you can use the Arrangement View to combine the best parts of each take into one perfect "supertake."

Of course, the nicest thing about this workflow in the Session View is that it allows you to quickly build layers and sections of a song without ever stopping Live. You can then audition all of your new clips and organize scenes to start arranging the sections of your song.

> **ON THE LEVEL:** Before you start an audio recording, check your input signal level to make sure that it's not too high or too low. The track's meters will show the volume of any incoming signal as soon as the track is armed. Play as loud as you plan to play during the recording while watching Live's meters. If the signal is too loud (the meters reach the top and turn red), it could distort, or clip, the recording. If the level is too low, your sound may become grainy when turning it up to match the rest of your song.
>
> If you're recording at 24-bit or more, you can record at lower levels and still have excellent audio quality, so this is generally recommended. If for some reason you need to record at 16-bit, it's much more important to get the highest level possible without clipping.

Session Record Button

The Session Record button (see Figure 4.6) is a multi-function button, which is relevant to the prior section because it can be used to record new clips. It's also relevant to the upcoming sections because it is used to overdub automation and MIDI in the Session View.

When you click on Session Record, it will start recording in the empty clip slots of the highlighted scene for any armed track in which a clip is not currently playing. Clicking it a second time will stop recording and begin playback of any newly recorded clips. Just like the Clip Record buttons, Session Record is quantized to make it easy to record properly timed loops.

Session Record's role in MIDI overdubbing recording automation will be discussed later in the section entitled "Automation and MIDI Overdub." Because this button does several different things, it provides a very streamlined workflow, but it also creates the potential for confusion. Make sure to take some time experimenting with this button as you learn about its different functions to avoid surprises later.

Figure 4.6 Session Record can be used to record new clips. It also enables MIDI and automation overdubbing.
Source: Ableton

Arrangement Record Button

The Arrangement Record button also handles several functions (see Figure 4.7). It's used to record new clips in the Arrangement View, as well as to overdub automation and MIDI. Arrangement Record is also used to initiate recording clips from Session into Arrangement. This might sound like a lot, and it is!

Figure 4.7 Arrangement Record is used to record new clips into the Arrangement. Like Session Record, it also has several other functions that are discussed later in this chapter.
Source: Ableton

Depending on your workflow, you'll probably use some of these functions more than others. So as you get familiar with the Live workflow, all of this will make sense eventually. For starters, though, you'll want to take some extra time to familiarize yourself with each of these functions as they are explained in the upcoming sections.

Recording in Arrangement View

If you've made recordings in just about any other DAW, from Pro Tools to Garageband, this way of working will be familiar. To record clips into the Arrangement View, just arm a track and click Arrangement Record. To stop recording, you can click Arrangement Record again, disarm the track, or simply press the spacebar.

In addition to allowing the type of recording described here, Arrangement Record also causes clips to be recorded from the Session into the Arrangement, which can take some getting used to. If you want to avoid this behavior, make sure that there aren't any clips playing in the Session before you record new clips in the Arrangement. This can be done by clicking Back to Arrangement or Stop Clips.

> **READY, SET, GO!:** The Count In feature can be accessed easily from the Control Bar by opening the Metronome's drop-down menu. Select the number of bars of count-in you want, and you're ready to go. The next time you start recording, Live will count you in with the metronome so you can get a clean start.

Punching In and Out

In the good old days of recording to tape, it was common to replace only a section of a recording using a technique called *punching*. If you had a good vocal track with a weak phrase, the engineer would wait until that moment, press Record while the singer replaced it, and then disable recording before erasing the next phrase. In digital audio, we do the same thing, but it's much less nerve-wracking since digital recording is nondestructive.

Punching in Live is easy. While playing back, click Arrangement Record to start recording, and once again to stop. No special steps are necessary. However, you can also make Live automatically begin recording at a specified point and stop at another. This is really handy if you're both the engineer and performer.

In Chapter 3, there's a brief introduction to setting these points, known as Punch In and Punch Out. They can be set visually by dragging the bracket that sits above the track display, or set numerically in the Control Bar. Once the points are set, punching is enabled with the two buttons located to either side of the Loop button, as seen in Figure 4.8.

When you click Record, Live will start running but will wait for the Punch-In time before it actually starts recording. It will continue recording until it reaches the Punch-Out point. You may, of course, use either Punch-In or Punch-Out by itself if you choose.

Figure 4.8 Configured as shown, Live will automatically begin recording at bar 21 and then stop recording four bars later. The two bent line icons are the Punch-In and Punch-Out switches.
Source: Ableton

MIDI Overdub

MIDI Overdub allows you to record additional note or controller data into a MIDI clip without erasing what's already there. This is a handy feature when it comes to programming drumbeats, since you can build them one piece at a time. For example, you could make a two-bar loop with just a kick drum and then play the additional parts (snares, hi-hats) layer by layer as the clip continues to loop.

MIDI Overdub has all sorts of uses. If a piano part is really tricky, you can record the left-hand and right-hand parts separately. Or you can build a drum part one drum at a time and generate variations while you're at it. For example, start with a simple drum pattern (perhaps just kick drum and hi-hat for the intro of your song); then use Duplicate to copy the clip and launch the copy. Now you can use MIDI Overdub to add snare hits. This will leave you with two MIDI clips: one with just kick and hats and the other with a snare added. You can then duplicate the MIDI clip again and layer on an additional part, such as a shaker or congas. Using this technique, you can build a collection of drum variations quickly.

To overdub MIDI into an existing MIDI clip, you must first arm the track for recording. Once you've done that, the procedure for MIDI overdubbing differs in Session and Arrangement.

Overdubbing in Session View

In the Session View, launch the clip you want to overdub on and arm the track. You'll be able to play your controller and hear what you're playing along with the clip. At this point, your playing isn't being recorded, so this is a handy way to practice before doing the overdubbing.

MIDI overdubbing is initiated by clicking on the Session Record button (see Figure 4.9). After doing this, you'll see the clip's launch button turn from green to red. Now any notes you play (or knobs you turn) on your controller will be recorded into the clip.

Session Record Is Enabled

This Clip Is Playing and Recording at the Same Time

Track Is Armed

Figure 4.9 MIDI overdub recording allows you to record into an existing MIDI clip without erasing what's already there.
Source: Ableton

Overdubbing in Arrangement View

In the Arrangement View, MIDI overdubbing is enabled with the MIDI Arrangement Overdub switch, shown in Figure 4.10. (It's on by default.) Once it's enabled, just arm a MIDI track, press Arrangement Record, and you're in Overdub mode.

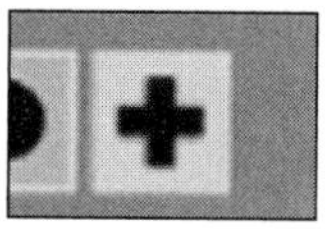

Figure 4.10 MIDI Arrangement Overdub enables overdubbing into Arrangement clips.
Source: Ableton

It's important to understand that recording in the Arrangement works differently and requires more caution than it does in the Session View. This is because you can destructively record *over* MIDI clips in Arrangement—something that is not possible in Session. In other words, if you arm a MIDI track and click Arrangement Record while MIDI Arrangement Overdub is *disabled*, you'll start recording a new MIDI clip that contains only your new performance.

Fortunately, Live has an Undo command!

Recording Automation

Nearly everything in Live can be automated. Want a synth part to slowly fade in over 32 bars? No problem, just automate the volume. Want an effect to kick in on every other snare drum hit? Automate the effect's Device Activator. Automation has been an important part of sound mixing for a few decades now. In contemporary electronic music, it's more important than ever because it's an essential tool for building evolving arrangements out of loop-based elements.

To record automation in Session or Arrangement, enable Arrangement Arm, shown in Figure 4.11. The basic process for recording automation is incredibly simple. Just move the controls you want to automate while recording. These could be mixer controls such as volume and pan, or effect and instrument device parameters, whether built-in, VST, or AU.

Figure 4.11 Automation Arm is the key to recording automation.
Source: Ableton

Session Automation

Session automation can be recorded while you record new clips, or it can be overdubbed afterward. In order to record automation, the Automation Arm switch must be enabled. It is turned on by default, so you may have already started recording automation without doing anything special.

The process of recording automation couldn't be easier. While recording a new clip, modify the device or mixer controls of your choosing. For example, while recording a new MIDI clip, tweak the filter cutoff of the virtual instrument you're using. The change to the filter is recorded into the clip alongside any notes you've played. Once you're done recording the automation, it can be viewed and edited in the Clip View as seen in Figure 4.12.

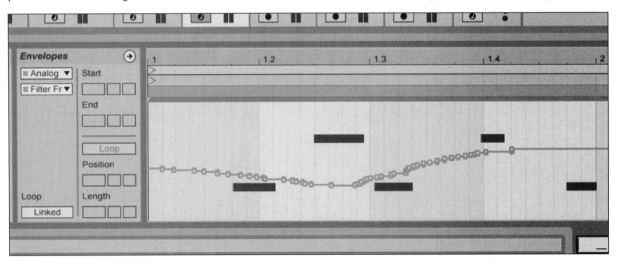

Figure 4.12 Session automation is viewed in the Clip View. This is covered in detail in "Automation Editing" later in this chapter.
Source: Ableton

Automation overdubbing is enabled with the Session Record button. Again, the basic process is simple. Make sure that Automation Arm is enabled, click on Session Record, and make some parameter changes. When you're done, click Session Record again to stop recording automation.

There's one very important preference you have to consider when overdubbing Session automation. It's in the Record/Warp/Launch tab of Live's Preferences, and is labeled "Record Session Automation in." When set to Armed Tracks, you'll only be able to overdub automation into tracks that are armed. The appeal of this setting is that it prevents you from unintentionally recording automation by forcing you to arm tracks.

The other setting, All Tracks, allows you to record automation into any clip, regardless of the track's Arm status. This setting is extremely flexible, and it comes with a different advantage: you can record automation without arming any tracks, so you don't have to worry about inadvertently overdubbing MIDI while you work.

If you find that you're generally focusing on one track at a time, recording clips and automation in a single pass, you're probably best by using the Armed Tracks preference. If you prefer to jump around, creating clips in many tracks, and then recording automation for several at a time, you'll find All Tracks easier to use. Like many workflow choices, it's a trade-off. The only way to find what's best for you is to experiment boldly and use Undo to clean up any messes you make.

Arrangement Automation

Just like in the Session View, the Automation Arm button must be enabled for automation to be recorded. While recording new clips, any parameter changes you make will be recorded and displayed, as seen in Figure 4.13.

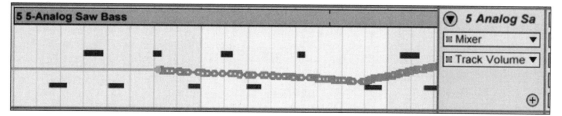

Figure 4.13 Arrangement automation shows up in the timeline as seen here.
Source: Ableton

Overdubbing automation into the Arrangement is also quite simple. Just enable Automation Arm, click Automation Record, and start twisting knobs and pushing buttons. However, there's one important caveat here. Unlike Session View, which can be set to record automation into only armed tracks, Arrangement automation is always recorded into all tracks. Not only that, but you must take extra care to make sure that you haven't unintentionally left tracks armed. For example, if you want to record some simple volume automation into an audio track you just recorded, you need to disarm the track beforehand. Otherwise, you'll end up simultaneously recording the automation *and* recording over the track! Probably not the desired result.

ALWAYS AUTOMATED: When recording clips from Session View into Arrangement View, automation will be recorded no matter what. If there's Session automation contained in the clips, it will always be recorded into the Arrangement. Additionally, manual tweaks made in any track in which you've launched a clip will be recorded, even if Automation Arm is disabled.

See "Recording from Session into Arrangement" later in this chapter for more information on this process.

Disabling and Re-Enabling Automation

When a parameter is being automated, a red "LED" (see Figure 4.14) appears next to it so that you know it's being controlled by automation. If you manually change an automated parameter, the automation will immediately stop, and the LED will turn gray to indicate that it's been disabled. The automation display (refer to Figures 4.11 and 4.12) will turn gray as well.

Figure 4.14 The small square next to the Filter Freq knob indicates that it's being automated.
Source: Ableton

Another thing happens when you manually change an automated control. The Re-Enable Automation switch turns orange, as seen in Figure 4.15. Clicking on this causes automation to resume for all automated parameters in all tracks and clips immediately.

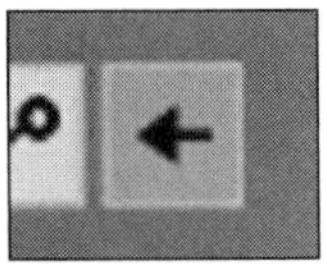

Figure 4.15 Click Re-Enable Automation to bring all your disabled automation back at once.
Source: Ableton

Re-enabling automation is an area where there's a difference between Session and Arrangement.. Session automation is automatically re-enabled whenever you launch a clip containing automation. In other words, Session automation can only be disabled if you manually change the automated parameter while the clip is playing back. The next time you launch the clip, its automation will be active.

> **DELETE AUTOMATION:** If you decide that you want to get rid of all automation for a given control, there's an easy shortcut. Just right-click on the control (knob, slider, and so on) and select Delete Automation from the context menu. Be aware that this is a very powerful command since it deletes all the automation for that control from the timeline and from all Session clips.

Using Scenes

In the studio, the Session View is conceived of primarily as a powerful sketchpad for creating parts and experimenting with ideas. And indeed, it shines in this capacity. However, unless you take some time to organize your ideas, it can quickly turn into an unwieldy mess. You think you'll remember which parts went well together and what order you were launching the clips in, but next week when you come back to it, you'll remember nothing. Trust me, this is based on a true story.

The ultimate solution to this problem is to create an arrangement in the Arrangement View. This is the place where you make final decisions about the flow of your song. That said, there's often an intermediate step where you want to organize your ideas and create sections before beginning the process of creating a final arrangement. This is where scenes really come in handy. On stage, scenes are a powerful tool, as well. Not only do they allow multiple clips to be launched simultaneously, but they can also be used to adjust tempos and time signatures automatically.

Scenes are horizontal rows of clips in the Session View. Drag clips that go together into the same scene and use the Scene Launch buttons (in the Master track) to launch them all simultaneously. As shown in Figure 4.16, this method can be used to build an arrangement that is both clear and very flexible. Scenes can be launched in any order and allowed to play for as long as you like.

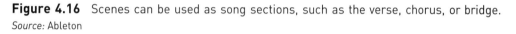

Drums	Bass	Pad	Melody	FX		Master
☐	☐	▷ IntroChord	☐	▷ Space		▷ *Intro*
▷ Minimal	☐	▷ IntroChord	☐	▷ Space		▷ *Intro 2*
▷ Beat 1	▷ Thump	☐	▷ Verse 1	☐		▷ *Verse*
▷ Minimal	▷ LudeBass	▷ IntroChord	☐	☐		▷ *Interlude*
▷ Beat 1	▷ Thump	☐	▷ Verse 1	▷ Magic		▷ *Verse2*
▷ Beat 1	▷ Thump	▷ BigChord	▷ Verse 1	☐		▷ *Chorus*

Figure 4.16 Scenes can be used as song sections, such as the verse, chorus, or bridge.
Source: Ableton

The song shown in Figure 4.16 is organized from top to bottom with the top-most scene being the intro and the song progressing downward. Each row can house whole musical sections, new song directions, or merely a slight modification in the piece currently playing.

If you run out of scenes, or just want to add a new one at a specific location, select Insert Scene from the Edit menu. The new scene will be inserted below the currently highlighted scene. You can also create a new scene containing clips you like in one step. When you come across a combination of clips that sound good together, select Create > Capture and Insert Scene to create a new scene that is populated with the currently playing clips.

To change the location of scenes as you create them, just click on the scene's title (or number) and drag it to the new location. To rename a scene, use Edit > Rename. Press Enter (Return) to accept the new name or Escape to leave it as it was. Or you can press Tab to rename the next scene down.

> **TWO SCENES ARE BETTER THAN ONE:** When working on a song arrangement, it can be really useful to make a copy of an entire scene and use it to create some variations. Click to the right of a Scene Launcher to select a scene and then use Duplicate to copy the scene directly below the scene you are working in. Now delete or modify clips in the new scene to create variations.

There are a number of different ways to launch and move between scenes. In addition to pressing the Scene Launch button, you can trigger a scene by pressing the Enter (Return) key, as long as the scene number/name is highlighted. Changing the highlighted scenes can be done with the arrow keys, so it's easy to navigate and trigger each scene from the computer keyboard without doing any special mapping.

Live also features a couple of Preferences specifically for working with scenes (see Chapter 2). When Select Next Scene on Launch is set to On, Live will automatically move down one scene every time a scene is launched with the

Enter key. The Start Recording on Scene Launch preference can be turned on to allow recording to be initiated by launching Scenes. By default, a track's Arm status is ignored when launching clips, so empty clip slots in armed tracks will simply cause the currently playing clip in that track to stop.

Programming Scene Tempos and Time Signatures

From time to time, you may want to make instantaneous jumps to different tempos while in the Session View. By naming a scene using a special convention, you can cause Live to change tempos when the scene is triggered. To switch the tempo to 85 BPM, just include "85BPM" in the name of the scene and launch it. The scene can be empty; you don't need to trigger any clips when you launch this scene if you merely want to change tempos. You can remove all the Clip Stop buttons (select them and press Ctrl (Cmd)+E) so that none of your clips are stopped.

One instance where programming scene tempos is particularly helpful is when you're organizing a large batch of clips into a Set so that a single Live Set contains multiple songs. One group of scenes may belong to one song at a given tempo, while another group of scenes represents a different song and tempo, and so on.

Scenes can also be named to create changes in the time signature. Time signatures are represented as fractions with the numerator (number of beats per bar) being any value from 1 to 99, and the denominator (type of beats) being 1, 2, 4, 8, or 16. Scene names can contain both time signature and tempo changes as long as the two values are separated by at least one character (see Figure 4.17).

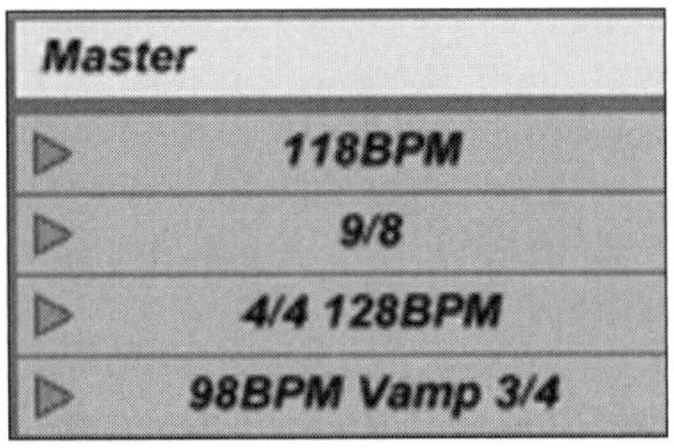

Master	
▷	118BPM
▷	9/8
▷	4/4 128BPM
▷	98BPM Vamp 3/4

Figure 4.17 Live is smart enough to recognize tempos and time signatures in scene names. Launching these scenes will cause the indicated changes to take effect immediately.
Source: Ableton

Removing Clip Stop Buttons

In Figure 4.18, you'll see that only some of the empty clip slots have square Clip Stop buttons. Removing the Clip Stop button from a clip slot will allow a playing clip on the track to continue playing when the scene is launched. To remove a Clip Stop button, right-click in a clip slot and select Remove Stop Button. Don't worry, you can get the Stop Button back by right-clicking again and selecting Add Stop Button.

This feature is particularly handy when working with longer clips. For example, let's say you have a long clip containing ambient sound effects in scene 1. You want them to keep playing in scene 2. If you copy the clip into scene 2, the sound effects clip will start over again from the beginning when the scene is launched. By removing the stop button from scene 2, you can allow the ambient effects to continue playing instead of restarting.

Beats	Keys	Bass
▶ ChillyBeat	▶ ChillySynth	▶ ChillyABass
	▷ NewSynth	▷ Bass2
▷ HardBeat2	☐	
☐	☐	☐

Figure 4.18 Launching the second scene in this example will allow the first clip (ChillyBeat) to keep playing, while launching new synth and bass parts.
Source: Ableton

Arrangement View

Where the Arrangement View fits into your workflow depends a lot on what you do. If you're primarily interested in producing music, it's absolutely essential. The Arrangement is where you really put the song together—beginning, middle, and end.

In fact, for many producers the Arrangement comes into play quite early in the production process. The Session View is great (maybe one of the greatest things ever) for the initial part of the production process, but even if you're clever at organizing ideas with Scenes, you'll find that laying your ideas from left to right forces you to make decisions and get clear on where a song is going. The beauty of Live is that moving to the Arrangement View doesn't mean you have to be done with the Session View. You can continue returning to it to compose new ideas and experiment with old ones.

If you're only using Live as a performance platform, the Arrangement will likely be of secondary importance to you. However, there are many exceptions to this. There are some performers who organize performances using the Arrangement View and take advantage of Live's unique locators, which can be launched like clips. There are also certain types of editing that are impossible in the Session, so you may end up using the Arrangement to prepare clips for performance.

There are a few methods for getting clips into the Arrangement. You can add files from the Browser and record new clips, just like you would in the Session. Or you can use the fun and interactive process of recording clips from the Session View.

Recording from Session into Arrangement

When Live 1.0 first hit the scene, there were two features that immediately made it stand out. The improvisational Session View really made eyes pop. But no less significant was the ability to perform with Session clips and capture every move—every launched clip, mixer adjustment, and device tweak—into the traditional timeline of the Arrangement View. To this day, it remains a uniquely fun and musical way to compose with a computer. Let's take a look at the process.

Start off by clicking Stop in the Control Bar twice. The second click sets the Arrangement playback position to 1.1.1. Next, click Arrangement Record and perform your song by launching clips, moving sliders, and turning knobs. Remember that Arrangement Record is also used to record brand new clips into the Arrangement, so make sure that no tracks are armed.

When you click Arrangement Record, recording will begin immediately. Depending on how you work, this may or may not be a problem. Here are a few methods to get a clean start.

> ▷ Use the Metronome's drop-down menu to select a count-off. This will give you a moment to get ready after pressing Arrangement Record.
> ▷ Launch all of the clips for the intro of your song and then click Stop twice. When recording begins, these clips will start playing back, and you can take it from there.
> ▷ Shift-click Arrangement Record. This arms recording, but does not start playback. As soon as you launch a clip, recording will begin.

When you're finished, press the Spacebar to stop, or click Arrangement Record to disable recording while playback continues. If you want to re-record a section or add new clips, just press Arrangement Record again. Newly launched clips will be recorded; clicking Clip Stop buttons will cause Arrangement clips to be erased. Everything else will be left alone.

When recording clips from Session to Arrangement, automation is *always* recorded, regardless of the Automation Arm status. Also note that if you launch Session clips containing automation, that automation will be recorded as well. After recording, this automation will no longer be shown in the Clip View (as Session automation is), but will instead be shown in the track display of the Arrangement View. For more information on viewing and editing automation, see the "Automation Editing" section later in this chapter.

When you're finished recording, take a look at the Arrangement View. The tracks will now be filled with clips, and any tracks containing automation will display a red automation line, as seen in Figure 4.19. However, you'll also notice that every clip is grayed out, and starting playback does not cause the arrangement you just created to play back. What's going on here? The answer lies with Back to Arrangement.

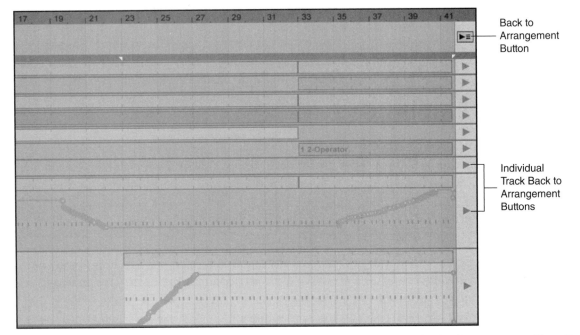

Figure 4.19 After recording, every clip launched in the Session appears in the Arrangement. The clips are grayed out, however, and the Back to Arrangement button appears above the upper-right corner of the timeline. This indicates that the Session clips are still in control.
Source: Ableton

SESSION TO ARRANGE (AND BACK AGAIN): As you work on your masterpieces, you'll sometimes want to manually drop a Session clip into the Arrangement View. To do this, click a clip and hold down the mouse button as you press and then release the Tab key. Now you can drag that clip to wherever you want it in your arrangement and drop it in. The same technique also works for dropping clips from the Arrangement into the Session.

Back to Arrangement

Since the Session and Arrangement Views share the same set of tracks, there has to be a way to determine which view will be in control. Remember, any track can only play back one clip at a time. This means it's an either/or situation. Either a track plays back Arrangement clips or Session clips, never both.

Ableton's scheme for handling this problem is to allow Session clips to automatically override Arrangement clips whenever they are launched. Arrangement clips are re-enabled manually via the Back to Arrangement buttons. When a Session clip is launched, any Arrangement clips in that track are grayed out to indicate that they are currently disabled. This explains the grayed out Arrangement mentioned above. Until you explicitly give control to the Arrangement, the Session stays in control.

There are two global Back to Arrangement buttons, both of which function identically. One is located in the Session View, next to the Stop Clips button in the Master track (see Figure 4.20). The other one appears conditionally in the Arrangement View, as seen in Figure 4.19. By default, the Session's Back to Arrangement button is gray, and the one in the Arrangement is completely invisible! As soon as anything is done to override the Arrangement, they both light up. Clicking on either one causes the Arrangement to take control immediately.

Figure 4.20 The Session View has a Back to Arrangement button in the Master track.
Source: Ableton

You can also give control to Arrangement tracks on a per-track basis. Whenever a Session clip is launched, a triangular button appears at the far right of the corresponding Arrangement track. In Figure 4.19, you'll see these arrows displayed in every track. Click on an arrow to re-enable Arrangement clips for that track only.

Bear in mind that you don't have to have anything in the Arrangement to "override" it. For example, when you first launch Live and are looking at a completely empty set, the Back to Arrangement buttons are gray. As soon as you launch a single Session clip, they turn orange. Clicking Back to Arrangement will stop playback of any Session clips you've launched because Live will give control to the tracks in the Arrangement View, which are currently empty.

Transport and Navigation

Before digging into the details of navigating and editing in the Arrangement, let's get some terms straight. The Arrangement View has several different areas and a few interface elements that might not jump out at you at first. Figure 4.21 shows them all.

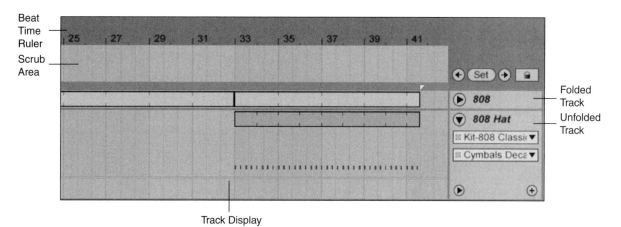

Figure 4.21 The majority of the Arrangement View is taken up by the track display.
Source: Ableton

The Beat Time Ruler displays bar numbers, and if you zoom in enough, it will show beats and sixteenths as well. When you float your mouse pointer over the Beat Time Ruler, it turns into a magnifying glass which can be used to zoom (by dragging vertically) and scroll (by dragging horizontally). To zoom from the keyboard, use the + and – keys. You can also scroll by holding down Shift and using the scroll wheel on your mouse.

Next is the Scrub Area, where the mouse turns into a speaker. Click to make the Arrangement play back from where you clicked. If Live is running when you click in the Scrub Area, playback will jump according to the global quantize setting. If you want Live to respond immediately, or you want to be able to drag the speaker for traditional scrubbing behavior, set Quantize to None in the Control Bar.

The final method for controlling the transport involves mousing over the Scrub Area of the Arrangement. When your mouse turns into a speaker icon, you can click, and Live will immediately begin playing from this location. You can even do this while the transport is running to jump to a different position in the arrangement.

There are two ways to view tracks in the Arrangement View: folded and unfolded (refer to Figure 4.21). A track can be unfolded by clicking on the downward pointing triangle next to the track name. Holding down Alt while clicking here will fold or unfold all tracks in the arrangement. The unfolded track can be resized easily by dragging up or down at the bottom edge of the track's Mixer section.

While keeping tracks folded is convenient for getting an overview of your arrangement, unfolded tracks are easier to edit. When a track is unfolded, a miniature waveform or MIDI display is revealed for the clips. I'll be referring to this area as the *display,* and the colored bar above it as the *title bar* of the clip. (These aren't official Ableton terms, but we've got to call them something.)

Insert Marker and Arrangement Selection

Unfolded clips are easier to edit because you can click within the display to place the insert marker, or click and drag to select a range of time within the clip (called the *arrangement selection*). If you want to make a selection within a folded track, you'll have to hold down Alt+Shift while clicking. In the upcoming sections, these will be mentioned quite a bit, and you'll see why they are important.

To place the insert marker, click anywhere in the track display, except in the title bar of a clip (see Figure 4.22). If you click in the title bar of a clip, the entire clip gets highlighted, and you set the arrangement selection instead (see Figure 4.23). The arrangement selection can also be set by clicking and dragging in the track display. To extend an existing selection, Shift-click at the location you would like to extend it to.

Figure 4.22 The Insert Marker shows up as a blinking cursor in the track display and a downward pointing arrow above.

Source: Ableton

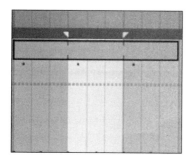

Figure 4.23 The Arrangement Selection is indicated by the pair of angled triangles above the track display. The Arrangement Selection can be set by dragging in an unfolded track or clicking on a clip's title bar.
Source: Ableton

Setting Playback Position

When you stop and start Live, it doesn't resume playback from where you stopped. Instead, playback begins from either the insert marker or the arrangement selection. (If you want to resume playback from where you last stopped, use Shift-spacebar.) If you want to temporarily play back from a different location, click in the Scrub Area to change the playback position without relocating the insert marker. To play back from the very beginning of the Arrangement (1.1.1), click Stop while Live is already stopped.

Looping

You can loop a section of your arrangement by enabling Loop in the Control Bar (see Figure 4.24). To the left of the Loop button is a numerical display indicating the bar and beat that the loop begins, while on the right you will see another numerical display showing the length of the loop. These values can also be edited by moving the brace that sits above the track display and dragging its edges to resize.

Figure 4.24 Turn on Loop to repeat a section of the Arrangement.
Source: Ableton

Often, you'll find that you want to set the loop points to match the exact length of a clip, or a series of clips, in your arrangement. To do so, select the clip(s) and use Edit > Loop Selection, which automatically sets the loop points to the position and length of the selection and enables Loop in one step.

You'll also notice there's a Select Loop command in the Edit menu. This enables you to create an arrangement selection across all tracks from the loop points. The more editing you do in the Arrangement, the more this will come in handy. For example, you might Select Loop and then use Duplicate to copy the part of the song you're currently looping.

Locators and Time Signature Changes

Locators are used to mark sections of a song, such as the start of a verse, chorus, or bridge. However, Ableton did not stop there—it has given you the ability to launch the locators like you would clips, thus allowing you to perform custom arrangements right in the Arrangement View.

Creating Locators

To place a locator, right-click in the Scrub area (the area directly above the top-most track) and select Add Locator from the context menu. Or you can set locators interactively using the Set button in the upper-right corner. This method will place a locator at the position of the playback cursor while Live is running or at the insert marker (or start point of the arrangement selection) when Live is stopped (see Figure 4.25).

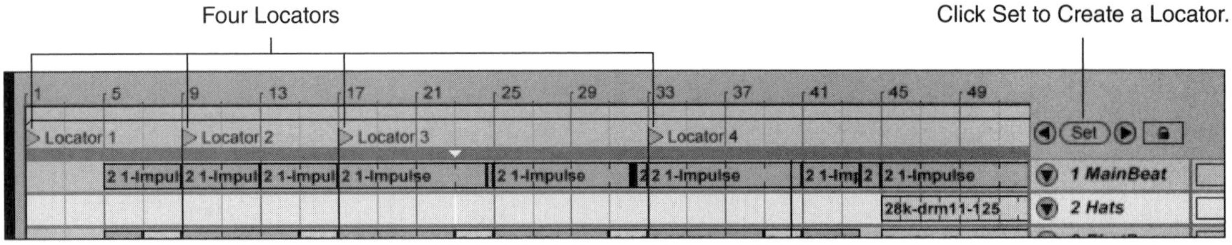

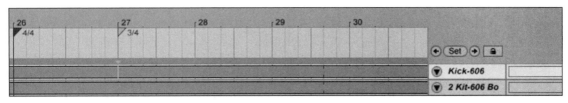

Figure 4.25 Every time you click Set, a new locator will be created at the current play position.
Source: Ableton

Each time you make a locator, it will be given the name Locator followed by a number. To give the locator a more useful name, right-click on the locator and choose Rename. You can change the position of locators after you've made them by clicking the locator and dragging it to a new location in the timeline. If you want to remove the locator, click to select it and then press Delete.

Jumping to Locators

The best part about locators is your ability to jump between them seamlessly while the arrangement is playing. All you have to do is click on a locator (it will begin to flash green) and playback will jump to that location, subject to global quantization. You can also use the two arrow buttons to the left and right of the Set button to jump to the previous or next locator.

What makes Live's locators unusually cool, though, is that you can assign MIDI messages and computer keys to these locators, just like any other control in Live. This means that the arrangement is now nearly as flexible as the Session View in that you can repeat sections of the song at will or jump to other areas as you see fit. Even the most complex of arrangements is now opened up for your experimentation, thanks to these locators.

Time Signature Changes

Time signature changes can be created by right-clicking in the Scrub area, choosing Insert Time Signature Change from the context menu, and typing in the time signature you want (see Figure 4.26). Editing and deleting a time signature change is done from the context menu as well. Just right-click on the time signature change and select Edit to alter the time signature or Delete to remove it.

Figure 4.26 Time signature changes in the Arrange View.
Source: Ableton

> **LOOP RECORD:** The Arrangement Loop can be quite handy for recording. For example, perhaps your song is done except for lead vocals. Create a loop around any part the singer is having trouble with and start recording. Go make a cup of tea while the singer sings it over and over and pick the best take (or edit together a few takes) when he's done.

Arrangement Editing

By editing the contents of the arrangement, you can fix mistakes, change the structure of your song, and creatively modify clips in ways that go beyond what's possible in the Session.

The standard Cut, Copy, Paste, Duplicate, and Delete can all be used in the Arrangement View to copy clips or automation. Paste will place the contents of the clipboard at the insertion marker, while Duplicate will place a copy immediately to the right of the selection. It's important to note that Duplicate operates on a range of time, not just the clips or automation. For example, you can select a full bar of time in a track, even though it only contains one short clip on the first beat, and use Duplicate to place a copy of the clip one bar later (see Figure 4.27).

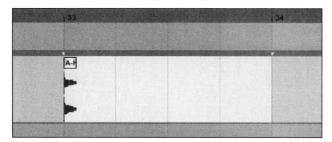

Figure 4.27 Selecting the clip and the rest of the empty bar allows you to duplicate both the clip and the empty space. This way the clip lands at the beginning of the next bar.
Source: Ableton

Drag clips by their title bar to move them. At the left and right boundaries of a clip, your mouse turns into a bracket (]), and you can click and drag the clip's edge to change its length. If an audio clip's Loop switch (in the Clip View) is enabled, you'll be able to resize the clip beyond its original length and cause it to loop as long as you want. Otherwise, you can only drag until the start or end of the audio file it references. MIDI clips can be extended indefinitely in either direction, which will just add empty space to the clip.

Cut Time, Paste Time, Duplicate Time, Delete Time

In the Edit menu, you'll also see a set of basic editing commands with the word "Time" appended. These commands work on all tracks simultaneously, based on the arrangement selection. While the standard editing commands operate only on clips and automation, these commands allow you to edit *time itself.* (Welcome to the future.)

Let's say you want to move the bridge of a song. It's currently after the second verse, and you decide you want it after the third verse. In the track display, select the range of time where the bridge is currently located. It doesn't matter what track you make the selection in, or even if there are any clips in that track. As long as you create an arrangement selection from the start of the bridge to the end, you're all set.

Cut Time will remove every clip in the bridge and slide over everything that happens after it to fill the gap. Now, place the insertion marker after the third verse, where you want the bridge to begin and use Paste Time to insert the clips you just cut. Live pushes the rest of the arrangement over to the right to make room for the clips you're pasting. Note that you must click in the *top-most track* when placing the insert marker. Live pastes the tracks from the top down, so if you click in any other track, the clips will get pasted into the wrong tracks.

This example should give you a pretty good idea of how Duplicate Time and Delete Time work as well. Duplicate Time places a copy at the end of the selection, shoving everything in the way over to the right. Delete Time simply removes an entire chunk of the song.

The keyboard shortcuts for these commands are easy to remember. Just add Shift to the key command for the standard version. For example, Cut Time is Ctrl (Cmd)+Shift+X. (The exception is Delete Time which is Ctrl(Cmd)-Shift-Delete). Take a moment to test out these commands and familiarize yourself with how they work. They are one of the most powerful features of the Arrangement View.

Insert Silence

Insert Silence is found under the Create menu. It's similar to the Time commands in that it allows you to insert empty space in the arrangement, moving clips and automation to the right to make room. Before using Insert Silence, you must create either an arrangement selection or place the insert marker at the location you want to add silence to. Depending on which you do first, the command will behave differently.

If you use Insert Silence after making an arrangement selection, it will place a range of empty space equal to the length of the selection. If you place the insert marker instead, Live will display the dialog shown in Figure 4.28 asking how much space you want to insert.

Figure 4.28 Type in the amount of space you want to insert.
Source: Ableton

Splitting and Consolidating Clips

You can break a clip into smaller clips using the Split function. To do this, it's easiest to unfold the track first. Once the track is unfolded, you can find the point at which you want to split the clip. Now click the location for your cut and use Edit > Split. The clip will be split into two clips (see Figure 4.29). These new clips will be completely independent of one another, meaning they can have their own unique clip settings, (such as transposition, warping, loop points, and so on).

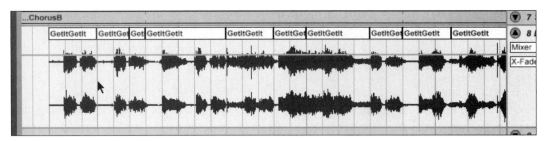

Figure 4.29 Just click and split to break clips into smaller ones for independent editing.
Source: Ableton

You can also join several clips into one clip for easier use. Select the clips that you want to join and select Consolidate from the Edit menu. Live will quickly render a new clip containing all the parts you had selected. When Live consolidates a clip, it creates a new audio file in your project folder, in *Samples > Processed > Consolidate*.

Bear in mind that Consolidate operates on a range of time, not just clips, so you can make new clips by combining empty space with existing clips. For example, you could use Consolidate to create a one-bar clip out of a mostly empty bar with a short audio clip in the middle (see Figure 4.30). This new clip could be copied to the first beat of any bar and retain the placement of the sample.

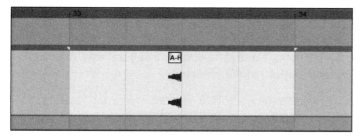

Figure 4.30 Consolidating this short sample into a bar-long clip makes it easy to copy to other locations while retaining the timing of the sample.
Source: Ableton

Automation Editing

Automation editing is important for a few reasons. First, no matter how well you perform automation while recording, there will be times when you want to change it later. Often, it's easer to make changes by editing instead of re-recording. There are also cases where it's easier to draw in automation manually rather than record it.

Automation is displayed as a line graph representing changes to a parameter over time. The meaning of the line shown in the automation track is determined by the parameter being controlled. In the case of level controls, such as Volume or Send, volumes increase as the line moves upward. For other controls, such as Pan, a line in the center of the track represents a center pan position. Lower values move the pan left, while higher values move the pan right.

Viewing Automation

Before you get into editing automation, though, there are a few things you need to know about viewing it. Session automation is shown in the Envelopes box of the Clip View (see Figure 4.31a). Arrangement Automation is shown in the track display, as seen in Figure 4.31b.

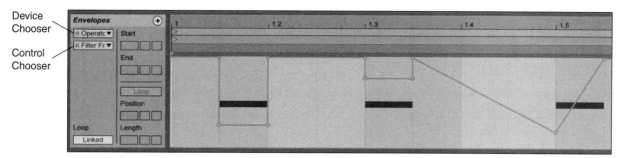

Figure 4.31a Session automation.
Source: Ableton

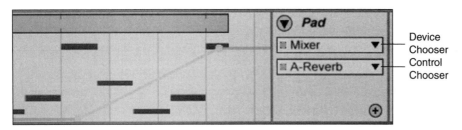

Figure 4.31b Arrangement automation.

Source: Ableton

With Session automation, it's only possible to view one automated parameter at a time. By default, the Arrangement also displays one parameter at a time, but it's possible to display many parameters at once using multiple Automation Lanes. Let's take a look at the basic method first, and then we'll get into multiple lanes.

As seen in Figures 4.31a and 4.31b, both Session and Arrangement have a pair of menus known as the Device Chooser and the Control Chooser. The Device Chooser displays the devices contained within the track as well as the Mixer. The Control Chooser selects a specific parameter from the device selected in the first menu. For example, to see the track's volume automation, you'd select Mixer in the first menu and Track Volume in the second menu. If an Auto Filter effect is loaded onto the track, you can view its Cutoff automation by choosing Auto Filter and then Cutoff Freq.

Live makes it easy to find automated parameters by placing a red LED next to devices and parameters containing automation. At the bottom of both menus, you'll also find the Show Automated Parameters Only command, which collapses the two menus into one and shows only automated parameters. You can select Show All Parameters from this menu to return to the default view.

If you select a parameter that has not been automated, a light, dotted line is displayed. Click on this line and use the editing techniques explained in "Editing Automation" to create automation manually.

SKIP THE CHOOSERS: Here's a trick that let's you view automation without navigating the automation choosers at all. First, select the view that contains the automation you want to see (Session or Arrangement). Then click on the Mixer or device control you want to view automation for.

For example, to view Arrangement Automation for the feedback of a Ping Pong Delay, switch to Arrangement and then click on the Feedback knob. The track will display the automation immediately.

Automation Lanes

In Arrangement View, it's possible to view more than one lane of automation at a time. The easiest way to view all of a track's automation is to right-click on the track name and select Add Lane for Each Automated Envelope from the context menu (see Figure 4.32).

If you want to view only certain envelopes, you can click the plus sign below the track name. This will add a new lane for whatever envelope you are currently viewing on the track. To add additional lanes, select a different envelope from the Device and Control Choosers, and click the plus sign. Conversely, each automation lane has a minus sign that can be used to remove the lane. Instead of removing lanes, you may just want to hide them. This can be done with the additional Fold button that appears at the bottom of the track's title bar.

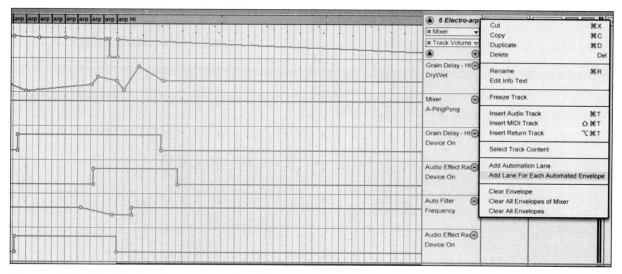

Figure 4.32 Use the plus icon in a track's title bar to add an automation lane. Use the minus icon in a lane's title bar to remove it. The Add Lane for Each Automated Envelope command will automatically create a new lane for each automated parameter.

Source: Ableton

Editing Automation

You can change the shape of the automation graph using two techniques, one of which involves the standard mouse pointer and another that uses Live's pencil tool, known as *Draw Mode*. (Toggle Draw Mode on and off with the B key.) In Draw Mode, you'll draw with the pencil, creating flat "steps" that are each the same width as the current grid setting (see Figure 4.33a). This will allow you to create tempo-synced automation effects, such as volume gates or timed effect sends. The pencil will overwrite any ramps that may have been made in the breakpoint mode in favor of its flat-step style.

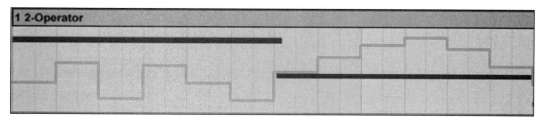

Figure 4.33a In Draw Mode, it's easy to create tempo-synced steps in your automation.

Source: Ableton

QUANTIZE KEYS: You can manually change the grid resolution with these keystrokes:

Ctrl (Cmd)+1: Makes the grid smaller.

Ctrl (Cmd)+2: Makes the grid larger.

Ctrl (Cmd)+3: Toggles triplet mode on and off.

Ctrl (Cmd)+4: Toggles the grid on and off. When the grid is off, you will be able to draw values anywhere.

You can also select different Adaptive or Fixed Grid modes by right-clicking (Ctrl-clicking) a track in the Arrangement View.

When Draw Mode is off, you will be creating breakpoint envelopes (see Figure 4.33b). The automation will be displayed as lines with little circles known as *breakpoints*. You can click on the lines to create or delete breakpoints, and you can drag the breakpoints around to reshape the graph.

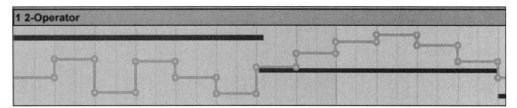

Figure 4.33b Turning Draw Mode off reveals individually adjustable breakpoints.
Source: Ableton

To move a chunk of automation, first drag to highlight all of the automation you want to move. Then grab a breakpoint and drag. Note that breakpoints cannot be dragged to the left or right of other breakpoints unless you hold down Shift, which will cause breakpoint to be deleted as you drag over them.

You can move a line segment in between two breakpoints by positioning the mouse on the segment and then holding down Shift while dragging. Or you can move the mouse just above or below the segment until it turns blue and then drag it. These same mouse techniques can also be used to move an entire range of automation up or down. Simply drag to highlight the range of automation you want to adjust and then drag the entire range when it turns blue. This method is handy because it prevents unintentional left/right movement.

There are a couple of other modifier keys you should know about for adjusting automation. Automation segments can be curved, as seen in Figure 4.34, by holding down Alt (Option) while dragging a segment. For making very fine value adjustments, hold down Ctrl (Cmd) while dragging a breakpoint or segment. Not only will you get a greater degree of precision, but left/right movement is constrained as well.

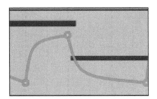

Figure 4.34 Automation curves in action. Double-click while holding Alt (Option) to restore the curve to a straight line.
Source: Ableton

Right-clicking on a selected range of automation reveals a special set of automation editing commands not shown in the Edit menu (Cut Envelope, Paste Envelope, and so on). The shortcuts for these commands are easy to remember because they're just the default key command + Alt (Option). For example, Cut Envelope is Alt (Option) + Ctrl (Cmd) + C. Automation is deleted with Ctrl (Cmd) + Delete.

> **WARP AND STRETCH:** Session automation can also be moved and resized using Warp Markers and MIDI Stretch Markers, both of which appear as handles directly above the envelope editor. Warp Markers often have to be created manually, while MIDI Stretch Markers appear automatically whenever a range of automation is selected. These will both be discussed in detail in Chapter 5, "Clips."

Lock Envelopes

To the right of the Scrub Area is a switch with a lock icon (refer to Figure 4.21). This is Lock Envelopes, which is used to lock automation to the timeline. By default, moving, copying, or deleting clips will move, copy, or delete automation as well. If you want to edit clips without editing automation, turn on Lock Envelopes. This will cause automation to remain at its current location, regardless of the movement of the clips.

Fades

Unless you've done a lot of audio editing, you may not realize what a big deal it is to be able to fade and crossfade audio clips automatically. Well, if that's the case, let me tell you—it is. While Live's Fades feature can be used for what is commonly thought of as a fade (a song slowly decreasing in volume or smoothly transitioning into another song), fades are also important to anyone who has to chop up audio. First, with digital audio there is always the "zero-crossing" problem. If a digital audio file is ever suddenly cut off anywhere other than the exact center of the waveform display (as seen in Figure 4.35), there will be an unpleasant popping sound.

Figure 4.35 Without a fade, this audio clip will pop when it ends.
Source: Ableton

In the real world, it's simply not possible to make every single edit at a zero crossing (and ever get anything else done, that is). To address this, most DAWs and audio editing programs have the ability to create fades to prevent popping when audio files are silenced or cut together.

This is particularly important when "comping" together takes (such as multiple passes of a vocal track). When doing this, it's sometimes necessary to make extremely precise edits—sometimes placing an edit in the middle of a word, for example. In these cases, crossfades are essential. By simultaneously fading out one piece of audio while fading in the other, these minute transitions can be made far more smooth and convincing.

Fades are not automation, but they appear in the Arrange View as if they were (see Figure 4.36). They are automatically created at every clip boundary, so depending on your workflow, you may not find yourself viewing fades very often. However, in cases where you're doing some intense editing, or you want to experiment with some creative crossfading, you'll need to view your fades so you can customize them.

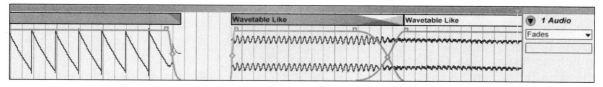

Figure 4.36 When a clip is followed by silence, a fast fade is automatically created to avoid clicks and pops. When two clips are adjacent to each other, a crossfade is created, causing the sounds to overlap and fade into each other.
Source: Ableton

Fades have two adjustable handles. The top handle controls the length of the fade. In the first fade shown in Figure 4.36, the top handle could be dragged to the left to create a longer, more gradual fade. The center handle controls the fade's slope, changing it to more of a "scoop" or a "bump" shape.

> **NO FADES ON ME:** Don't like fades? In Live's Preferences, there's a setting called *Create Fades on Clip Edges* in the Record/Warp/Launch tab. If you turn this off, not only will Live stop creating fades at clip boundaries, but it will also allow you to delete existing fades. Select the fade and pres Ctrl (Cmd)+Delete, or click the top fade handle and then press Delete.

Exporting Audio

After you have finished your Live song—and you like the way it sounds—it is time to get it out of your computer, burned to CD, and onto the streets. Before you can start burning CDs, though, you need to render your arrangement to a stereo audio file. Figure 4.37a shows the Export Audio/Video dialog (formerly known as Render to Disk) that appears when you press Ctrl (Cmd)+R. Figure 4.37b shows the only difference in this dialog when it is invoked from the Session View: the Length value.

Figure 4.37a The Export Audio/Video dialog in Arrangement View.

Source: Ableton

Figure 4.37b The Export dialog in Session View differs only in that the length of the output file must be specified in the Length field.
Source: Ableton

In both the Session and Arrangement Views, the Export Audio/Video dialog presents several important decisions to make. To begin, you will need to know the exact length of the section of audio you are rendering. If you are rendering from Session View, then you are likely rendering only a four-, eight-, or sixteen-bar section, whereas in the Arrangement View, you may well be rendering an entire song and can select the amount of desired rendering time by highlighting the portion of the arrangement you want to render (or its entirety). For instance, if you want to render a four-minute song, simply drag (highlight) the entire length of the song on any track.

Note that you also need to select which output to render, selected in the Rendered Track box. For creating a final mix, you should select the Master output. You also have the option to render any of the individual tracks or the Render All Tracks option, which will render each of your tracks individually all at the same time. This last option can be extremely useful if you want to export individual tracks for mixing in another audio sequencer, such as Pro Tools or Logic.

Remember that rendering the Master output will include only the output that is routed to the Master track. If you want to create a submix of a few tracks, you can solo those tracks, and only those will be heard in the final mix. Also, don't forget that if you have any tracks bypassing the Master and being routed directly to outputs on your audio interface, they won't get included at all.

To render from Session View, the steps are as follows:

1. Determine how long you want your loop or rendered audio section to be. There is no need to render more than one repetition of the audio segment; however, you can often make your music more interesting by embellishing the repeated loop and then rendering both the original and the varied loop as two loops.
2. Launch all of the clip(s) you want to be rendered. Once you've got them all playing, stop the sequencer.
3. Select File > Export Audio/Video to call up the Export Audio/Video dialog and type in the length of the file to be rendered, as determined in Step 1.
4. Click OK or press Enter, and select the drive/folder where you want to save your new loop.

To render from the Arrangement View, do the following:

1. Select the portion of the arrangement that you want to render. This selection can be made by click-dragging on any track, clicking on a clip, Shift-clicking to select a series of clips, or adjusting the loop brace to the desired length and clicking on its top bar.
2. Select File > Export Audio/Video to call up the Export dialog. Note that the range you have selected in Step 1 is displayed at the bottom of the dialog.
3. Select the Rendered track. Select Master to create a final mix, select an individual track, or select All Tracks to export all tracks individually.
4. Click OK or press Enter, and select the drive/folder where you want to save your new loop.

By default, the Rendered Track menu is set to Master. The Master track is where all of your individual tracks are summed together into a single stereo signal, so this is what you would use to output a final mix. The next option in this menu, All Tracks, is incredibly useful if you want to mix in another program. It creates individual files for every single track in the Set. The rest of the menu entries allow you to choose a single track for export.

The rest of the options in Export Audio/Video are as follows:

▷ **Normalize**: Analyzes the exported file to find the highest peak; then increases the volume of the file by the amount necessary to make this peak 0dB. This makes the file as loud as possible without clipping. Leave it off for most applications.

▷ **Render as Loop**: Primarily used to export loops with reverbs and delays. Live calculates the decay tail of the effect that would occur *after* the exported file ends and renders it at the *beginning*. This avoids the problem of the decay cutting off abruptly when looping the exported file.

▷ **Convert to Mono**: Exported file is mono instead of stereo.

▷ **File Type**: WAV and AIFF files are identical in sound, size, and just about every important way. Windows does not natively support AIFFs (though most pro audio programs do), so use WAVs if you need universal compatibility. If you want to make an MP3, the conversion must be done in a different program after you export one of these formats.

▷ **Sample Rate**: If you're exporting audio that will be sent out for mixing or mastering, you should select the highest sample rate used in your set, typically the same as the In/Out Sample Rate in the Audio tab of Preferences. If you're exporting audio that's going straight to consumer formats like MP3 or CD, use the standard rate of 44100.

▷ **Bit Depth**: When exporting for consumer formats, bit depth should be set to 16. When exporting for mixing or mastering, higher bit depths are typical. Live's internal bit depth is 32, therefore, any audio that is processed within Live is technically 32-bit. Bear in mind, however, that 32-bit files are very large and not supported by all programs. For most pro audio applications, 24-bit is just fine.

▷ **Dither**: Dithering adds low-level noise to digital audio to hide the distortion that occurs when reducing bit depth. It is commonly accepted that when outputting at 16 bit, some dithering should be used (try POW-r 2 as a default for most pop and electronic music). If you're outputting at 24 bit, Triangular is the safest dither method to use, although some say not to use any at all. Search the Internet for endless pages of incomprehensible discussion on the topic.

▷ **Create Analysis File**: When this setting is activated, Live will also create an ASD file in addition to the rendered audio file. This is helpful when exporting files that will be reimported into Live, since the ASD file contains waveform display data and information, such as tempo.

▷ **Export to SoundCloud**: SoundCloud is an Internet service for sharing your music. If you have an account with them, this option streamlines the process of uploading your song.

IMPORTANT NOTE! START TRANSPORT ON RECORD: As this book was on its way to the printer, Ableton added an important new preference to the Record/Warp/Launch tab: Start Transport with Record. This preference affects the behavior of both of Live's Record buttons. When set On (the default), recording behaves as described in the rest of this book.

When Start Transport with Record is set Off, clicking Arrangement Record or Session Record will prepare Live for recording without starting playback. To begin recording, you must then press Play. (This behavior will be familiar to users of prior versions of Live.) Additionally, Session Record will not initiate clip recording as described in the "Session Record Button" section of this chapter.

Clips

C LIPS ARE THE MUSICAL BUILDING BLOCKS OF LIVE. As such, you'll eventually want to gain a deep knowledge of their inner workings, and this chapter is designed to help you do just that. From simple tweaks, like clip name and color, to the far-out manipulations possible with Warp Markers and grooves, there's an awful lot going on in the Clip View that you need to know about.

Common Properties of Clips

While MIDI and audio are very different animals, there are a number of behaviors and settings that are common to both types of clips, all of which will be discussed here. The Clip View is divided into several different areas: the *editor* on the right, which displays audio waveforms, Warp Markers, MIDI notes, and envelopes; and several parameter boxes to the left: the clip box, which is always shown, and the Launch, Sample (audio clips), Notes (MIDI clips), and Envelopes boxes, all of which can be shown or hidden using the switches in the lower-left corner. See Figure 5.1.

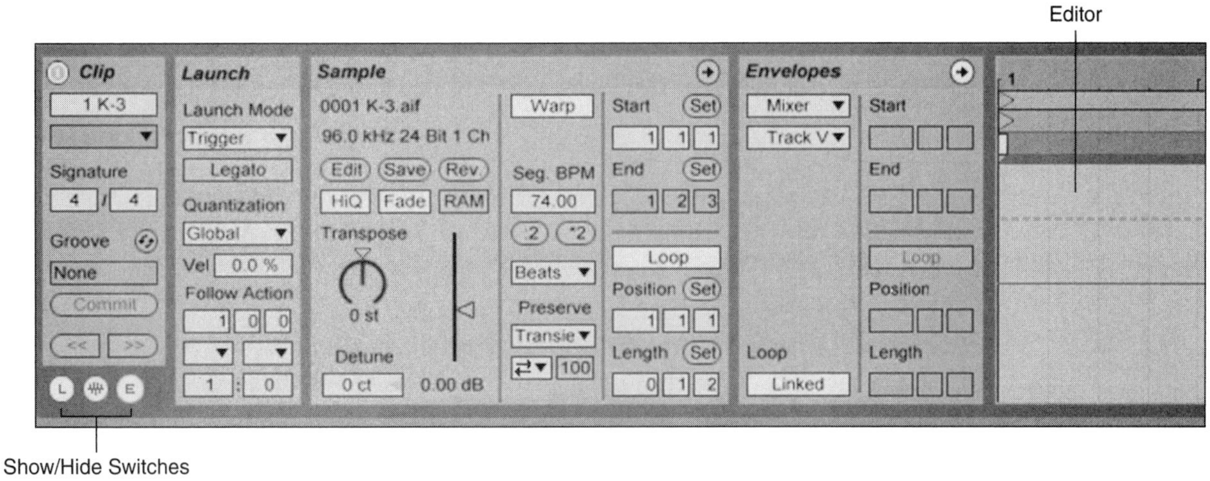

Figure 5.1 The Clip View contains multiple sections that can be shown and hidden using the icons at the lower-left corner of the window. An audio clip is shown. For MIDI clips, the Sample box is replaced by the Notes box.
Source: Ableton

Be aware that the editor is used to view both audio/MIDI data and the envelopes of a clip. Click in the title bar of the Sample or Notes box to show audio or MIDI in the editor and in the title bar of the Envelopes box to show envelopes. If you're not focusing on envelopes, it's a good idea to hide the Envelopes box. This will save space and help avoid any confusion.

The Clip Box

The clip box is always visible in the Clip View (see Figure 5.2). Here you'll be able to adjust some basic properties of the clip and enable a groove if you choose.

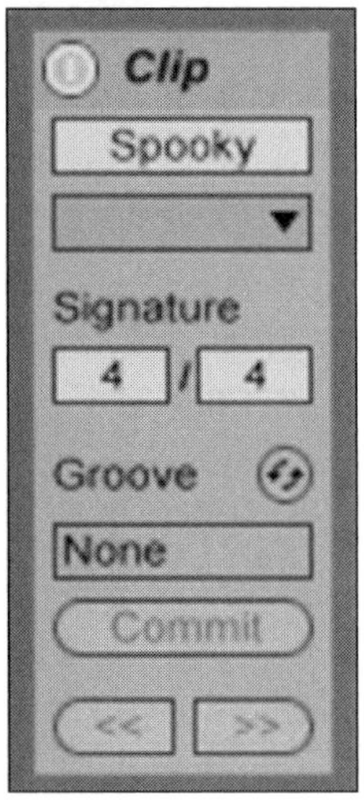

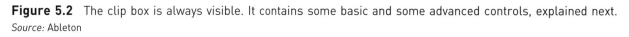

Figure 5.2 The clip box is always visible. It contains some basic and some advanced controls, explained next.
Source: Ableton

Clip Activator

The circular "power switch" in the upper-left corner can be used to disable the clip. This is handy if you want to leave a clip in place, but signify that it is not being used. It is particularly useful when working in Arrangement View, because it will allow you to mute a clip but leave it in place in case it is needed later. Clips can also be deactivated by selecting them and pressing zero on your computer keyboard, or by selecting Deactivate Clip from the context menu.

Clip Name and Color

The first two settings in the Clip section (see Figure 5.2) are purely cosmetic—they have no impact on the behavior or sound of the clip. The first field is the Clip Name, which can be as many characters as you want. Clips can also be named using the Rename command, and colors can be selected by right-clicking on a clip and using the color chooser.

If you create a clip by dragging a file from the Browser, the clip will be named the same as the file. When you record a new clip, it will be given the name of the track in which it is created. To help keep multiple takes (recordings) in order, Live adds a number to the beginning of the clip (and file) name as each new one is created. If you use long clip names, you'll only see the first nine characters in Session View when using the default track width. This can be remedied by dragging the right edge of a track's title bar to widen the track.

Clip color may seem like a bit of aesthetic fluff at first, but color coding your clips can be a huge benefit in performance or when working on complex productions. For example, you could make all your bass parts shades of blue in your songs or use colors to indicate different genres in your DJ set.

Time Signature

The clip's Time Signature (labeled *Signature*) determines the numbering of the grid markers in the editor. What it does *not* do is change the time signature, tempo, or any other audible aspect of the clip. This parameter is strictly to make the editors visually coherent when working in different meters.

Clip Groove

The Groove section is one of the more complex (and mind-blowing) features found in the Clip View. Using Live's Groove features, you can modify the timing and dynamics of your clips in unlimited ways. Groove is a deep topic that requires a good knowledge of clips, so it's explained in a separate section later in this chapter.

Clip Nudge Controls

Next are the Clip Offset Controls, which are composed of two buttons at the bottom of the Clip Box. These controls allow you to offset a clip easily by a quantized value or to sync clips manually without quantization. These controls work differently than the Tempo Nudge controls. Clip Nudge changes the offset of a single clip relative to Live's master tempo, while Tempo Nudge momentarily changes the master tempo and thus the playback tempo of all clips.

Pressing the two arrow buttons (the Nudge buttons) will perform the shift. (The clip should be playing when you do this.) Each time you press an arrow, the start and playback positions of the clip will change by an amount determined by the Global Quantize setting. (Don't confuse this with the clip's Launch Quantization, which will be explained next.) If the Global Quantize is set to 1 Bar, the clip's start location will be shifted by 1 Bar with every click of the Nudge buttons. If you want to offset by a smaller amount, select a smaller Quantize value. With Global Quantize set to None, the Nudge buttons will offset the clip by minute increments, allowing you to make your clip sit just the tiniest bit ahead of or behind the beat.

For an example, let's say you're DJing with Global Quantize set to 1/16, rather than 1 Bar, in order to occasionally offset a track to create a new groove. The Clip Nudge controls could be used while pre-listening to correct the placement of a track that was launched a little too early or too late, or to experiment with different offsets before bringing the track in. Or you could launch a track with Global Quantize set to 1 Bar and then change it to None and nudge the clip so it rushes or drags a tiny bit.

> **THE THIRD CONTROL:** While it looks like the Nudge controls are limited to only two buttons, there is a third control that can be accessed only through MIDI assignment. When you enter the MIDI Map mode (Ctrl [Cmd]+M), you'll see a tiny box appear between the arrow buttons. Click this box and twist a knob on your MIDI controller. Now you can twist the knob to perform the nudge. You should use an endless encoder knob for this.

> **KEEP THE GROOVE:** After you've nudged a track to perfection, you may want to be able to recall exactly how much you've nudged it so it can be played back exactly the same the next time you launch it. To do this, select Capture and Insert Scene from the Create menu. This will make a copy of whatever clips you currently have playing back and create a new scene with just those clips in it. Any tracks that you've nudged will have their Start markers moved by the amount they were nudged.

The Launch Box

In Live, we use the term *launch* to indicate the playing back of a Session clip. Launching is a customizable behavior that offers a variety of creative options. These options are set in the Launch Box, which is shown or hidden using the L icon in the lower left-hand corner of the Clip View.

Launch Mode

The Launch mode (see Figure 5.3) determines what happens when a clip's launch button is pressed, or the clip is launched via MIDI or the computer keyboard. Be aware that the behavior of the Launch modes is linked to the Quantization setting (explained next). To experiment with the different modes, I recommend that you set Quantization to a relatively low value (such as 1/16), as it will make the differences in the modes much easier to understand.

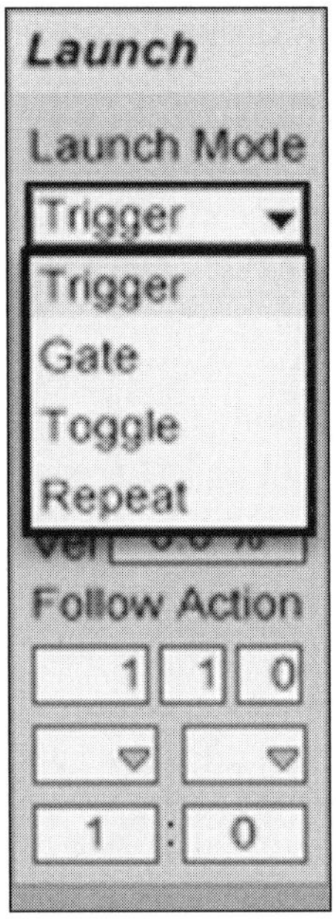

Figure 5.3 Launch modes are a powerful and simple way to get creative with clips.
Source: Ableton

▷ **Trigger:** The most common Launch mode for use in most performance situations is Live's Trigger mode. Each time you fire a clip, it will launch. Once a clip is launched and playing, you will be able to stop its play-back only by pressing one of the Clip Stop buttons located in the same track. This mode ignores the up-tick (release) of the mouse button, computer keyboard key, or MIDI note. Each clip can be fired as rapidly as the quantization will allow, and each time the clip is fired, it will restart the clip from the beginning, even if it was already playing.

▷ **Gate:** When triggering a clip in Gate mode, you will hear the sound only for as long as your mouse or key-board key is depressed. This is an excellent setting for dropping in snippets of sound without playing the entire clip. In short, holding down your left mouse button (or MIDI/computer-keyboard key) will play the clip continuously until you let up.

▷ **Toggle:** With Toggle mode engaged, the Clip Launch button basically turns into an on/off switch for the clip. If you launch a clip that is playing, it will stop. Launch the stopped clip, and it will begin playing. This also works at the scene level if you trigger a scene with clips set in Toggle mode. Each time you trigger the scene, clips that are playing will stop, and stopped clips will start. Bear in mind that stopping of the clip will respect the current quantization, just the way launching does.

▷ **Repeat:** Repeat mode is a way of retriggering a clip by holding down the mouse or assigned key/MIDI note. Any time the mouse or key is held, the clip will continuously restart itself at the rate specified by the clip's Quantize setting. If the setting is 1/4, holding down the mouse/key will cause only the first beat of the clip to play over and over again. When the mouse or key is released, the clip will play through its entirety like normal. This mode can create fun stutter effects, but should be used sparingly—probably not a good choice for default behavior.

Legato Mode Switch

Below the mode menu is the Legato switch. When enabled, the clip will begin playback from the relative position of the currently playing clip in the same track. For example, let's say you have two eight-bar clips set to Legato mode. The first clip is launched and allowed to play for two bars before the second one is launched. Instead of playing from the beginning, it starts at bar 3 since that's where the previous clip would have been had it been allowed to keep playing.

This feature allows you to switch between several different clips, dipping in and out of various sections of each clip. With low launch quantization values, this feature makes it possible to generate a large number of variations from a relatively small number of clips.

Clip Quantization

You may be familiar with quantization as a technique to correct the timing of MIDI performances. However, the Quantization menu in the Launch Box deals with something called *launch quantization*, which is quite a different animal. It still deals with correcting timing, but only in terms of launching and stopping clips (as the name suggests!). Proper Clip Quantization settings ensure that clips will start on time and in sync with each other, even if they are triggered a little early by us sloppy humans.

When you launch a clip, Live waits to play it back until the next quantization interval is reached. For example, with a quantization setting of 1 Bar, the clip will wait until the downbeat of the next bar to begin playing. In the interval between when a clip is launched and when it actually begins playing back, the Clip Launch Button blinks. With quantization set to None, a clip will start playing the instant it is launched.

Quantization is selected from the drop-down menu shown in Figure 5.4. By default, clips are set to Global, which causes the clip to follow the Quantize setting in the Control Bar. In Live's Preferences, it's possible to change the default quantization to a value other than Global, but for most applications you probably don't want to do this. It's handy to have most clips follow global quantization and override that behavior only when necessary.

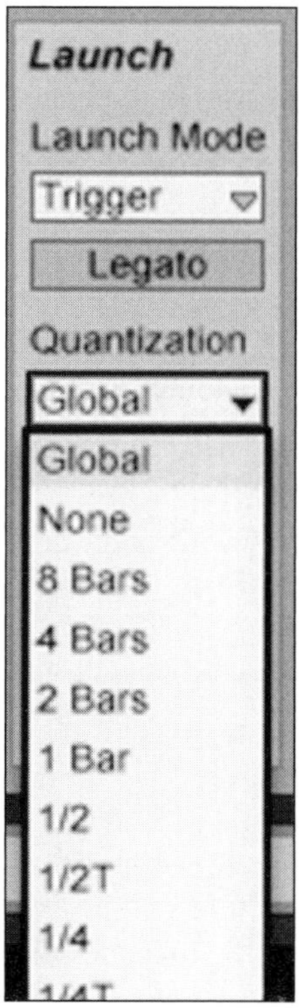

Figure 5.4 The Quantize settings for a clip.

Source: Ableton

Velocity

Just below the Quantization box is the Velocity Amount. This value works only for clips launched by MIDI. It uses the incoming velocity level of the MIDI note to set the playback volume of the clip. At 0%, the velocity has no effect on clip playback volume—it plays at its original level. At 100%, the clip's velocity sensitivity will be extreme—probably too sensitive for most situations. This works for both audio and MIDI clips.

Follow Actions

Live's Follow Actions allow an amazing level of automation within the Session View. Using Follow Actions, you can set rules by which one clip can launch another. Any particular clip can launch clips above and below it, replay itself, or even stop itself—all based on odds and a time period that you can program. You can think of Follow Actions as a virtual "finger" that launches for you. Follow Actions open up so many creative possibilities that you'll find a list of potential applications listed in Chapter 13, "Live 9 Power."

Follow Actions work on *groups* of clips, which are clips arranged above and below one another in the same track (see Figure 5.5). An empty clip slot inserted between two clips divides them into separate groups. Follow Actions cannot be used to trigger clips in different groups or tracks.

Figure 5.5 The track on the left features one group of clips, while the track on the right has two groups.
Source: Ableton

The time and conditions for a Follow Action are set in the three sections at the bottom of the clip's Launch window. The first section, the Follow Action Time, determines how much time elapses between when the clip is launched and the Follow Action occurs. Figure 5.6 specifies that the action Play Next will be performed after one bar elapses.

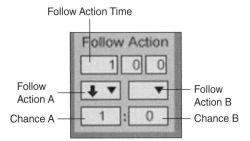

Figure 5.6 These parameters determine the Follow Action behavior of the clip. If Chance A and B are both set to a non-zero value, Follow Action A or B is randomly chosen, based on their ratio.
Source: Ableton

The options in the Follow Action menus are as follows:

▷ **No Action:** No action is performed. This is the default action for all new clips. With No Action selected in both menus, no Follow Action will occur.

▷ **Stop:** Stops playback.

▷ **Play Again:** Relaunches the currently playing clip.

▷ **Previous/Next:** Triggers the clip above or below the current one. If the clip at the top of a group triggers the Play Previous action, it will "wrap around" and trigger the bottom clip of the group and vice versa.

▷ **Play First/Last:** Triggers the top or bottom clip in a group. If the top clip in a group triggers the Play First action, it will relaunch itself.

▷ **Any:** Launches a randomly chosen clip from the group. Live might retrigger the same clip with this option.

▷ **Other:** Launches a *different* randomly chosen clip from the group. The same clip will never be launched.

What makes Follow Actions particularly interesting is the ability to create two possible actions for each clip. Live will choose between Follow Action A and Follow Action B at random, but this randomness can be constrained using a mathematical ratio.

Chance A and Chance B are used to set the odds that each action will occur. By default, the odds are 1:0, meaning that the Follow Action on the left will always be performed. Odds of 0:1 will cause the right Follow Action to always be performed. Odds of 1:1 will give you a 50-50 chance of either action being performed. You can put in any values you like, such as 2:3 or 1:200.

Bear in mind that whenever No Action is encountered, no further Follow Actions will occur, even if the clip is looped. This is because Follow Actions are only evaluated after a clip is *launched*. If you want to create a chance that a clip will either continue to loop or launch another clip, use Play Again instead. This way, the clip will continue to evaluate its Follow Actions.

PLAYING THE ODDS: Note that odds are calculated afresh every time a Follow Action is performed. If you have a clip with Follow Action odds of 1:1 and Live chooses the left Action the first time, it does not mean that Live will choose the right Action the next time. Just as it is possible to roll the same number on a die time after time, it is quite possible for Live to choose the left Follow Action five times in a row, even with 1:1 odds.

Sample/Notes

The next box in the clip view differs for audio and MIDI clips. Audio clips display a box called *Sample*, while MIDI clips have a box called *Notes*. The left sides of these boxes differ in the Sample and Notes boxes, but the right sides contain identical parameters for adjusting the clip's playback range and loop length.

Start and End

A clip can contain more audio or MIDI than you actually want to play back. In other words, you may have a four-bar clip but decide to use only the first bar. You may have a five-minute song from which you isolate a great drum fill in the middle. These adjustments are made using the Start, End, and Loop controls.

Start determines where the clip begins playback. The Start position is shown both as a numeric value and as a right-pointing flag in the editor to the right. End determines where the clip stops playback when the Loop switch is disabled. This is an important point, so I'll also say it a different way: when Loop is enabled, End has no effect. This parameter is displayed as a left-pointing flag in the editor, and as a numeric value directly below Start. Both of these values can be edited by dragging the flags or by editing the numeric values directly, as shown in Figure 5.7.

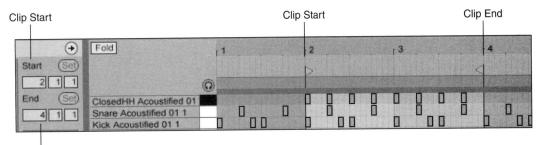

Figure 5.7 You can define a smaller section of a clip to use by setting the Clip Start and End Markers.

Source: Ableton

CLIP TRANSPORT: You can start playing a clip from any point you choose without having to move the Start Marker. To do this, simply hover the cursor just above the editor, which turns into a speaker icon. When you click, the clip will begin playing from the closest location allowed by the clip's Launch Quantization. In other words, if the clip's Quantize setting is set to 1 Bar, you'll be able to start playback from the beginning of any bar in the clip. This makes it easy to jump to any point in a track, even during a performance, since the jumps are quantized.

Loop Settings

The loop settings consist of three controls: Loop, Position, and Length. The first of these, Loop, is a large switch that enables or disables the loop. The second two controls determine where the loop begins and how long it is. These parameters, Position and Length, are displayed as numeric values and as a brace running along the top of the editor (see Figure 5.8).

Dragging the right edge of the brace changes the Length while dragging the left edge will change both Length and Position simultaneously. Drag the brace from its center to change the Loop Position while leaving its Length the same. A single click on the Loop brace will select it and allow you to adjust it with the arrow keys. The left/right keys will move it by the grid size, and the up/down keys will move it by the current Loop Length.

Live also lets you define the loop points as the clip is playing by pressing the buttons marked "Set" next to Loop Position and Loop Length. These buttons are both quantized to the value in the global Quantize menu, so it's easy to interactively create perfect loops.

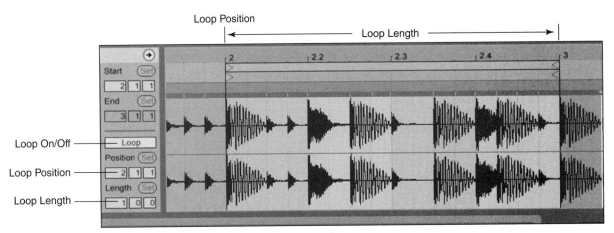

Figure 5.8 It's easy to loop any portion of the audio or MIDI within a clip.

Source: Ableton

Bear in mind that Start and Loop Position can be adjusted independently. This means that you can have clips that don't begin to loop right away, as seen in Figure 5.9.

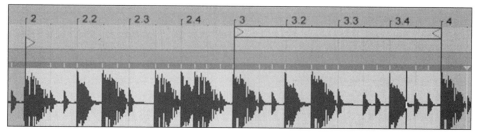

Figure 5.9 A clip can be set to loop at a different point than it initially plays back from.
Source: Ableton

This is useful in a variety of situations. For example, imagine you have a drum loop that starts with a crash cymbal. Instead of looping the entire clip, resulting in the crash cymbal sounding every time the clip repeats, you can specify a loop area after the crash cymbal. This way you'll hear the crash the first time you trigger the clip, but you won't hear it again until you relaunch the clip. Or, in a DJ set, it can be very useful to set up a song to play from the beginning, and then loop somewhere toward the end to buy you extra time when mixing into the next song.

It's also possible to place the clip Start within the loop, at a point other than the loop start (see Figure 5.10). By offsetting loops from each other, a great deal of rhythmic variation is possible. To get a feel for this, try launching a drum loop and a bass loop on two different tracks. While the loops are playing back, move the Start position of the bass loop and listen to how the groove changes.

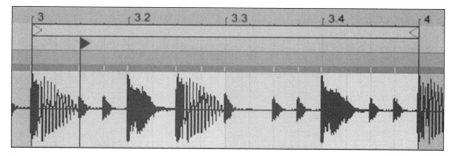

Figure 5.10 Try offsetting the clip's Start to create loop variations.
Source: Ableton

ORANGE DIGITS: When adjusting loops, you may occasionally find numbers in the loop settings or Start/End display that are orange. This means that the number displayed is not exact. For example, if a loop length is listed as 1.0.0 with the last 0 in red, the clip may actually be 1.0.01 beats long. A loop this long will at first sound correct, but will drift over time since it's a tiny bit too long.

This can be fixed easily by typing in the correct number and pressing Enter.

Editing Multiple Clips

Many of the clip parameters explained here can be edited for multiple clips simultaneously. When you select multiple clips, only the controls that can be changed for all selected clips will be shown (see Figure 5.11). Controls that are set to different values will display an asterisk (*) instead of a value.

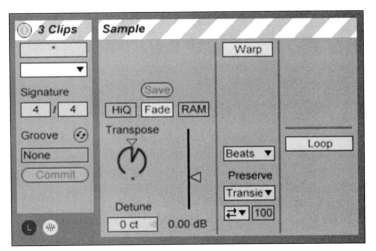

Figure 5.11 Edit multiple clips simultaneously and save yourself some time.

Source: Ableton

Some of the options, such as Clip Name and Clip Color, will be set identically for all clips. For example, if you change the Clip Name to Hot Drums, all of the selected clips will take on the same name. This same behavior is true for nearly all of the available fields when editing multiple clips.

The Transpose, Detune, Velocity, and Volume settings of audio clips, however, can be adjusted by a relative amount. For example, if the Transpose setting of one clip is –2 and another is +3, turning up the Transpose knob 2 ticks while selecting both clips will result in the first clip being set to 0 while the second clip is set to +5. To reset a control of all selected clips to the default value, select the control and press Delete.

MIDI Clips

If you're using Live to compose music, you'll probably be using MIDI clips extensively. Whether you're performing with a controller or drawing in parts from scratch, you'll need to know your way around the MIDI clip. In this section, we'll take a closer look at their properties and at MIDI editing in particular.

Editing MIDI Clips

MIDI is incredibly flexible. Recorded notes can be effortlessly transposed to different pitches, extended or shortened, and moved to a different location in time. When you edit MIDI clips in Live, you not only have the ability to change the notes that were recorded, but also to create new ones by hand. In fact, many producers prefer to draw parts directly into the clips instead of playing them, when programming drum parts, for example. It allows them to create specific performances, such as perfectly repeating 1/16 notes that are all the same duration and velocity. Editing data by hand also allows you to create precise automation, such as perfect volume fades and quantized filter modulations.

If you ever want to create a MIDI clip entirely through editing, there's no need to record at all. Just double-click in an empty clip slot to create an empty MIDI clip and edit away.

Adjusting the Grid

All editing in a MIDI clip is governed by the timing grid. Anytime a note is created or moved, it will snap to the grid values. If your grid is set to 1/4, you'll be able to align the MIDI notes only to the 1/4 note of the clip. You can also change the grid settings, allowing you to make more precise rhythmic adjustments. You can even turn the grid off completely for free-form editing.

Live has two grid modes: Adaptive and Fixed. The grid mode can be selected by right-clicking anywhere in the Note Editor and selecting from the context menu. Adaptive mode, the default, simply changes the grid value according to the zoom level. The grid values get smaller the more you zoom in on your MIDI notes. Fixed grid keeps the resolution at the value you select, regardless of the zoom level. Changing the Fixed grid resolution can be done with the key commands outlined next. As you execute these key commands, you'll see the grid value change in the MIDI data window (see Figure 5.12), reflecting your modification. Note that before using the following key commands, you must click on the grid to select it; otherwise, you might be adjusting the Quantize menu in the Control Bar.

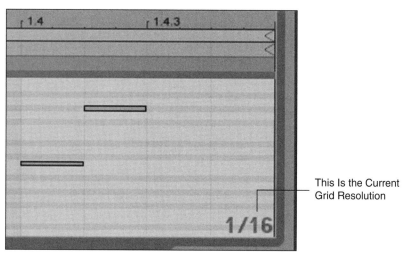

This Is the Current Grid Resolution

Figure 5.12 The current grid setting is 1/16. Notes will snap to 1/16-note timing when dragged, and any notes drawn will default to a duration of 1/16.
Source: Ableton

▷ **Ctrl (Cmd)+1:** This will decrease the value of the grid. If the grid was set to 1/16 before, it will be 1/32 after using this key command.

▷ **Ctrl (Cmd)+2:** This has the opposite effect of the command above. A grid value of 1/16 will change to 1/8 after using this command.

▷ **Ctrl (Cmd)+3:** This key command toggles Triplet mode on and off. A previous setting of 1/8 will turn to 1/8T (1/8-note triplet) after pressing these keys. Use this key command again to switch Triplet mode off.

▷ **Ctrl (Cmd)+4:** This turns the entire grid on and off. When the grid is off, the grid value display will turn gray. You will be able to place MIDI data anywhere you like while the grid is off. To re-enable the grid, use this key command again.

Editing Notes and Velocities

After you've got your desired grid timing selected, you're ready to start manipulating MIDI notes. Live displays MIDI notes in a style known as a *piano roll*. This term comes from the old player pianos that were programmed using rolls of paper. These rolls had small slots cut into them, each representing a specific note on the piano keyboard or one of the other instruments mounted inside. A note that played for a long time was triggered by a long slot in the paper. As the paper rolled by mechanical sensors, it triggered servos to play notes on the piano.

Viewing MIDI Data

The Piano Roll View in Live features a lane for each note on the MIDI scale. When looking at Figure 5.13, you'll see an image of a piano keyboard at the left side of the window. From each of these keys is a lane extending to the right where notes can be placed. Notes placed in these lanes trigger their corresponding key in the scale. Turn on Preview to hear notes as you draw or move them.

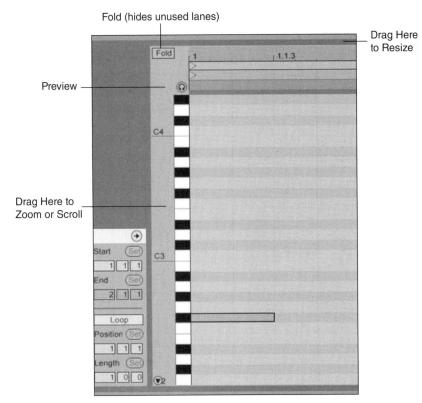

Figure 5.13 The MIDI editor can be resized, and the piano roll zoomed and scrolled, so you can always see what you need to see.

Source: Ableton

You can zoom in and out of the vertical piano keyboard, thus allowing you to see more or less of the 128 possible notes in the MIDI scale. Zoom in by moving your mouse over the piano keyboard at the left of the window. When the mouse changes to a magnifying glass, you can drag horizontally to zoom and vertically to scroll. To enlarge the editor, move your mouse above the editor until it becomes a splitter and then drag upward. If you want, you can make the editor take up the entire screen and use Shift-Tab when you need to see the clip grid or track display.

> **INTO THE FOLD:** Live's MIDI display has a unique feature that hides any lanes that don't contain MIDI data. When the Fold button (located just above the Piano Roll display) is activated, the display will be condensed, and you'll see only the lanes that contain notes.

Basic Editing

There are two methods for editing MIDI data: with the standard mouse pointer, or with Live's pencil tool, known as Draw Mode. To enable Draw Mode, click the pencil in the Control Bar or simply press the B key on your keyboard (see Figure 5.14). A short press toggles Draw Mode on and off, while holding B will temporarily enable Draw Mode and restore the standard mouse pointer when you release it. This technique works in reverse as well, temporarily enabling the standard mouse pointer while in Draw Mode.

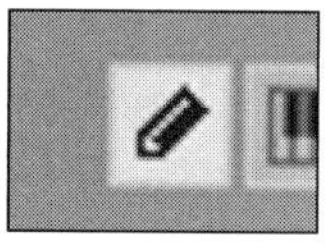

Figure 5.14 Enable Draw Mode to draw and erase notes with a single click.
Source: Ableton

When Draw Mode is on, you can add notes in the editor by single-clicking. The notes you create will automatically be set to the length of the current grid setting. If you continue to hold the mouse button after you create the note, you can drag up and down to set its velocity. If you click and drag horizontally, the pencil will create a series of notes in that lane, which is great for hi-hat patterns. (You can also drag up and down to set the velocities of the whole group.) Clicking an existing note with the pencil will erase it.

While Draw Mode is very convenient for many editing tasks, there are a few things you can only do with the standard mouse pointer. For example, you can click and drag notes to relocate them, or draw a marquee around a group of notes to select them, and then move or edit them as a group. Once notes are selected, they can also be moved using the arrow keys. To create a MIDI note with the standard mouse pointer, double-click in the editor. Double-clicking an existing note will erase it.

Regardless of which mode you're in, the mouse will change into a bracket-shaped (] or [) trimmer tool when moved to the edge of a note. This tool is used to change the length of notes. When dragging with this tool, the note length will change smoothly at first, only snapping to the next grid line when dragged very close to it. Once it snaps to the next grid line, it will continue to snap, only allowing you to make edits sized to the grid. Not to worry, just hold down Ctrl (Cmd) while dragging to disable the grid.

Note lengths can be adjusted from the keyboard by holding down Shift and using the left/right arrow keys. Add Ctrl (Cmd) to disable the grid while resizing.

> **QUICK SELECT:** There's a quick shortcut for selecting every instance of a particular pitch or drum in a MIDI clip. Just click in the piano keyboard (or next to the drum name if you're using Drum Rack or Impulse) to select all of the notes in that lane.

The area directly above the note editor will display a highlighted area called the *selection area* whenever a selection is made. A selection can be made by clicking on a note, Shift-clicking to select a range of notes, or clicking and dragging to draw a selection marquee. Note that it's even possible to create a selection area without selecting any notes, simply by dragging in an empty area of the editor. The length of the selection area is particularly important when using commands that operate on a range of time.

For example, when Duplicate is used on MIDI notes, the copy will be placed at the end of the selection area. Therefore, the notes shown in Figure 5.15 will be placed at the beginning of the next beat. The note editor also supports the Cut Time, Paste Time, Duplicate Time, Delete Time, and Insert Silence commands described in the Arrangement Editing section of Chapter 4. These commands will replicate or remove ranges of time according to the current selection area.

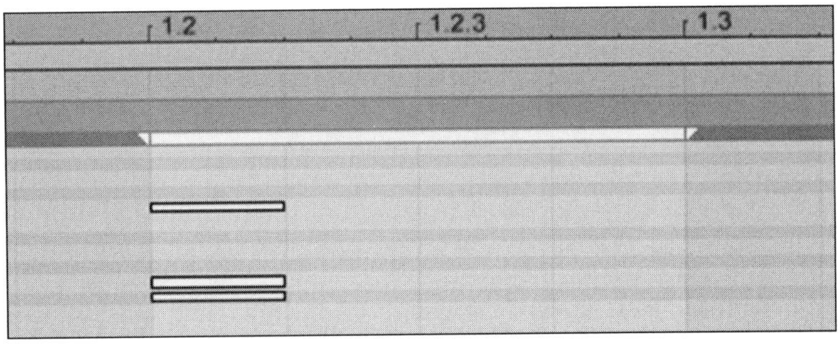

Figure 5.15 Even though all the notes are on the first 1/16 note, the selection area shown is a quarter note long. The Duplicate command could now be used to place a copy of these notes at the start of the next beat.
Source: Ableton

Clicking in an empty area of the editor inserts a blinking cursor, which is useful if you're using the standard Cut, Copy, and Paste commands. Once you've cut or copied a selection, click to place the cursor before pasting to determine where the notes will be placed.

Bear in mind that whenever you've selected a group of notes, they can all be edited simultaneously. Not only can you move them, but you can also resize them, or you can scale their velocities all at once.

Editing Velocity

Directly below the note editor is the velocity editor. Typically, changes in velocity will result in a change in the volume of the note. However, this behavior is actually controlled by the instrument receiving the MIDI, and you'll find that some sounds are velocity sensitive while others are not. Some presets will map velocity to other values such as filter cutoff. To learn more about mapping note velocity, read up on Live's instruments in Chapter 8, "Live's Instruments."

The velocity editor can be folded or unfolded, and resized by dragging the lower boundary of the note editor (see Figure 5.16). When Draw Mode is turned off, the velocity of each note is represented by a vertical line with a small circle at the top. To adjust the velocity, just drag the circle up or down. With Draw Mode on, the circle disappears, and you can draw velocities directly into the velocity editor.

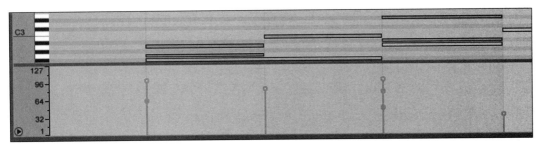

Figure 5.16 The velocity lane can be enlarged by dragging at the top, or hidden by clicking the fold switch in the lower-left corner.
Source: Ableton

Since multiple notes can occur in different lanes at one time in a MIDI clip, it's possible for the velocities of multiple notes to be stacked on top of one another, making it difficult or impossible to change the velocity of a particular note. To work around this, select the note in editor first, and you'll then be able to edit its velocity. If you use the Draw Mode in the velocity lane, you will not be able to specify which note to edit when two or more occur at the same time. Instead, you'll set all the notes to the same velocity.

Fortunately, there's also an easy shortcut for editing velocity that works whether or not Draw Mode is turned on. Just hold down Ctrl (Cmd) while holding the mouse pointer over a note, and it will change into a splitter. Drag the splitter up or down to change the velocity. Since Live color-codes notes to show their velocity, you may not have to use the velocity editor at all, and can just fold it to save space on your screen.

> **RISE AND FALL:** With Draw Mode turned off, hold down Ctrl (Cmd) and draw a ramp in the velocity lane to create a range of increasing or decreasing note velocities. To set a range of notes to the same velocity, select them and drag up or down until all notes are at the maximum or minimum. When you move back toward the center, they will all remain at the same velocity.

Stretch Markers

With one exception, creating a selection area causes a set of handles called MIDI Stretch Markers to appear above the editor. (No markers appear when you select only simultaneously occurring notes.) These can be used to flexibly adjust the duration and timing of the selection. If the Envelopes view is showing, these markers can also be used to adjust automation or modulation (see Figure 5.17).

Figure 5.17 MIDI Stretch Markers allow you to do some elastic editing to both notes and envelopes.
Source: Ableton

Dragging the markers works similarly to moving notes, in that they move smoothly at first and then snap to the grid once the first grid line is reached. The way they adjust notes, however, is unusual and can take some getting used to. The marker that is moved will adjust the notes, while the other marker acts as an anchor. The way the notes are adjusted depends on which direction you drag. If you drag a marker to increase the size of the selected area (you drag it *away* from the other marker), the notes are elongated and their timing is slowed down. Dragging a marker toward the other one compresses the timing and duration of the notes. If you continue to drag the marker, you can actually drag it *past* the other one and reverse the order of the notes.

MIDI Editing Buttons

In the Notes box, there are several buttons used for MIDI editing, as well as a handy Transpose function (see Figure 5.18).

Figure 5.18 There are a few MIDI editing buttons in the Notes Box.
Source: Ableton

Transpose

This nifty box shows you the range of the selected notes in the clip, or all notes if none are selected. For example, if you program a melody that runs from middle C to the G above, Transpose will display C3-G3. Drag up or down in this box to transpose the notes up or down, or type in a numeric value. For example, typing in –7 will move the notes down seven semitones (a perfect fifth). Alternately, you could move the notes this same amount by typing the new bottom pitch (in this case F2) or the new top pitch preceded by a minus sign (–C3).

Play at Double Tempo/Half Tempo

These buttons can be used to exactly halve or double the playback speed and the duration of selected notes. If no notes are selected, all of the notes are adjusted, as is the clip's loop length. The first thing you might notice about them is that their markings seem counterintuitive. The reason that Play at Half Tempo is marked *2 is that playing something at half tempo means it takes *twice as long to play.*

Reverse and Invert

Want to hear what your MIDI sequence sounds like backward or upside down? These buttons have got you covered. The results that these buttons produce are often in the strange and twisted category, but sometimes that's just what you need. Like the double/half buttons, these operate on selected notes or the entire clip if none are selected.

Force Legato

Legato is an Italian word that's used to signify that notes should be played or sung such that they are smoothly connected to one another. This button provides an easy way to move the end of every selected note so that it reaches the start of the next one. If no notes are selected, the entire clip is modified.

Duplicate Loop

This button addresses one of the most common needs in MIDI programming, duplicating an entire pattern. A very common workflow is to program a one-bar loop, then double it and add variations to create a two-bar loop. This process can be repeated indefinitely, having the two-bar loop become four bars and so on.

Quantizing Your Performance

Quantizing is the process of aligning events to a timing grid. When quantizing a MIDI clip, you're making sure that the notes are aligned (fully or partially) to the grid. Quantizing can be done either while you record or after the fact.

If you want to quantize while recording, you'll have to visit the Record Quantization submenu (under the Edit menu). After you select a quantization value here, any recording you make will be perfectly aligned to the rhythmic subdivisions you have selected. Figures 5.19a and 5.19b show how this works. This is a dream come true when programming drumbeats, since every recording will be rhythmically tight. Live can quantize notes to a grid of 1/4 notes, 1/16-note triplets, or anything in between.

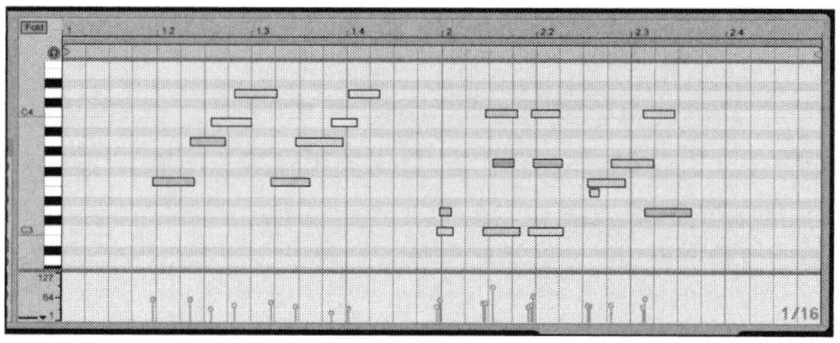

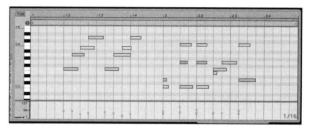

Figure 5.19a Here are some unquantized MIDI notes.
Source: Ableton

Figure 5.19b The same part recorded with quantizing. Notice how each note's left edge is aligned with one of the grid lines.
Source: Ableton

Of course, most music does not demand strict rhythmic quantization. Many musicians prefer to keep the natural feel of a performance, only using partial quantization or none at all. You can turn off Live's automatic quantizing by choosing No Quantization from the Record Quantize menu. For many situations, this is the best choice, since it's easy to quantize later if you choose.

> **THE UNDO TWO-STEP:** When Live is set to quantize a recording automatically, you'll still be able to undo the quantizing in case you left it on by accident. The first time you press Ctrl (Cmd)+Z after recording, the recorded notes will move to their original, unquantized locations. The second Undo will erase the clip, allowing you to make another.

To quantize an existing clip, first select the notes you want to quantize. If you want to quantize the entire clip, you can simply click in an empty part of the editor; when no notes are selected, Live assumes you want to quantize the whole thing. Then select Quantize Settings from the Edit menu (see Figure 5.20).

The first value at the top sets the quantize grid. Generally, this should be set to the smallest subdivision that occurs in the part. In other words, if you've played a part containing 1/8 notes and 1/16 notes, you'd select 1/16. If you select 1/8, the Quantize function will move the 1/16 notes to the closest 1/8 note and mess up the part. The Current Grid option will quantize to the size of the grid shown in the MIDI editor.

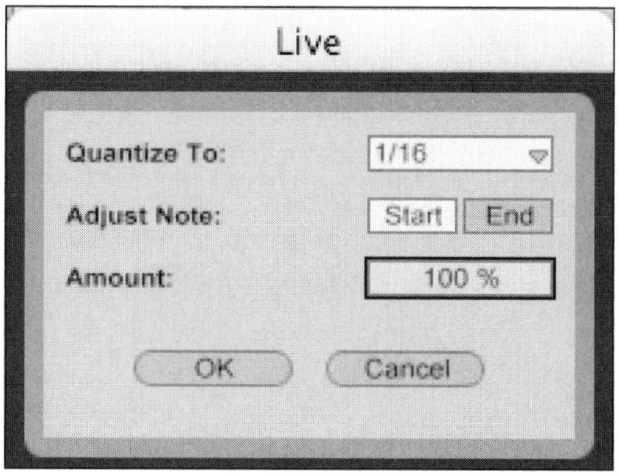

Figure 5.20 Live's Quantize dialog box will tailor the method by which Live quantizes your notes.
Source: Ableton

Below the Quantize selection is the Adjust Note selection, with two buttons labeled Start and End. By default, only Start is enabled. This means that Live will change only the start location of a note when it quantizes—the length of the note will remain the same. If you enable End as well, Live will make sure that the note ends on a grid subdivision, too. This is handy for rapid-fire synth bass sequences, because each note will be on beat *and* the same length. If you wanted, you could deselect Start, making Live fix only the end of each note.

The last parameter in the dialog box is the Amount value. Normally, this is set to 100%, which forces every note to the nearest grid subdivision. If you set this value to 50%, Live will move the notes only halfway to the proper place. The result is a tighter performance, but one that is not completely rigid.

> **PARTIAL QUANTIZING:** Sometimes you may not want to quantize an entire clip. Maybe the hi-hat feels just right, but the snare is a bit too wonky, or maybe one section needs to be quantized to straight 1/16s and another section to 1/16-note triplets. In this case, just select the notes you want to quantize by dragging over them in the editor or Shift-clicking on individual notes. Now quantization will be applied to these notes only.

After you've set up your quantize settings, you can immediately apply them to any MIDI clip without opening the Quantize window by using the Ctrl (Cmd) + U keyboard shortcut. When combined with the Current Grid setting in the Quantize dialog, this shortcut can be a real time-saver!

Step Recording

Live offers yet another way of creating MIDI clips: step recording. Step recording allows you to place notes into a MIDI clip from your controller keyboard without having to perform them in real time. This technique can only be used to add notes to an existing MIDI clip, so either you'll be using it to overdub notes into a clip you've recorded, or with empty clips that you've created by double-clicking in an empty clip slot.

To do step recording, you need to arm the MIDI track for recording and turn on the Preview switch in the MIDI editor. Now, notes or chords can be added by holding down keys on your controller and then pressing the right arrow key to determine the length of the notes. The right and left arrow keys are also used to navigate through the clip, so pressing the right arrow without holding down notes allows you to enter rests or skip ahead to another part of the clip entirely.

When in the MIDI map (see Chapter 11, "Remote Control"), you'll notice two arrows appear below the fold switch. These can be remote-mapped to allow you to step back and forth through your MIDI clips from your controller, without using the arrow keys on your computer's keyboard.

Program Change

Program change messages are used to recall presets on the destination MIDI device. By setting the Program and Bank values in the Notes Box (see Figure 5.21), each clip can recall a different preset from the same instrument when it is launched. Hardware instruments are typically configured so they automatically respond to program changes. Software instruments vary. Some will work automatically, while others may require special configuration in order to recall presets. Live's built-in instruments don't respond to program changes, so this is a technique for third party plug-ins and hardware devices only.

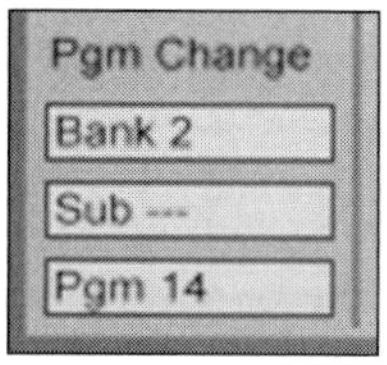

Figure 5.21 Use the Program Change settings to automatically recall presets when a clip is launched.
Source: Ableton

A Program Change is a MIDI message with a value between 0 and 127 and refers to a memory location in your MIDI device's sound bank. The way a manufacturer maps the Program message to the memory slots is entirely up to them, but generally a Program Change of 0 will cause the first sound on the instrument to be loaded. So, using the Program Change message, you can recall up to 128 presets.

But what if your device has more than 128 sounds? That's where the Bank Change message comes into play. A bank holds 128 programs. So you can recall any sound in your MIDI device by first specifying the containing bank followed by the program number. Some devices require that banks be specified with two numbers, the Bank and Sub-bank. Thus the presence of the Sub setting below Bank in Figure 5.21.

Importing and Exporting MIDI Files

Live stores all MIDI data and parameters for MIDI clips within the Live Set. You can see the individual MIDI clips and tracks within the Browser. While audio clips must play a specific audio file stored on a hard disk, the MIDI clips don't require any sort of external support file that you need to keep track of. When you import a MIDI file, Live copies the data from the MIDI file into the Live Set. Live will never use the original MIDI file again, so should that file be changed or lost, the Live Set will still play perfectly.

Live imports MIDI parts from Standard MIDI Files (SMFs), which come in two flavors: Type 0 and Type 1. Unless your MIDI file has only one part in it, Type 0 won't do you any good in Live—all the parts are squished into one track. Type 1, on the other hand, has the MIDI parts split into separate tracks for each instrument. There will be a track for the bass, some for the drums, and tracks for any other part in the song, all of which will be displayed below the MIDI file when you open it in the Browser. Live lets you import these tracks into new clips by dragging the tracks into your session or arrangement like regular clips.

If you've got a song in another software, or perhaps something stuck in an older hardware sequencer, and you want to transfer it to Live, SMFs will usually take care of the job. The format has been around for a long time, so you can be assured of compatibility; however, SMFs don't necessarily retain *everything* from a computer project. When exporting songs done in other programs, application-specific features such as automation won't appear in an SMF export.

If you need to take the MIDI part from a clip and send it to another Live Set or a different program, you can export the MIDI data as an SMF. Select the clip and choose Export MIDI clip from Live's File menu. You'll be prompted to give a name and destination for the exported data. Choose a location and name and click Save.

Audio Clips

You may be surprised to discover just how creative you can get with audio in Live. Obviously, if you're going to be recording live instruments and vocals, audio clips will be a big part of your life. But even if MIDI is the backbone of your compositional process, you'll still find that manipulating audio can produce a broad array of weird and wonderful results for your tracks. Live's warping features can be used to synchronize any sample to the tempo of your track. And, of course, if you're going to be DJing with Live, you'll need to have a solid understanding of working with audio.

The Sample Box

Before digging into the details of warping, let's take a closer look at the Sample box (see Figure 5.22), which contains a number of audio specific controls.

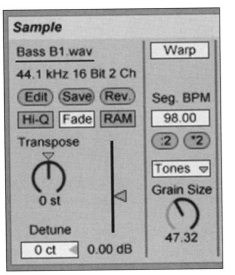

Figure 5.22 The Sample box contains controls concerning audio speed, pitch, volume, and warping. In the Arrangement, you'll notice that the Fade switch does not appear, and there's an extra switch marked Slave.
Source: Ableton

Edit

Clicking the Edit button will open the audio file in the sample editor you have selected in File/Folder preferences. Audio editors are useful for performing a variety of operations on your audio files, particularly when you want to edit *destructively*. Now, this may not sound very appealing at first, but there are times that you want to make a change that permanently affects the audio file itself. Modifying the Sample properties in Live only changes that audio file's playback characteristics. That's why it's called *non-destructive editing*.

While you are editing your sample file, the Clip View's waveform display will say Sample Offline. When you finish editing, just save your changes and return to Live. The newly edited sample will be loaded into the clip.

Save

By default, adding an audio file to Live causes an analysis (.ASD) file to be created in the same folder as the audio file. This file contains basic information about the file, including the data needed to draw the waveform display in the Clip View. When you click Save, *all* of the current clip settings (warping, loop settings, and so on) are written into the analysis file. The next time you add the audio file to a Set, these clip settings will be recalled automatically.

Reverse

Live's Reverse feature (the Rev. button) is not instantaneous—don't expect it to be. It is, however, a whole lot of fun when used properly. Click the Reverse button, and Live will create a new audio file—a reversed version of the original. This new audio file will be named the same as the original, but it will have the letter "R" added to the end.

Okay, so it's not truly a Reverse button, as in "play the sample backward." Instead, the Reverse button means "play a backward version of the sample." This means you'll have to wait for the "R" file to be made the first time you reverse, but from that point on, Live will just choose the original or reversed file to play, allowing you to switch directions almost instantaneously. Because of the nature of the Reverse feature, you may want to avoid using this button during live performances. Instead, I recommend you make two clips: one normal and one reversed.

Hi-Q

This button simply switches the audio clip between high-quality and low-quality interpolation (used for transposition). If this button is on, the clip will play using better pitch shifting and resampling algorithms, but it will also place a slightly heavier strain on your CPU. I recommend leaving this option on for all clips (setting Default SR & Pitch Conversion to "High Quality" in Preferences > Audio will make this the default) and turning it off only if you have a slower computer, and you need to save every bit of CPU power.

Fade

To help an audio file loop seamlessly (no clicks or pops when the file loops around), Live can perform a quick (4ms) volume fade at the end of the clip. I recommend leaving this option on as the default, unless the downbeat transient seems too quiet. It is possible that the fade can soften the initial attack of the downbeat (for instance, shaving the attack of a one-shot sample), so you may need to turn this off from time to time. Because the Arrangement View contains a more sophisticated set of tools for creating fades, this option is not available there.

RAM

Live streams audio files from disk as they play. With each additional audio clip that plays, the computer will have to stream another file from disk. Your hard disk can stream only a finite amount of data per second, and when Live requires more than the disk can provide, you get audio dropouts. When you hear audio problems, check to see if the Hard Disk Overload Indicator (the letter "D") in the right-hand corner of the Control Bar is lighting up.

To alleviate this, you can load audio clips into your computer's RAM, which is accessed much faster than the hard disk, by pressing the RAM button. Remember to be conscious of the size of the files you're loading into RAM. Even if you're using only 10 seconds of an 8-minute file, Live will still load the whole file into memory. The problem with this feature is that your operating system may decide to swap contents from RAM to hard disk. Live has no control over when this happens, so you may not always see the performance benefit you expect from using the RAM switch. If rapid access to audio files is a major concern for you, purchasing a solid state drive (SSD) is probably a better option.

Transpose and Detune

The Transpose and Detune controls (see Figure 5.23) change the playback tuning of the clip (without changing its playback speed). Transpose shifts pitch in semitones, while Detune adjusts it in small steps known as *cents* (one-hundredth of a semitone).

While transposing generally produces artifacts in the audio, small shifts in pitch can often be made with acceptable sound quality as long as you use the appropriate Warp mode for the audio you're transposing. The Complex Pro mode can produce some very high-quality results when transposing, at the cost of high CPU usage. There's more about Warp modes in the "Warping" section.

> **GOING WAY OUT:** Although Transpose is useful to make a loop match the key of your song, you'll discover that wild new sounds can be found by tweaking the tuning up or down by multiple octaves and experimenting with different Warp modes. Once a sample is altered this much, new textures and sounds can emerge. Take time to experiment!

Clip Gain

The Clip Gain slider, which is unlabeled and located just to the right of the Transpose knob, is used to adjust the individual volume of a clip. This is a very convenient way to balance audio levels without using automation. Just bear in mind that you're changing the volume of the audio *before* it flows through effect devices. This is particularly important when using gain-sensitive effects (such as compression and distortion), which produce different results depending on the volume of the incoming audio.

Warping

Warping is the term used to describe Live's time-stretching and compressing technique. The technique of warping an audio file to match the tempo, groove, and pitch of a song involves many parameters, but the most important of these is the Warp button at the top of Figure 5.23. With Warp off, the clip plays the audio at its original tempo. However, once Warp is engaged, you can change the playback speed and pitch of the audio independently, as well as make adjustments to its timing and groove.

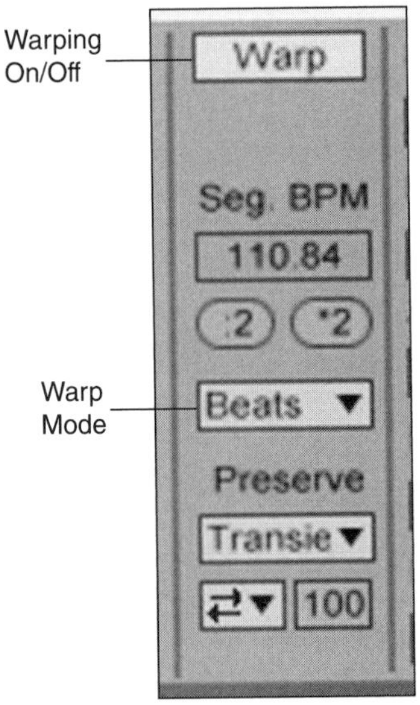

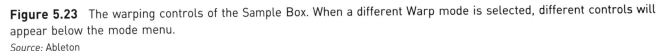

Figure 5.23 The warping controls of the Sample Box. When a different Warp mode is selected, different controls will appear below the mode menu.
Source: Ableton

In order for Live to work its warping magic, it needs some information about the audio it's working with. For example, to match a file to the current master tempo, Live needs to know the original tempo of the file so it can determine how much to speed it up or slow it down. For music with a completely steady tempo, this is a simple matter. However, in cases where the music wasn't played to a click track or programmed with a sequencer, it's a bit more complicated, since the actual tempo changes from bar to bar. It might only fluctuate by a fraction of a BPM, but it still matters.

When working with short, properly cut loops, Live can typically determine the necessary information for warping automatically. However, there are many cases where you'll need to specify where important timing events occur using Warp Markers (see Figure 5.24). You might do this to move an individual note with bad timing, or even to dramatically change the timing and sonically mangle a chunk of audio. If you're trying to sync up a song with a constantly fluctuating tempo, this can require quite a few Warp Markers, but don't worry. Live's *Auto-Warp* feature can usually be coaxed into doing most of the work for you.

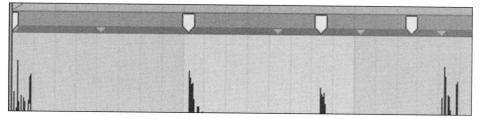

Figure 5.24 Warp Markers are the key to total timing control (or intentional timing madness!).
Source: Ableton

Before getting into the nitty gritty of working with Warp Markers, let's explore the warping controls within the Sample Box.

Segment BPM

Segment BPM calculates the tempo of the audio in a clip, based on the position of its Warp Markers. This value is then used by Live to set the playback speed. Let's start off with a simple example. If Live's tempo is set to 70 BPM and Segment BPM is 70, then Live will not change the playback speed of the audio. If the tempo is changed to 140 BPM, however, Live would know from the Segment BPM value that it needs to play the audio at double its original speed to match the master tempo.

What makes Segment BPM potentially a bit complicated is the fact that it refers not just to the entire clip, but also to the segment of audio in between two Warp Markers. Click on a Warp Marker to display the Segment BPM of the audio in between the selected Warp Marker and the one preceding it. Strictly speaking, however, this only applies to audio with a fluctuating tempo, or cases where Warp Markers have been used to alter the original timing of the audio. For audio with a completely steady tempo, only one Warp Marker is necessary, and the Segment BPM will reflect the tempo of the entire clip.

Half/Double BPM

The two buttons below the Segment BPM window will either double or halve the tempo of the clip. Pressing the *2 button will multiply every Segment BPM by two. The result is that the clip will play at half speed. This may be counterintuitive, but remember that you're not telling Live to "play this clip at twice the speed," but rather you're telling it "the actual tempo of this audio is twice as fast." Pressing :2 will have the opposite effect. This is helpful when Live incorrectly guesses the length and tempo of a new audio clip. For example, if Live identifies a 170 BPM drum 'n bass loop as 85 BPM, a click of the "*2" button will fix this immediately.

Warp Modes

Choosing the correct Warp modes is essential for clean, musical warping. The Warp mode affects the way in which Live approaches stretching and pitch-shifting your audio clips. Six different Warp modes are available in the audio clip's Warp section: Beats, Tones, Texture, Re-Pitch, Complex, and Complex Pro. Each mode also features a special set of controls that will appear below it. We will cover these below. Also, don't forget that you can simply turn off Live's Warp Engine altogether and play the sample at its default speed and pitch. Here's a list of what kinds of different sounds you can expect when choosing among these six Warp modes.

BEATS

Beats mode is a great mode for rhythmic loops, percussive samples, and even entire songs. You will usually want to use Beats mode with percussion, drums, and sounds characteristically containing minimal sustain. This includes samples that you might not think of as beats, such as a funk rhythm guitar part or perhaps a minimal techno track. When Beats mode is used with sounds that are too textured or lack rhythmic definition, you may hear artifacts.

> **DEFINITION OF TRANSIENT:** The Transient setting is a critical element of Live's beat-warping functionality. But what is a transient to begin with? A transient is the short, sharp attack portion of a sound. A transient occurs at the instant a stick hits a drum, or a string is plucked. The soft attack of bowed strings may have no transient. In warping terminology, *transient* is often used to mean a chunk of audio (such as an entire snare hit) with a transient at the beginning.

Beats mode looks at your audio as a series of segments, the size of which is determined by the Preserve menu. The default value in the Preserve menu—Transients—uses the location of the clip's transients to time-compress or stretch the audio (see Figure 5.25). Conceptually, the way this works is quite simple. When Live detects transients in a drum loop, it is identifying each hit in relationship to its position in the bar: this kick drum occurs on beat 1, this snare drum occurs at beat 2, and so on. Live then knows where to put each drum hit, regardless of the tempo, just like it does with a MIDI file.

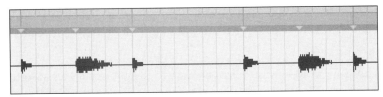

Figure 5.25 The small gray triangles above each beat indicates where Live has detected the transients.
Source: Ableton

For most rhythmic material, preserving transients will produce the best results. The other options in the Preserve menu provide compatibility with earlier versions of Live and allow you to tell the Warp engine to look at the audio as a series of evenly spaced segments (such as 1/8 or 1/16). If you have a one-bar loop with the Transient value set to 1/16, Live's default behavior will be to treat the file as if it were sixteen equally sized segments. Live then plays these chunks back as if they were sixteenth notes at the current tempo.

Next, let's further examine what happens to your audio when you speed it up or slow it down. If the beat being warped needs to be sped up to match the tempo of Live, the segments will be moved closer together. As this happens, Live will time-compress the end of each segment, making the duration of each drum hit slightly shorter, so the decay doesn't get cut off due to the faster tempo. If the beat is getting slowed down, Live has to either stretch out the playback of each segment or leave a space between segments, since the original decay of the hit won't be long enough to fill the space at the slower tempo.

To stretch out the decay, Beats mode loops the last portion of the segment—the fading sound of the transient. If you're thinking that this might end up sounding a little strange, you're right. It is, however, the best solution, given that Live is doing all of this time stretching in real time. That said, it is generally easier to speed beats up without noticeable artifacts than it is to slow them down.

Live gives you full control over how this looping is done via the Transient Loop Mode menu (see Figure 5.26).

▷ **No Loop** (single arrow): Live plays each segment to its end without doing anything to fill the space until the next segment plays. This yields extremely clean results (because there's no looping); but, it may leave audible spaces in between each note or drum hit. Let your ears decide whether or not this is acceptable or desirable.

▷ **Loop Forward** (double forward arrows): Loops the decay of each segment forward. This mode tends to produce glitchier results and works more like an effect.

▷ **Loop Back-and-Forth** (bidirectional arrows): Live loops the decay of the segment forward and backward in order to fill empty space at slowed-down tempos. Generally speaking, this mode will yield the most artifact-free stretching. This is the default setting.

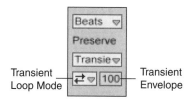

Figure 5.26 Transient Loop mode and Transient Envelope have a big impact on the results when changing the tempo or pitch of a clip.
Source: Ableton

The numeric box next to Transient Loop Mode is the Transient Envelope. This value determines if a fade should be applied to each audio segment. In No Loop mode, reducing this value can be used to create dramatic gating effects, even when you're playing the audio at its original tempo. Playing with this value is highly recommended! When Transient Loop Mode is set to either of the looped modes, lowering the envelope tends to produce less dramatic results, but can still be very useful for smoothing out time-stretching artifacts.

TONES

Tones mode is based on a technique called *granular resynthesis*. As a file is played back, it is broken into grains. The idea is that when you loop a grain, you get a continuous tone that represents that sound "frozen in time." By splitting the audio into grains and spreading the grains apart, Live slows down the tempo of the audio playback; however, since each grain is still played at its original pitch, there will be empty space between each grain. Looping each grain fills space to time-stretch the file.

Of course, looping each grain isn't necessary when speeding up playback of a file. As the grains are brought closer together, they will overlap one another. Each grain will therefore cut off the one before it, resulting in a continuous sound, but with one playing faster than before. For this reason, you'll probably find that you have better success speeding up loops or transposing them down (both methods use the same process) than slowing them down or pitching them up, which requires looping the grains.

With careful setting of the Grain Size value, you can achieve nearly transparent warping. Tones such as bass guitars, synthesizers, vocals, keyboards, or other long-sustaining instruments will usually sound much less processed when playing in Live's Tones mode. You can adjust Live's Grain Size to help reduce undesirable audio artifacts.

TEXTURE

Texture mode is built for atmospheric sounds with no definite pitch, but it can also work well on other complex sounds, such as orchestral samples and keyboard pads. Like Tones mode, Texture mode is based on granular resynthesis. In an effort to cloud the repetitive artifacts from looping grains, a Flux value is added that, when increased, allows Live to randomly change the grain sizes used in the process. This also adds a sense of stereo imaging to mono files.

RE-PITCH

Re-Pitch mode is more like vinyl DJing—Live will alter the pitch of the sample, depending upon the playback speed. This mode produces no artifacts and thus usually sounds the best, especially if the sample is played close to its original tempo. Re-Pitch merely alters the file playback speed, which results in pitch changes.

COMPLEX AND COMPLEX PRO

Designed for use on entire songs, the Complex modes are the ones to go for when none of the other modes produce sufficient quality. Complex Pro comes in particularly handy when transposing audio with vocals, since it allows you to change the pitch (within reason) without making the singer sound like a chipmunk or a troll.

The magic of these modes comes at the cost of higher CPU usage, with Complex Pro being the more power hungry of the two. Unless you're strapped for computer power, or you like the artifacts produced by Complex mode, you should generally use Complex Pro for its higher sound quality. Just be aware that the Pro version can strain Live enough to produce glitches in the audio output without the CPU meter reporting abnormally high usage. If your computer is having a tough time keeping up with the added load of the Complex mode, you can Freeze the track (see Chapter 7) or resample the clip (see Chapter 6).

Warp Markers

Warp Markers are the pins that fix audio events to a specific moment in time. An audio clip always has a minimum of one Warp Marker, which by default is placed at the very beginning. In the simplest situations, this is all that's needed. In the more complex scenarios, numerous Warp Markers can be used to radically reshape audio, changing the timing and duration of numerous individual segments. If you have an audio file that has sloppy timing, you can use a few Warp Markers to move individual hits to just where you want them.

Setting up Warp Markers can be done manually or by using Live's Auto-Warp technology. When working with short audio files, such as prerecorded loops, Live automatically detects the tempo with a high degree of accuracy. If you're a DJ you'll probably be using Auto-Warp extensively to prep your music library to play back in sync. For rhythmically imprecise material or material that you want to dramatically change, you'll be creating and moving Warp Markers manually.

When a piece of audio requires manual adjustment to get it to sync up (or to get it mangled to perfection), these are the tools you'll be working with. First, let's get our terms straight:

▷ **Transient:** Transients appear as small gray triangles above the waveform display. They are automatically created by Live for any audio clip with its Warp switch turned on. Transients can be manually inserted or deleted from the editor's context menu or by Alt(Option).

▷ **Warp Marker:** Locks a segment of audio to a location on the timeline. They appear as yellow markers directly above the waveform display. Warp Markers can be created by clicking anywhere in the waveform display or just above it.

▷ **Pseudo Warp Marker:** When the mouse is moved over a Transient, a gray Pseudo Warp Marker temporarily appears. When dragged, these markers will become permanent Warp Markers if they are followed by any existing Warp Markers. Otherwise, they can be dragged to adjust the timing of the clip, and will return to being normal Transients when released.

Ableton describes Warp Markers as being "pins" that can be used to attach a piece of audio to a certain point in time. This is a great way of looking at it. So, in order to correct the timing of the audio shown in Figure 5.27, the first thing you would do is double-click to create a Warp Marker above the late snare hit. Dragging the hit so it lands on beat 1.2 moves not just the snare hit, but also all of the audio before and after it (see Figure 5.28). The first hit, however, stays locked in place because of its Warp Marker, although its decay gets compressed slightly to compensate for the fact that the snare hit has gotten moved earlier.

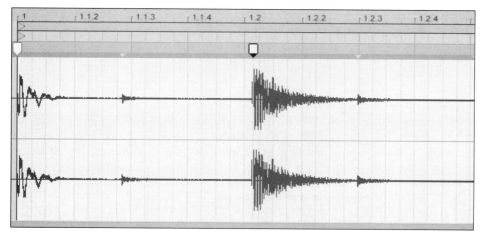

Figure 5.27 There is always at least one Warp Marker in an audio clip when the Warp mode is engaged. Transient markers temporarily become Pseudo Warp Markers when you hold the mouse over them.
Source: Ableton

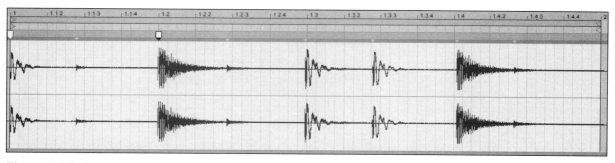

Figure 5.28 When the snare hit is moved to beat 1.2, the hits to either side are also moved slightly earlier.
Source: Ableton

Now, let's say you want to move the hi-hat accent between beats 1.1 and 1.2 so it lands right on 1.1.3. Just grab the Pseudo Warp Marker that appears when you mouse over the transient and drag it to 1.1.3. You're done! The existing Warp Markers keep the other hits locked down while you move the hi-hat into place (see Figure 5.29). There's a shortcut that allows you to create three Warp Markers in one click for just this purpose. Just hold down Ctrl (Cmd) before double-clicking to create a new Warp Marker.

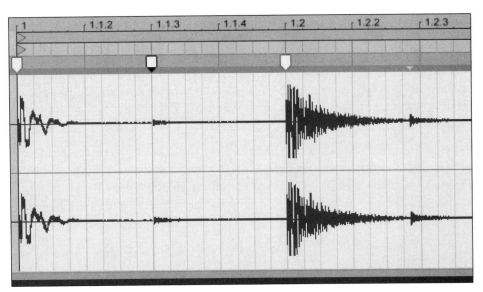

Figure 5.29 With the hits at 1 and 1.2 locked into place, you can move the hit in between without throwing anything else off.
Source: Ableton

This process can be repeated indefinitely to put every hit just where you want it. (Although, if you're just looking to get every hit perfectly lined up with the grid, refer to the "Quantize" section later in this chapter.) Another possibility when you're working manually with Warp Markers, though, is to create a completely new rhythm by dragging hits to locations other than those for which they were originally intended. Figure 5.30 shows the same audio clip warped to play a completely different rhythm.

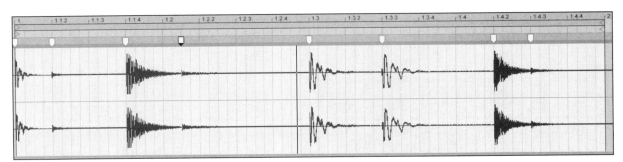

Figure 5.30 Warping can be used to turn a boring beat into a syncopated masterpiece.
Source: Ableton

> **WARP 'EM ALL:** If you're looking to do some serious mangling with Warp Markers, drag in the editor to select a range (or use Ctrl (Cmd) + A to select the whole clip) and use Insert Warp Marker from the Create menu. A Warp Marker will be created for each transient in the range.

Auto-Warp

When working with longer audio files, Live uses a technology called *Auto-Warp* to analyze the file and insert Warp Markers where needed. This process, however, is not perfect and you may still have to adjust the Warp Markers manually. There are two ways to use auto warping: first, let Live do it automatically, and second, manually invoke it using the Warp commands from the context menus.

By default, Live will analyze and add Warp Markers whenever you add a long audio file to your set. In the Record/Warp/Launch tab of the Preferences screen, you can disable this behavior by setting "Auto-Warp Long Files" to Off. Depending on the material you're warping, you may find it quicker to manually invoke Auto-Warp—because the Warp commands let you give Live hints about the contents of the file and how to place the Warp Markers.

> **TEMPO TIP:** Before using Auto-Warp, it's a good idea to set the tempo of your Set to the approximate tempo of the audio you're importing. For example, if you're preparing a techno DJ set, try setting the tempo to 127 BPM. (If you're not sure what tempo to use, tap the tempo in while playing the audio back unwarped.) This prevents Live from detecting a tempo that is half or double the desired result. Live uses the current tempo as a hint, so if you import the techno tracks I just mentioned while Live's tempo is set to 70 BPM, they'll end up warped as being 63.5 BPM. They'll be in sync with the clock, but will play back at double their original speed when Live is set to 127 BPM! (This may cause you to lose your residency at the club.) To fix this problem if it occurs, use the Half or Double BPM buttons explained earlier.

The Warp commands are accessed by right-clicking in or above the waveform display and selecting one of the following options.

▷ **Warp from Here:** This tells Live to analyze the clip starting at the selected location and continuing to the right. It will attempt to detect tempo based on the audio, tracking fluctuations and placing Warp Markers as needed. Everything to the left of the selected marker will remain intact.

▷ **Warp from Here (Start at X BPM):** This option uses the current project tempo as a starting point and attempts to detect any tempo variations that occur later. If you've already determined the approximate tempo of the audio file using Tap Tempo, this option will often yield good results when the standard Warp command fails.

▷ **Warp from Here (Straight):** This mode attempts to set the tempo of the clip using one Warp Marker only. This should be used only when warping music that you know to have a completely steady tempo. This command is very handy because it prevents Auto-Warp from becoming confused by syncopations which otherwise might cause it to incorrectly detect a tempo fluctuation and place incorrect Warp Markers.

▷ **Warp X BPM from Here:** This simply sets the current Warp Marker to the current tempo of the Set. If there are any Warp Markers to the right, they will be erased in the process.

▷ **Warp as X-Bar Loop:** If you already know that the file you're working with has an even number of bars, you can select this option to automatically turn the clip into an even loop. The number shown here will depend on the current project tempo. If Live determines that it will have to do the least amount of warping to turn the clip into a one-bar loop, as opposed to a two-bar loop, the program will display "1" in place of "X" in the menu item above. If you increase the project tempo by almost double, Live will see that it is now easier to make the clip a two-bar loop and will suggest that by showing "2" in place of "1" in the menu option.

Note that there are also a number of other options in this context menu to help you work with your sample files, including the important "Set 1.1.1 Here" command. This command will renumber the grid to start from beat 1 at the selected location.

Quantize

One of the cool features that comes with Live is the ability to quantize audio clips, much the way you can with audio. While viewing a clip's waveform display, select Quantize Settings from the Edit menu. The Quantize To setting specifies the location on the grid to which transients should be moved. In other words, if this value is set to 1/16, Live will find each transient most closely adjacent to the 1/16 note divisions of the grid and automatically move them there. Setting Amount to a value less than 100% will yield partial quantization. In the prior example, 70% quantization would cause each accent to be moved 70% of the way to the nearest 1/16th, rather than all of the way.

Once you've got your Quantize settings set, just click OK. You can also use the Quantize command Ctrl + U (Cmd + U Mac) to apply quantization to a clip using the previously set Quantize settings.

Setting Warp Markers for Multiple Clips

If you have two or more clips based on audio files of exactly the same length, Live will allow you to set Warp Markers across multiple clips simultaneously. This is especially convenient when you are working with a multitrack recording of a performance, and you want to give all the tracks exactly the same warp timing. You can do this quite easily by simply selecting all of the clips you want to work with in the Arrangement View before making your warp adjustments. The Warp Markers you set here and their timing will automatically apply to all of the other clips you have selected.

For example, here's a good technique you can use for syncing up a live band recording with Live's tempo. First, import each track from your original multitrack recording onto a separate audio track in Live, and then make sure that they are all exactly the same length. Select all of them in the Arrangement View. Then find the track that is rhythmically simplest and clearest to insert your Warp Marker settings. Using a separate bass drum track often is the easiest way to go; a stereo drum mix will work as well. Once you have set the timing of this track, all of the other tracks also will follow.

> **WARPING WORK-AROUND:** You can still warp multiple clips, even if the underlying audio files aren't of the same length. You just have to generate new audio files first. Line up the files in the Arrangement View and trim them until they are the same length. If you need to make a clip longer, hold down Shift and highlight both the clip and the necessary amount of empty space in the timeline. Then use the Consolidate command to write new audio files of the specified length.

Tempo Master/Slave

If you are in the Arrangement View, you will see another control just above Seg. BPM: the Tempo Master/Slave switch (see Figure 5.31a). This control allows you to designate any clip as the tempo master by toggling its Master/Slave switch to Master. The current tempo master clip will always play as if Warp were *off*, but will cause the master tempo to follow the timing of the clip's Warp Markers instead of the other way around (see Figure 5.31b). This means that all warped clips will follow the timing fluctuations of the Master clip.

Figure 5.31a   Master/Slave only appears in Arrangement View. Click the switch to toggle between Slave and Master.
Source: Ableton

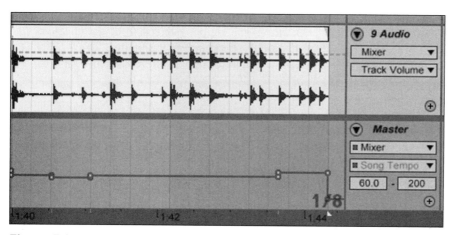

Figure 5.31b Because the clip above is set to Master, pseudo tempo automation appears in the Master track based on the location of the clip's Warp Markers.

Source: Ableton

Let's say that you have a piano recording that you want to add some additional programmed parts and loops to. It's a well-played part with a mostly steady tempo, but since it wasn't recorded to a click track, there is some natural variation to the time. One way you could use warping in this context is to straighten out the timing of the piano track by adding Warp Markers so the piano lines up perfectly with the sequencer tempo. However, if the piano has a nice feel, this could make the whole recording feel rigid and dull.

Instead, you could add a Warp Marker to the downbeat of each bar in the piano part and set the clip to Master. Now, Live's tempo will breathe with the pianist's rhythm, and all of your MIDI clips and warped loops will breathe along with it!

If you toggle the Master/Slave switch back to Slave or delete the clip, the tempo automation will stop, and the former tempo will resume. If you want to keep the tempo information from the clip, right-click on the Control Bar's Tempo field and choose the Unslave Tempo Automation command. All clips will then be set to Slave, and the tempo information will become standard automation in the Master track.

Bear in mind that if you set more than one clip to be the Tempo Master, the bottommost one will be in control, and the others will be ignored. When Live's *EXT* switch (visible only when an external tempo source is enabled) is enabled, the Master/Slave switch has no effect and will appear to be disabled in all clips.

Clip Modulation

To the right of the Sample Box (for audio clips) or the Notes Box (for MIDI clips), you'll find the Envelopes Box. (If it's hidden, click the "E" icon in the lower left-hand corner to reveal it.) Click in the title bar of the Envelopes Box to make the editor display envelopes. To return to the standard display, click in the title bar of either the Sample Box or the Notes Box.

Within the editor, there are two different types of envelopes that can be edited: automation and modulation. Automation envelopes are what this book has discussed so far. Modulation envelopes are very similar in that they can be used to automatically change device or mixer parameters, but they are very different in a few other respects.

TERMINOLOGY: In previous versions of Live, a clip's *modulation* was simply referred to as a *Clip Envelope*. *Envelope* itself is just a generic term to describe how a parameter changes over time. Since Live 9 introduced automation to the Clip View, you need to specify what type of envelope you're referring to: automation or modulation.

First, modulation is *relative* as opposed to automation, which is *absolute*. In Figure 5.32a, you'll see an automation envelope for the mixer volume. The first breakpoint is highlighted, and a box appears above, showing that the breakpoint is set to a value of –8 dB.

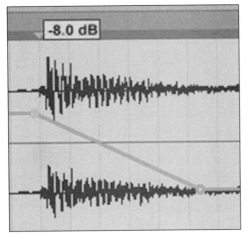

Figure 5.32a Automation is used to set absolute values.
Source: Ableton

In Figure 5.32b, you'll see a modulation envelope for the same parameter. It's roughly the same size and shape, but notice that the value displayed for the first breakpoint is 65%. What's going on here?

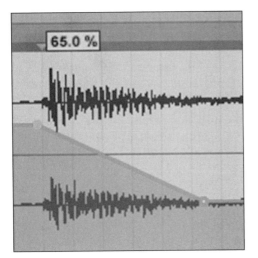

Figure 5.32b Modulation makes relative changes to a control's state. Modulation envelopes are displayed with a shaded area below to differentiate them from automation.
Source: Ableton

When you automate a control, you're specifying absolute values, such as "set the volume to –8dB." When you modulate a control, you're specifying a relative change to the control's current value, such as "set the volume to 65%." For most device and mixer controls, the current position is considered to be 100%, and you can modulate it all the way down to its lowest possible value, which is considered 0%.

Therefore, unlike automated controls, you can freely make manual adjustments to modulated controls. Manually changing an automated control causes the automation to be disabled, while manually changing a modulated control simply causes the range of the modulation to change.

Another feature of modulation envelopes is that they can be used to tweak some properties of audio clips, such as the transposition and clip gain. You can even modulate the clip's playback position (Sample Offset) as a way to create variations and glitches.

A final, and very important, difference between automation and modulation is the relationship to the Arrangement View. When Session clips containing automation envelopes are recorded into the Arrangement, the automation is recorded into the timeline and no longer appears in the Clip View. Modulation, on the other hand, remains in the clip. This is because modulation and automation can actually be used simultaneously. Figure 5.33 shows automation slowly sweeping a filter's cutoff frequency from low to high, while a clip's modulation moves the frequency rhythmically above and below its automated value.

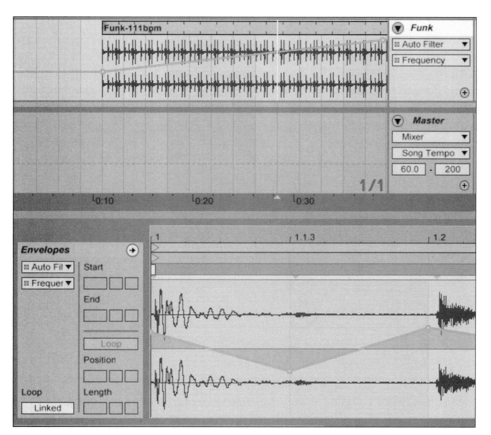

Figure 5.33 Here's an example of automation and modulation being used in conjunction.
Source: Ableton

Modulation cannot be recorded using the methods explained in Chapter 4, "Making Music in Live." It can only be programmed manually in the editor. The editing techniques for modulation are identical to that of automation. You'll be using breakpoints and Draw Mode, and with a few exceptions, anything that can be automated can be modulated as well. With the release of Live 9, Ableton has hidden modulation envelopes by default. Before you can program modulation for a control, you'll have to reveal it in the editor. There are a few ways to do this.

In the Session View, launch the clip you want to add modulation to. Then right-click on the control you want to modulate and select "Show Modulation" from the context menu, as seen in Figure 5.34. If you want to add modulation to an Arrangement clip instead, just select the clip before right-clicking on the control. You can also reveal modulation by first navigating a clip's Device Chooser and Control Chooser menus to show the automation for a particular control (see "Automation Editing" in Chapter 4). Then you'll be able to select Show Modulation from the editor's context menu.

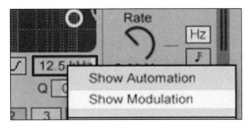

Figure 5.34 Show Modulation can be accessed from a control's context menu, or from the editor in the Clip View.
Source: Ableton

Once you've created modulation, it will be accessible from the Control Chooser. In Figure 5.35, there's some modulation programmed for the Frequency parameter of an Auto Filter. Notice that there is an item called Frequency Modulation listed, which reveals the modulation envelope, and another called Frequency, which reveals the automation envelope for the same control.

Figure 5.35 Once modulation is programmed, you can get back to it easily from the Control Chooser.
Source: Ableton

When modulation is affecting a parameter, it doesn't directly change the knob, slider, or number box the way automation would. Instead, it makes a subtler indication. Knobs will highlight the area of the knob's range that's being modulated, while sliders will display a small dot indicating the current modulated value.

Modulating Audio Clip Properties

As mentioned previously, it's possible to modulate some properties of audio clips. These deserve special mention since they're fundamentally different than the device and mixer adjustments discussed in Chapter 4. Revealing the modulation for clip properties is easy. Just select Clip in the Device Chooser, and they'll appear in the menu below.

Volume

The Volume Modulation envelope changes the clip's gain. It provides an easy way to quickly cut chunks out of a loop or make small dynamic changes. Because it doesn't interfere with any automation or manual volume changes you may make to the track, it's very simple to use at any point in the production process (see Figure 5.36).

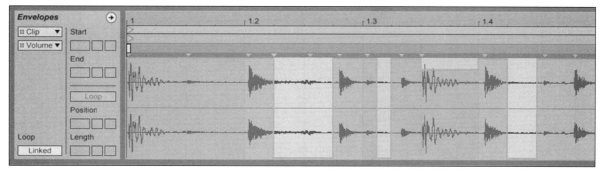

Figure 5.36 This modulation changes the playback volume of various hits in this drum loop, silencing some completely and cutting others short.
Source: Ableton

Transposition

The Transposition Modulation envelope will modulate the location of the Transpose knob, allowing you to program pitch changes, slides, or entire harmonic progressions for the clip. Because changing the pitch of a clip often produces interesting artifacts, this can be used as a sound design tool as well. Transposition begins as a flat line. Every line above zero is one semitone up, while every line below zero is a semitone down, as seen in Figure 5.37.

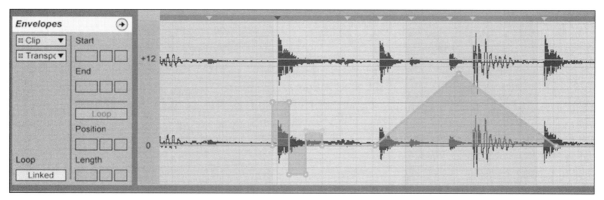

Figure 5.37 Transposition can be modulated up or down by 48 semitones.
Source: Ableton

Be aware that to make smooth pitch slides, you'll have to be using a Warp mode other than Beats, which only allows one transposition change per transient. Also notice that you can scroll the range of the editor vertically by dragging the scale at the left, or you can enlarge the editor (by dragging upward at the top) to reveal the full range of +/–48 semitones.

Sample Offset

Sample Offset allows you to manipulate the clip's playback position as it plays back. The horizontal grid lines represent sixteenth notes. The area above the center line moves the playback position forward, while the area below moves it backward (see Figure 5.38). Sample Offset only works when a clip's Warp mode is set to Beats.

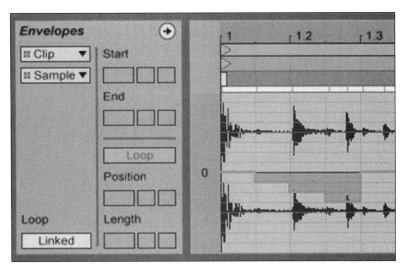

Figure 5.38 This Sample Offset modulation causes the first drum hit to repeat four times. The first step down causes playback to jump back one sixteenth, the second step causes a jump of two sixteenths, and so on.
Source: Ableton

Bear in mind that the value in the Preserve menu will determine the size of the chunks that get offset. If Preserve is set to Transients or 1/4, you'll get some unusual results if you make a lot of sixteenth note offsets. However, unusual results is generally what you're going for with this envelope, so take your time and experiment. If you're looking to do some meticulous micro-editing of your beats, you'll be happier doing it in the Arrangement View.

MIDI Controller Envelopes

In addition to all of the types of automation and modulation discussed so far, MIDI clips also have the ability to send standard MIDI control messages such as Pitch Bend, Modulation, Volume, and Foot Pedal (sustain). Control messages can be recorded from a MIDI controller during any recording, regardless of whether or not Automation Arm is enabled. That's because technically they are not automation at all—these messages are recorded as MIDI data, just like the notes are. For this reason, MIDI control messages also can't be viewed or edited in the track display of the Arrangement. They appear within the clip only.

To reveal controller envelopes, select "MIDI Ctrl" in the Device Chooser. The Control Chooser will then display a long list of MIDI control messages (see Figure 5.39).

Figure 5.39 MIDI controller envelopes can be edited just like standard automation.
Source: Ableton

When you look through the list of available MIDI controllers, you'll see some of them have already been named, such as Volume, Breath, Pan, and Expression. This is because part of the MIDI standard defines certain controller numbers for certain musical tasks. Controller 10 is generally Pan. Controller 7 is usually Volume, and so on. Whether these controllers actually have any effect will be determined by the MIDI device on the receiving end. Just about any virtual or hardware instrument will respond to pitch bend, but beyond that, you'll need to look at your MIDI device's manual, specifically the MIDI implementation chart (usually at the end of the manual), to see a list of the MIDI controllers and messages for the instrument.

Unlinked Envelopes

Until this point, we've been talking about editing loops of a given length. After all, a loop is, by definition, a repeating sample or phrase. That is just what loops do—they loop. And by default, each envelope in a clip is the same length as the clip itself, allowing you to create repetitive automation or modulation patterns that recur every time the clip repeats itself. However, by *unlinking* an envelope you can create modulations or automations with lengths and loop points independent of the clip, which gives you a mind-boggling array of options.

Sometimes, you may want to extend a given loop beyond its original borders. For instance, you have a repetitive two-bar drum loop, and you really wish that you had an eight-bar loop to make it sound more lifelike and less repetitive. One way to accomplish this is by *unlinking* the clip's envelopes. By changing the length of an envelope so that it is different from the length of the clip, you can introduce just this kind of variation to your loops.

Anytime you click the Unlink button (see Figure 5.40), the audio or MIDI note display disappears from the editor, because the envelope is now an independent entity with its own length and looping properties. These points are adjusted using a loop brace and familiar looking Start, End, Position, and Length controls in the Envelopes Box—but in this case, you're affecting the envelope only. Feel free to make an unlinked envelope of eight bars over a two-bar loop, or one that starts on beat one, goes for four bars, and then starts looping.

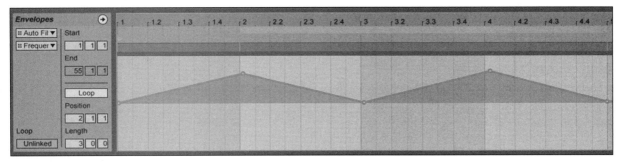

Figure 5.40 The Start/End and Loop properties of the envelope are enabled when Unlink is activated.
Source: Ableton

Bear in mind that each envelope, be it modulation or automation, can be linked or unlinked as you choose. This means you can have envelopes of many different lengths all happening simultaneously. You can also create envelopes of odd lengths that will change their position in relationship to the loop points of the clip over many bars. Imagine taking a two-bar MIDI clip and modulating a synth's filter with an envelope 7 bars long, while modulating the parameters of a delay and a distortion using envelopes 3 and 5 bars long. To the average listener, the pattern would be nearly impossible to discern, and the modulations would sound random.

Audio to MIDI

Live provides several ways to start with an audio clip and create a MIDI clip from it. The Convert to New MIDI Track features are new to Live 9, while the Slice to New MIDI Track feature has been around for a while now. Slice to New MIDI Track provides an easy way to chop up a sample and trigger it via MIDI, while the various Convert modes actually analyze the musical information in the audio and generate a MIDI clip based on it.

Convert to New MIDI Track

This feature comes in three flavors. There's a method optimized for melody, one for harmony (chords), and another specifically for drums. What these functions do is analyze the audio clip to detect pitches and transients and generate a MIDI sequence from them. This sequence can then be used to trigger the sound of your choice. So, for example, you could record yourself singing a melody and then convert it to a MIDI track and have the melody played by a synthesizer.

Generally speaking, you shouldn't expect this feature to extract parts from fully mixed songs. It's much more well suited to converting individual parts. It's also best not to expect a high degree of precision in the conversions, although you may sometimes. The conversion process is very sensitive to a wide variety of factors, and it's better to expect a conversion to give you a starting point, rather than a finished product.

On the other hand, as a tool for generating raw material that you'll make new parts out of, you may have a lot of fun with this feature. Take a melody and convert it using the drum's algorithm or the harmony algorithm, for example. Obviously, not everything you get from intentionally misusing the technology will be great, but occasionally it will get the creative juices flowing.

The basics of using these commands is very simple. Right-click on an audio clip and choose Convert Harmony to New MIDI track, Convert Melody to New MIDI track, or Convert Drums to New MIDI track, depending on the audio you're converting. All of the methods create a new track with a default instrument loaded and a new MIDI clip generated from the analysis. After the conversion, you can swap out the instrument to customize the sound. You can also drag an audio clip to an existing MIDI track, and a dialog will appear giving you the three conversion choices.

▷ **Convert Drums to New MIDI Track** analyzes audio, assuming it contains drums, and produces a new MIDI clip that will play a similar pattern on a Drum Rack. Generally, this technique does a very good job of identifying clear kick, snare, and hi-hat parts. However, it will falter, depending on how unusual and complex the drum sounds are. Not to worry, though, with a bit of editing this conversion method produces very usable results on a wide variety of material.

▷ **Convert Melody to New MIDI Track** will typically generate usable results if the source has strong transients and the signal is steady in pitch. Complex, modulating synthesizer tones and weak vocal performances (or emotional ones with a lot of note sliding and other vocal artifacts) will produce less accurate results.

▷ **Convert Harmony to New MIDI Track** is the fussiest of all of the methods. Even with a solo keyboard or guitar part, it will often generate chords containing strange extra notes or leave notes out entirely. Your mileage will vary greatly, depending on the material you feed it, so keep it simple and be prepared to edit the results.

Slice to New MIDI Track

Slice to New MIDI Track is a whole different animal than the conversion methods discussed earlier. This method breaks the original audio into slices and then creates a new track containing a MIDI clip to trigger the slices in order.

To invoke this command, right-click on a clip and select Slice to New MIDI Track from the context menu. Next, you'll be presented with a dialog offering a couple of options (see Figure 5.41). The first menu allows you to choose how many slices your audio should be divided into. A good value to start with here would be whatever value you would use for the Transients setting in Beats mode. If the beat is based on 1/8th note divisions, try slicing at this value. There's also an option to slice at Warp Markers. This means that anywhere you've created a Warp Marker, a slice will be created. In other words, you can control how many slices are generated by adding Warp Markers before doing the slicing.

Figure 5.41 The Slice to New MIDI track dialog. Make sure to experiment with the different slicing presets!
Source: Ableton

The Slicing Preset menu gives you a few presets that will affect the MIDI track that gets created. To fully understand these options, you'll need to know a bit about Drum Racks and Sampler so you may want to explore Chapter 8, "Live's Instruments." The first option, "Built-In," creates a MIDI track containing a Drum Rack. Each slice of the loop will be mapped to a pad in the Drum Rack, and a MIDI file will be generated to play the slices back. The Drum Rack comes equipped with some preprogrammed Macros for tweaking the envelope and the loop properties of each slice. Try turning Loop Length up and Loop Compress down for some buzzing glitchy madness.

Many of the other options in the menu place the slices into Zones within a Sampler instead. These presets use a wide variety of Sampler's modulation options to generate sonic variation. Make sure to try out your keyboard's modulation wheel while using these presets, as many of them are programmed to respond to it. Ableton updates these presets when new versions of Live are released, so don't be surprised if the contents of this menu change from time to time.

After you've clicked OK and waited for a few seconds, you'll have a brand new MIDI track all loaded and ready to go. Just launch the new MIDI clip, and you'll hear your loop playing back just as if it were the original audio clip. This is where things get interesting. Try rearranging, deleting, or adding MIDI notes, or try creating a brand new clip and using individual slices to program a beat! Also, make sure to check out the macros that have been programmed for you in the new Drum Rack.

For most rhythmic material, selecting Transient in the top menu will yield good results. Occasionally, you might find that Live is chopping the audio into too many slices. For example, sometimes Live will place a transient in the middle of a drum hit, causing it to be chopped into two separate drum pads in the resulting MIDI track. If this happens, examine the transients and right-click on any that you think are unnecessary and use the Delete Transient(s) command. For completely customized beat slicing, use Warp Marker as the slicing division after placing a Warp Marker at each segment you would like sliced.

Groove

Before we get too far into discussing Live's groove features, let's talk a little bit about the concept of groove in general. Simply put, musical parts that have a certain amount of rhythmic variation or imprecision, as well as changes in dynamics, often have a more compelling feel than parts that are perfectly quantized and even in volume. This is not to say that absolute precision always sounds bad; but sometimes, it's useful to contrast extremely tight tracks against looser ones. There are also cases where a robot-like beat is just the thing. It all depends on the musical context.

Using music technology to adjust the timing of a beat automatically is not new. Many classic drum machines, like Roland's TR-909, have a shuffle control. The shuffle control delays certain beats of a sequence to create a shuffle or "swing" feel. A swing is a very simple type of groove. To create a 1/8th note swing, all you have to do is slightly delay every other 1/8th note in a beat (starting with the second). The more you delay the alternate 1/8th notes, the more intense the swing will be.

While a swing control on a drum machine isn't news, Live's Groove Engine does a few things that are downright futuristic. Not only can Live apply a traditional shuffle to both MIDI *and* audio clips, but it can also quantize audio to correct timing or *remove* swing, as well as apply a whole variety of other grooves, such as those associated with samba and rumba. Far from simply being able to delay certain beats to add swing to a loop, the Groove Engine can shift individual beats in either direction and add some randomization to the timing as well. Grooves can also contain velocity changes, which can be used to modify dynamics as well. This could be a simple matter of making the downbeat of a bar slightly louder than the other beats, or it could be a complex flow, rising and falling throughout the bar.

To apply a groove to a clip, press Hot Swap Clip Groove, as seen in Figure 5.42. This will cause the Browser to display the groove files in Live's Library. Now you can browse until you find the groove you're interested in. If you're new to working with grooves and shuffles, open up the Swing folder and select one of the groove files contained within to get started. If you're an experienced percussionist, or perhaps a user of Apple's Logic Pro or Akai's MPC-series drum sequencers, you'll be happy to find all sorts of familiar grooves contained within the other folders.

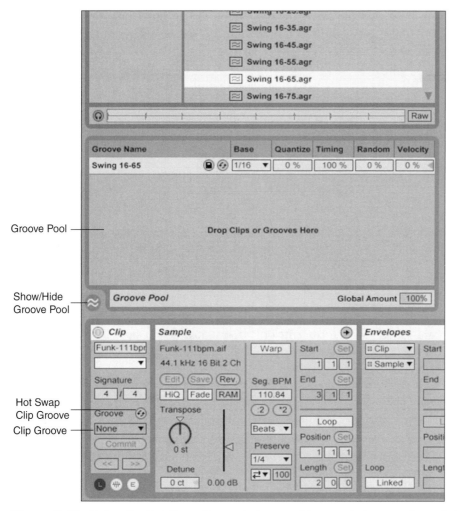

Figure 5.42 Using the Hot Swap Groove button enables you to browse through Live's Groove Library. After you select a groove, you can customize it in the Groove Pool. Click the wavy lines above the Clip View to open up the Groove Pool. You can also drag grooves directly from the Browser into the Groove Pool.
Source: Ableton

After you've selected a groove by double-clicking it, you should hear it take effect immediately, and it will appear in the Groove Pool. The Groove Pool displays one row for each groove that is used in the current Set. For each groove, the following parameters are available:

▷ **Base:** In order to shift the timing of certain beats in a clip, Live needs a point of reference. For example, if Base is set to 1/16, it will examine every 1/16 note chunk of a clip and evaluate how much (if at all) the accents within it need to be moved to match the timing of the Groove.

▷ **Quantize:** This setting determines how much real-time quantization is applied to the clip, based on the setting of the Base parameter. In other words, if Base is set to 1/16, then Live will first quantize the clip to 1/16 notes, *before* making the timing adjustments contained in the Groove file. At percentages lower than 100%, Live will move each accent only a portion of the way to the nearest 1/16. Doing this allows you to keep some of the clip's original timing before applying the groove to it.

▷ **Timing:** This is where you tell Live how much to apply the Groove's timing to the clip. At values lower than 100%, the clip's accents will be moved only part of the way to the locations specified in the Groove. At 0%, no timing adjustments will be made.

▷ **Random:** By increasing the Random value, you add timing randomization to the clip. A little randomness can emulate the natural timing variations that occur with live musicians. Unless you're looking to create some serious chaos, this setting is best used at lower values.

▷ **Velocity:** This setting determines how much the velocity fluctuations in the Groove should be applied to the clip. Be aware that some Grooves in the Library don't contain any velocity information, so changing this value won't have any effect. Note that this value can be set to negative values to invert the velocity as well. When applying grooves to audio clips, velocity creates volume fluctuations. (This is usually the case with MIDI clips as well, but that's ultimately determined by the instrument.)

▷ **Amount:** This is the Global Groove Amount. It sits at the top of the Groove Pool and is applied to all Grooves in the Set. It acts as a global control for the Timing parameter in each of the grooves. Note that Amount can be set to values greater than 100% to move all Groove Timing percentages above their specified amount.

When you've applied a groove to a clip, not only does it appear in the Groove Pool, but it also becomes available to every clip in your set. To apply the groove to additional clips, just select it from the Clip Groove menu. In Figure 5.42, Clip Groove appears as a grayed-out box that reads "None." After there are grooves in your Groove Pool, this turns into a menu.

BEHIND THE GROOVE: If you want to examine the contents of a groove, just drag it out of the Browser or the Groove Pool and drop it into a MIDI track. What you'll find is that a groove file is really just a MIDI clip that Live uses as a template for timing and dynamics. Try it!

Commit

One thing that's great about working with grooves is that they are applied in real time as the clip plays. In other words, no direct changes to the clip itself are made. Adjustments to the groove can be made continuously as you work on a track, and these changes will immediately affect any clips utilizing that groove.

However, there may be cases where you want to apply a groove to a clip in a more permanent way. To do this, press the Commit switch directly below the Groove menu in the Clip Box. In the case of a MIDI clip, this will actually move individual notes to conform to the groove and apply any necessary changes in velocity. For audio clips, Live creates Warp Markers to apply timing variations and a volume envelope to create changes in dynamics.

ANALYZE THIS: Want to create your own grooves for use with Live's Groove Engine? Just drag an audio or MIDI clip into the Groove Pool. Live will analyze the clip and create a new groove file based on the timing and dynamics of the clip. If you want to save this new clip to the Library, right-click in the Groove Pool and select "Browse Groove Library." Now, you can drag the groove from the pool into the Browser, and it will be saved for use in future sets.

Tracks and Signal Routing

O NE OF LIVE'S OFTEN UNSUNG FEATURES IS ITS INCREDIBLY FLEXIBLE ROUTING. If you're just getting started as a producer, you may not have use for everything described in this chapter right away. However, if you're coming to this chapter with some experience, I predict you'll enjoy how easy it is to route multiple MIDI tracks into one instrument or record from one track to another.

In the following pages, we'll be exploring some track types that haven't been discussed yet (such as Groups and returns) and looking at some interesting uses for regular audio and MIDI tracks. We'll also take a look at ReWire, which is a brilliant utility for sending audio between different applications and synchronizing their sequencers.

A lot of the techniques presented here involve use of the mixer's Input/Ouput section, so make sure to visit the View menu and have it displayed when following along. Figure 6.1 shows an audio and a MIDI track with this section shown, so make note of the chooser names, since I'll be referring to them quite a bit.

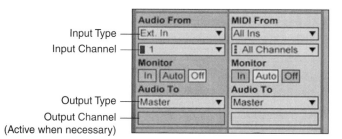

Figure 6.1 To be a routing ninja, you need to know your way around Input/Output.
Source: Ableton

The Master Track

The Master track is created automatically and cannot be deleted. By default, all tracks route their output to the Master (see Figure 6.2), where they get mixed together. It also serves as the final stop to process the sound before is gets sent out to the speakers. For example, it's common for performers and DJs to use the Master track for effects, and for producers to sweeten a final mix with some compression and EQ. (That said, until you're an experienced engineer, it's probably best to leave the Master track empty when producing.) Devices (audio effects only) can be dropped into the Master track just like any other track. Instead of clip slots, however, the Master track contains Scene Launch buttons, which are described in Chapters 3, "Live Interface Basics," and 4, "Making Music in Live." This track also has some special controls in the Mixer and Input/Output sections, which we'll take a look at next.

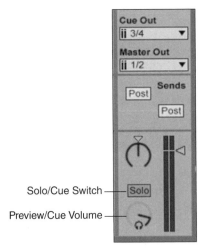

Figure 6.2 Your entire mix will pass through the Master track before heading out to the speakers.
Source: Ableton

When audio leaves the Master track, it goes to the output specified in Master Out. This can be any enabled output on your audio interface (see "Audio" in Chapter 2, "Getting Live Up and Running"). Just make sure that your monitors (or the sound system) are connected to the output specified in Master Out, and you're all set.

Above Master Out is Cue Out, which specifies the output that will be used for previewing, cueing, and the metronome. Next to the Master's volume slider, you'll find the Preview/Cue volume knob, which adjusts the volume of Cue Out.

By default, Cue Out will be set to the same outputs as the Master Out, and for many studio setups this is just fine. However, if you select unique outputs for your Cue Out, a number of possibilities arise, most of which are useful for performance. For example, by sending Cue Out to the headphone output of your audio interface, you now have the ability to preview files in the Browser, or hear the metronome without those signals going out of the Main Out and into the sound system.

Another thing that happens when Cue Out and Master Out are set to different values is that the Solo/Cue switch is activated. Click on it to select either Solo or Cue. When Cue is active, the Solo buttons on the audio tracks will turn to Cue buttons (headphone icons). When you press a Cue button, Live will route that track to the Cue output, so you can hear it through your headphones.

Bear in mind that Cue works independently of the volume fader. In other words, clicking Cue does not stop the signal from going to the Master (or wherever else you may be sending it). In a DJ setup, you'd need to keep the track's volume fader down in order to cue a song without sending it out to the dance floor.

Return Tracks

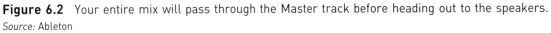

By default, there are two return tracks in a new Live Set. You can add more (up to 12) by choosing Insert Return Track from the Create menu. Return tracks are lettered (A–L) instead of being numbered, and can be shown or hidden under the View menu. You'll probably find these tracks mostly useful for effects processing, but you may discover other uses for them as well.

Return tracks don't host clips. Instead, the signal is routed to them using send knobs (see Figure 6.3). You don't have to do anything to create a send knob; they are added automatically every time a return track is created. Sends can be hidden or shown independently of return tracks, so visit the View menu if you don't see them on your screen.

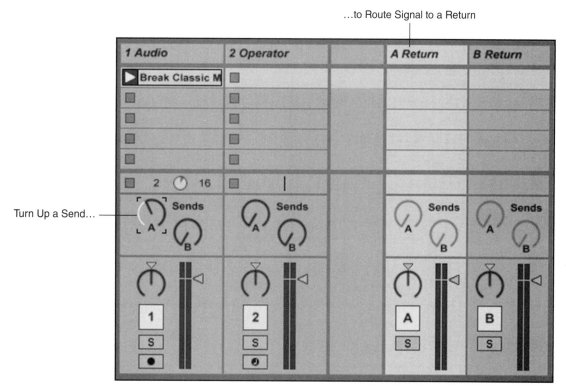

Figure 6.3 Each return track has a corresponding send knob in every track.
Source: Ableton

Let's say you have a drum loop playing on track 1. If you turn send A all the way up, the drum loop will now be sent at full volume to return A, while still playing out of track 1. In this case, the result will be to double the volume of the drum loop, since it will now be playing out of two tracks. Obviously, that's not a very interesting result. However, if you put effects on return A, you can route any signal through these effects by turning up send A. For a full discussion of using effects on return tracks, see "Insert vs. Send/Return" in Chapter 7, "Using Effects and Instruments."

By default, sends are *post-fader*. This means that they pass signal to the returns *after* the track's volume control. So turning down a track's volume by 6dB will also turn down the signal being sent to any return tracks by 6dB. With the volume fader all the way down, the returns will be silent as well. As shown in Figure 6.4, a send can be configured *pre-fader* instead, which means that the send is completely independent of the volume fader and will pass the signal, regardless of the track's volume.

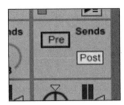

Figure 6.4 Sends can be set to either pre- or post-fader by using these switches in the Master track.
Source: Ableton

Under the Options menu, there's an item called Solo in Place, which is checked by default. For most applications, you'll probably want to leave it this way. With Solo in Place enabled, you'll be able to solo a track without muting any return tracks that receive a signal from it. With it disabled, soloing a track causes all returns to be muted.

Finally, note that one of the options for a track's Output Type is Sends Only. This is an easy way to prevent the signal from going to the Master track, so it's only heard when a Send is turned up. This is an unusual configuration, but there are occasionally (primarily performance) situations where this is handy.

> **YOU SEND ME:** Notice that even return tracks have sends, but, by default, the sends on return tracks are disabled. To enable them, right-click the Send knob and select Enable Send. Any send in Live can be disabled by right-clicking it and choosing Disable Send. The Send control will now appear grayed out.

Group Tracks

Think of a Group Track as a track that contains other tracks. The audio from the tracks within the group flow into the group track instead of directly to the Master (although this can be customized if you want). Unlike audio, MIDI, and return tracks, group tracks are not created from the Create menu. Instead, they are created by first selecting one or more audio or MIDI tracks and then selecting Edit > Group Tracks.

One use of Group Tracks is for traditional submixing, such as you might use with drums. For example, let's say you have each of your drums on an individual track. In this case, it's very helpful to be able to adjust the volume of all of the drums simultaneously, as well as to be able to process the drum mix with some compression. Group Tracks make the process incredibly easy.

Not only do they simplify submixing, but Group Tracks offer other advantages as well. First, notice the Fold switch (the small triangle) in the title bar of the Group Track. This allows you to hide or show the tracks as desired. And, of course, since this is Live, there's also a twist for live performance. If you look closely at the Group track in Figure 6.5, you'll notice that some of the slots contain triangular play buttons, which can be used to launch an entire row of clips contained within a group. Group tracks also contain stop buttons that can be used to stop all clips in the group.

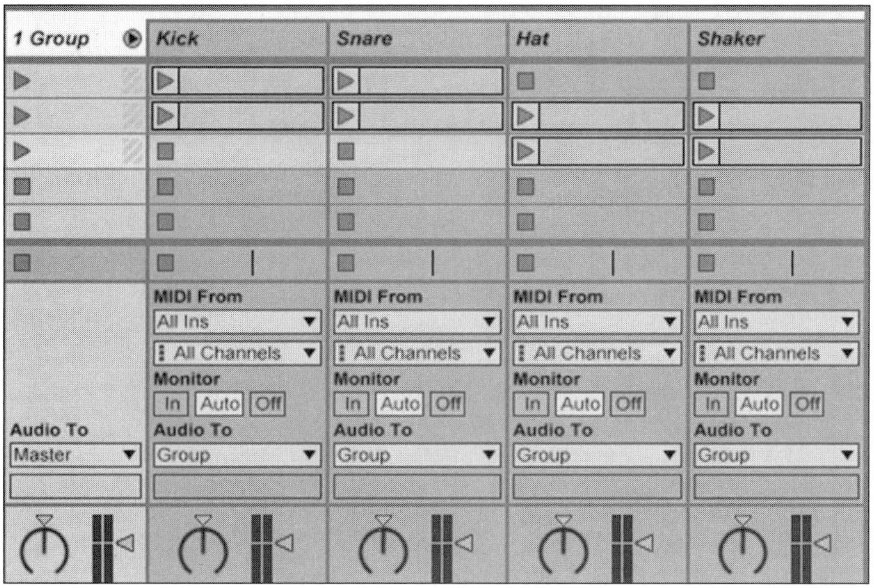

Figure 6.5 Group Tracks contain audio and MIDI tracks.
Source: Ableton

If you ever want to add an additional track to a group, just drag the track until it is adjacent to the other grouped tracks. Conversely, tracks can be removed from groups by dragging them away. Also, be aware that if you delete a Group track, all of the tracks within it will get deleted as well. If you want to ungroup the tracks within a group, right-click on the title bar of the Group track and select Ungroup from the context menu.

When tracks are grouped, their Ouput Type automatically changes from "Master" to "Group," as seen in Figure 6.5. If a track is routed somewhere other than Master before grouping, its output routing will be left alone, and it won't pass through the Group Track. With Live's flexible routing, you can easily take advantage of folding or Group Launch buttons and still send the signal wherever you want.

> **GROUP IN A GROUP?:** If you're wondering whether it's possible to put a Group Track within a Group Track, the answer is no. However, you can get some of the same benefits by creating a submix within a group. Submixing is explained in the "Submixing and Multing" section.

Audio Routing

If you explore Live's Input Type and Output Type menus, you'll discover that tracks can receive or send audio to other tracks. For example, you could create an audio track that records the output of another track while you launch clips and tweak effects.

In Figure 6.6, you'll see the input of track B has its Input Type set to track A. In the Input Channel chooser below, you'll see three options: Pre FX, Post FX, and Post Mixer. These options allow you to choose where in the signal path the audio is routed from or *tapped.*

Figure 6.6 Track B is configured to record from Track A. The Input Channel menu gives you the power to tap the signal with or without effects.

Source: Ableton

> ▷ **Post Mixer**: The signal is tapped after it is processed by any effects and passed through the mixer. Any changes to panning or volume made in the mixer affect the signal.
> ▷ **Post FX**: The signal is tapped after the effects in the Track View, but before the mixer. Changes to panning or volume made in the mixer do not affect the signal.
> ▷ **Pre FX**: Taps the signal directly, before any effects or mixing.

Submixing and Multing

In Figure 6.7, pay attention to the Output Type choosers, and you'll see the "source" tracks are routed into an audio track called *DESTINATION*. This is commonly known as a *submix*. You may notice that all I've done is to manually create the routing behavior of a Group Track—several tracks are mixed together before being sent to the Master. Unlike Group Tracks, however, this method makes it easy to record the submix. Just click Arm and start recording in the destination track to create a new audio clip from the submixed tracks.

Source 1	Source 2	Source 3	DESTINATION
■	■	■	■
■	■	■	■
■ │	■ │	■ │	■ 🎤
Audio From	**Audio From**	**Audio From**	**Audio From**
Ext. In ▼	Ext. In ▼	Ext. In ▼	Ext. In ▼
■ 1 ▼	■ 1 ▼	■ 1 ▼	■ 1 ▼
Monitor	**Monitor**	**Monitor**	**Monitor**
In Auto Off	In Auto Off	In Auto Off	In Auto Off
Audio To	**Audio To**	**Audio To**	**Audio To**
DESTINATION ▼	DESTINATION ▼	DESTINATION ▼	Master ▼
Track In	Track In	Track In	

Figure 6.7 Three tracks, all routed to a single destination. The track called DESTINATION is a regular old audio track. Some DAWs make you use special tracks for this sort of thing, but not Live!

Source: Ableton

Multing is a recording engineer abbreviation for multiplying—sending a signal to multiple destinations simultaneously. It's conceptually the opposite of submixing. Instead of sending multiple sources to one destination, you're sending one signal to multiple destinations. This is done by creating a new audio track and setting the Input Type to another track in the set. In Figure 6.8, there are three destination tracks receiving the signal from a single source. Notice that the source track still passes the signal directly to the Master, due to its Output Type setting.

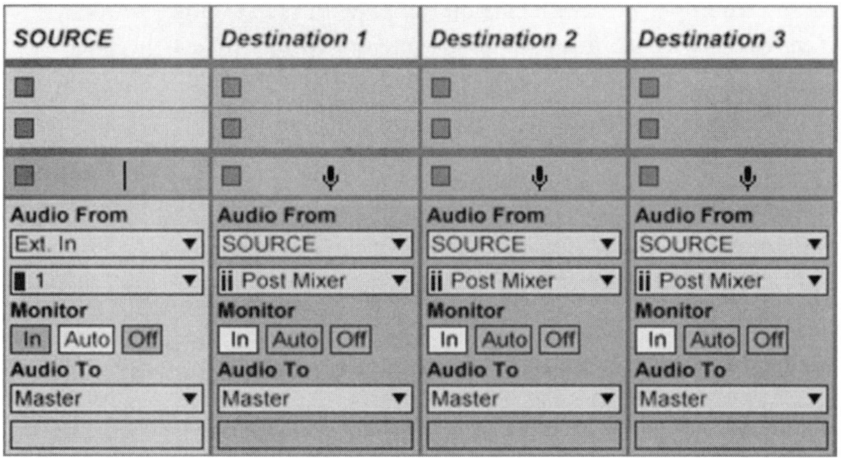

SOURCE	Destination 1	Destination 2	Destination 3
▣	▣	▣	▣
▣	▣	▣	▣
▣ |	▣ 🎤	▣ 🎤	▣ 🎤
Audio From	**Audio From**	**Audio From**	**Audio From**
Ext. In ▼	SOURCE ▼	SOURCE ▼	SOURCE ▼
▉ 1 ▼	‖ Post Mixer ▼	‖ Post Mixer ▼	‖ Post Mixer ▼
Monitor	**Monitor**	**Monitor**	**Monitor**
In Auto Off	In Auto Off	In Auto Off	In Auto Off
Audio To	**Audio To**	**Audio To**	**Audio To**
Master ▼	Master ▼	Master ▼	Master ▼

Figure 6.8 The three "destination" audio tracks are all receiving the signal from the track called SOURCE.
Source: Ableton

Whether you are submixing or multing, bear in mind that you must either arm the destination track (if its Monitor status is Auto), or set its Monitor status to In. Otherwise, the signal will not be passed through. Review the "Input/ Output" section in Chapter 3 for more information on monitoring.

Resampling

Another handy option you'll find in the Input Type menu of every audio track is Resampling (see Figure 6.9). Selecting this input allows you to record a new clip from the output of the Master track This is a quick and easy way to grab audio from whatever is going on in Live at the moment. Mute tracks you don't want to record, or solo the tracks you want recorded and go! When resampling into a track, its output is automatically muted to avoid feedback.

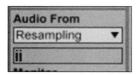

Figure 6.9 Select Resampling as the source for an audio track to record Live's main output.
Source: Ableton

Virtual Outputs

Some of Live's built-in devices and some third-party plug-ins have multiple virtual outputs, which can be useful in a variety of ways. For example, perhaps you're using Impulse (Live's basic drum instrument), and you want to send each drum to a separate track for individual processing. Or maybe you're using a multitimbral instrument like Native Instruments' Kontakt, which can load multiple instruments simultaneously. Virtual outputs make it easy to monitor or record each sound separately.

They're easy to miss, however, unless you know where to look. Whenever you load an instrument with virtual outputs into a MIDI track, the virtual outputs will become available in Input Type menus for the audio tracks in the Set. Let's take a look at an example using Impulse.

Take a look at Figure 6.10. You'll see a track containing an Impulse drum kit along with several audio tracks. Each of these tracks has its Input Type set to the Impulse track, while the Input Channel for each audio track is set to an individual drum. With these inputs selected, the drums will be sent to the individual audio tracks, instead of the Impulse track. You can now place different effects on each drum, or record the drums to separate audio clips (or both!).

When working with plug-in devices, there will typically be an additional step where you must configure the plug-in to send different sounds to different virtual outs. Consult the plug-in documentation for more information.

Figure 6.10 When Input Type is set to a track containing an instrument with virtual outputs, Input Channel will display the individual outs.
Source: Ableton

> **SUPERGROUP:** After creating separate tracks to process the virtual outputs of an instrument, it is often helpful to group them together by using a Group Track. This way, you get the best of all worlds: individual tracks for each sound, a track for group effect processing and volume adjustments, and the ability to fold all the tracks into the space of a single track.

External Outputs

So far, every technique discussed here has to do with routing signals to various destinations within Live's mixer. It's also possible to route tracks directly to physical outputs on your interface. To do this, select Ext. Output as a track's Output Type, and set Output Channel to a specific output.

One common scenario for routing to external outputs is DJing with Live using a standard DJ mixer. In Figure 6.11, you'll see two tracks configured to send their outputs to tracks 1/2 and 3/4, respectively. By connecting these two stereo pairs to channels on a mixer, you can mix and cue just like you would if you were using two turntables or CD players.

Figure 6.11 Send tracks to individual outputs on your audio interface to mix using a hardware mixer.
Source: Ableton

Advanced MIDI Routing

Just as audio signals can be routed between tracks, so can MIDI signals. All of the core concepts of routing are covered in the previous audio routing section, so you may want to read through that before digging into these MIDI techniques.

In some cases, the MIDI routing process is very similar to that of audio routing. For example, to send a MIDI signal to multiple tracks, simply create additional MIDI tracks and set their Input Type to the track sending MIDI, as seen in Figure 6.12.

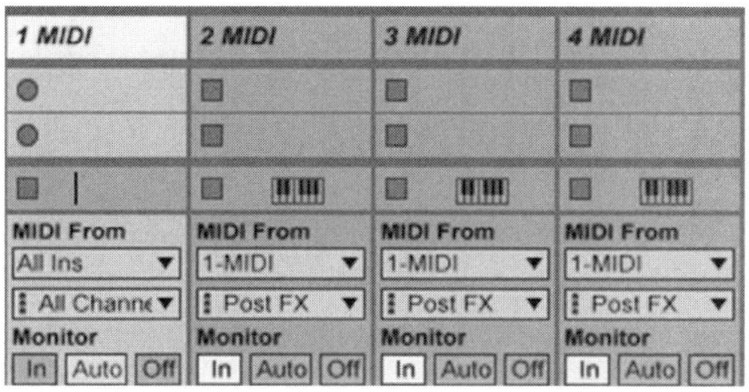

Figure 6.12 The three tracks to the right will all receive MIDI from the clips playing in track 1-MIDI.
Source: Ableton

Using this configuration, you could program clips in track 1-MIDI and have them trigger instruments in all four tracks. (A similar result can be produced using Instrument Racks, but some prefer this technique.)

Routing multiple MIDI tracks to a single instrument is a bit different than its counterpart in the audio world, submixing. In Figure 6.13, you'll see a track configured to send signal into a track called 1 MIDI. Notice that there are two choices in the Output Channel menu. The first is the track's input (Track In), while the other is an input that feeds directly into the instrument in the track (in this example, Operator is loaded).

Figure 6.13 This configuration allows you to pass MIDI directly into the Operator on track 1 MIDI.
Source: Ableton

If Track In is selected, you'll have to make sure 1 MIDI has its monitoring set up correctly (Monitor = In, or Monitor = Auto and the track is armed). With this setup, the monitoring status of the destination track will prevent you from being able to play any clips in that track. If Operator is selected, the monitoring status is ignored, which means that the destination track can trigger Operator with its own clips while additional tracks feed MIDI into Operator as well.

Sound complicated? Well, yes, it is a little. This does allow for some interesting programming techniques, however. For example, you could have a four-bar legato bass loop playing in the Operator track while occasionally triggering additional notes from a second track to create slides and variations.

Just like instruments can have multiple virtual outputs, some have multiple inputs. For example, if you repeat the above experiment with a Drum Rack in the source track instead of an Operator, you'll see that the Output Channel menu allows you to route the MIDI to a specific drum within the Rack. This same technique can be done with some plug-in devices as well. If you're working with a plug-in with virtual inputs and outputs, your best bet may be to program it using the External Instrument device, which is explained in Chapter 8, "Live's Instruments."

ReWire

These days, most music applications are incredibly powerful and don't have any serious limitations that would prevent you from using them to create a piece of music from start to finish. However, every program has its strengths, and some producers find it useful to use different programs for different things. For example, you might create some loops in Reason, and have them play alongside your song in Live. Or perhaps you're working on a Pro Tools session and you want to take advantage of Live's warping features or built-in instruments.

All of these things can be done by importing and exporting audio between the programs, but sometimes it's easier to use ReWire, which allows you to link together multiple pieces of music software. With this technology, audio and MIDI stream seamlessly from one program into the other, and the transports and tempos of the two applications are linked, making them act like one mega-program.

For the most part, ReWire is very transparent to use. You don't need to install or configure it separately, and it launches automatically when needed. Its behavior is determined by the order in which you launch your music applications and how you route signal within the applications themselves.

Masters

In any ReWire setup, there is always one program designated as the *ReWire master*. The ReWire master is the program that will be communicating with the computer's audio hardware and will accept audio streams from other ReWire applications. When a ReWire compatible application is opened, it checks to see if any other ReWire compatible applications are already running. If not, it gets designated as the master. Therefore, always launch the program you want to be the master first.

Slaves

All ReWire compatible programs launched after the Master will be designated *ReWire slaves*. Slaves don't actually communicate with the computer's audio hardware at all. Instead, their audio outputs are routed to the ReWire Master application. Since the audio is being passed through the Master application, you will not hear the slave application unless you configure the application's internal routing properly. The exact method for doing this varies from application to application. In Live, the process is very simple and will be explained below.

Using ReWire with Live

Live can act as both a ReWire master and a ReWire slave. Not all programs have the capability to function in both modes. For example, Steinberg's Cubase SX can only function as a ReWire master. Propellerhead's Reason can only be used in slave mode. So if you wanted to use Live and Cubase together, Cubase would be the master and Live would be the slave. If you wanted to use Reason, Live would be the master and Reason would be the slave.

Using Live as a ReWire Master

When Live is used as a ReWire master, its operation is essentially identical to when it's being used without ReWire. The main difference is the routing. You'll need to configure Live to receive audio from the slave application, and you may need to send MIDI into the slave as well.

To receive audio, create an audio track and set its Input Type to the slave, as seen in Figure 6.14. What you select in the Input Channel depends a bit on how you have the slave application configured. By default, Live will select the slave application's main stereo out. ReWire supports up to 64 virtual outputs, which can be used if you want to route individual instruments from the slave into different tracks in Live.

Figure 6.14 Here outputs 1 and 2 from Reason are inputs for an audio track.
Source: Ableton

After you have selected the ReWire source for a track, you can record the audio from the slave application as a new clip or simply monitor the source. ReWire synchronizes the programs, so clicking Play in Live will cause the parts from the slave to play right along in time. Just bear in mind that, while ReWire is itself very light on system resources, running multiple audio applications can be very taxing on CPU and RAM.

ReWire can also be used to send MIDI from the master to the slave. This allows you to control compatible applications the way you would control a virtual instrument in Live. Select the ReWire application in Output Type and the specific device in Ouput Channel (see Figure 6.15).

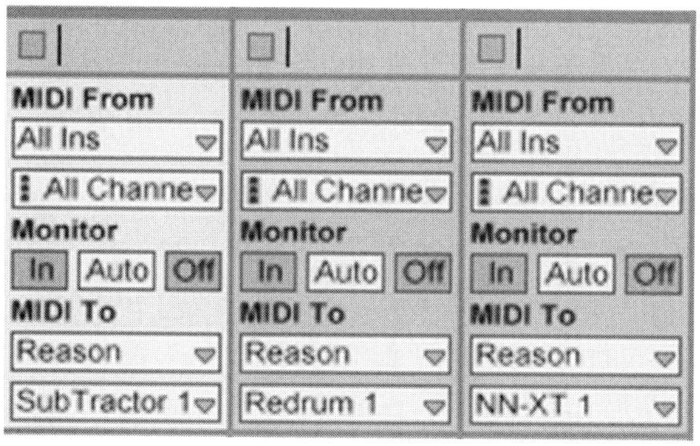

□	□	□
MIDI From	**MIDI From**	**MIDI From**
All Ins	All Ins	All Ins
All Channe	All Channe	All Channe
Monitor	**Monitor**	**Monitor**
In Auto Off	In Auto Off	In Auto Off
MIDI To	**MIDI To**	**MIDI To**
Reason	Reason	Reason
SubTractor 1	Redrum 1	NN-XT 1

Figure 6.15 These three MIDI tracks are being routed to the Subtractor, ReDrum, and NN-XT modules in Reason. They can now be programmed and automated using the power and convenience of Live's clips.
Source: Ableton

Bear in mind that a destination channel will be listed only if there are devices or elements in the Slave application that are active and able to receive MIDI messages. For example, if you load an empty rack into Reason, there will be no output devices listed in the lower box. If you make a few devices, like a Subtractor, ReDrum, and NN-XT sampler, these devices will be individually selectable in the lower box of the MIDI track's Input/Output section.

Not all ReWire slave applications are capable of receiving MIDI input from the master application. If a program is not able to receive MIDI, it will not be listed as an available output destination in the MIDI track.

Remember, in order to hear the results of your MIDI messages sent to the slave, you'll need to have an audio track set up to monitor the return signal from the slave. So instead of the MIDI track outputting the audio (as would happen when a virtual instrument is loaded onto a MIDI track), you'll need another audio track to hear the results. This means that the MIDI info leaves on one track, and the audio returns on another.

EXTERNAL INSTRUMENTS—INTERNALLY: The External Instrument device handles sending MIDI to a ReWire application and receives the audio back from that application in the same track. It's as easy as dropping an external device into a MIDI track and configuring it, using the same settings you would for a ReWire track. For a complete explanation of External Instruments, see Chapter 8.

Using Live as a ReWire Slave

The exact steps for opening Live as a ReWire slave depend partly on the master application you use. In some cases, you may need to enable ReWire channels in the master application before Live is launched; otherwise, Live may not open in slave mode. Be sure to check the master application's manual for recommendations on how you should do this. The only hard and fast rule, though, is that the ReWire master must be launched before Live. When Live launches as a slave, you'll see this noted on the splash screen during launch.

When using Live as a slave, you'll notice many subtle differences in available options throughout the program. The first thing to be aware of is that Live will be sending audio to and receiving MIDI from the master program instead of your audio and MIDI hardware.

Another difference will be the available output routings for audio in the mixer. When looking at the Master Out, and all of the individual track Output Type menus, you'll find that the list is populated with ReWire busses instead of the outputs of your audio interface. These are the pathways that lead from Live into the master application. By default, Live will send all of its audio out of the Mix L/R bus. If you want, however, you can send different tracks into different busses and have the master application receive these on different tracks.

Note that ReWire also gives you the capability to access Ableton's built-in instruments from the master application. However, note that this will not work with any plug-in instruments, which cannot be loaded into Live when in slave mode.

Let's look at how to set up Pro Tools to run with Live as a slave. (The procedure for setting up ReWire varies from host to host, so consult your sequencer's documentation if you're working with a program other than Pro Tools.) First, start Pro Tools and open a new session. Then insert the Ableton Live ReWire plug-in and select Mix L – Mix R, as seen in Figure 6.16.

Figure 6.16 Configuring a track in Pro Tools to receive ReWire input from Live.
Source: Ableton

Now you are ready to work with Live. Go ahead and open the application; you should see the message "Running as ReWire Slave" in Live's splash screen as it starts up. Looking over at the master track in your Live Set, you'll see that the master output is set to Mix L/R, the same input we selected in Pro Tools. Even before there is sound coming out, you'll be able to see ReWire at work. Notice that pressing Play in either Live or Pro Tools causes both sequencers to start running, and that changing the tempo in Pro Tools causes Live's tempo to change as well. Now you can drop some clips into Live or open an existing Set in Live, and you'll hear Live's Master output through Pro Tools.

If you want to control Live's instruments from Pro Tools, there are a few additional steps. First, create a MIDI track and place one of Ableton's instruments on it—for this example, we'll use an Operator. Next, create a MIDI track in Pro Tools. (If you haven't done so already, the order of the steps isn't important here.) Set the output of your MIDI track in Pro Tools to the Live track, as seen in Figure 6.17. That's it!

Figure 6.17 Any instruments loaded in Live will show up as valid outputs in the master application.
Source: Ableton

If you want to route tracks from Live directly into individual tracks in the host, just select a ReWire bus for a track's output in Live, and create a track in your host to receive audio via this bus. Figures 6.18 and 6.19 show how to do this in Pro Tools.

Figure 6.18   Choose a ReWire bus as the output for a track in Live.

Source: Ableton

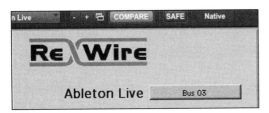

Figure 6.19   Receive audio from the same ReWire bus on a track in Pro Tools.

Source: Ableton

Using Effects and Instruments

Gone are the days when having an arsenal of effects and instruments meant owning piles of keyboards, stomp boxes, and rack units, labeled with tape and connected with miles of cable. Every piece of gear needed for the music production process, from the first drum beat to the last dab of reverb, now exists in software form. Sure, there's still lots of hardware out there that is fun to use and sounds great, but for the most part it's no longer a necessary part of making great music.

Device Types

In this chapter, we'll be getting acquainted with how software effects and instruments, generically referred to as *devices*, are used in Live. Some devices are *built-in*, meaning they come with Live and can't be used directly within any other music program. Others are *plug-in* devices, meaning they are made by companies other than Ableton, and are designed such that they can be used in just about any music program you've got.

Instruments are just what they sound like: devices for *creating* sound. These fall into two categories: *synthesizers* that generate sound, and *samplers* that play back audio files and don't have the ability to generate sound from scratch. If you're new to this realm, these two types may sound very different, but in fact they have much more in common than you may think. Both use similar sets of sound-shaping tools (such as filters) and modulators (such as envelopes) for designing sounds. Instruments can only be used in MIDI tracks.

Effects come in two flavors: Audio and MIDI. Audio Effects are the most common type and can be used in any type of track, processing the audio coming from audio clips, or the sound coming out of an instrument. Audio Effects are used in a wide variety of ways: to remove unwanted frequencies (EQ), to create the sound of a room or a stadium (Reverb), or to mangle a sound into something radically different (Frequency Shifter). MIDI Effects can only be used in MIDI tracks. They transform a performance *before* it reaches an instrument. This could be turning a single note into a chord (Chord) or turning a chord into a melodic pattern (Arpeggiator).

This chapter will also give you the lowdown on Racks, which are used for combining multiple devices into an easy-to-use bundle. If you're a beginner, you'll primarily interact with pre-made Racks from the Library, and you'll enjoy how they provide instant tweakability, while hiding the complexity within. For more advanced users, Racks are a bottomless pit of wonder, offering endless possibilities for creative routing and customization.

For a complete reference of every built-in device in Live, see Chapters 8, "Live's Instruments," 9, "Live's Audio Effects," and 10, "Live's MIDI Effects."

Using Devices

Devices are accessed from the Browser (see Figure 7.1), as described in Chapter 3, "Live Interface Basics." The Audio Effects, MIDI Effects, and Instruments views are dedicated solely to Live's built-in devices. Sounds is a special view that shows all of Live's factory Instrument (and Instrument Rack) presets organized by type, while Drums is a hybrid view that is used for accessing both Drum Racks and drum samples. The Plug-ins view displays any third-party effect or instrument devices you've installed on your computer. Max for Live devices are like built-in devices because they can only be used in Ableton Live, but they are also like plug-ins because additional devices can be downloaded and added to your collection.

With a few exceptions that will be covered later in this chapter, devices function identically, regardless of whether they are built-in, plug-in, or Max for Live. Just bear this in mind as you read through the chapter. Unless otherwise specified, any reference to an effect or instrument applies to all types.

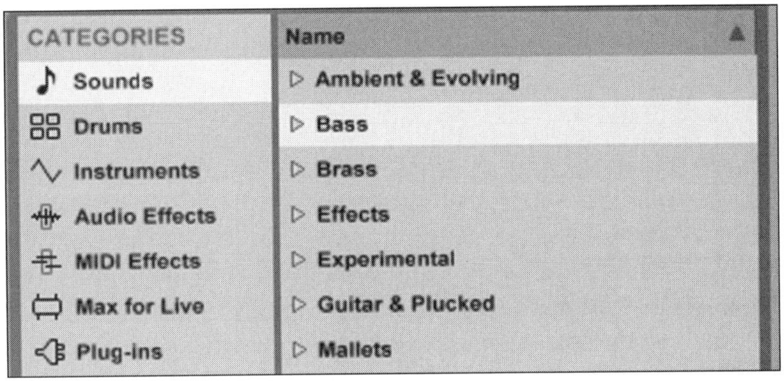

Figure 7.1 Devices are accessed from any of the categories shown here. Sounds (highlighted above) displays Instrument and Instrument Rack presets.

Source: Ableton

From Browser to Track

Adding a device from the Browser is easy. There are several different ways to load devices onto a track, all of which work identically in both the Session and Arrangement views.

1. Drag a device from the Browser and drop it anywhere on a track, as shown in Figure 7.2.
2. Select the destination track by clicking on it, and then double-click the desired device or plug-in shown in the Browser.
3. Double-click the title bar of a track to expose its Track View; then drag and drop the device directly into the Track View (see Figure 7.3). When loading effects, the benefit of this method is that you can drop the device directly into any position in the effects chain.
4. Instead of dragging the device out of the Browser, click on the triangle to the left of the device to reveal its presets. Now, drag or double-click the preset instead of the device. (There's more on presets below.)

Drag from the Browser....   ....and drop into a Track

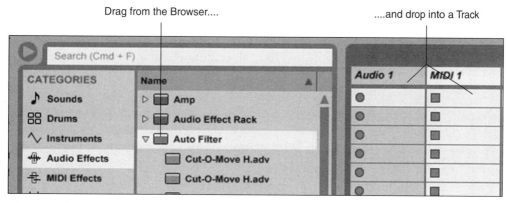

Figure 7.2 Click and drag a device from the Browser to a track.
Source: Ableton

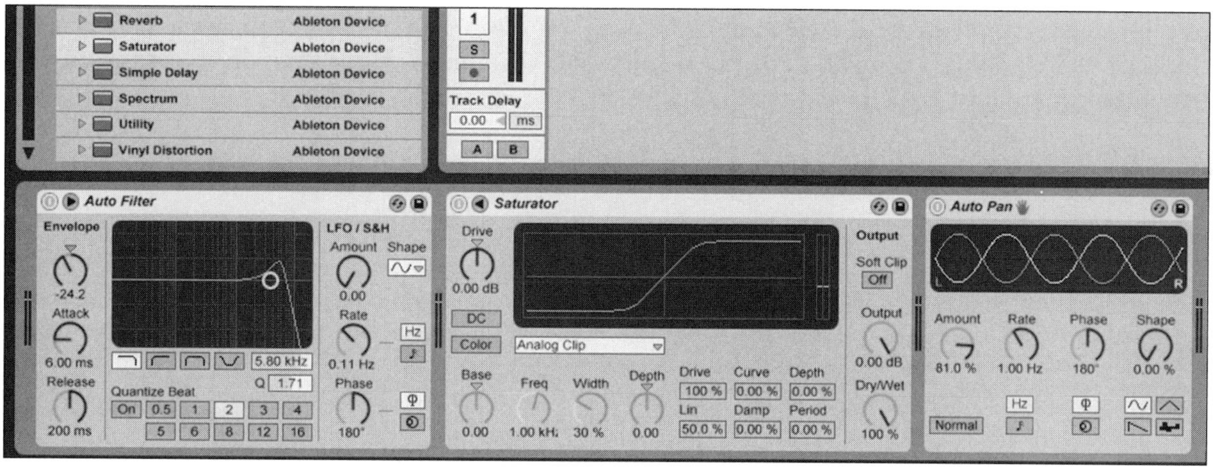

Figure 7.3 By dragging devices straight into the Track View, you can insert them at any point in the chain that you want.
Source: Ableton

There's no fixed limitation on how many effects you can place in a track. The only limitation is your CPU power (and your sanity). Instruments, on the other hand, have a very serious limitation: there can only be one in any MIDI track. When you add an instrument to a MIDI track that already contains one, the new instrument replaces the old one. (Spoiler alert! In the section on Instrument Racks, I'm going to tell you how to put more than one instrument in a MIDI track, but for now, just go with it.)

THE BIG PICTURE: You'll quickly discover that it's very easy to add enough devices to a track so that they can't all be seen at one time. When this happens, the devices will simply scroll off to the right. At the lower right-hand corner of your screen, you'll see a miniaturized image of all of the devices in the track, with a black rectangle indicating the devices that are currently in view. Just like in the Arrangement View, you can slide the rectangle around to view different parts of the device chain.

My favorite trick for keeping devices in view, however, is folding them. Just double-click in a device's title bar, and it will collapse sideways, taking up a fraction of the screen space that it did before. It's easy to keep your devices folded and just unfold the one you're working with at the moment.

Inside the Track View

As first mentioned in Chapter 3, the Track View is the name for the area in which devices appear. If you want to become a device master, you'll need to know your way around the Track View. In case you've forgotten, remember that you can always get to the Track View by double-clicking in a track's title bar or by using the Shift-Tab keyboard shortcut.

Activate/Deactivate and Edit

Every device has a circular Device Activator switch in the upper left-hand corner, which can be used to deactivate or *bypass* the device (see Figure 7.4). When deactivated, instruments produce no sound, and effects pass the signal through unchanged. When using effects, it's often important to temporarily bypass a device so you can hear exactly what's going on with the sound. Also bear in mind that a deactivated device uses no CPU power, so this can also be a useful technique when trying to determine if a particular device is overloading your system.

Clicking in the title bar of a device selects it and allows you to use commands from the Edit menu. (Also, note that once a device is selected, you can select the adjacent devices using the left and right arrow keys.) Cut, Copy, and Paste can be used on devices, as can Duplicate. The Rename command works as well, allowing you to give a descriptive name that specifies how a device is being used. Finally, if you decide you want to permanently remove a device, just click in the title bar to highlight it and press Delete.

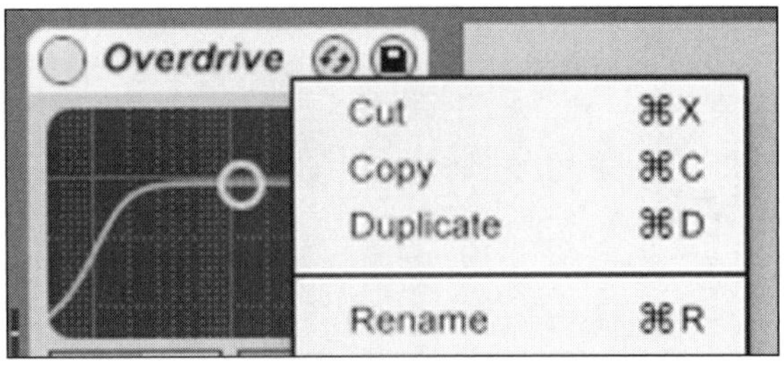

Figure 7.4 Bypass devices by clicking the circular switch in the upper left. Also note the standard editing commands available in the context menu.
Source: Ableton

Signal Flow

It's critical to understand that, once added to a track, effects process any signal passing through the track. A common misunderstanding is to think of putting an effect "on a clip." That's not how it works. When a clip plays back, its signal passes through every device in the Track View before arriving at the mixer. Therefore, the effects will transform the signal for *every clip in the track*.

Signal flows through the Track View from left to right. In the case of effects, this simply means that the output of a device is passed on to the next device to the right, and so on. This is an important point because the order that effects are placed in can have a big impact on the final result. To change device order, just click on the title bar and drag the device to a different position. Make sure to experiment!

MIDI tracks can host MIDI Effects, Instruments, and Audio Effects, which make them a bit more complex than Audio tracks, which can only host Audio Effects. MIDI Effects always appear to the left of the Instrument (since they process the MIDI before it reaches the Instrument), while Audio Effects appear to the right (since they process the audio coming out of the instrument).

Take a close look in the track view, and you'll notice a small level meter in between each device. Audio Effects have an audio level meter before and after the device, which helps you track how the effect may be changing the signal's gain. MIDI Effects display a dotted meter that shows the presence of MIDI data. Some MIDI devices can perform MIDI "filtering," which blocks some MIDI messages, so if your MIDI data is disappearing, these meters can help you determine where the problem is.

Finally, Instruments have a MIDI meter to the left and an audio meter to the right, showing you MIDI coming in and audio flowing out (see Figure 7.5). It's possible to have a situation where an instrument is producing no signal (a sample playback device with no sample loaded, or a synthesizer with all its oscillators turned off, for example), so this is another case where these handy meters can save you some headaches when diagnosing a signal flow problem.

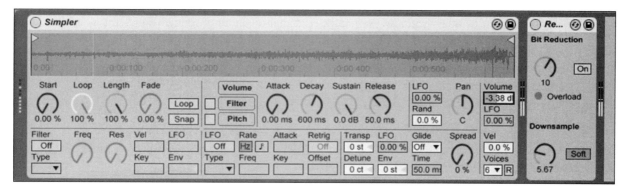

Figure 7.5 There are meters to either side of each device to show the signal flow. Notice the dotted meter to the far left shows MIDI data entering the Simpler. To the right of the Simpler, there's an audio meter showing sound exiting the Simpler and entering the Redux effect.
Source: Ableton

MIX IT UP: The question often arises, what do you do if you only want an effect on a certain clip and not on the others? The simple answer is to put the clip (or clips) on a separate track and add only the effects appropriate to those clips.

It's also possible to temporarily turn effects on and off by automating an effect's Device Activator (also known as the "Device On" parameter). This can be a very useful technique, but still it's often easier (and less confusing) to simply use a separate track to provide special effects where needed.

Insert vs. Send/Return

There are two primary ways that audio effects are used. The most common method is to use the effect as an *insert*, which means you insert it directly into the path of the signal you want to process. If you drop an effect into an audio track, MIDI track, or Group track, you're using it as an insert. The other way to get an effect into your mix is to put it on a Return track.

One of the big differences between these two methods is the relationship of the processed (*wet*) signal to the unprocessed (*dry*) signal. When an effect is used as an insert, the wet signal typically *replaces* the dry signal, unless the effect has a Dry/Wet knob for blending the two signals together. For example, if you place an EQ on a track and turn a few knobs, you're no longer hearing the unprocessed signal at all, which makes sense: the reason you use an EQ is to transform the sound such that it contains more of the frequencies you want, and less of those you don't.

On the other hand, when you use a reverb or delay effect, you're typically looking to keep the dry signal intact and *add* the ambience that the effect provides. This means that when a reverb is used as an insert, the Dry/Wet knob is extremely important since it will determine not just how much of the effect you hear, but how much of the original signal you hear as well.

This approach has a particular problem. As you increase the Dry/Wet knob toward 100%, you're not just adding effect, you're simultaneously *decreasing* the amount of dry signal. Sometimes, it's important to be able to set the level of the dry signal, and then independently adjust the level of the effect. For example, if you want to put a large amount of reverb on a snare drum, you typically don't want to turn down the level of the drum itself, you just want to crank up the reverb and leave the drum alone! Enter the Return effect.

When an effect is used on a Return track, you *add* the processed signal to the unprocessed signal and gain the flexibility that comes with having dry and wet on separate tracks. For time-based effects such as reverb and delay, this is a perfect scenario. With other effects, such as EQ, this approach rarely makes sense since the goal is to replace the unprocessed signal with the processed one.

Sends and returns are covered in detail in the "Return Tracks" section of Chapter 6, "Tracks and Signal Routing," if you need more information.

Using Return Effects

To get started with this method, add an effect to a Return track, just like you would with any other track. To get signal to flow through the effect, turn up the associated Send knob on the track you want to process. For example, place the Reverb device on Return A and turn up Send A on your snare drum track to add some reverb to the snare (see Figure 7.6). How much you turn up the Send determines how much signal is sent to the Return, and how much of the effect is added. Keep in mind that the Send knob does not *divert* signal to the Return track—it *copies* the signal to the Return track. This means that the output volume of the source track will stay the same, regardless of the Send knob position.

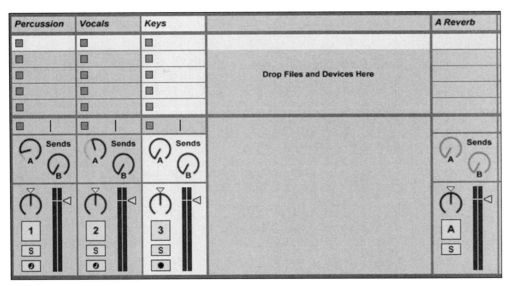

Figure 7.6 Return tracks are particularly handy when working with reverbs and delays. In this example, there's a Reverb on Return track A. Notice that the Send knobs turned up in the Percussion and Keys tracks add some effect to these tracks.

Source: Ableton

There's a Send knob on every track, which you can adjust to add varying amounts of effects to any track. For our snare drum example, you might crank the Send up high to add a dramatic effect, while turning it to a low level on the hi-hat track for a subtle ambience. This is not only convenient, but it's also CPU efficient. Plug-in reverbs in particular can be very demanding on your processor, and using many instances can place an unnecessary burden on your computer. Using the Send/Return approach allows you to share one device between many tracks.

There's one important caveat to observe when placing effects on returns: *always set the effect to 100% wet.* If the effect has a Dry/Wet knob, turn it all the way up. If the effect has an independent Dry control, turn it all the way down. Do whatever it takes to ensure that the effect on the Return track is outputting *only processed signal.* The unprocessed signal is unnecessary, since it's still being output from the original track. If you allow return effects to pass any unprocessed signal, you'll get the undesirable and confusing result of increasing the volume of the unprocessed signal whenever you turn up a Send.

PRE OR POST?: On the right side of the mixer, there is a button labeled Post for each Send knob. These buttons determine whether the Send knobs take their signals *pre-fader* or *post-fader.* Post-fader is the default setting for each track, which causes the amount of signal sent from the Send knob to vary based on the track's volume slider. If you're fading down a vocal part that is sending to a reverb, the amount being sent to the Reverb will also diminish, causing it to fade out as well.

The pre-fader position (click the Post button to turn it to Pre) causes the Send level to remain the same, even if the track's volume is adjusted. This is particularly handy when using compression in a return track (a technique called *parallel compression*). Since compressors behave very differently depending on the level of the input signal, it's handy to have independent control over the volume of the send and the track.

You'll see that the Return track itself also has Send knobs. This allows you to output a portion of the returned effect to another Return. The Return track can also send back into itself, allowing you to create feedback loops (watch your volume!). Because of the feedback risk, the Sends on Return tracks are disabled by default. If you right-click on a Send, you can enable it from the context menu.

DUB STYLE: There's loads of fun to be had with delay effects in Return tracks. For example, place a Ping Pong Delay in Return A, with a fairly high Feedback setting. Now, momentarily crank the Send knob up and down for various tracks in your song to create dramatic effects on individual drum hits or other musical phrases. Use this technique as a live performance effect, or record the Send movements as automation in the studio.

Third-Party Plug-Ins

While Live offers an impressive collection of devices right out of the box, you may also want to use plug-in effects and instruments from other manufacturers. Live supports the VST and Audio Units (Mac OS X only) plug-in standards, allowing limitless expansion possibilities for your virtual studio.

Plug-in effects and instruments are not separated into multiple views as they are with the built-in devices. To tell them apart, notice that plug-in instruments have a small piano keyboard in their Browser icon, while effects do not (see Figure 7.7). Audio Units are automatically organized by manufacturer, while VSTs can be manually organized by creating folders in the VST plug-in folder. (This can't be done in the Browser, so you'll have to use your computer's file management system.)

Figure 7.7 The piano keyboard lets you know that Kontakt 5 is an instrument. Guitar Rig 5 is an effect.
Source: Ableton

Unlike built-in devices, plug-ins use a separate window to display their parameters. When you load an external plug-in, Live displays a generic X-Y object in the Track View (see Figure 7.8), the axes of which can be set to any of the plug-in's parameters via the menus below. Clicking the wrench icon opens up the plug-in's custom graphical interface.

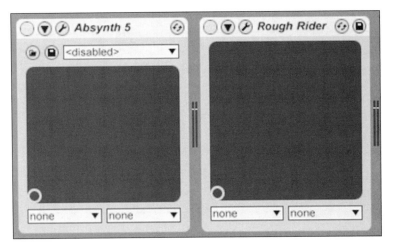

Figure 7.8 Plug-ins show up as generic placeholders. On the left there's a VST instance of Absynth. The Rough Rider to the right is an Audio Unit.
Source: Ableton

Warnings

By using a third-party plug-in, you are incorporating a new piece of program code into Live. Usually, this is nothing to worry about. However, a buggy plug-in can malfunction in all sorts of ways. In the worst cases, this could mean outputting high-volume digital noise or causing Live to crash. Just because a plug-in works well in another host is no guarantee that it will behave the same way within Live. There's nothing to be afraid of, though. Download and experiment to your heart's content. Just be sure to test at low volumes, save your work often, and never *ever* try out an untested plug-in on a gig!

If Live determines that a plug-in has caused a crash, it will offer to disable the plug-in so it doesn't happen again. However, there may be cases where you need to do this manually. This is a simple matter of removing the plug-in from the plug-in folder. (See "Installation Tips" in Chapter 2, "Getting Live Up and Running," for more information on plug-in locations.)

Managing Presets

Most effects and instruments can produce a wide variety of results. Some devices (Redux, for example) have limited functionality and a small set of parameters to match, while others (like Operator) have so many parameters that even experienced users may be endlessly surprised by the sounds that can be produced. To improve the usability of complex devices, we have *presets*: a collection of parameter settings that can be instantly loaded to configure the device for a particular sound.

Knowing how presets are loaded, managed, and created is important for producers of every skill level. At first, you load a device's presets to become familiar with what it can do and get up and running quickly. Once you've gained some expertise with programming the device (or you've stumbled on something cool-sounding through experimentation and dumb luck—my favorite method), you can save your sound as a preset for easy recall later.

Managing Presets (Built-In and Audio Unit)

For Live's built-in devices, all preset management is done via the Browser. Just click the triangle to the left of the device icon to reveal the device's presets, often categorized for easy browsing (see Figure 7.9). These presets can be added directly into tracks, as explained earlier, or added by hot-swapping them into an existing device (see the "Hot Swapping" section).

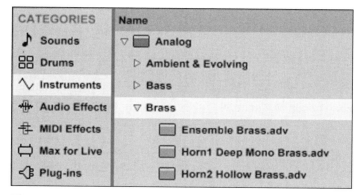

Figure 7.9 Unfold devices to reveal their presets.
Source: Ableton

Audio Unit presets are a little different. Just like built-in devices, there's a triangle for unfolding the device, but you won't see any presets here until you create some yourself. Factory presets for AU devices are accessed through the plug-in's GUI. Consult the manufacturer's documentation for more information on this. To save your own AU presets, you can either use the plug-in's preset management interface, or you can save them into Live's Browser, as explained below.

Saving presets is useful for two reasons. One is simply a matter of organization. Let's say you find an Operator preset you like. Rather than having to remember its name, wouldn't it be handy to save it to a separate location where you keep all your favorites? The other reason is to preserve settings you've programmed yourself. Either way, you'll be using the User Library.

At the far right of the device's title bar is a small floppy disk icon, the Save Preset button. Clicking this button causes a new preset to appear in the User Library (see Figure 7.10). Type in the name that you want and press Enter. If you make further edits to the preset and press the Save Preset button again, just press Enter without typing a new name to overwrite the preset with your new settings.

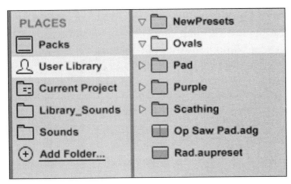

Figure 7.10 When you save a preset, it goes to the User Library. You can create folders to organize them however you want.
Source: Ableton

The User Library can be organized in any way you like. Right-click to bring up the context menu and select New Folder; then drag around the presets just like you would in your computer's file management system. Make a folder for your favorite factory presets and another for your own, or organize them by type of sound or by the colors the sound makes. It's up to you!

> **NAME GAME:** If you name your preset folders to match those of Live's built-in preset folders (for example, "Ambient & Evolving," "Bass," "Pad," and so on), your presets will automatically appear alongside the factory presets in the Categories area of the Browser.

If you right-click in the title bar of a built-in device, you'll see an additional way to save a preset: the Save as Default Preset command. If you select this, the device's current settings will be saved and used whenever a device is added to a track.

Managing VST Presets

The preset management scheme for third-party VST plug-ins is straightforward and similar to the methods employed by other DAW programs. Live can store the current settings of a plug-in using the preset icons at the top of the plug-in window (see Figure 7.11).

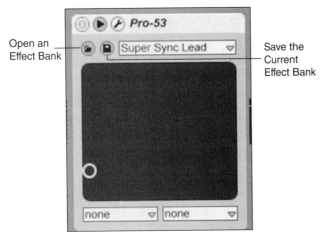

Figure 7.11 Preset management buttons found in each VST plug-in's title bar.
Source: Ableton

The drop-down menu in the plug-in window contains a list of previously stored presets for the effect (or instrument), including those provided as starters from the manufacturer. Selecting a preset from the menu will load it and replace the settings currently being used by the plug-in. If this menu is inaccessible, it's because the manufacturer has integrated preset management directly into the graphic interface of the plug-in (accessed with the wrench icon in the upper-left corner of the plug-in window).

While presets for built-in devices are automatically stored in the Library, VST presets can be saved anywhere you want. Just click in the floppy disk icon (refer to Figure 7.11) and choose a location on your hard drive. It's probably a good idea to choose a centralized location for these preset files so you don't lose track of them.

Hot-Swapping

There's an icon containing two arrows in a circle that you'll find in the title bar of every device and in a few other spots within certain devices as well. This is the Hot-Swap button, which is used for loading device presets, swapping out devices, and loading content into Drum Racks, Simpler, and Impulse. Hot-Swap mode is entered by clicking the icon or by pressing Q on your keyboard. To exit Hot-Swap mode, you can press Q (or Esc) or click on the X that appears in the title bar of both the Browser and the device being swapped.

Device Swapping

In the upper-right corner of every device, you'll find a Hot-Swap button (see Figure 7.12a). When activated, the Browser will jump to the available presets for that device. Double-clicking on a preset or highlighting a preset and pressing Return will load it into the device. The biggest advantage to this feature is being able to swap out sounds using only the keyboard. Use the up/down arrow keys to navigate in the Browser, the left/right arrow keys to open/close folders and switch views, and finally Return to load the sound.

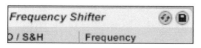

Figure 7.12a The Hot-Swap button is just to the left of the floppy disk icon (the Save button).
Source: Ableton

When using a device's Hot-Swap button, the Browser's title bar turns orange and displays "Swapping <device type>" (device type being Instrument, Audio Effect, or MIDI Effect), as shown in Figure 7.12b. This is to indicate that Hot-Swap mode allows you to do more than just load a new device preset. You can actually load any device or preset of the same type. So, for example, you could replace a Filter Delay with a Reverb, or a built-in synth-like Operator with a plug-in synth like Massive.

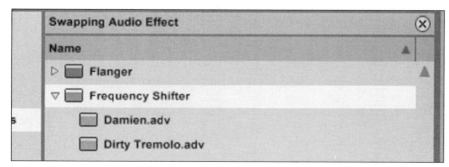

Figure 7.12b The Browser in Hot-Swap mode.
Source: Ableton

Content Swapping

Hot-Swapping can also be used to load content into Impulse, Simpler, and Drum Racks. To reveal the Hot-Swap buttons, float your mouse over a sample slot in Impulse or the sample display in Simpler. The Q shortcut doesn't work to swap samples in these devices (you'll end up swapping device or preset instead), so you'll have to use the mouse. Once you're in Hot-Swap mode, everything works the same, except that the Browser will only display sample files.

Drum Racks are a little different. In a Drum Rack, Q can be used to swap out the contents of a pad as long as it's highlighted first. You can highlight a pad by clicking on it or by using the arrow keys to navigate between pads. You can also use the D key to toggle between highlighting the Drum Rack itself and the last selected pad. This way, you can swap out drum kits or build an entire drum Rack from scratch entirely from the keyboard.

When swapping pads, the Browser allows you to select either sample files or instruments (either built-in or plug-in), since Drum Racks are relatives of Instrument Racks, which are used to host other devices. Instrument Racks are covered in detail later in this chapter, while Drum Racks are covered in Chapter 8.

Racks

Racks allow multiple devices to be grouped together to create a custom "superdevice" that can be treated as if it were a single device. There are Racks for each of Live's device types: Audio Effect Racks, which contain audio effect devices, MIDI Effect Racks for MIDI devices, and Instrument Racks, which can contain not only instrument devices, but also MIDI and audio effects. In some ways, Racks are just like other devices: there's an Activator switch in the upper-left corner, which bypasses every device in the Rack, a Save button for saving the Rack as a preset, and a Hot-Swap button for selecting a different Rack.

Live comes with numerous preset Racks, and there are many available from third-party content developers as well. Rack presets are explored just like any other type of preset in the Browser. For example, to browse for audio effects, just unfold Audio Effect Rack (in the Audio Effects view), and you'll see various effects organized by type. Instrument Racks appear in two different areas of the Browser: under Instrument Rack in the Instruments view and also in the Sounds view.

Rack Basics

Racks have three parts, which you can reveal or hide as necessary: Macros Controls, Chain List, and Devices. Use the buttons at the left edge of the Rack to hide or show the different sections (see Figure 7.13).

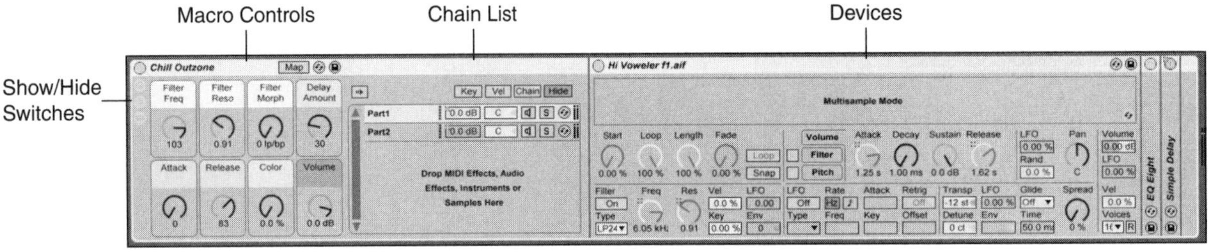

Figure 7.13 A fully expanded Instrument Rack.
Source: Ableton

When working with preset Racks, you'll primarily interact with the eight Macro knobs, which allow you to tweak selected parameters of the devices contained within, without having to understand the details of how every device works. To create your own Racks (or modify presets beyond what the Macros will allow), you'll need to work with the Chain List and the individual devices as well.

A Chain is a lot like a track in that it has basic mixer controls: volume, pan and an activator switch (see Figure 7.14). Just like a track, a Chain can contain multiple devices, which process audio in series from left-to-right fashion. However, bear in mind that despite the fact that the Chain's controls appear to the left of the Devices, they process the signal *last*, after the final device within the Chain. When a Rack has multiple Chains, they operate in parallel, a concept I'll explain next.

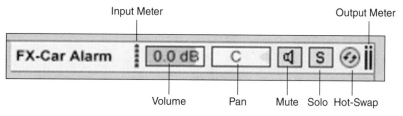

Figure 7.14 A Chain has all the mixer controls of a track.
Source: Ableton

The Rack's devices show up to the right of the Chain List. Bear in mind that you can only view the devices for one Chain at a time. For Racks with multiple Chains, click on the Chain you want to edit and its devices will appear in the Devices area.

To create a Rack from scratch, drag the Instrument Rack, Audio Effect Rack, or MIDI Effect Rack from the Browser into a track. As you can see in Figure 7.15, there's not much to look at in an empty Rack. You add devices to the Rack by dropping them directly into the Rack's Chain List or Devices area. When a device is first added into a Rack, a Chain is automatically created.

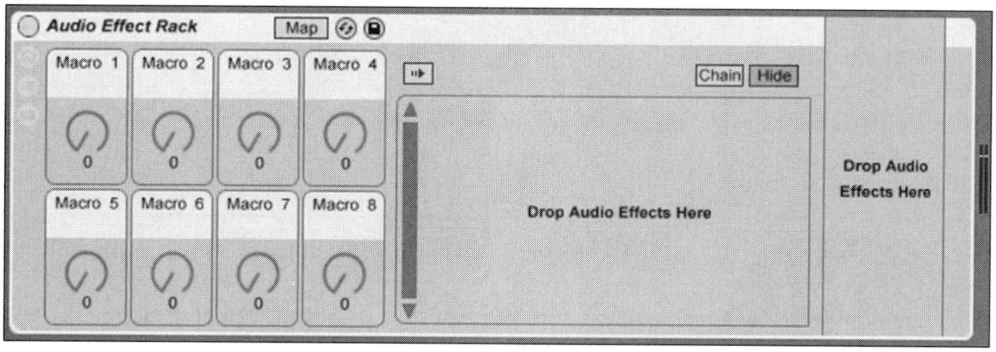

Figure 7.15 An empty Audio Effect Rack.
Source: Ableton

> **GROUP IT:** You can also place devices in the Track View into a Rack by using the Group command from the Edit menu (or a device's context menu). To group multiple devices into a Rack, first select all of the devices by Shift-clicking their title bars. To remove a Rack and leave its individual devices in the track, highlight the Rack and select the Ungroup command in the Edit menu or the context menu.

Chains

When adding additional devices to a Rack, you can drop them into the Devices area or directly on a Chain. However, you can also create a new chain by dropping a device into the *drop area* of the Chain List. In Figure 7.16, this is the part of the Chain List that reads "Drop MIDI Effects, Audio Effects, Instruments or Samples Here."

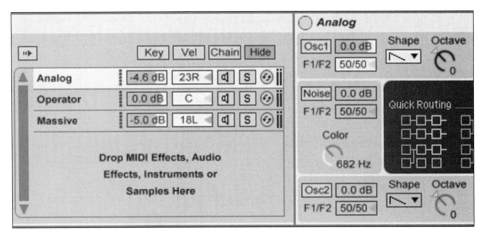

Figure 7.16 A layered Instrument Rack utilizing two built-in instruments and a VST instrument. All three instruments will play simultaneously when MIDI input is received. The Chain controls are used to balance the levels of the Chains and pan them left or right.

Source: Ableton

Chains are processed in *parallel*, which means that the incoming signal is split and passed to each chain independently. In other words, if you have an effect Rack with five chains, then you have five *copies* of the incoming signal going to five different device chains. In the case of Instrument Racks, this means that you can create layered sounds by simultaneously triggering multiple instruments, processing each instrument with different effects.

Also bear in mind that Racks can contain other Racks. So even if you're a novice sound designer, you can create massive sounds by layering multiple Rack presets together. If this has you rubbing your hands together and cackling like a mad scientist, you've got an idea of how powerful this is. (If you're not, don't worry—head to the laboratory for some experimenting, and you will be soon.)

> **EMPTY CHAINS:** Chains can also be created manually by using the Create Chain command in the context menu of the Chain List. This is handy for creating an empty chain. This might not sound useful at first, but in Audio Effect Racks it can sometimes be very useful to have a chain that passes the dry unprocessed signal to blend with the effects in the other chains.

With layered Racks, the mixing features of the Chain List become particularly important. This is where you'll balance the levels of each layer and use the Activator and Solo switches as you work to help zero in on different parts of the sound. The chains for an Instrument Rack can also be viewed directly within the Session View. The title bar of a track containing an Instrument Rack will have an Unfold button next to the track name. Clicking this reveals the Chain Mixer, a mini-track for each chain in the Rack (see Figure 7.17). Clicking in the title bar of any of the tracks in the Chain Mixer will cause the devices for that Chain to be displayed in the Track View, which can be quite handy when managing complicated Racks.

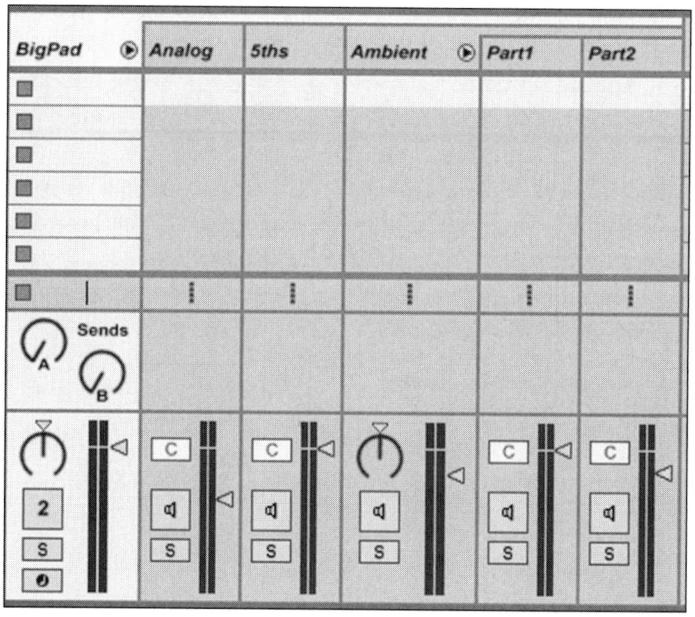

Figure 7.17 The Chain Mixer contains chains named Analog, 5ths, and Ambient. The chain called Ambient contains another Rack (!), so it can be unfolded as well, to show the chains within.
Source: Ableton

Macro Controls

With the potential to include a large number of devices, a large Rack can become cumbersome to navigate. The Macro Controls address this issue by giving you a set of eight freely mappable controls.

To assign Macro Controls, click the Map Mode button at the top of the Rack (see Figure 7.18). Clicking this button highlights every controllable parameter of every device in the Rack, and switches the Browser into mapping mode so it displays all current mappings for the Rack.

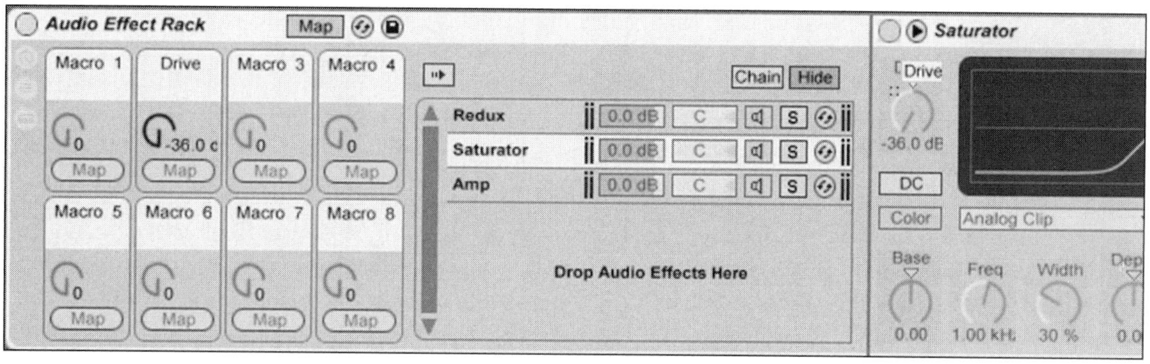

Figure 7.18 In Map mode, you can select a device parameter, and then click the Map button below a Macro Control to assign it. Notice that the Saturator's Drive control is already mapped.
Source: Ableton

Click a parameter and then click on the Map button under one of the Macro Controls to assign it. (If you click on a control that's already assigned, the button will read Unmap instead.) Just like MIDI controllers, a Macro knob can be mapped to control many parameters simultaneously. For example, you could control the filter cutoff of all of the synths in an Instrument Rack with a single knob.

While in Map mode, the Browser displays all of the mappings for the Rack, as seen in Figure 7.19. This is handy when designing complex Racks, and also allows you to edit minimum and maximum values for the mapped parameter. For example, in Figure 7.19, you could adjust the Min and Max values for the Saturator's Drive, so it only ranges from –12 to +12dB. Bear in mind that you can set Min to be *greater* than Max, thereby inverting the behavior of the Macro Control so it turns the value down as you turn the knob up.

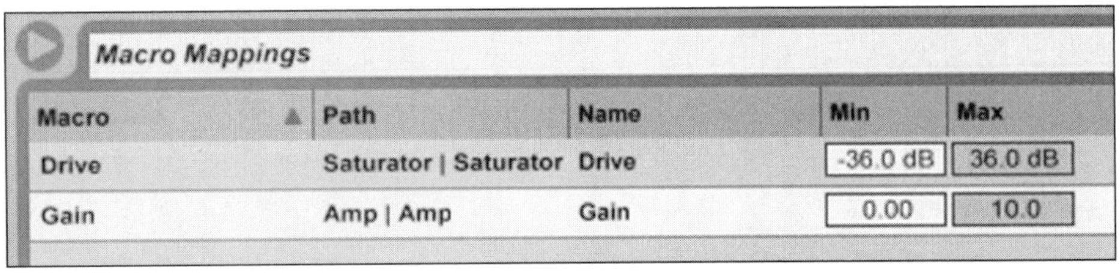

Macro Mappings				
Macro ▲	Path	Name	Min	Max
Drive	Saturator | Saturator	Drive	-36.0 dB	36.0 dB
Gain	Amp | Amp	Gain	0.00	10.0

Figure 7.19 In Map mode, the Browser displays mappings. You can edit minimum and maximum values here, or right-click and select Invert Range to swap Min and Max.
Source: Ableton

After making your Macro assignments, click the Map button in the Rack's title bar to exit Map mode.

> **IN CONTEXT:** It's possible to edit Macro Control assignments without ever entering Map mode. Just right-click on the device parameter you want to map, and you'll see a full set of mapping commands in the context menu.

Zones

Racks can be further customized with Zones, which allow you to dynamically activate and deactivate chains or even crossfade between them. For example, you could create a multi-effect Rack that allows you to switch between effects with the turn of a knob, or create an Instrument Rack that routes different note ranges to different instruments. There are three zone types: Chain Select, Key, and Velocity. The Chain selector exists in every type of Rack, while Key and Velocity only pertain to Instrument Racks.

The Chain Selector

Above the Chain List, you'll see a button marked Chain. Click on this to expose the Chain Select Editor. This editor consists of two sections: the Chain selector, a vertical orange bar at the top that can be dragged horizontally, and the Zone Editor that allows you to create a map of active chains. The position of the Chain selector determines which chains will be active. If there is a Zone directly below the Chain selector, the associated Chain will be active; otherwise, it will not.

By default, the zones for each chain are lined up at the far left of the editor, with the Chain selector directly above (as seen in Figure 7.20). If you grab the Chain selector and drag it to the right, the Rack will immediately go silent. Zones can be moved by grabbing them from the center and dragging, and resized by dragging at the edges. (The mouse pointer will turn into the bracket-shaped "trim" tool that you see when resizing clips in the Arrangement.)

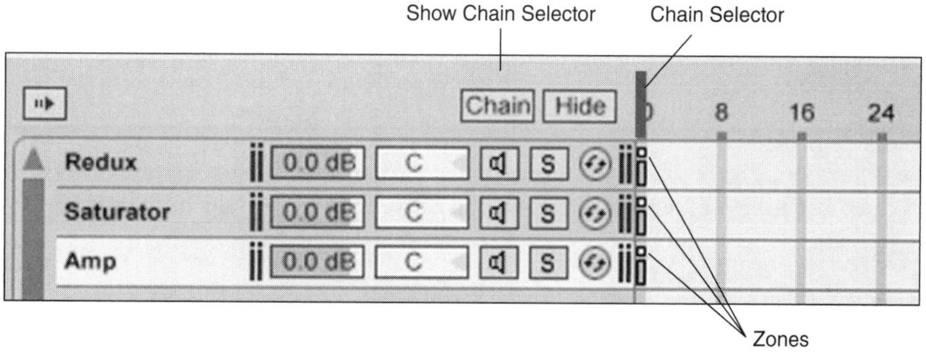

Show Chain Selector   Chain Selector

Zones

Figure 7.20 Click the Chain switch to reveal the Chain Select Editor at the right.
Source: Ableton

If the Zones are arranged as seen in Figure 7.21, the Chain selector can be used to switch between Chains by dragging it across the top of the editor. The Chain selector can be MIDI-mapped or mapped to a Macro knob so you can select Chains without having the editor open.

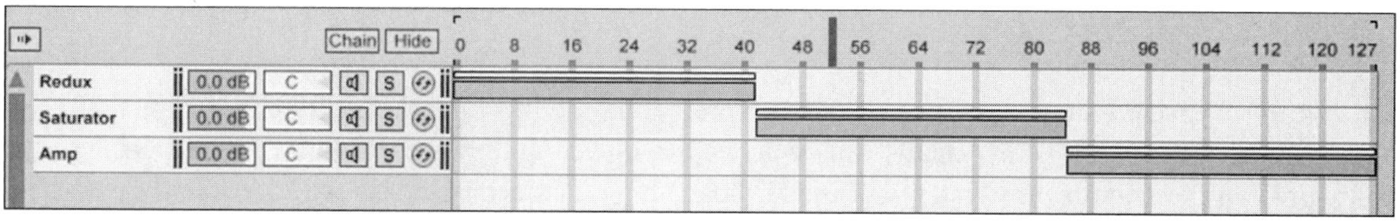

Figure 7.21 In the configuration shown, only one Chain will ever be active at a time (since none of the Zones overlap). With the Chain selector in its displayed position, the Saturator chain will be active.
Source: Ableton

It's also possible to have Zones fade in and out as the Chain selector is moved. To create fades, hover the mouse over the edge of a Zone until it turns into a bracket, and then move it upward slightly until the small bar running along the top of the Zone is highlighted. Click and drag to create a fade as seen in Figure 7.22.

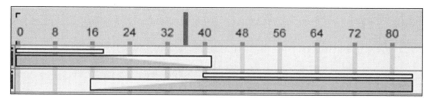

Figure 7.22 Fades can be used to gradually increase or decrease the volume of a Chain as the selector is moved. With the Chain selector in the position shown, the top Chain is turned almost all the way down, while the Chain below is near full volume.
Source: Ableton

Key & Velocity

Instrument Racks feature two additional Zone editors for further customization: Key and Velocity. These Zones are accessed by the buttons marked Key and Vel directly above the Chain List. Key Zones are used to activate chains based on the incoming MIDI note, while Velocity Zones will activate chains based on incoming MIDI velocity.

Key Zones are handy for creating performance presets (left-hand triggers a bass sound, right-hand triggers piano), while Velocity Zones allow you to create expressive sounds, adding or switching layers as the keys are struck harder. These Zones are moved, resized, and faded just like the Zones in the Chain Select Editor, so make sure to read the preceding section if you haven't already.

Across the top of the Velocity Zone Editor (see Figure 7.23), you'll see numbers from 1 to 127, representing the incoming velocity. The Zones below are used to specify which chains will be active for a given velocity range.

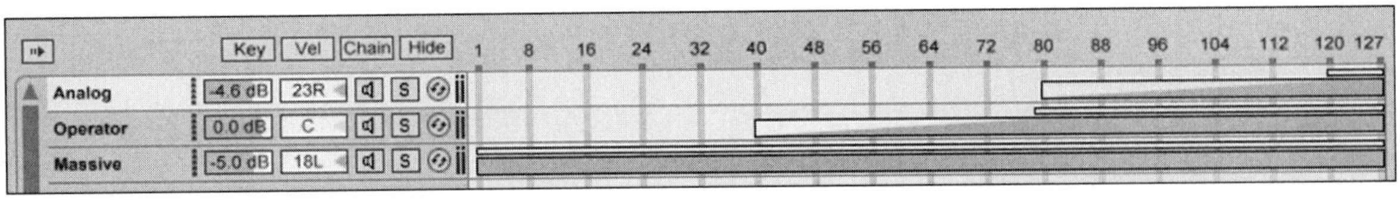

Figure 7.23 In this example, the Operator chain only sounds when the velocity is over 40, and only reaches its full volume at velocities over 80. The Massive chain sounds at all times, regardless of velocity.
Source: Ableton

In Figure 7.23, we are using Velocity Zones to filter the MIDI data coming into the Rack and determine which instrument it will trigger. In this image, the lowest velocity notes will trigger the FM8 instrument, and the highest velocities will trigger Absynth 4. Notes within a middle range of velocities will trigger both instruments simultaneously.

Across the top of the Key Zone Editor is a piano keyboard representing the incoming MIDI note (see Figure 7.24). The Zones below are used to specify which chains will be active for a given note range. In Figure KEYZONE, you'll see a Rack configured so the bottom three octaves of the keyboard trigger an acoustic bass sound, while the remainder of the keyboard triggers piano.

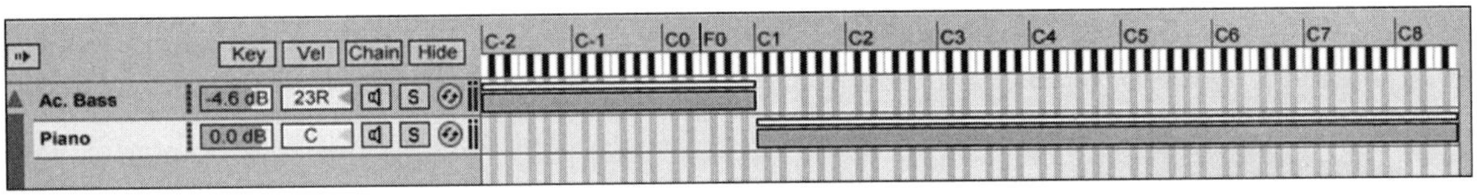

Figure 7.24 Key Zones in action. The lower range of the keyboard is directed to the top Chain, while the other Chain handles input from the rest of the keyboard's range.
Source: Ableton

When you're done working with Zones, click the Hide button to hide the editor.

Freeze and Flatten

Devices use CPU power. Some use more than others, but overall it's just a fact of life. For the most part, the usage of CPU power is managed pretty efficiently. For example, a virtual instrument won't drain the CPU unless it's playing. Not only that, but it will use less CPU power to play one note than it will to play 10 notes simultaneously. However, even with a powerful computer, you'll still encounter situations where your computer is struggling to keep up with all the devices you're using. The Freeze function will help you manage these situations.

Freeze works by temporarily rendering a track's output to an audio file. A frozen track uses much less CPU power, but is limited in how much it can be edited. Let's take a look at how this works.

The easiest way to invoke the Freeze command is to right-click in a track and select Freeze Track from the context menu. You'll have to wait a moment while Live processes the audio—obviously, tracks with long clips (or a large number of clips) will take longer. When finished, the track will look more or less the same. You'll see all the original clips and devices, but key editing features are turned ice-colored, indicating that they are "frozen" and not editable. In the Arrangement View, you'll also notice a crosshatched region immediately following any clip being processed with delay or reverb. This indicates that the effect tail has been rendered as well (see Figure 7.25).

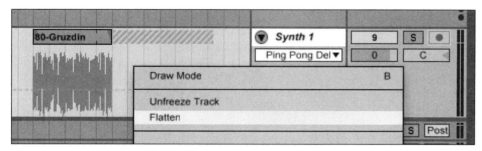

Figure 7.25 A frozen track in the Arrangement View. Notice the slashes to the right of the clip indicating the tail of a delay effect. Right-clicking on a frozen track reveals the Unfreeze and Flatten commands in the context menu.
Source: Ableton

What happens behind the scenes is that Live disables all of the clips and devices in the track and plays back the temporary audio files instead. All standard editing functions (Cut, Paste, Duplicate, Consolidate, etc.) and most track controls (output routing, volume, pan, etc.) still work, but most detailed editing (such as changing device or clip parameters) is impossible. Adding new devices to frozen tracks is prohibited as well.

If you need to tweak frozen parameters, you can unfreeze the track (again, right-click the track and select Unfreeze Track) to immediately restore the track to its original state. You can now use the track as normal and refreeze the track when you're done.

CAN'T FREEZE?: Be aware that there are a few cases in which tracks can't be frozen, and you'll get an error message explaining why the track can't be frozen. If you get an error because you're using a sidechained device (such as Compressor), you can work around this by first grouping the track you want to freeze (see Group Tracks in Chapter 4, "Making Music in Live") and moving the sidechained device to the Group Track. Alternately, you can render un-freezable tracks by using Resampling or track-to-track recording, as explained in Chapter 6.

Next to Unfreeze Track, you'll also see the Flatten command, which is used to commit to the frozen version of the track. Flatten converts the frozen track into a standard audio track and populates it with the temporary audio clips that were created when the track was first frozen. Now you can edit and tweak the audio to your heart's content and even add new effects for further sonic exploration.

DRAG IT: Sometimes you may want to get your hands on some of a track's frozen audio without flattening the track. To do this, just drag any frozen audio or MIDI clip to an audio track. Like magic, the frozen audio appears in the new track, ready for editing or further effects processing.

Delay Compensation

Just as all devices use CPU power, all devices generate latency. When a signal passes through an effect, it takes the device a small amount of time to perform the processing, and the result is a slight delay. By default, Live compensates for this delay so it's not something you usually have to worry about. However, because there are rare cases where delay compensation can cause sync problems, it can be turned off by unchecking Delay Compensation under the Options menu. There are also cases where Live cannot automatically compensate for all of the latency generated by a plug-in. If this occurs, you can use Track Delay to manually compensate.

When Live is compensating for devices that generate large amounts of latency, you will find that virtual instruments respond sluggishly, and any audio signals you monitor are noticeably delayed. Check "Reduced Latency When Monitoring" under the Options menu to compensate for this.

Live's Instruments

L IVE FEATURES EIGHT VIRTUAL INSTRUMENTS: Impulse, Simpler, Operator, Sampler, Analog, Electric, Tension and Collision. Impulse and Simpler come free for all Live users, while the others are included in the Live Suite or must be purchased separately.

Under the Instruments view of the Browser, you'll actually see 11 items, three of which aren't exactly instruments, but are included in the same category nevertheless. Drum Racks and Instrument Racks both work in conjunction with other virtual instruments to make customized meta-instruments, ranging from the very simple to the mind-bogglingly complex. External Instrument is a handy utility for easy integration of hardware instruments and multi-timbral plug-ins.

General Principles

Before getting into a discussion of each individual instrument, it's important to mention some concepts and functionality that are common to all instruments. Make sure to read this section thoroughly first, and refer back to it as necessary.

Live's instruments are a deep topic that an entire book could be devoted to. Instead of endlessly listing every parameter of every device, I've made an effort to draw attention to the most important aspects of each instrument to help you through the hardest part of the learning curve. Bear in mind that sound design and synthesis are subjects that go far beyond the discussion of any individual instrument. If you're new to this topic, you may want to explore the excellent (and free!) Sound on Sound series "Synth Secrets" located on the Web at www.soundonsound.com/sos/allsynthsecrets.htm.

Modulation

Modulation is just a fancy term for *changing something*. For example, instead of saying that you got a great sound by repeatedly changing the filter frequency, you can impress your friends by talking about your awesome *filter modulation*. Modulation always has a source and a destination. In the above example, the filter's cutoff frequency is the destination. The source could be an instrument's built-in envelope or LFO, or it could be a standard MIDI message, such as velocity or pitch bend.

In all of Live's instruments, you'll find numeric boxes that are used to specify modulation amounts. For example, in Figure 8.1, you'll see a Volume knob with a box below marked Velocity. This box is used to specify how much a note's velocity will affect the instrument's volume. At zero, every note will come out at the same volume, regardless of how hard you bang on your MIDI controller. As you increase this value, you'll find the instrument starts to behave like a piano—the harder you strike a key, the louder the output. You'll find that 50% is a good value to start with, but you should experiment and adjust to your taste and playing style.

Figure 8.1 Modulation boxes like the one shown here are used to route a modulator to the parameter they sit near. This example shows the very common routing of MIDI velocity to output volume.
Source: Ableton

You'll see boxes marked Velocity (or sometimes Vel) all over the place in Live's instruments, because velocity can be mapped to many parameters other than volume. For example, turning up the value of a Vel box located near a Pan control allows you to move the sound from left to right as the velocity increases.

Figure 8.2 shows Analog's filter section. Here we see that the cutoff frequency has three modulation sources: LFO2, Key, and Env. Turning any of these to a non-zero value engages modulation. The greater the value, the greater the depth of the modulation, and the more it deviates from its original value. Key is used to make the modulation respond to the pitch of the input note—the higher the note, the more the cutoff frequency will increase. The LFO and Env controls are used to apply modulation generated by the built-in LFO and envelope sections.

Figure 8.2 Many instrument parameters can be modulated by multiple sources simultaneously. However, when learning, it's best to start with one at a time.
Source: Ableton

To fully understand these last two, you'll need to know a bit more about these types of modulation sources, which will be explained next. There are other modulation types I'll be mentioning as well, and it can be a lot to absorb. Don't worry—as long as you understand the basic principle of assigning a destination to a source, you'll eventually get it all. Start simple, take your time, and experiment.

LFOs and Envelopes

All of Live's instruments contain LFOs and Envelopes for generating modulation. While they vary a bit from instrument to instrument, they all have many things in common.

LFOs (Low Frequency Oscillators) are typically used to generate repetitive modulations, such as vibrato, tremolo, and the rhythmic "wobbles" heard in a lot of contemporary electronic music. All of Live's instruments have a selectable waveform to determine the shape of the LFO. Sine waves produce the smoothest effect, while sawtooth and square waves can be used to generate modulations with more rhythmic aggression. At the bottom of each instrument's wave menu is a random LFO style, sometimes referred to as *noise* or *S&H* (sample and hold).

All of Live's LFOs can be synchronized to the current tempo, or set in Hertz (cycles per second). For Hertz, click the button marked Hz, or to synchronize, click the button marked with a musical note. The Rate knob will update to display either cycles per second or note divisions, depending on the mode you select.

Envelopes are used to create modulations that begin when a note is pressed and conclude when it is released. Most of Live's instruments have envelopes for volume, filter frequency, and pitch. Depending on the instrument, there may be additional envelopes or assignable envelopes that can be used to control any parameter you want. If you're new to working with envelopes, the volume envelope is the one you should master first.

Most of the envelopes you'll encounter use the traditional four-stage design: Attack, Decay, Sustain and Release (ADSR). Some instruments have additional envelope stages, which will be explained in the individual instrument sections. However, if you're not sure how these work initially, don't sweat it. Just focus on the ADSR, and you'll be fine.

Here's a brief explanation of how a volume envelope works. Once you've wrapped your head around this, you'll have no trouble understanding the other envelopes, as long as you're willing to be patient and do some experimentation.

As soon as a MIDI note is received, the Attack stage begins. This stage determines how long it takes the sound to reach its full volume. Turned all the way down, the note will sound instantaneously, while high values will cause the note to fade in slowly. The Release stage happens as soon as the note is released. This stage determines how long it takes for the note to fade to silence once you release it. When turned all the way down, the note will be silenced immediately, while long values will cause it to linger on long after you've stopped playing your keyboard.

Decay and Sustain work in conjunction with each other. Decay specifies how long it takes for the volume to reach the Sustain level. The trick here is to understand that Decay is a measurement of time, while Sustain is a parameter value (in this example, volume). To best understand how this works, turn Sustain all the way down. This means that the Sustain level is *silence*. Now you can use the Decay control to adjust how long it takes for the note to decay to silence. Once you've got a grip on this, try setting Sustain to –12db, Decay to 50ms, and Attack all the way down. This creates a percussive transient every time you play a note, since the first 50ms of the note is 12dB louder than the note's sustain.

Filters

All of Live's instruments contain a variety of filter types, often in both 12 and 24dB/Octave variations. These numbers refer to the severity or *slope* of the filter. The higher the number, the more steeply the filter reduces the frequencies outside the filter's range. Generally, this means a more intense or aggressive effect, especially with high resonance values. Some of Live's instruments use the following abbreviations: LP (low pass), HP (high pass), and BP (band pass). So, HP24 means a high-pass filter with a 24dB/Octave slope. A few instruments have special filter types, which I'll explain as necessary. If you're totally new to filters, I recommend reading the "Auto Filter" section in Chapter 9, "Live's Audio Effects," for more explanation of fundamental filter concepts.

Global Parameters

All of Live's instruments use a handful of common commands, such as polyphony and pitch bend range, that aren't particular to the instrument's specific synthesis or sampling style. So instead of covering them with each instrument, I'll start out with this handy reference that can be applied to all of them. Just bear in mind that each synth does not have every single one of these parameters.

    ▷ **Detune:** Makes fine pitch adjustments to the entire range, to a maximum of 50 cents (one half of a semitone).
    ▷ **Error:** Introduces a random amount of tuning variation to each note (as might happen with an unfretted string instrument, like a cello).
    ▷ **Glide:** Same as Portamento (see below). For instruments that offer a choice between Glide and Portamento, use Glide to get the classic monosynth glide described below, and Portamento for polyphonic operation.
    ▷ **Pitch Bend:** Controls how much the instrument will respond to pitch bend messages. Adjustable from 0 for no response at all to 12 or 24 semitones, depending on the instrument.

▷ **Portamento:** Causes each note to slide into the next at a rate determined by the Time parameter. For the classic portamento behavior of old monosynths, set Voices to mono when enabling this setting. With Legato enabled, only notes that overlap will slide together. The Proportional setting will automatically adjust the portamento time so that larger intervals slide longer than shorter ones.

▷ **Priority:** Determines how the instrument handles the maximum number of voices (set by the Voices parameter) being exceeded. When more notes are sounded than Voices permits, Priority will tell the instrument which notes to prioritize (and which to cut off): High (cuts off the lowest notes first), Low (cut off the highest notes first), or Last (cuts off the oldest notes first).

▷ **R (Retrigger):** This function of the Retrigger switch varies, depending on context. In the case of an LFO or Envelope, this button determines whether or not each MIDI note will restart the LFO or Envelope from its starting point. For example, for a pad with long evolving envelopes, this Retrigger probably isn't a desirable behavior—you want to be able to hold notes down, and have any additional ones you add pick up the envelope at its current position. When this switch appears in the global section of an instrument, it can be turned off to allow one note struck multiple times to use more than one voice instead of retriggering the same voice. This only applies to sounds with long release times in the volume envelope, and it can generally be left on.

▷ **Semi or Transpose:** Transposes the entire range of this instrument in semitones.

▷ **Spread:** A simplified version of Unison (see below) that creates a detuned stereo output.

▷ **Stretch:** Allows the adjustment of the instrument's temperament. Increasing this value will change the tuning such that higher notes are slightly sharper and lower notes are slightly flatter, which for pianos can result in a more natural and brilliant overall sound.

▷ **Unison:** Duplicates the final output of your instrument. Unless used in conjunction with the Detune or Delay parameters, all this does is make the signal louder. Slight detuning will create a chorusing effect, while larger values can be used to create strange, out-of-tune harmonies. Delay increases the effect by delaying the unison layer up to 100ms.

▷ **Voices:** Controls how many notes can sound at once. Reducing the number of voices will save CPU power. When set to Mono (one voice), any note played will cut off any currently playing note. This is useful for emulating the behavior of classic monosynths.

Impulse

Impulse is Live's basic drum instrument (see Figure 8.3). Where Drum Racks offer endless flexibility, Live's more limited Impulse offers instant usability due to its sparse controls and simple design.

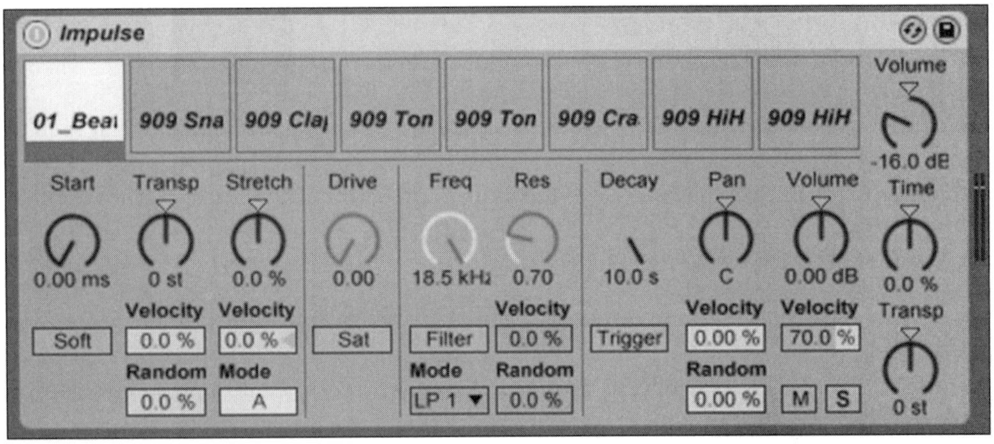

Figure 8.3 The clean and crisp Impulse interface sports eight slots for samples. Clicking the slot displays its editable parameters.

Source: Ableton

Sample Slots

The upper portion of Impulse is made of eight squares, or sample slots, each of which can hold one sample, and can be triggered via MIDI or with the mouse. When you hover the mouse over a slot, a play button is revealed, along with a small rectangular Mute switch on the left, and a Solo switch to the right. To load a sample, drag an audio file from the Browser into one of the slots. You can also load samples by using the Hot-Swap button in each slot, or you can even drag in audio clips directly from Session or Arrangement.

Each slot has a full set of editing controls, but you can only edit one slot at a time—the knobs below are used to edit the currently selected slot. In other words, before editing a sample, you must first click on the slot containing it.

The MIDI notes assigned to trigger the eight cells are the white keys between C3 (middle-C) and C4 (one octave above middle-C). However, when you're editing the MIDI data of a clip playing Impulse, the normal piano keyboard will be replaced with the names of the samples assigned to each note.

HAS ANYBODY SEEN MY KEYS?: If you're using a small MIDI controller or the computer keyboard keys, you may find yourself bashing away on the notes but hearing nothing from Impulse. This frequently occurs when the keyboard has been transposed to the wrong octave. With Impulse, any notes outside the range C3 to C4 are ignored.

If you're using the computer keyboard for MIDI input, the Z and X keys will transpose the keys. When transposing the keyboard, you'll see the current key range listed at the bottom of the screen. To transpose the range of your MIDI controller, consult its documentation.

Note that slot 8 (the farthest to the right) has one parameter that none of the other slots has: the Link switch. This links slots 7 and 8 together, so they cannot play at the same time. This is typically used for open and closed hi-hat samples, which classic drum machines (and actual drumsets!) do not allow to sound simultaneously. When enabled, triggering slot 7 or 8 will immediately cut off the sample playing in the other slot.

Start, Transpose, and Stretch

Now that you know how to trigger the samples, let's look at how to change the sound using the playback parameters offered in Impulse. The first section of controls affects the sample itself: it can be tuned, time-stretched/shortened, and have its front-end cut off. Pitch can be randomized or modulated by input velocity. The Soft button performs a fade at the beginning of the sample to soften its attack.

Transpose works as you'd expect, raising or lowering the pitch of the sample. Stretch is a bit more interesting, and is used to elongate the sample or shorten it. Long stretch times generate some weird artifacts, so make sure to experiment with this one and try it out while adjusting Transpose as well.

The Mode button changes the stretching method. In Mode A, Impulse waits a brief moment before stretching in order to ensure that the stretching doesn't distort the attack of the sound. For punchy drum sounds, this is especially important. Mode B, on the other hand, begins stretching the instant the sample starts to play. Ableton recommends Mode A for sounds that are lower in pitch, such as kick drums, and Mode B for higher-pitched sounds like hi-hats.

Turning up Start causes the sample to play back from a position later in the file. This can be used creatively to chop off the beginning of a sound, or to correct for empty space at the beginning of a sample file.

The Soft button is somewhat related to the Start dial in that it affects how Impulse plays the beginning of the sample. When Soft is off, Impulse simply plays the sample the instant it is triggered. When Soft is turned on, Impulse will perform a short fade-in. The result is that the attack of the sample is softened without changing the length of the sound. If you try this with the kick drum, you'll hear that the "snap" at the beginning of the sound is softened, while the beefy punch of the drum remains.

Notice that Transpose and Stretch can both be modulated by velocity, while Transpose also has a Random modulator beneath it. Turn this up to apply pitch randomization to the sample. A small amount of this can add subtle life and variation to an otherwise static sample.

Saturation

The Saturation section is the simplest to use of the five controls in Impulse. Engage the Sat button and turn up the Drive to achieve overdriven percussion sounds. Small amounts of distortion can be helpful when you need to add some edge or aggression to a sample, while large amounts can mangle a sound beyond recognition. Give it a try!

Filter

Click the Filter button to engage this section. The Mode menu is used to select the filter type, while the Freq and Res knobs set the cutoff and resonance. Notice that the resonance can be randomly modulated, just like Stretch. Note that the filter is applied after the saturation stage. This is because distorting a sound can yield some unwieldy high harmonics, which you may want to tame with a low-pass filter.

Volume, Pan, and Decay

This section is used to set the output level (Volume) and stereo position (Pan) for each individual sample. The Decay knob shapes the tail end of a sample. If the button below the Decay knob is in Trigger mode, the Decay knob will dictate the fade-out time from the moment the sample is triggered. It doesn't matter how long you hold the pad or key that is triggering the sample—the decay time will always be whatever value is specified by the Decay knob. This is classic drum machine behavior.

In Gate mode, the fade-out won't begin until a MIDI Note Off message is received (when you lift your finger off a key). With long decay values, you may not notice any difference between these two modes. But with short values, it becomes more obvious. For example, try using Gate mode with a Decay time of 50ms. You'll find that this allows you to create variations in your drum parts by editing the length of the MIDI notes. Try making some snare hits longer than others or varying the length of hi-hats to keep things interesting. In Trigger mode, this won't work—all the hits will be reduced to a 50ms blip, regardless of the note length.

At the bottom of this section, you'll find buttons marked M and S for muting or soloing the current slot.

Global Volume, Time, and Transpose

The Global section contains a master Volume knob, plus master Time and Transp (transpose) knobs. These last two knobs function just like the Transpose and Stretch knobs described previously, except that they apply to the entire kit.

Simpler

When it comes to quick sample playback and manipulation, nothing is simpler than Simpler. What is Simpler? A simple sampler, of course. However, don't be fooled. Simpler offers a wealth of creative possibilities within its humble interface, such as independent Pitch, Filter, and Amp Envelopes, as well as portamento and other effects.

Overview of the Interface

The Simpler interface looks quite similar to Impulse, but it has one large sample window instead of eight sample cells (see Figure 8.4). Simpler works with only one sample at a time, and its contents are displayed in this main window. You can zoom in and out on the waveform by clicking it when you see the magnifying glass cursor appear and dragging up and down with the mouse.

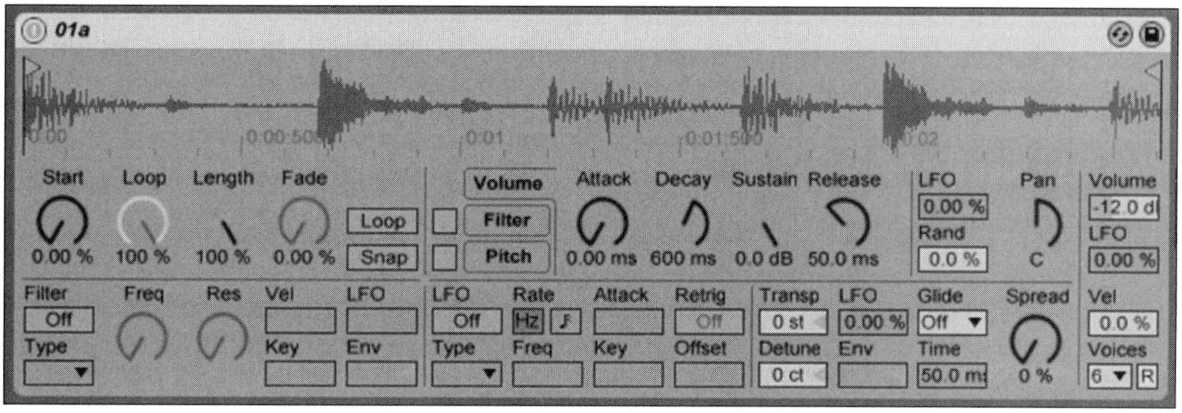

Figure 8.4 Simpler is the go-to instrument for quick and easy sample playback.
Source: Ableton

Simpler can be loaded with a new sound by dragging a sample from the Browser, or an audio clip from the Session or Arrangement View. Since Simpler is designed to hold just one sample, any new sound dragged into the instrument will replace the previous one. The sample you load into Simpler can be triggered from any MIDI note. C3 (middle-C) will trigger the sample at its original pitch, while higher and lower notes will transpose the sample up or down. Please note that Simpler does not use the Warp engine—changing pitch without changing time. Instead, the sample is simply slowed down or sped up to lower or raise the pitch.

> **MULTISAMPLE MODE:** When using Simpler presets, you may find the sample display window empty, reading "Multisample Mode" instead. This is the result of a clever Ableton hack that allows Simpler presets to be created in Sampler, which allows multisampling. If you own Sampler, you can get under the hood and fully edit these presets by right-clicking in Simpler's title bar and selecting "Simpler > Sampler."

Sample and Loop controls

The upper-left corner of Simpler contains the knobs you'll use to set all the basic parameters for sample playback. Any changes you make with these knobs will be shown graphically in the Sample Display window. However, there are also two parameters that can only be set in the display: the absolute start and end points. These are represented by two flags, which should look familiar from the Clip View (see Figure 8.5).

Figure 8.5 Simpler can only play back the audio enclosed within the start and end flags. The audio that gets played and looped is determined by the Start, Length, and Loop controls.
Source: Ableton

The first three knobs change the start position, loop length, and end position of the sample. When Start is set to 0%, playback begins from wherever you've placed the (right-pointing) start flag in the Sample Display. Length specifies how much of the sample can be played. When this value is set to 100%, playback can continue as far as the (left-pointing) end flag in the display.

With the Loop switch enabled, the Loop knob becomes active. It specifies how much of the sample will loop, expressed as a percentage from the end (as specified by Length). The Fade knob applies a crossfade to the loop's connection points to smooth out any pops you may encounter when the sample starts over. The Snap button helps prevent these pops by forcing the start and end points of the Loop area to snap to a zero crossing.

Although it might not be apparent at first, some of the controls in this section are extremely expressive to adjust in real time. For example, altering the loop length and start positions on the fly can change the timbre and tone of the sample in wild and wonderful ways.

Envelopes

The next set of controls to the right are Simpler's envelopes. There are three envelopes available: Volume, Filter (cutoff), and Pitch. The names of these three envelopes are clickable tabs, which can be used to bring up the associated envelope for editing. The Volume envelope is always active, while the Filter and Pitch envelopes must be activated by clicking the square switches to the left.

Note that to activate the Filter envelope, you must also engage the Filter button (described below). Also, bear in mind that to hear the effect of either the Filter or Pitch envelope, you must also assign an envelope amount in the Filter or Pitch section, as explained below.

Pan

To the right of the Envelopes section is the Pan control. Panning can be modulated with the LFO and randomness. When Random is turned up for the Pan control, a new position in the stereo field is chosen every time a note is triggered. To generate continuous movement without triggering new notes, you'll have to use the LFO.

Filter

The Filter is located in Simpler's lower left-hand corner, and is engaged by clicking the Filter button. It contains the basic Freq (cutoff) and Resonance controls, along with a Mode menu for selecting the filter type. The remaining controls are used to assign modulators to the cutoff frequency. The Env knob scales the amount of Filter Envelope signal used to change the filter cutoff. The higher the value, the more the envelope causes the cutoff frequency to deviate from its original value.

Key is used to change the cutoff value of the filter based on the pitch of the incoming MIDI note. The higher the pitch, the higher the filter cutoff will be. This helps emulate real sounds, which get brighter as their pitch increases. The LFO knob determines the amount of LFO signal used to modulate the cutoff. Notice that the Env and LFO amounts are disabled unless their associated modulators are engaged.

LFO

To the right of the Filter section is the LFO (engaged with the LFO button). Depending on the assignments you make, it can be used to modulate the Filter Frequency, Pitch, Pan, and Volume. The shape of the LFO is selected from the Type menu. The Rate section changes the speed of the LFO.

The LFO speed can be further modified with the Key value. Turning this up means that higher notes will have a faster LFO speed than lower ones. You can also use the Attack value to have the LFO gradually fade in instead of starting immediately when a key is pressed. This is great for lead sounds where you'd like to introduce vibrato after you've held a note for a moment.

Retrig and Offset are used to manipulate the position of the LFO. When Retrig is on, a new LFO cycle will start every time a MIDI note is received. With Offset, you can change the overall position of the LFO, which is particularly useful when using it in synced mode. For example, 1/4 note LFO could be offset 180 degrees so the peaks occur in between every beat instead of directly on them.

Pitch

Immediately to the right of the LFO section is the Pitch section, the majority of which is explained in the Global Parameters section at the beginning of this chapter. The LFO box sets the amount of LFO modulation to apply to the pitch of the sample, also known as *vibrato*. Similarly, the Envelope box sets the amount of pitch modulation applied by the Pitch envelope. Bear in mind that the Envelope and LFO amounts are disabled unless their associated modulators are engaged.

Volume

At the far right, you'll find Simpler's Volume control along with amounts for the various modulators that can be assigned to it. Velocity is explained in the Modulation section at the top of this chapter.

Operator

Introduced in Live 4.1, Operator is Ableton's first add-on instrument. Operator is a very flexible instrument, which allows you to use three different types of synthesis to craft your sounds: FM, subtractive, and additive.

Overview of the Interface

Operator represents a slight departure from the user interface scheme set forth by Impulse and Simpler. While Operator still conveniently sits within the Track View (see Figure 8.6), it does not display all information and parameters at once. Operator is a deep and complex synth, so many of the parameters have been consolidated into the center window of the interface.

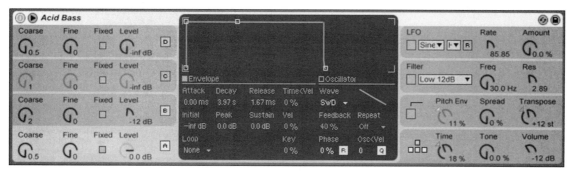

Figure 8.6 The Operator interface has two sections: the center window (the display) and the eight sections surrounding it (the shell).
Source: Ableton

Looking at the interface, you'll see a large center window, called the *display*, surrounded by eight sections, collectively referred to as the *shell*. The shell sections are (clockwise from the lower-left corner): Oscillator A, Oscillator B, Oscillator C, Oscillator D, LFO, Filter, Pitch, and Global. If you click on one of these sections, the display will change to show its associated parameters. Try it—click anywhere within the oscillator A section. The display will show a graphic envelope, as well as a myriad of values below it. If you click on the Pitch section, a different set of information will be shown in the display.

Ableton has placed the most tweakable parameters of Operator into the shell so that you can access them at all times. The more intricate details are neatly tucked away within the display. If you'd like, you can even hide the display, leaving only the shell exposed, by clicking the little triangle in the upper-left corner of the interface. Also, along the top title bar are the standard controls for recalling and saving presets.

Creating and Shaping Sounds

So how do you operate Operator? It depends on what type of synthesis you're trying to achieve. As you're about to see, Operator can pull off both subtractive and FM synthesis, and it has some additive synthesis features as well.

The Algorithm

Click on the Global section in the shell. (This is the area in the lower-right corner containing the Volume and Tone controls.) The global parameters will now be shown in the display (see Figure 8.7). If you've been clicking around through the other sections in Operator, you'll notice that this display is different from the others. Gone are the graphic envelopes, and in their place is a collection of colored squares.

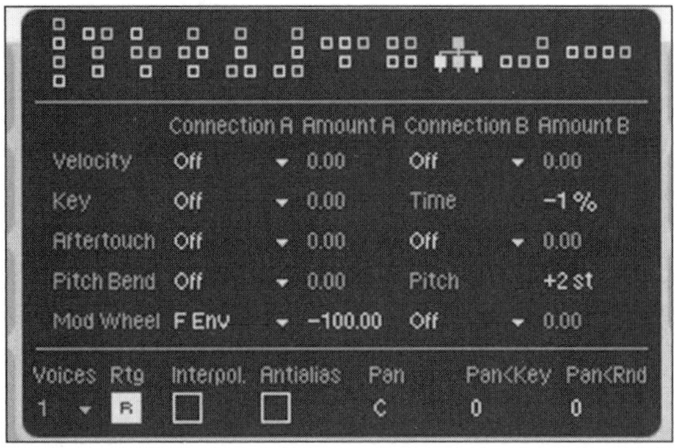

Figure 8.7 The global parameters of Operator.
Source: Ableton

While the term *algorithm* may conjure up images of mind-bending calculus formulas, you'll be pleased to know that Operator provides a simple way to visualize an algorithm using the assortment of colored squares in the display. By default, the upper-left algorithm will be active (its squares are solid colors, as opposed to outlines). Notice that the colored letters in the oscillator section to the left are the same colors as the squares in the algorithm's display. The colored squares are therefore a map, or flowchart, of how the oscillators interact with each other.

You can read an algorithm from the top down, but I also like to look at it from the bottom up from time to time. If you look at this first algorithm starting at the bottom, you'll see that the bottom square is a yellow A. This is oscillator A. You'll also see that there is a little yellow line extending downward from this square. This line shows that oscillator A will be outputting a signal that you can hear.

If you look at the next block above A, you'll see a green square with a B inside. This block has a line extending downward from it, too, but it connects to oscillator A instead of being an output. This means that the waveform created by oscillator B will be used to change the frequency of oscillator A, which is output to your speakers. In this arrangement, oscillator B is called a *modulator*, and oscillator A is a *carrier*.

Knowing this information, you can now see what parts oscillator C and oscillator D play in this algorithm: They are additional modulators. Oscillator D will modulate oscillator C, which modulates oscillator B, which modulates oscillator A—the carrier.

Now look across to the right. The eighth algorithm over is shaped like a box. When you select this algorithm, you will see the familiar arrangement of oscillator B modulating oscillator A. The difference this time is that oscillator C is now a carrier—you will hear the waveform it generates, modulated by oscillator D. You can think of this as a dual-FM synth where you can create two unique waveforms simultaneously, which can be used in layers to thicken your sound, or to create two independent sounds that interplay with each other.

The next algorithm to take special note of is the horizontal arrangement at the far right. When using this algorithm, you will no longer be using any of the oscillators as modulators—they'll all be sent directly to the output. In this, each oscillator will output its own unique waveform, which can be mixed together and filtered, very much like a classic analog synth.

Below the algorithms is the routing matrix, which gives you enormous modulation flexibility. We'll discuss this after we've gone over more of the basics of Operator.

The Oscillators

Leave the algorithm set to the default vertical arrangement, and click on operator A in the shell. The algorithms in the display will now be replaced with an envelope and additional parameters. These are all of the control parameters for operator A. By default, each operator is set to produce a sine wave with instantaneous attack and release. Try playing a few notes to hear this for yourself.

In the shell, all you can set is the tuning and volume of the oscillator. (You can also click the colored ABCD buttons to turn the oscillators on and off.) Tuning and volume have a tremendous impact on the sounds resulting from FM synthesis, so these controls have been made easily accessible. Tuning has two modes: Variable and Fixed. The Variable setting (the default) causes the operator to change frequency, based on the notes you play. The Fixed setting (enabled by clicking the Fixed box of an operator) causes it to ignore incoming note information and will instead sound at the specific frequency that you set in the shell.

When in Fixed mode, the two tuning options will be Freq and Multi, which stand for frequency and multiplier, respectively. The operator's frequency is determined by multiplying the Freq by the Multi value. If the frequency is 100Hz and the multiplier is one, the resulting frequency will be 100Hz (100Hz × 1 = 100Hz). If the frequency is 245Hz and the multiplier is 10, the operator's frequency will be 2,450Hz.

When in Variable mode, the oscillator frequencies are no longer shown. Instead, you are presented with Coarse and Fine adjustments, which express the operator's frequency as a ratio of the base frequency. An operator with a Coarse setting of 2 will sound an octave higher than one with a Coarse setting of 1. An operator with a Coarse setting of 0.5 will sound an octave lower. You can use the Fine adjustment to create ratios that are fractions, such as 1.5 (Coarse 1, Fine 500) or 2.25 (Coarse 2, Fine 250).

Tucked away in the display is a parameter named *Wave*. The option below it is currently set to Sin—a sine wave. Click on Sin to open a menu with all of the available wave shapes. Try out a few of them to hear how they sound.

The saw and square waves have multiple shapes, denoted by a number after the name. The number in the waveform name tells you how many harmonics were used to create the wave shape. In the case of Saw3, only three harmonics were used: the fundamental, the second harmonic, and the third harmonic. As a result, the Saw3 waveform still resembles a sine wave more than a sawtooth wave. As you go further down the menu of waveforms, you'll see saws with greater numbers of harmonics. Saw64 uses 64 harmonics to generate the sawtooth wave, and sounds like a traditional analog sawtooth, while D signifies a digital sawtooth—the brightest of the bunch. This same numbering scheme is true for the square waves as well.

The Oscillator Display

Once you dig into FM synthesis with Operator, you'll find that the various algorithm/waveform/tuning options offer a wide array of wild and complex tones. But there's even more flexibility available—Operator also allows you to visually edit the built-in waveforms by graphically adding and subtracting harmonics.

Above the Envelope display, click on the box marked Oscillator, next to the box marked Envelope. This changes the display to show you the harmonics of the waveform being used for the currently selected operator. If Sine is selected from the menu below, you'll see exactly one bar all the way to the left of the display. This tells you that the wave is composed of a simple fundamental pitch with no higher harmonics. Now try selecting Saw3 from the menu. This is the sawtooth wave we discussed earlier, composed of only three harmonics. With Saw64, you'll see harmonics cascading across the display, illustrating the complex sound of a true sawtooth wave.

Once you have a basic understanding of what you're looking at here, things get really interesting. When your mouse floats above the harmonics display, it turns into a pencil, allowing you to freely alter the wave's harmonics. Try it—start slowly, increasing or decreasing the right-most harmonics to make the sound brighter or darker. Then go crazy with it, drawing or deleting harmonics as you please. Notice that as you do this, the waveform display below changes as well, and the Wave menu now reads User.

This makes for a truly overwhelming number of options for programming this synth. If you're new to Operator, it might make more sense to get a handle on simple FM before you start building all sorts of custom waveforms. However, the mad scientist in you may win the day and demand a purely experimental approach to sound design. That's OK, too!

FM in Action

Enough talk, already. It's time to hear what all of this sounds like. Load up an Operator in its default state and play a note—you should hear a single sine wave. You are hearing oscillator A by itself. Now, while holding the note, turn up the level of oscillator B. As you do this, you will hear the sound of oscillator A change. This is because oscillator B is modulating oscillator A, resulting in what are called *side bands*. Oscillator A becomes more and more brilliant (more upper harmonics) as you increase the level of operator B, increasing the modulation amount. If you turn oscillator B back down again, oscillator A will revert to a sine wave.

Conceptually, this is the opposite approach seen in traditional subtractive synthesis where one starts with a bright complex wave, such as a sawtooth, and then removes high harmonics with a low-pass filter. With FM synthesis, we can actually start with a harmonically simple sound like a sine and add high harmonics by adding modulation.

For your next experiment, turn up oscillator B again and then play with the Coarse knob. The result will be another constant tone, but one with a different harmonic structure. As you turn up the Coarse knob, you will be changing the frequency ratio between oscillators A and B in whole numbers (for example, 1 to 2, 1 to 3, 1 to 8, and so on).

Things start to get strange, however, when you begin to change the Fine adjustment. Hold a note and slowly increase the Fine setting. With a small change, the sound will go "out of tune," and with a large change will become "without tune." This is because the frequencies of the modulator and carrier are no longer at a musically coherent (whole number) ratio. Next, try switching oscillator B into Fixed mode and play some notes. As you play across the range of the keyboard, you'll get constantly changing inharmonic modulations, which are the result of the modulator staying at a fixed pitch while the carrier's pitch changes.

But enough math for now. If you want to explore the principles behind FM synthesis further, there are many scholarly works on the topic. For now, all that's important to know is that messing with fine-tuning or switching modulators into Fixed mode moves you out of the realm of the melodic into sci-fi weirdness, synthetic percussion, and all-out mayhem.

A HIDDEN MODULATOR: While the Operator algorithms select which oscillators will be modulators for others, there is another hidden modulation you can perform as well. Click on an oscillator's section to show its parameters in the display. If it's not currently being modulated by any other oscillators, you'll notice that the Feedback parameter becomes enabled. This uses the output of the oscillator as a modulation input for itself. If you start with a sine wave and turn the Feedback parameter up to 50%, the result will be nearly identical to a sawtooth wave. If you have a waveform other than sine selected, the result will be extremely strange. Try it out!

The Envelopes

Each oscillator has its own volume envelope. Not only that, but the Filter and Pitch sections also have their own envelopes, as does the LFO. That's seven envelopes for a single voice! That's quite a lot compared with Simpler, which has only three envelopes per voice.

You heard in the previous experiments how the volume of a modulator would affect the timbre of the carrier. Therefore, using an envelope to change the volume of a modulator will allow you to change the harmonic content of a sound as it plays, like using a filter envelope in subtractive synthesis.

Continuing on with the experiment we started earlier, crank up oscillator B to full volume and modify its volume envelope so it decays to silence very quickly (an example of this envelope shape is shown in Figure 8.8). The sound now has some motion to it—it has an aggressive attack that quickly decays into the fundamental sine wave. This is because oscillator B plays at full volume when you strike a note, but it quickly fades out after the initial attack. This is what creates the harmonic complexity at the beginning of every note.

The remaining parameters in the display for an oscillator govern how velocity and key-follow will affect the operator's pitch and level. For starters, the Vel parameter will modulate the operator's volume based on velocity—positive values will cause the operator to increase in volume as you play harder, while negative values will attenuate the operator the harder you play. If you use this setting on a modulator, it will have a similar effect to applying velocity scaling to a Filter Envelope in subtractive synthesis. The harder you play, the more FM modulation will result, thus causing a brighter sound. The Key parameter will cause the operator to play louder or softer (depending on the value you use) as you move into the higher registers of your keyboard. This is similar to the key-follow found in the filter sections of many subtractive synths.

The LFO

Moving to the right side of the Operator interface, you'll find the LFO section right at the top. On a synthesizer, an LFO is used to create repetitive automations for other parameters of the synth. On a subtractive synthesizer, LFOs will often be used to modulate the filter cut-off or the volume. The LFO of Operator can do this and much more.

To activate the LFO, turn it on with the little box to the left of its Waveform menu in the shell. Once active, you'll see all the parameters appear in the display. Pay close attention to the four lettered boxes matching the oscillators. By default, these are all turned on, and the four oscillators will all have their pitches modulated by the LFO. To get a feel for what you can do with this LFO, try turning off the routing to your carrier oscillator(s), and route the LFO to the modulators only.

An interesting feature of Operator's LFO is that it's not relegated to low-frequency (slow speed). The LFO's range can be adjusted with the tiny drop-down menu next to the wave shape. The options are *L* for low-frequency mode, *H* for high-frequency mode, and *S* for sync. In high-frequency mode, you can run it into audio range, thus making it available as another audio oscillator for your FM experiments.

The Filter

Coaxing your desired tone from an FM synth is not easy, especially for beginners. However, generating a complex waveform with FM is easy. The filter allows you to treat this complex FM waveform as the starting waveform for subtractive synthesis, taking advantage of the simplicity a classic filter offers. Thanks to Operator's FM capabilities, your arsenal of waveforms is nearly limitless.

Like the LFO, the filter must be turned on before it will have any effect. Do this by clicking the box just to the left of the Filter-Type menu. You'll see the center display spring to life with color, indicating that the filter is active. The filter contains the same six-parameter envelope as the operators and LFO that will modulate the Filter Cutoff frequency. The amount of envelope modulation is set with the Envelope parameter. The other parameters in the display determine how key position and velocity will affect the filter.

Operator has a total of 14 filters types, eight of which are the standard Ableton filters. The additional filters are the Ladder and SVF types in low, band, and hi-pass versions. These filter types both offer distinctly different pleasing tonal qualities, with the SVF offering the capability to self-oscillate with high-resonance values, and the Ladder type producing a sound modeled on some classic analog filter designs. (Moog comes to mind.) Make sure to experiment with them all.

In addition to the new filter types, Operator's filter also includes a saturator/waveshaper (found in the display). The Shaper menu offers you four types, two of them being classic saturation (Soft and Hard), and two being more unusual digital-sounding effects (Sine and 4-bit).

The Pitch Settings

Below the Filter section is the Pitch section, which contains an envelope, as well as some other unique pitch-related controls. To make the Pitch Envelope work, you'll have to switch it on using the switch at the left and turn the Pitch Env dial as well. You can use both positive and negative values here, so it's possible to reverse the effects of the envelope.

As with the LFO, you can choose which oscillators will be modulated with the Pitch envelope. Often, it's not necessary to modulate all the oscillators. Of course, if you don't modulate them all, you might get inharmonic results. However, this can be desirable on the attack of a sound, such as when making drum sounds.

> **CUT IT SHORT:** Make sure to explore Operator with your mouse's right button—it's jam-packed with all sorts of shortcuts. For example, the Frequency knob's context menu includes a Play by Key option that configures the filter to track the keyboard perfectly, while the oscillator display has an Export AMS option that exports a custom user waveform to an audio file with an .ams extension that can be used as a sound source for Sampler.

In the display of this section, you'll find the Glide setting, which is explained in the "Global Parameters" section at the top of this chapter.

The Global Settings

The last section of Operator contains Global Settings for the instrument. You're already familiar with the algorithms contained there, but there are still a few more things you should know.

First, the Time control. This knob adjusts the speed of all of the envelopes in Operator simultaneously. You can slow them down dramatically or speed them up to a point where you hardly notice them. This is a great tool for performing final tweaks to a sound you've mostly finished designing. It's also a great dial to tweak on presets, or to automate to add expressiveness to a sound.

To the right of the Time knob is the Tone knob, which is a handy way to tame high frequencies. Sometimes, a sound will sound okay at one pitch, but may sound harsh when played an octave or two higher. This is because FM synthesis is capable of producing extremely high overtones, which may sound unpleasant. Grab the Tone knob to get this under control.

Within the display for the Global Settings, below the algorithms, is Operator's routing matrix. This setting allows many different parameters to be modulated in a variety of ways, making this synthesizer dramatically more powerful than it was before.

The first item to notice here is located in the "Connection B" column and is marked Pitch. This is the Pitch Bend range, which is explained in the "Global Parameters" section.

Running vertically along the left side of the display are the various modulators that Operator can respond to: Velocity, Key, Aftertouch, Pitch Bend, and Mod Wheel. The menus and numeric values that appear across each row are for routing these modulators to specific parameters. For example, let's say you want the velocity of incoming notes to control the overall volume of Operator. To do this, just set Connection A in the Velocity row to Volume and set Amount A to specify how velocity sensitive you want the volume to be (70% is a good default value). Now, what if you want the velocity to control the waveshaper, too, so as you play harder, the notes also become more distorted. No problem: just set Amount B to Shaper Drive and set the amount as desired. Get the idea? You can use any of these five modulators to control two different parameters of your choice simultaneously.

Below the routing matrix, you'll see seven more parameters. The three parameters on the right are used to set the pan position of Operator's output, along with Key and Random modulator amounts. The Interpolation and Antialias controls are mostly there for backward compatibility with older versions of Operator, which did not have these settings. Leaving them on results in a smoother, more polished sound, at the cost of a slightly higher CPU load.

Sampler

Sampler is Simpler's big brother: a fully featured multisampling instrument with a full complement of modulation, filtering, and mapping options (see Figure 8.8).

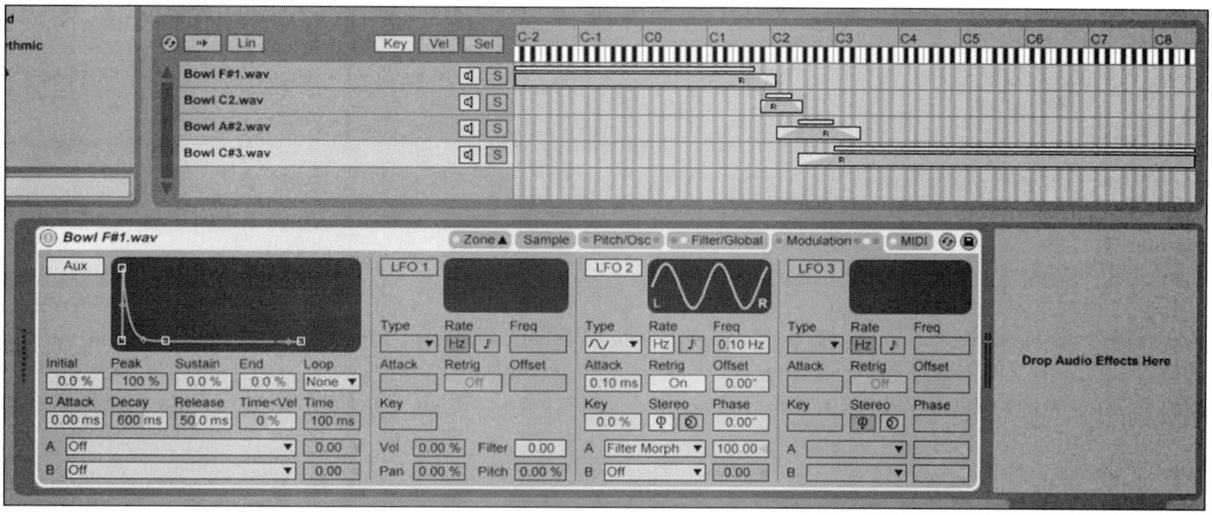

Figure 8.8 Ableton's Sampler unfolds to show a layer/zone editor.
Source: Ableton

Although Live has had basic sampling functions since the introduction of Simpler, Sampler vastly expands Live's sampling capabilities by introducing support for multisampling, as well as a wide range of sound-design and modulation options. What does this mean? Unlike Simpler, Sampler can hold many samples at once. Instead of simply transposing a single sample up or down the keyboard, multisampling uses many samples to capture the sound of an instrument at multiple points in its frequency and dynamic range.

The theory and practice of multisampling could fill an entire large book on its own. Setting up the intricate sample mapping required to accurately re-create the sound and feel of a complex acoustic instrument like a violin is an advanced topic that we can't really cover here in any depth. That's OK, because the main reason you'll encounter multisampling is with presets such as Live's Grand Piano. There are other, simpler creative uses of multisampling as well, which you can use to create your own sounds that have nothing to do with emulating acoustic instruments.

Looking at the Sampler interface, you'll see that its functions are organized into a number of different tabs, including Zone, Sample, Pitch/Osc, Filter/Global, Modulation, and MIDI. Let's have a look at each of these and see how they work.

The Zone Tab

Clicking the Zone tab brings up Sampler's Zone Editor. It's used to map samples across key and velocity ranges, and it appears above the main Sampler interface, as seen earlier in Figure 8.9. The Zone Editor opens in its own special window, directly above the Track View.

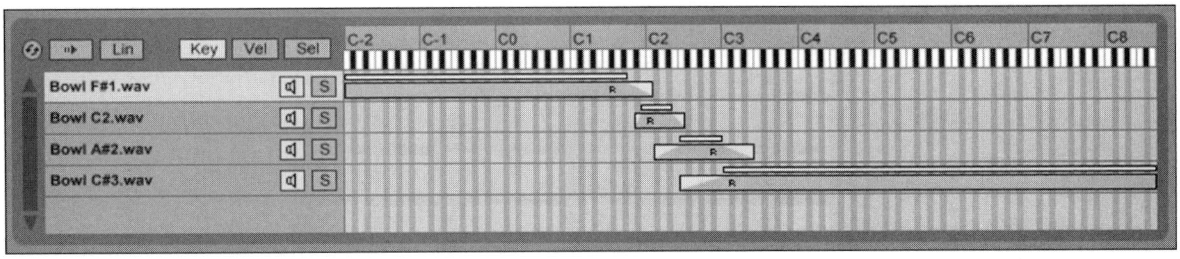

Figure 8.9 The Zone Editor showing key zones with crossfades.
Source: Ableton

On the left side of the Zone Editor is the sample layer list. All of the individual samples belonging to a given instrument will appear here, referred to as *layers*. For very large multisampled instruments, this list might be hundreds of layers long. (Note that selecting any layer by clicking it will load its sample into the Sample tab for examination.)

The next thing we'll look at is the Key Zone Editor, which is displayed by selecting the Key switch above the list. In Figure 8.9, I have created a custom instrument by importing four "kitchen bowl" samples; you can see here in the Zone Editor how the different samples are mapped across the keyboard. Samples are triggered only when incoming MIDI notes lie within their key zone. By default, the key zones of newly imported samples cover the full MIDI note range. Zones can be moved or resized by clicking and dragging in the middle or from their right or left sides. Zones can also be faded in or out over a number of semitones at either end by clicking and dragging the narrower small line above (refer to Figure 8.9). This makes it easy to set up smooth crossfades from zone to zone.

The Zone Editor can also be used to trigger samples according to velocity range. In Figure 8.10, there is a pad sound composed of three long samples, overlapped by velocity. The combination of samples you will actually hear when a note is played depends on the velocity of the triggering MIDI notes.

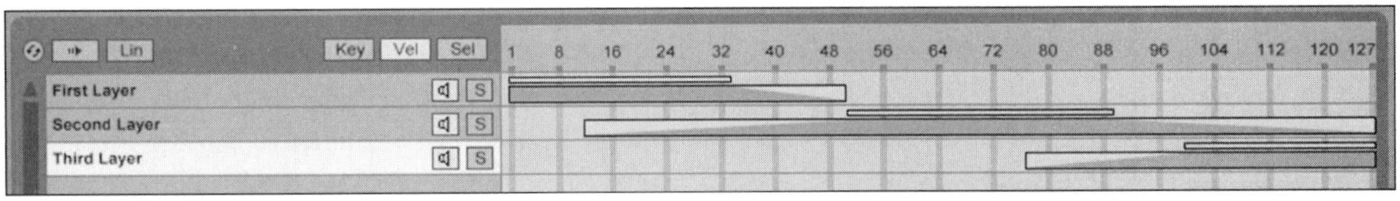

Figure 8.10 Velocity mapping in the Zone Editor.
Source: Ableton

The last option is the Sample Select Editor, which is shown by clicking the Sel switch. This is a very Ableton touch, and works like the Chain Selector in an Instrument or Effect Rack. As the sample selector (the horizontal orange bar above the editor) is moved from left to right, it enables the sample in the range shown in the editor. The Sample

Selector has 128 steps, so it's perfect for mapping to MIDI CCs. In the example shown in Figure 8.11, the selector can be moved to enable one of the three layers shown.

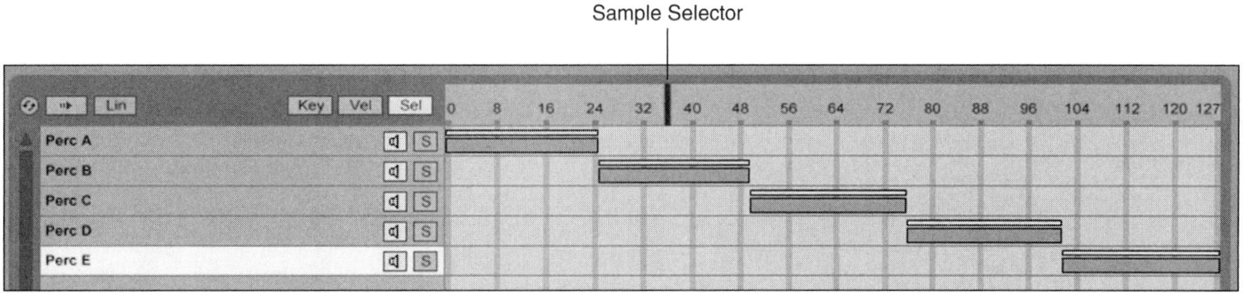

Sample Selector

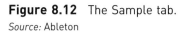

Figure 8.11 By using the Sample Select Editor, you can have loads of different samples at your fingertips just by turning a knob on your MIDI controller.
Source: Ableton

The Sample Tab

The Sample tab is where you can set the playback characteristics of individual samples. A large part of this tab is devoted to displaying the waveform of the sample you currently have selected (see Figure 8.12). The name of the sample is displayed below in the Sample drop-down chooser box. You can select a particular sample to edit by clicking it in the Zone Editor window, by using this chooser, or by clicking the Hot-Swap button next to the chooser, which will take you to the Browser and show you a list of samples used in the current instrument.

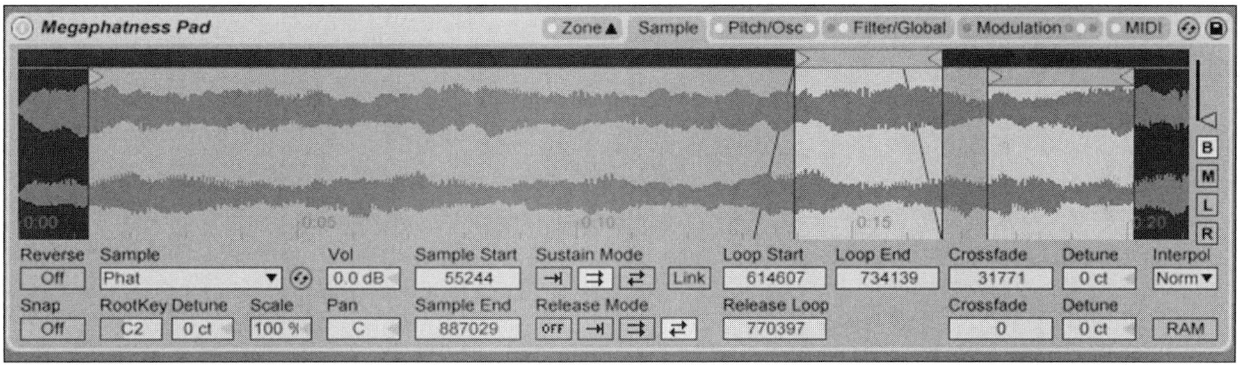

Figure 8.12 The Sample tab.
Source: Ableton

At first glance, the Sample tab appears similar to the display of Simpler, and it serves a similar function. However, Sampler gives you more power to control how each of your samples plays back and loops. Note that the settings in the Sample tab will affect only the sample (or multiple samples) that are currently selected in the Zone Editor.

▷ RootKey sets the reference pitch for the current sample. When a given sample is triggered by an incoming MIDI note matching the RootKey, it will be played back at its original pitch. MIDI notes higher or lower than the RootKey will transpose the sample accordingly.

▷ Detune makes fine adjustments to the sample tuning, +/−50 cents.

▷ Volume adjusts sample volumes individually.

▷ Pan adjusts the left-right position of individual samples.

▷ The Reverse button causes the entire multisample to play backward when triggered. In this case, sample playback begins from the sample end point and proceeds backward to the sample start point.

▷ When the Snap button is engaged, the start and end points of your sample will snap to the waveform zero-crossing points in order to avoid clicks or pops in playback.

To the right, the rest of the controls in the Sample tab work together with the Global Volume envelope in the Filter/Global tab to determine how your samples should be played back.

The Sample Start setting determines where the playback of the sample will begin when triggered, while the Sample End setting determines where playback will end.

Sustain and Release

The Sustain and Release modes are selected with the various arrow buttons located at the center of the area below the sample display. These determine how sample playback works during their respective phases of the ADSR volume envelope.

There are three Sustain Modes: On (single arrow), Loop (double arrow), and Loop Back and Forth (bidirectional arrows). When On is selected, the sample will play from beginning to end, until either it reaches the Sample End or the volume envelope (on the Filter/Global page) comes to the end of its release stage, whichever comes first.

With Loop enabled, the sample will play from the beginning until the loop end, at which point it will revert to the loop start and continue looping. Loop Back and Forth differs only in that when it reaches the loop end point, it will play backward until it reaches the loop start. Toggling the Link button automatically sets the sample start to the same point as the loop start and prevents them from being set to separate values.

Activating one of the looped Sustain Modes also allows you to modify the Release Mode, which determines what will happen during the release phase. When set to Off, the sustain loop simply continues through the release phase of the volume envelope. When set to On (single arrow), however, the sustain loop is disabled during the release phase, and the sample plays through to the end point.

Selecting one of the loop modes enables the Release Loop (notice the second loop brace to the right—refer to Figure 8.12), a separate loop with an end point fixed to the Sample End value. With either Loop (double arrow) or Loop Back and Forth (bidirectional arrows), the sustain loop is deactivated during the release phase, allowing the sample to play through to the end, at which point it loops back to the Release Loop point, until the end of the release phase.

Sustain Loop Crossfade (labeled *Crossfade*) sets fades at the loop boundaries in order to smooth out the loop. You can also use Sustain Loop Detune (labeled *Detune*) to make small adjustments in pitch as desired.

The Interpol (interpolation) control lets you decide which algorithm you want Sampler to use when transposing samples. You can choose from No, Normal (the default), Good, Better, or Best Interpolation. Your choice here can have a significant impact on the overall quality of sound coming out of Sampler, but you also need to remember that selecting Better or Best will increase the hit on your CPU.

You can engage the RAM mode switch if you want to load the entire multisampled instrument into your computer's RAM memory instead of streaming it from disk in real time (the default mode). This can be used to alleviate any disk overload problems you encounter when using Sampler, but if you have many samples loaded into RAM, this will eat up your available memory quickly and affect the performance of your computer/software adversely. (By default, Sampler will load only the beginning of each sound into memory at first and then stream the rest of the sound from your hard drive as it plays.)

The next tabs include a number of controls that shape and modify the sound of your samples. Let's look at what you can do with them.

The Pitch/Osc Tab

The Pitch/Osc tab (see Figure 8.13) contains a range of controls for Sampler's Modulation Oscillator and Pitch Envelope, which are used to modulate the audio output from the playback in the Sample tab.

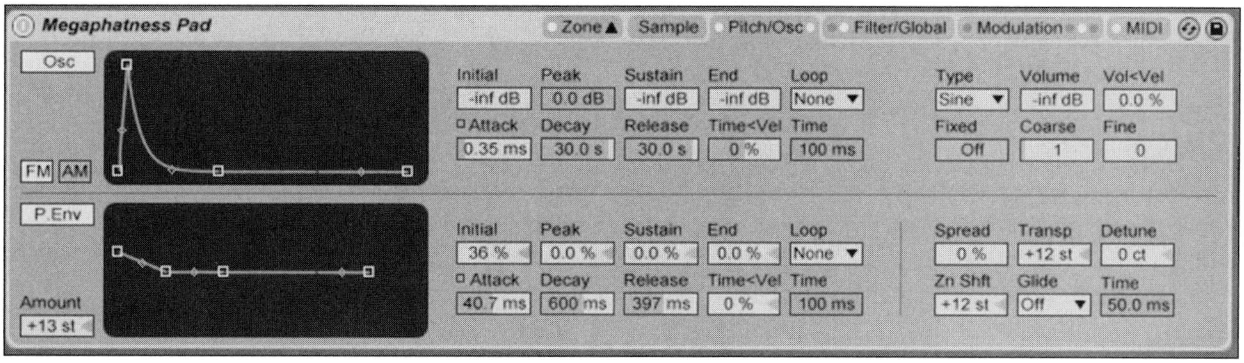

Figure 8.13 The Pitch/Osc tab.
Source: Ableton

The Modulation Oscillator

The upper part of the Pitch/Osc tab is occupied by the controls for Sampler's modulation oscillator. This oscillator makes no sound of its own, but it is used instead to modify your samples via frequency or amplitude (FM or AM) modulation. You can toggle between these two modes using the FM and AM buttons on the left side of the interface. If you use the modulation oscillator for amplitude modulation, you are affecting the volume; you can use this to create interesting tremolo effects or other more radical changes in volume. Used for frequency modulation, the modulation oscillator can transform your samples by creating FM-style effects reminiscent of Ableton's FM-based synth Operator, described in the previous section.

The Modulation oscillator's control interface features an image of an envelope at left, showing the ADSR envelope stages for the oscillator. If you select a long attack time here, then the effect of the oscillator will fade in slowly. You could use this with AM oscillation to create a tremolo effect that slowly fades in after a note is struck, for example. You can change the envelope settings by moving the breakpoints of the envelope itself or by adjusting the values in the readouts.

There are a range of waveforms to choose from for the modulation oscillator, including a selection of basic sine, sawtooth, and square waves. You can choose these in the drop-down chooser labeled Type. You can also adjust a number of parameters here to affect the speed and synchronization properties of the waveform, whether or not it is synced with the tempo of your project.

The Pitch Envelope

The lower part of the Pitch/Osc tab contains an additional set of controls for a separate pitch envelope. There is a graphical display for editing, as well as numerical controls. This envelope can be used to create pitch changes in your samples. The setting just to the left of the envelope, labeled Amount, will adjust the total amount of pitch-shifting effect in semitones.

The Filter/Global Tab

The Filter/Global tab (see Figure 8.14) contains the controls for Sampler's powerful morphing filter, as well as a Global volume envelope. Both of these affect the master output of Sampler.

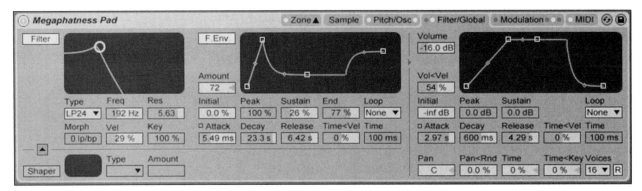

Figure 8.14 The Filter/Global tab.

Source: Ableton

The Filter

The filter in Sampler has a number of different modes available, including a Morphing filter (M) with 12dB and 24dB varieties, as well as standard low-pass, band-pass, and high-pass types. The Morphing filter is interesting in that it can smoothly transition from one filter type to another; for example, from low-pass to high-pass, sweeping across the frequency spectrum and resulting in some unusual filter shapes along the way. Try routing the Morph control to an external MIDI controller and automating it for some very interesting filter effects. The SVF filter type behaves like the Morphing filters, but it provides different tonal characteristics.

Of special notice in the filter section is the Shaper below. This offers the same distortion/waveshaping modes offered by Operator, with the additional option of changing its position in the signal path. Click the arrow directly above the Shaper switch to apply waveshaping before or after the filter. Try this out, and you'll see this is no small distinction. Just changing the order of operations here has a big impact on the sound.

The Volume Envelope

The volume envelope is a global envelope; it will affect how the final output of Sampler is heard. You have standard Attack, Decay, Sustain, and Release controls here, as well as an Initial setting that allows you to specify the volume at the moment the envelope is triggered.

Also notice the small blue handles in the graphical display, in between those representing the ADSR values. These can be dragged to change the envelope shape from linear to exponential. When dragged, you'll notice the controls below refresh to show numeric values for the slope you're drawing.

The Modulation Tab

The Modulation tab (see Figure 8.15) gives you four different modulation sources you can use to continuously modulate and change nearly any parameter in Sampler. There is a Modulation Envelope here, as well as three separate LFOs and a familiar range of controls.

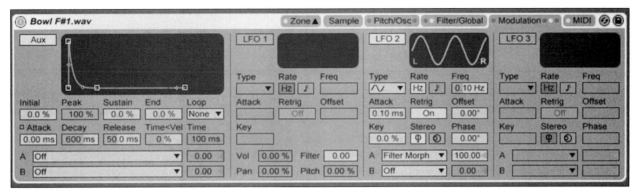

Figure 8.15 The Modulation tab.
Source: Ableton

Aux Envelope

The left-most section of this tab is the interface for the auxiliary envelope, which can be used to apply ADSR modulation to a variety of Sampler's parameters. It can be switched on by using the Aux button on the left edge of the interface. If you click the drop-down choosers labeled A and B at the bottom of this part, you will see a long list of other parameters in Sampler. Any of these can be selected as a destination to be modulated by the envelope. The A and B choosers enable you to select two simultaneous modulation targets to be affected.

LFOs

There are three LFOs here you can also use to modulate a wide variety of parameters in Sampler. The first one, labeled LFO1, has four particular global parameters: Volume, Filter, Pan, and Pitch. The other two, LFO2 and LFO3, can be freely assigned to a list of parameters in Sampler; just as with the Modulation Envelope, the A and B choosers enable you to select two simultaneous modulation targets to be affected by each LFO.

Each of these LFOs can be set up to sync to the tempo of your Live Set or be timed in cycles per second. You can choose which of these behaviors you want from each LFO by clicking on the Hz (Hertz) button or on the small button with a picture of a musical note just to the right of it. Then use the control to the right of this (labeled Freq or Beats, depending on which mode you have selected) to set the exact frequency of the oscillator. You can select from a variety of standard waveforms for each LFO, such as square, sawtooth, and sine waves.

Additionally, the LFOs can be forced to start from the beginning of the cycle every time a key is pressed by enabling the Retrig switch. With this turned off, the LFO will run freely. The Offset control is particularly useful when using a synced LFO. For example, let's say you're modulating a low-pass filter so that it rises to its peak value on every quarter note. By changing Offset to 90, you'll invert the pattern, so the peak frequency occurs on every offbeat instead.

The MIDI Tab

I'm sure you won't be surprised when I tell you that the MIDI tab (see Figure 8.16) is the place where you set up MIDI modulation routings for Sampler. Here, you can use various MIDI parameters as modulation inputs and use them to affect various parameters in Sampler. Let's look at how to do this.

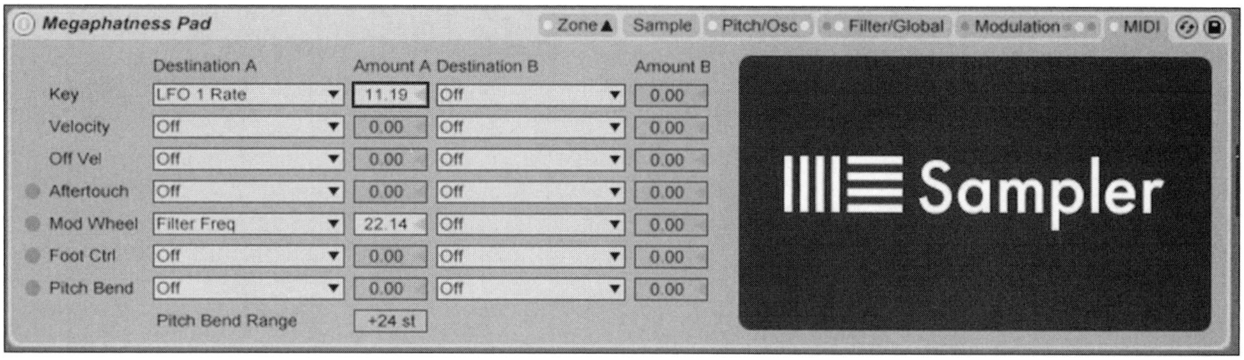

Figure 8.16 The MIDI tab.
Source: Ableton

The interface here allows you to take the MIDI input from a number of specific parameters. The MIDI parameters available as sources for modulations are listed along the left-hand edge of the tab, including Key (pitch), Velocity, Off Vel (release velocity), Chan Pres (aftertouch), Mod Wheel, and Pitch Bend. Any of these input sources can be mapped to two different modulation destinations simultaneously, using the Destination A and Destination B drop-down choosers. You can set the amount of modulation with the Amount A and Amount B controls. By routing the Velocity parameter to control volume, you can make your samples play back more loudly or softly when those channels receive higher or lower MIDI velocity messages, or, for example, when you play harder or softer on your MIDI controller keyboard. (Note that you can also do this with the Vol<Vel control on the Filter/Global page.)

Importing Third-Party Instruments

As mentioned previously, if you already own any collections of multisampled instruments in AKAI, GigaStudio, Apple ESX24/Garageband, SoundFont, or Kontakt format, you can import these into Sampler for easy access in Live. To import a third-party instrument preset into Sampler, locate the file in the Browser and double-click to convert it to a Sampler preset. If this doesn't work, you may be able to open the preset by dragging it from the Browser and dropping it onto Sampler. You can see all of your imported instruments in the Instruments view under Sampler > Imported.

Some more complex multisampled instruments will be converted to Instrument Rack presets using multiple instances of Sampler in order to better translate the sound of the original. For most multisample formats, Live will import the audio samples into the Library, where they will appear as new samples under Samples > Imported. However, note that in the case of Apple EXS24/GarageBand and Kontakt multisample formats, Live will create new Sampler presets that reference the original WAV or AIF sample files. This means that they will not work if you remove the original WAV or AIF samples. (However, Live's File Manager also offers the option to collect and save these external samples into the Library, if desired.)

The AAS Instruments

The remainder of Live's built-in instruments are developed in partnership with Applied Acoustic Systems, a software company that specializes in modeling technology. Physical modeling concerns itself with creating mathematical equations that imitate or "model" the behavior of real-world acoustical events. Three of these synthesizers—Collision, Electric, and Tension—are based on familiar physical processes: hammers hitting tone bars and guitar picks plucking strings, for example. Analog, on the other hand, models behavior that goes on under the hood of an analog synthesizer, so from a synthesis standpoint, it's going to be a bit more familiar.

While this may sound fairly pedestrian, get ready for a major paradigm shift if you've never worked with a physical modeling synth before. Because you'll be working with controls that model physical events, you'll need to be aware that many of the parameters affect each other dramatically. Especially in the case of Tension, it's possible to create patches that don't create any sound at all! You'll need to think more in terms of inventing and playing an instrument, rather than twiddling knobs. (Will a very smooth bow moved very quickly across a violin string with very little force produce any sound? What if you move it slowly?)

Electric

Electric, the simplest of the physical modeling instruments, is an electric-piano emulator (see Figure 8.17). Instead of reproducing actual electric pianos through sampling, physical modeling is used instead. This means that sound is produced via mathematical equations representing the various physical aspects of the instrument itself.

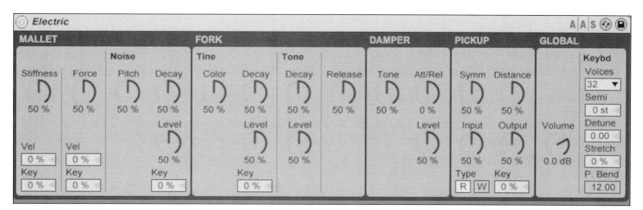

Figure 8.17 Electric gives you the power to design a wide array of electric pianos.
Source: Ableton

Electric's interface is divided into four sections dedicated to different aspects of how an electric piano produces sound: the mallet, the metal fork that gets struck by the mallet, the damper that controls the tine's resonance, and the magnetic pickup that converts the sound into electricity. The fifth section, Global, deals with overall instrument settings that aren't electric piano specific.

Mallet

This section controls the characteristics of the mallet, or hammer, that causes the metal fork to vibrate. Stiffness represents how hard the surface of the mallet is, so lower values will produce a gentler attack, while higher values will tend to make the sound more percussive and less full bodied. Force is the speed at which the mallet hits the fork, with higher values tending to produce more overdrive and "growl." Since both of these controls affect how much the fork is made to vibrate, they interact with each other closely. For example, both values affect the overall volume of the sound, but in different ways. A very hard mallet hitting the fork with a small amount of force will tend to produce a hard attack, but a relatively weak overall sound. A soft mallet hitting a fork very hard will produce a much fuller sound at a similar volume to the first setting, but with a much weaker attack. Both of these parameters can be modulated by both the velocity and the pitch of incoming MIDI notes. This is where physical modeling gets interesting. It's fairly intuitive to see that modulating the force with velocity will create a real-world situation, whereby more force is applied as you strike the key harder. However, we are also given the option of making our electric piano's hammers get harder as we play louder (or softer if you want).

The Noise subsection models the noise of the hammer hitting the fork, so it also affects the attack of the piano sound. Noise, however, is independent of the tone that the fork produces. Think of it as an additional percussive attack that you can blend in using the Level control to give the sound more definition. To get a better understanding of how Noise affects the sound, turn both of the Level controls in the Fork section down to 0% and play with the noise Pitch and Decay.

Fork

Some electric pianos, such as those made by Yamaha, use actual strings to produce sound—just like an acoustic piano. The most familiar electric piano sound, however, is the sound of a hammer striking a metal tuning fork—the design of the famous Rhodes piano. The tuning fork consists of two distinct parts: a stiff metal wire (the "tine") and a tuned metal resonator (the "tone bar"). The tine is struck by the hammer, and it causes the resonator to vibrate, creating a distinct pitch.

To understand how the Tine and Tone subsections of the fork work, start by turning the Level control for Tone to 0% and the Level and Decay for the Tine to 100%. This will allow you to hear clearly only the Tine portion of the sound. It sounds very much like you might imagine a hammer hitting a stiff wire—a high frequency "ping" with very little body to the sound. Increasing the Color control will bring out more of the higher frequencies, while reducing it will make the sound darker. The Decay control can be used to make the sound range from a short percussive hit to a drawn-out ring.

Once you have a handle on the Tine part of the sound, the Tone section is fairly self-explanatory. This is obviously the sound of the tuned resonator that produces the lion's share of the piano's tone. Again, you can get familiar with this aspect of the piano's sound by turning down the Level control in the other sections and listening to it by itself. The Decay control adjusts how long the note rings out while the key is held down, while the Release determines how long the note rings after the key is released. Don't expect to hear long release times like you would with a synth, however. Because we're modeling the behavior of a vibrating piece of metal in contact with a damper (see below), the release time is necessarily fairly short.

Damper

In a real electric piano, the dampers control the sustain feature of a note. When a key is struck, the same mechanism that moves the mallet also moves the damper away from the fork so it can resonate. When the key is released, the damper moves back into place, causing the tone bar to stop ringing. In the Damper section, you can control both the hardness of the damper surface and the noise made by the dampers moving back and forth.

As the Tone value is increased, harder dampers are modeled, and the damper noise becomes brighter and more pronounced. The Att/Rel knob controls whether damper noise is heard on the attack or the release of the note, with −100% being attack only, 100% being release only, and 0% being both. To hear what the Damper section is doing, it's easiest if you crank the Att/Rel knob to 0% or greater so it sounds when the note is released. The damper noise on the attack is much harder to hear since it is masked by the attack of the piano. Also, it's important to note that the amount of damper noise heard can be affected greatly by the Pickup settings.

Pickup

Much like an electric guitar, the vibrations produced by a mallet-striking fork are converted into an electrical signal through the use of a pickup, so they can be amplified. The Pickup section customizes the design and position of the pickup, which has a huge impact on the final sound. Before looking at the knobs, you'll want to turn your attention to the pickup type (the R and W buttons in the lower left-hand corner of the Pickup section). When set to W, the pickups have the high-end bite typical of the electrostatic pickups in a Wurlitzer piano. The R setting has the pronounced mids and full low-end associated with a Rhodes piano's magnetic pickups.

To get familiar with the Symm and Distance controls, start out with Distance at 100% and Symm at 0%. Symm controls the pickup's symmetry in relation to the fork. At 50%, the pickup is centered directly in front of the tine. Moving the knob to the left moves the pickup increasingly above the tine, emphasizing the higher harmonics, while moving it to the right shifts the pickup position lower, emphasizing lower harmonics. Note the dramatic change as you sweep symmetry from 0 to 100%.

Distance controls how far from the fork the pickup is. The farther away the pickup is from the fork, the more spectrally balanced the sound will be, while moving it closer will emphasize the frequencies produced by the part of the fork it is closest to and will produce more overdrive. Adjusting the distance has a different effect, depending on what type of pickup you are using. In the case of the W pickup, decreasing the distance will increase the high-end bite and decrease the amount of bass overall. The R pickup works a little differently. First, watch your speakers and your ears, because decreasing the distance of the R pickup increases the volume of the sound. As the R pickup is moved closer, there is an overall increase in drive and intensity in the highs and mids without much low-end attenuation.

Global

The Global section gives you control over the overall characteristics of Electric. For information on this section, see the "Global Parameters" section, earlier in this chapter.

Tension

Tension is the most interesting and unusual beast of the AAS Ableton instruments (see Figure 8.18). As a "string-modeling" synth, it takes the modeling concepts that you saw in Electric to a whole different level. Where Electric models a specific type of instrument, Tension applies modeling generically to the entire range of stringed instruments, ranging from cellos to pianos. The many parameters offered by this instrument also give you the opportunity to create some bizarre-sounding instruments that could never exist in the real world.

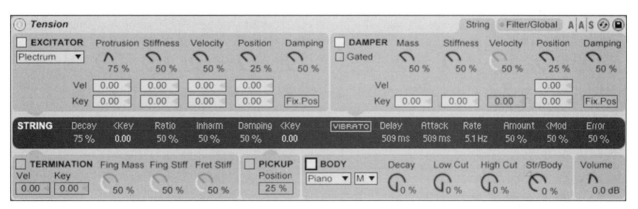

Figure 8.18 Tension allows you to create stringed instruments of many different types, including oddities such as a violin played with piano hammers.

Source: Ableton

The Tension interface is broken into several sections modeling different aspects of a stringed instrument: the Excitator that causes the string to vibrate; the Damper that reduces the string's vibrations; and the Termination, which emulates the effects of fingers and frets, the type and size of the instrument's body, the pickup for emulating electric instruments, and finally the string itself. Tension also features a second page of parameters for the filter and other aspects of the instrument not related to string modeling.

Note that each section has an on/off switch next to the section name, allowing you to bypass a set of parameters completely. While learning how to use Tension, it's going to be helpful to turn off other sections while learning a new one. It's a necessary evil (or benefit) of modeling that many parameters closely interact with each other. For example, a bow that is applied to a string with very little force will only produce sound if the bow is moved very slowly. There are many such interactions in this instrument.

Excitator

This section deals with one of the most fundamental aspects of any stringed instrument: the physical relationship between the string and the object that "excites" it into motion. Here you can choose to use a bow, a piano hammer, or a plectrum (pick) to get your sound going. Depending on the Excitator you choose from the menu, you'll be presented with different parameters for defining the object you've chosen and the way that it's used. With this section turned off, you'll probably get no sound at all out of Tension, although it is possible to create sounds that consist of damper noise and the string's decay.

For a bow, you'll first see the parameters for Force (how hard the bow is pushed against the string) and for Friction (the amount that the bow material naturally resists the string). Velocity determines the speed at which the bow is moving, while Position moves the bow all the way from the string's end (0%) to its midpoint (50%).

Hammers have a totally different set of parameters. You can adjust the mass and stiffness of the hammer, followed by the speed at which it hits the string (Velocity) and the hammer's location (Position). The final control, Damping, controls the stiffness of the mechanism that brings the hammer into contact with the string. At higher values, the action is very "springy," so the hammer bounces right off the string, allowing it to vibrate loudly. At lower values, the hammer action is very stiff, muting the string somewhat as it lands firmly upon it.

Hammer (bouncing) simulates a hammer that is dropped onto the string and allowed to bounce multiple times. Again, here you see a complex interaction of forces. Generally speaking, the velocity is going to have the largest effect on how much the hammer bounces, with low values producing little volume, a series of rapid bounces that can become as subtle as a slight buzz, and the highest values emulating the behavior of a hammer dropped from a very great height, producing a long trail of bounces with several seconds between the initial attack and the first bounce.

A plectrum is a fancy name for a guitar pick. It has the same set of parameters as a hammer, with the exception of protrusion, which replaces mass. Protrusion specifies the amount of the surface of the pick that comes in contact with the string. Lower values mean just the tip of the pick is being used to pluck the string, while higher values use more of the pick and result in a louder sound.

Damper

The Damper section controls how the string is made to stop vibrating. In the case of a piano, it emulates the behavior of the felt dampers coming into contact with the strings when the key is released (and the sustain pedal is off). In the case of a guitar, the damper could be the guitarist reducing the pressure on the string with the fingering hand or using the palm of the strumming hand to mute the strings.

Looking at the Damper's controls, you'll see that they are the same as those of the hammer in the "Excitator" section. This makes sense, because the sound produced by the damper is affected by all of the same qualities—the overall mass, the stiffness of the damper's surface, the velocity with which it comes into contact with the string, and its position along the length of the string. The final control, Damping, determines how stiff the damper mechanism is.

String

Here is where you'll set the properties of the string itself. The Decay and Ratio work closely with one another. The Decay setting controls both the string's initial decay time (right after the attack) and the release time (after the key is released). With Ratio set to 0, the string's decay will begin after the note is struck and continue to decay naturally, regardless of how quickly the key is released. At 100, the note will decay naturally as long as the key is held down, but will cut off abruptly as soon as the key is released. To get a better sense of this, set Decay to a high value and then experiment with different Ratio values, making sure to test each value with both a long key press and a short one.

The Key value can also be used to control how much note pitch will modulate the decay time. The trick here is that since you're modeling real-world strings, lower notes will always decay longer than higher ones. (Just imagine what happens when you hit the lowest note and the highest note on a piano with the sustain pedal on.) The Key control modulates this natural behavior. So by raising this value, you can make the higher notes ring longer and the lower notes shorter than they usually would. Lowering the Key value will exaggerate the instrument's natural decay behavior.

The Inharmonic and Damper controls both affect the tone of the instrument in dramatic ways. Inharmonic controls how much the upper partials of the string are out of tune with the harmonic series. As opposed to a theoretical perfect string that produces a perfectly pure tone, strings in the real world have inharmonic qualities. Depending on the Excitator you are using, you'll notice different effects from increasing this value. With a bow, the upper frequencies of the sound will become more like noise, whereas a hammered string will simply begin to sound more out of tune with itself as the higher harmonics are detuned.

Termination and Pickup

Termination applies to stringed instruments that are fingered. In other words, an individual string is "terminated" or ended on one of its ends by a finger, and possibly a fret, as opposed to a piano or a dulcimer, where the strings are fixed between two pegs and tuned to the desired pitch.

The Finger Mass refers to the force that is being applied with the finger. At lower values, the pitch becomes less distinct as the string is terminated in a less stable fashion. If Fret Stiffness is increased with a low Finger Mass setting, you will hear the string buzzing against the fret, much like it did during your first guitar lesson. With a low Fret Stiffness, you'll generally get a less distinct pitch from the string—unless, that is, you increase the Finger Stiffness to compensate for the lack of clear frets on the neck.

Switching on the Pickup section changes the sound from that of an acoustic instrument to the output of a magnetic pickup. The Position control changes the location of the pickup. At 0, the pickup is placed at the string's termination point, much like the bridge pickup on an electric guitar. As the value is increased to 50, the pickup is moved closer to the midpoint of the string, more like an electric guitar's neck pickup.

Body

The Body serves two purposes in the creation of our modeled string instruments. First, the instrument body acts as an amplifier of the strings' vibrations, which can add additional fullness and a longer decay to the sound. The Body also filters the frequencies that it radiates, further coloring the final sound.

To get an understanding of the different body types, try experimenting with different ones, first setting High and Low Cut to 0 and setting the Str/Body ratio to 100 (all body sound, no direct string sound). Turning up the Decay as well will tend to exaggerate the effect of the body and make its effects even clearer. As you might expect, a piano body offers the smoothest response across the frequency spectrum, while the violin body tends to bring out the higher frequencies more. Next to the Body Type menu, there is a menu to select the size, ranging from extra small to extra large. Larger body sizes tend to make the instrument sound more diffuse and farther away, while smaller sizes make the instrument sound closer and more present.

Filter/Global

The Filter section (see Figure 8.19) is located on Tension's second page of parameters and consists of a multimode filter that can be modulated with both an envelope and an LFO. In addition to the common filter types, you'll also find a formant filter (F6 and F12 in the Filter menu), which is a filter modeled on the resonance of the human vocal tract. Adjusting the resonance of this filter sweeps through the vowel sounds A, E, I, O, U and is capable of producing some very powerful resonant frequencies, so be prepared to lower the output volume, or you may find yourself running into some nasty distortion. Below the Frequency and Resonance controls, you'll find additional controls to specify how much you want these values to be modulated by the envelope and the LFO.

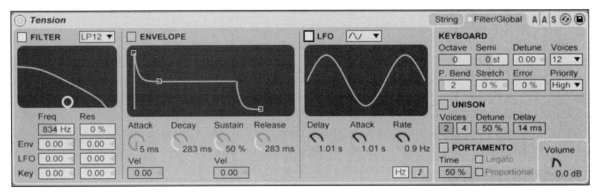

Figure 8.19 The Filter section can be used to give some additional flavor to your modeled string instruments.
Source: Ableton

For the Global parameters, see the "Global Parameters" section earlier in this chapter.

Analog

Analog is Ableton's take on a classic subtractive synthesizer (see Figure 8.20). Two oscillators and a noise generator feed two filters and two output amplifiers. There are two independent LFOs that can be used to modulate nearly any aspect of the sound, and each module has its own envelope section as well. So much has been written about the principles of subtractive syntheses that instead of covering all of this ground for the millionth time, we're going to focus most of our energy in this section on what makes this little synth unique.

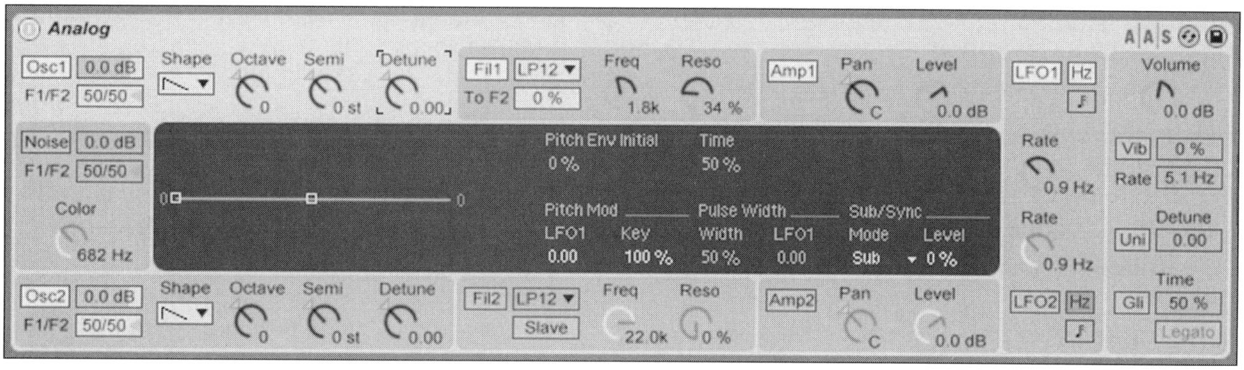

Figure 8.20 Analog is a powerful analog-style subtractive synthesizer.
Source: Ableton

Analog's interface is similar to Operator in that it is divided into a series of modules that surround a center window that will be updated to provide additional parameters for whichever module is currently selected. Again, here we will use the terminology *shell* to refer to the basic controls in the outer ring of the interface and *display* to refer to the center window.

The modules for Analog are as follows: two oscillators, a noise generator, two filters and amplifiers, the LFOs, and finally the Master. Clicking anywhere in any of these modules will change Analog's display to show its envelopes, LFO routing, or any other parameters that may apply. Finally, also note that the name of each section (for example, Osc1) is also a switch that can be used to turn the module on or off.

Oscillators and Noise

The oscillators are where the sound begins. In the Osc modules, you can select the shape of the waveform, adjust its volume and tuning, and set whether it gets routed to Filter 1, Filter 2, or both. The default value for filter routing is 50/50, meaning the signal is split equally between both filters. Dragging up or down in this control will show the ratio of how much signal is distributed to each filter until the display reads F1 (Filter 1 only) or F2 (Filter 2 only), at which point the signal is no longer split between the two filters.

With the Osc1 or Osc2 module selected, the display contains controls for adjusting the oscillator's pitch, pulse width, and optional Sub or Sync oscillator. The graphical display on the left displays the pitch envelope, which is used to make the oscillator's pitch rise or fall into its target pitch. This display corresponds to the Pitch Env Initial (the starting pitch) and Time (how long it takes to reach the final pitch) controls, seen to the right. Below, you can determine if the pitch is to be modulated by the LFO. The LFOs are "hardwired" to their corresponding oscillators—Osc1 can only be modulated by LFO1, and Osc2 can only be modulated by LFO2.

The Pulse Width section is only enabled when a square wave is selected as the waveform shape. Try sweeping this from 0 to 100, and you'll hear the tone go from being narrow and pinched to big and fat. Modulating the Pulse Width with the LFO is a great way to add some subtle movement to your sound. Note that unless the LFO is actually switched on, the LFO modulation amount will be disabled.

Hidden within each Oscillator module is a second oscillator that can be controlled via the Sub/Sync section. When Mode is set to Sub, an additional note will sound one octave below the pitch of the main oscillator. The volume of the Sub tone is set by the Level control. If you want some real nastiness, however, try setting Mode to Sync. When set to Sync, the additional oscillator is not heard directly. Rather, it is used to control the main oscillator by forcing it to restart from the beginning of the waveform for each cycle of the Sync oscillator. This changes the harmonic content of the main oscillator, with the pitch and intensity increasing as you increase the Ratio (the frequency of the sync oscillator).

Finally, in between the two oscillators is the Noise module, a sound generator that produces white noise. Noise has many uses—not only in producing percussion sounds, but also for adding a bit of extra attack or texture to an otherwise dark sound. All of the controls for Noise are located in the shell. The filter routing works just like it does for the oscillators, and the Color control is a simple low-pass filter that can be used to reduce the high-frequency content of the noise.

Filters and Amplifiers

Once the sound wave leaves the Oscillator module, it proceeds on to the filters. While filters are an essential part of most sounds, strictly speaking they do not need to be used. Both Filter modules can be turned off, and Analog will work just fine. Which filter will be used to shape your sound is determined by the filter routing in the Oscillator modules.

While the two filters are essentially identical, they do have a few subtle differences. Both have menus for selecting a filter type and the usual frequency and resonance controls. The first difference between the two is that Filter 1 has a control called To F2, which can be used to send the output of Filter 1 to Filter 2. This gives you the option of running the two filters in series (one after another) instead of in parallel. To fully understand what is possible here, it's also important to understand that the filters and the amps are hard wired to each other—in other words, Filter 1 is passed to Amp 1 automatically, while the same holds true for Filter 2 and Amp 2. So, even if you route Filter 1 to Filter 2, it will still be going to Amp 1.

Let's look at an example. For starters, we'll assume that you have both filters and both amps turned on, and that both of your oscillators are routed to Filter 1 only. Filter 1 is set to send 100% of its signal to Filter 2. This causes the output of Filter 1 to be sent both to Amp 1 *and* Filter 2, because the "To F2" control is a send—it taps the signal and passes it to the second filter without interrupting the signal flow to Amp 1. This means that if you want to truly hear the filters operate in series, you need to turn Amp 1 off completely. Now the signal will flow from Filter 1 to Filter 2 to Amp 2 and then on to the master output. If you leave Amp 1 turned on, you'll hear a combination of the output of Filter 1 along with the output of Filter 1 and Filter 2 running in series.

Filter 2 features a Slave switch, which allows its cutoff frequency to be controlled from Filter 1. With Slave enabled, the Frequency control of Filter 2 controls the difference between the two cutoff frequencies. This could be used to create a dual filter with two peaks that are always the same distance apart. Then, whenever Filter 1 is modulated, whether manually or by an LFO, Filter 2 will follow it.

With either of the filters selected, Analog's display will display options for the envelope (see below), as well as a few other options. Selecting a drive mode will cause the filter to overdrive, with the Asymmetrical modes tending to create a more harmonically rich-sounding distortion and the Symmetrical modes being a bit on the nastier side. The Freq Mod and Res Mod sections specify how much the filters frequency and resonance are modulated by the LFOs, the pitch (Key), and the envelope. The display looks nearly identical when the Amp modules are selected, the only difference being there is no Drive control, and the Modulation section applies to Volume and Pan.

Filters and Amp Envelopes

Since the envelope sections for the filters and the amplifiers are identical in design, we'll discuss them both together. The envelope is an ADSR (Attack, Decay, Sustain, Release) envelope that can be adjusted either by dragging the breakpoints in the graphical display or by changing the values in the numerical display to the right. In the numerical part of the Envelope display, you'll see one special value in addition to the usual ADSR values: Sustain Time. The standard Sustain value is a decibel level—the volume that the note sustains while you hold the key down. By default, Sustain Time is set to "inf," meaning that the note will sustain indefinitely as long as the key is held. Sustain Time specifies a length of time that the note will decay over, even if the note is held down.

At the far right of the envelope display, you'll see the Loop menu, which creates some very interesting variations to your sound. By selecting one of the Loop modes, you'll be telling Analog to repeat a part of the envelope instead of playing it through start to finish. AD-R will repeat the Attack and Decay portions of the envelope until the key is released, while ADR-R will repeat the Release portion as well. This makes it possible to use the envelope as more of an LFO, cycling through a series of values. When ADS-AR is selected, the envelope works normally until the key is released, at which point the Attack portion repeats before the Release, which could be used to create an additional swelling or short attack at the end of each note.

Looking to the left, there are a few switches above the graphical display that are worth mentioning. First, the Linear and Exponential switches are used to control the type of slope that occurs between the envelope's breakpoints. Linear slopes are increments or decrements in value that change at a constant rate over the time of the envelope segments (which is a fancy way of saying they are straight lines!). Exponential slopes start out as straight lines but curve more dramatically toward their destination point as they get closer. Because exponential curves tend to approach their target value very quickly before curving, they sound shorter than linear envelopes. The Legato switch may take a moment to understand, but it's well worth it. When enabled, instead of the envelope starting over every time a new note sounds, the envelope will continue if the two notes overlap. In other words, if a new note is played while another is held down, the new note's envelope will start at the existing note's envelope position instead of beginning from the attack phase. Finally, the Free switch can be used to bypass the Sustain portion of the envelope. Since the envelope will now jump from the decay to the release phase, it will always be the same, regardless of how long the note is held. The most common example of a Free envelope is a percussion sound—a short attack and decay phase immediately followed by a release.

> **MAKING FILTER ENVELOPES WORK:** If you're finding that adjusting the filter envelope isn't doing anything, it's probably because you haven't entered a value in either of the envelope (Env) fields for the filter. Unlike the volume envelope (which works automatically), you have to specify how much the filter envelope should be modulating the filter's frequency or resonance, or it won't do anything at all! In the display, enter an envelope amount under Freq Mod or Res Mod to specify how much the filter should be modulated by the envelope. Bear in mind that the frequency or resonance value shown in the shell is the starting value for the filter. The Env field can then be set to a positive or negative value to indicate whether the envelope should be increasing or decreasing that value as the envelope plays.

LFO

The two LFOs are completely independent of each other and can be used to control a variety of other parameters, as discussed in the previous sections. The only control here is the Rate, since the LFO amount is controlled within the module that it is being used to modulate. The rest of the controls for the LFO are located in the center window.

Use the Wave and Width selectors to control the shape of the LFO. When the Triangle wave is selected, the Width control can be used to change the wave shape to ramp up or ramp down. With Rectified selected and Width at 50%, the LFO is a square wave, while modulating Width in either direction changes the pulse width. Retrig (the R switch) controls whether or not the LFO starts over (is "retriggered") with each key press.

Offset is used to adjust the phase of the wave. With a tempo-synced LFO, this could be used to move the peaks of the wave that occur before or after the beat. Delay will wait a specified length of time after a keypress to begin the LFO, while Attack will cause the amplitude of the wave to fade in over the amount of time specified.

Global

Most of Analog's Global parameters are covered in the "Global Parameters" section earlier in this chapter, but a few things warrant special attention. The first switch in this section turns Vibrato on or off. Vibrato is a simple LFO that modulates the pitch of the oscillators. Only two controls are available here: the Amount, which controls the depth of the modulation, and the Rate, which controls the speed. The last switch in this section is marked "Gli" for Glide. For information on Glide, refer to the "Portamento" section, earlier in this chapter.

At the left-hand side of the display, you'll see some colored boxes. These are Quick Routing schemes, which can help speed the process of setting up a new patch. Unlike the similar-looking algorithms in Operator, these shortcuts are just timesavers—all they do is set the filter routing and turn the amplifiers on and off. For example, clicking on Quick Routing 4 (in the lower right-hand corner) sends both oscillators into Filter 1, the output of Filter 1 into Filter 2, and turns off Amp 1 so that only the output of Amp 2 is heard.

Collision

Collision takes the concept of designing percussion sounds to a whole new level (see Figure 8.21). Just as Tension can be used to create either familiar stringed instruments or otherworldly beasts, Collision is just as much at home producing the sound of a marimba or, let's say, a hybrid hand drum/metal tube with a decay of 25 seconds!

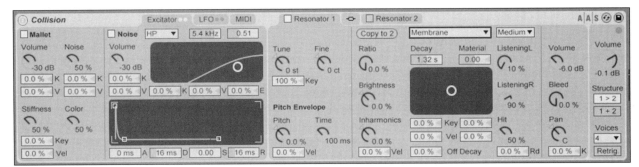

Figure 8.21 Collision: Ableton's percussion powerhouse.
Source: Ableton

Before getting too deeply into the unique details of Collision, I recommend that you at least read over the section on Electric. It's a far simpler instrument that covers some of the important concepts of physical modeling, and since an electric piano is essentially a percussion instrument, it's particularly relevant here. Tension also contains some important concepts that we'll be discussing here, too. In particular, Tension uses the concept of a designable Excitator—namely, an object with changeable characteristics that is used to strike a resonating object. In the case of Tension, the struck object is some sort of string. In Collision, it's a variety of different objects associated with different kinds of percussion instruments. For the initial experiments here, find the menu in the Resonators section that contains the different resonator types and set it to Plate.

The first similarity to Electric that you'll notice in Collision is the presence of percentage boxes marked Key and Vel (sometimes K and V to save space), located below a number of the controls. These are here to map the controls so they follow the velocity of the incoming MIDI messages or the pitch. Negative values are allowed here as well, so you can have controls change in inverse proportion to velocity and key.

Excitators

The Excitator section of Collision is broken into two parts: Mallet and Noise. Mallet is fairly straightforward. Looking at the far left, you'll see Volume and Stiffness. Stiffness controls the relative softness or hardness of the mallet. You'll find that as you increase it from 0%, the sound generally gets louder and brighter up until around 60%, after which the sound continues getting brighter, but the overall loudness is decreased as it starts producing fewer low harmonics. The Volume control simply controls the overall level of the Mallet excitator. The only reason this is needed is because there is a second, entirely independent excitator, and you may need to balance the relative levels of the two. For now, just make sure that it is turned up loud enough for you to hear Collision's output clearly.

Moving over to the next column of knobs, you'll see Noise and Color. *Noise* refers to the sound that is made by the mallet coming into contact with the resonating object. So, for this to make sense, you have to think of the sound as containing two distinct sounds—the initial impact of the objects colliding, followed by the resonance of the struck object. Like the Mallet's Stiffness control, the Noise parameter tends to decrease low harmonics and overall volume above 60%. Try this experiment: Park the Stiffness and Color controls at about 50% and Noise at 0%. Slowly increase the Noise control until you can start to hear a flinty "chiff" sound in the initial impulse. Now, turn down the Stiffness. You'll hear the fundamental pitch of the resonator get less distinct and the noise component of the sound will become much clearer and more noticeable. Next, sweep the Color control back and forth, and you'll be able to clearly hear how this adjusts the harmonic content of the noise.

The next section over is the Noise excitator, which can be turned on by clicking in the box next to the word *Noise*. This is a slightly strange beast because, while it acts as a physical object that causes the resonator to vibrate, it does not have any real-world counterpart. Rather, it's an imaginary object that consists only of a burst of noise. It can be used in conjunction with, or instead of, the Mallet excitator. Just bear in mind that you must use one or the other if you want Collision to produce any sound at all.

For now, turn off the Mallet excitator so you can hear the Noise section on its own. You'll find that this produces a similar sound to the Noise control we worked with previously, but it is far more customizable. When you first turn it on, you may not notice much sound coming out. If this is the case, increase the Volume control and also have a look at the Filter section immediately to the left. As you increase the cutoff frequency of the low-pass filter (using either the graphical or the numeric display), you'll be able to hear the noise more clearly, and you'll also notice the sound of the resonator getting brighter as well. The Filter section contains your basic filter types, along with an LP+HP filter, which combines a high-pass and a low-pass filter to produce a very flexible band-pass type filter.

What makes the Noise section really interesting is the envelope below. By adjusting the phases of the ADSR envelope, you can create a completely different pallet of sounds as a long, sustained noise signal vibrates the resonator, more like a bow than a mallet or stick. Try increasing the Attack to one or two seconds, and you'll hear what I mean (Figure 8.26 shows this configuration). Also, take a look above the Envelope display, and you'll see that there's a percentage box marked E below the Filter display. This applies the envelope to the filter frequency as well. If you need more info on ADSR Envelopes, brush up on them in the sections on Simpler and Analog.

Resonators

Continuing over to the right, you'll get into the Resonators section, which has the biggest impact on the overall sound. First, you'll come to the pitch section, which contains some controls that should be relatively familiar. *Tune* controls the overall tuning of the instrument in semitones, while *Fine* tunes Collision in cents (100ths of a semitone). Notice that below the Tune knob it is mapped 100% to Key, which makes it fully responsive to the notes on your

MIDI keyboard. Adjusting this value will allow you to make some more unusually tuned instruments. For example, with Key set to 50%, a movement of a semitone on your keyboard will only produce a change of a quarter tone in Collision, and so on.

The Pitch Envelope controls determine whether or not Collision reaches its target pitch immediately after it receives note input, or if it slides into the final pitch. Time determines the length of the slide, while Pitch controls how much higher or lower the initial pitch is than the target.

If you're new to synth programming and really want to get a handle on this instrument, this would probably be a good time to stop reading for a bit and make sure that you really know how to get around the controls we've dealt with so far. The rest of the controls in the Resonator section are very important because they're going to introduce a lot more complexity, and it's often easier to digest this sort of material in chunks.

The next section determines the physical properties of the Resonator, in other words, the primary component of the instrument itself. If you've followed along with the previous experiments, this would be a good time to switch back to the Mallet excitator and turn the Noise section off, just to keep things simple. The easiest aspect of the Resonator to set is the type, which is specified in the menu you set to Plate at the beginning of this section. Six of the resonator types fit into three categories: beams, planes, and cylinders. There's also a string type resonator, which in terms of its parameters is identical to the beams.

Beams are not what get emitted from your light saber—instead, think of the beams in your ceiling. These are the bars that you strike when playing a xylophone or vibraphone. Marimba is simply a special type of beam that has a deep arch cut out from the bottom. Membrane and Plate are two types that I'm describing as planes because they are both thin, flat surfaces—Membrane being a flexible material stretched tightly, such as a drum head, and Plate being flat pieces of metal. Finally, Tube and Pipe are both cylindrical objects, the only difference being that Pipe is open at both ends, while Tube is closed.

The controls below vary somewhat, depending on the type of resonator you've selected. The simplest resonator is Tube, so let's look at that first. The only controls available here are Decay and Radius. Decay is common to all the resonators and is probably the simplest to understand: This is how long it takes for the resonator to decay to silence. Radius determines the width of the Tube and has a major impact on the high harmonics produced. A low radius produces a subtle subby sound that could sound great layered in with a kick drum or bass sound. Switching over to Pipe, you may not notice much of a difference in the sound. The only difference in the controls available here is Opening, and when this control is at 100%, it's nearly identical to Tube. As you decrease Opening from 100%, you'll hear a high-frequency buzzing in the sound get louder and more complex.

For all of the other resonator types, the Radius control is replaced by Material. While this control represents a different physical property, in practice, it is very similar. Going from low to high values takes you through a range of tonal possibilities from dark and deep to extremely bright. You'll also notice that when selecting a resonator other than the two cylinders, the Quality menu becomes enabled. This feature controls how complex the harmonics generated by Collision are and therefore the CPU usage.

The remaining physical property controls are as follows:

  ▷ **Ratio:** This control only exists for the Membrane and Plate types and controls the overall shape and size of the resonator. Higher values produce much more complex harmonics and produce a less distinct pitch. This control interacts heavily with the Quality menu, which determines how complex the overtones can get.
  ▷ **Brightness:** Acts like a master tone control. Low values heavily favor low harmonics and can produce some serious volume, so watch your ears!

▷ **Inharmonics:** This is a pitch control for the overtones produced by the resonator. The most important thing to know about this control is that it is extremely sensitive (especially with Quality set to Full) and sometimes produces unexpected results. Try adjusting this control using your arrow keys, 1% at a time.

▷ **Listening:** Labeled ListeningL and ListeningR, these controls are easiest to understand if you think of them as controlling the placement of a pair of microphones being used to record your virtual percussion instrument. They both affect the tonal characteristics of the sound and the stereo field. When they are set to the same value, you'll get a mono sound, while adjusting them to opposing values gives you a much wider sound.

▷ **Hit:** If you've ever played drums, you know that they produce a very different sound, depending on where you hit the skin. The Hit control moves the point of impact from the center to the edge as you increase its value. This produces a minimal change for all of the resonators except Membrane and Plate.

▷ **Bleed:** Increasing the Bleed mixes in more of the unprocessed sound of the excitator. With Quality set to full, this doesn't have much impact since the excitator tends to get lost in the harmonics. With Quality set to basic, however, turning this value up can create some very interesting timbres.

The only other controls that you may find unfamiliar here are the Structure switches, which brings us to an important aspect of Collision. You actually have two resonators (selectable via the tabs at the top of the interface) to work with when designing your sound. Structure determines whether the output of Resonator 1 will be sent to Resonator 2 for further processing (1>2), or if both resonators will act in parallel as if they were being struck simultaneously by the same excitator (1+2).

By default, Resonator 2 is turned off, so you'll have to click on its on/off switch in the tab if you want it to be used. Also, you can edit both resonators simultaneously by clicking the link icon in between the two tabs or make both identical by using the Copy button above the Ratio control. Be aware that using both resonators (especially when running in series) can produce some serious gain, so be careful when you turn on Resonator 2.

The LFO and MIDI Tabs

You may think of LFOs as primarily being useful for sounds, like strings and pads, where you can use them to give a sound motion. But for designing traditional percussion sounds, LFOs offer some interesting options. For example, with Retrig off and a nice slow Rate, you can use an LFO to modulate a resonator's Pitch or Hit parameter, so that every time you strike a note, it has a slightly different quality (see Figure 8.22).

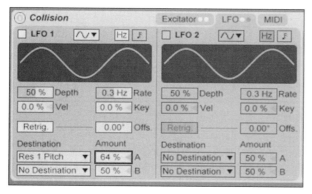

Figure 8.22 An example of Collision's LFO in action.
Source: Ableton

The LFO and MIDI sections of Collision are very similar to those of Sampler, although the MIDI mapping implementation for Collision is much simpler. Please refer to the "Sampler" section, earlier in this chapter, for a further discussion of these controls.

Drum Rack

For many of us, Drum Racks are one of the best things to happen to drum programming in a long time. A Drum Rack is an Instrument Rack that is customized for…drum roll, please…programming drums. While Drum Racks have much in common with standard Instrument Racks, they have a number of unique features. We'll focus on those features in this section.

What's particularly interesting about Drum Racks is that they have no built-in synthesis or sample playback capabilities. As opposed to powerful, complex plug-ins like Battery and Stylus RMX, a basic Drum Rack is incredibly simple. The beauty of the Drum Rack is that it can be powerful and complicated, but it doesn't have to be. Instead of having to deal with piles of features from day one, you get to decide how involved your Drum Racks are. When you're learning, you can keep them simple. As you get more comfortable, you can turn them into programming monsters using Macros, nested Racks, effects, and MIDI devices.

Pads and Chains

When an empty Drum Rack is dropped onto a track, it appears as 16 pads, each one displaying the name of the MIDI note it is mapped to (see Figure 8.23). While only 16 pads can be displayed at a time, there are actually 128 pads available—one for each possible MIDI note. The grid to the left of the pads shows an overview of all 128, while the black square highlights which 16 are in view. Drag the square to show a different group of pads.

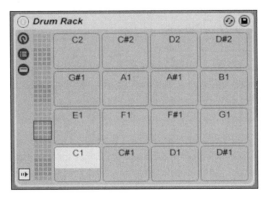

Figure 8.23 An empty Drum Rack.
Source: Ableton

> **PAD CONTROL:** If you use a pad controller that's listed as one of Live's supported control surfaces (such as the Akai MPD32), you're in for a treat. Select your controller in the Control Surface menu in the MIDI tab of the Preferences dialog. Then record-arm your Drum Rack track, click in the title bar, and the 16 pads on your controller will always stay mapped to the 16 pads that are in view for the Drum Rack. If it's not working, make sure that you are on the default preset for your controller (try preset #1). If it still doesn't work, you may need to do a preset dump. Check the documentation to determine how your device receives dumps; then click the Dump button next to your controller in the MIDI Preferences tab. Live will transmit the data to configure your controller properly.

Creating a basic drum kit with a Drum Rack is easy. Just drop a drum sample from the Browser onto any pad. Once you've dropped the sample, the pad will be updated to display the sample name instead of the note name. A play button for previewing the sample will appear, as will mute and solo switches. To see what's going on under the hood, you'll need to look at the Chain List and the Devices of the Rack (see Figure 8.24). The buttons for showing these are to the left side of the pads and look and function identically to those on a standard Instrument Rack. It's also possible to display the Device View by double-clicking on a pad.

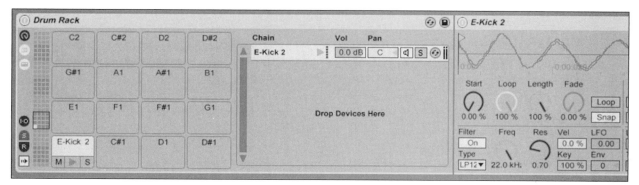

Figure 8.24 Our new Drum Rack with chains and devices shown.

Source: Ableton

First, notice the far right-hand side of the Rack. As I mentioned a moment ago, Drum Racks have no built-in sample playback capability, so here you'll see that Ableton's solution to this is to automatically create a Simpler when a sample is dropped onto a pad. The Simpler offers loads of options for tweaking the playback of the sample, so this is an excellent solution. There's no reason, however, that you need to use the Simpler to play back your samples, nor is there any reason that your Drum Racks need to be based on sample playback. You can just as easily drop a synth onto a pad and use synthesis to create your drum sounds.

Once you've picked out some samples or synths and gotten a basic drum kit together, you can start customizing your sounds with effects. Drop a Saturator into your snare chain to add some extra bite, or a Velocity device into your hi-hat chain to generate some random velocity variations. See where this is going? Your Drum Racks can become completely customized beasts with features that can rival any drum program out there. Your imagination is really the only limit.

It's also important to note here that a pad isn't limited to triggering only one sampler or synth. Want to create a sound that consists of several layers of samples, or synths, or both? No problem. You can create a layered sound in one step. Simply drag samples or devices to a pad while holding down Cmd (Mac) or Ctrl (PC). Live will automatically create a nested rack with one chain for each sample or device (see Figure 8.25). Triggering the pad will play all of the chains simultaneously.

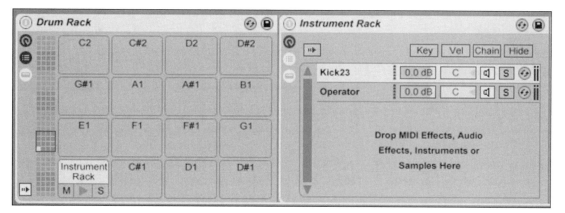

Figure 8.25 Here's a chain in a Drum Rack that triggers both a kick drum sample and an Operator, for some low-end madness.

Source: Ableton

> **MIX IT UP:** As your Drum Racks grow in size and complexity, you may want to use the Chain Mixer, which is accessed by clicking the triangular "unfold" button located in the title bar of the track containing the Drum Rack. This feature (explained fully in the Racks section of Chapter 7, "Using Effects and Instruments") can make navigating a complex Drum Rack much easier.

Advanced Settings

Whenever the Show/Hide Chains button is highlighted, a few buttons that are unique to Drum Racks appear in the lower left-hand corner (see Figure 8.26).

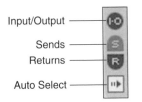

Input/Output

Sends

Returns

Auto Select

Figure 8.26 These buttons give you access to some custom features of Drum Rack Chains. They are only visible when the Show/Hide Chains button is highlighted.

Source: Ableton

The first button shows additional Input/Output options for the chains. With this turned on, you can view the MIDI routing options and choke groups for each chain (see Figure 8.27). The Audio To setting is only used for Return Chains, which we'll discuss later. The next two buttons, marked S and R, are for viewing the sends and returns. (Yes, Drum Racks have their own Send/Return bussing system!) The last button is an arrow icon called *Auto Select,* which makes it easy to find and view the chain you want by automatically highlighting the chain for the last pad that was triggered.

MIDI Routing

When the Input/Output section is in view, it's possible to adjust the MIDI routing of the chain. The Receive menu specifies what MIDI note triggers the chain. This is determined automatically when you drop a sound source onto a pad. If you change this value, you'll see the change reflected in the pad display. In other words, if you've dropped a sample called *Kick1* onto pad C1 and then change the MIDI Receive for this chain to D1, you'll see Kick1 jump to that pad. Each pad is hardwired to its note and location.

The Send setting is much more flexible. Here you can choose what note is sent to your sound source. By default, it's set to C3, which is the Simpler's default root note. So a C3 will play back the sample at its original pitch. Modifying this setting could be useful if you want to use a pitched sine wave as part of a kick sound. Change the Send note so the pitch matches the key of your song.

Choke Groups

Occasionally, it's necessary to configure some of the sounds in your kit so that playing one stops or "chokes" the other. The classic use for this is hi-hat. With a real-world drum kit, you cannot have an open and closed hi-hat sound happening at the same time. Whenever the closed hi-hat plays, the open one should stop immediately, and vice versa.

If you've used the Impulse drum machine, you may already know that it has one choke group hardwired to cells 7 and 8. Just press the Link switch on pad 8, and the two pads automatically choke each other when played. Drum Racks offer the flexibility of 16 different choke groups, which can be assigned to any group of pads. To set up the choke group, choose a choke group number from the Choke menu (refer to Figure 8.27) and assign it to all of the sounds you want included in the group. It doesn't matter which number you use—just make sure to use the same number for each sound. Now triggering any of the sounds in the group will automatically cut off any of the others.

Sends and Returns

To use the built-in sends and returns of a Drum Rack, you first have to create a Return Chain (just like in Live's mixer, where you created a return track, and the Send knobs were automatically created). First, show the Return Chains by clicking the button marked R at the lower left-hand corner of the Drum Rack. Now, you can drag an effect in to create a new chain, or you can right-click in the drop area and select Create Chain to create an empty Return Chain. More on why you would want an empty Return Chain in a minute. You can create up to six Return Chains.

After you've created a Return Chain, you can view the sends (see Figure 8.27). Now you can dial in as much effect as you want for each drum individually. By default, the output of your returns will be mixed in with the output of the Drum Rack. This, however, can be changed so that the output of the returns is routed to a return track in Live's Mixer. This could simply be for convenience, or this routing could be used to send your drums to an effect in one of the Mixer's return tracks.

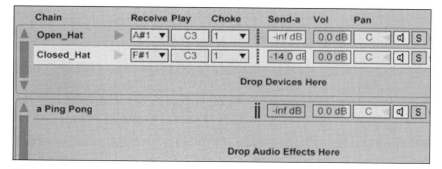

Figure 8.27 In this example, the open and closed hi-hats are both assigned to Choke group 1. Notice also the "Send-a" column, which shows us the open hi-hat is being sent to the Ping Pong Delay.
Source: Ableton

For example, let's say you have a reverb on return track A in Live's Mixer. You have a Drum Rack in which you want to add a bit of this reverb to just the hand claps and nothing else. To do this, just create an empty Return Chain and send the hand claps to it. Then, in the Audio To menu of the Return Chain, set the output to return track A, where your reverb is located.

> **EXTRACTION TEAM:** Once you're finished programming your drums, you may want to split each drum out to its own individual track. To do this, just right-click in the title bar of a drum in the Chain Mixer or the Chain List and select Extract Chains. Now you've got a new track with just that one drum and a new MIDI clip containing just the part for that drum. This technique is particularly useful if you need to render each drum to an individual audio track for mixing in another program.

External Instrument

External Instrument allows you to control an external synth from a MIDI track and make it behave like a virtual instrument track. Make sure to read through this section even if you don't have any hardware instruments. This device is also useful to anyone who uses instruments via ReWire, or plug-ins with multiple virtual outputs, such as Native Instruments Battery or IK Multimedia SampleTank.

Before the External Instrument device was introduced, sequencing external MIDI synthesizers always required two tracks: a MIDI track to control the synth and an Audio track for returning the audio from the synth. Not only does External Instrument allow this entire setup to be done with one track, but it takes advantage of Live's delay compensation as well.

After dropping External Instrument into a MIDI track, use the MIDI To menus to specify the port to which your hardware is connected (and the MIDI channel, if necessary). Arm the track for recording and play a few notes—the hardware should register the MIDI input. Next, make sure that your hardware is connected to an input on your audio interface and select this input in the Audio To menu (see Figure 8.28). Voila! You should now begin to receive audio into the track.

Figure 8.28 This External Instrument device is configured to send MIDI to a synth connected to the Analog Experience output port, and to receive audio from the synth through inputs 1 & 2.
Source: Ableton

As mentioned earlier, you can also use this device to make working with some software instruments easier as well. Any multitimbral instruments in the Set will appear in the routing menus as if they were hardware (see Figure 8.29). Instruments accessible from any currently loaded ReWire slave application will also appear here. To use these instruments with the External Instrument device, just configure the MIDI To and Audio From menus to the virtual ports on your software instruments.

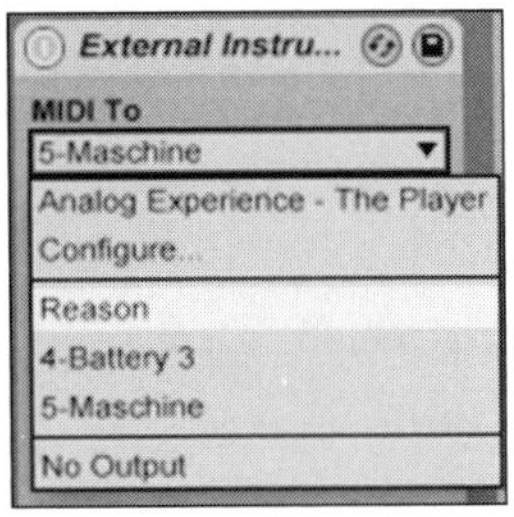

Figure 8.29 External Instrument can also transmit MIDI and receive audio from multitimbral plug-ins and ReWire applications such as Reason.
Source: Ableton

> **FREEZE!:** When it's time to record the audio from External Instrument into the Set, use the Freeze command. Live is smart enough to know when you're freezing a track that's communicating with external hardware, so it invokes a real-time process to record the audio through your soundcard's inputs.

Live's Audio Effects

What are audio effects? The question is nearly impossible to answer. Ranging from subtle mixing tools to extreme sound manglers, effects are used in every part of the music production process. A delay may be an integral part of a synthesizer sound, a distortion unit may be used to give a snare drum some extra bite, and equalizers and compressors may find their way onto nearly every track in a song during final mixdown. In this chapter, I'll discuss all 34 of Live's effects, giving some tips as to how each might be used along the way. But don't take my word for it, using effects is all about experimentation. So get in there and make some noise!

EQ and Filters

The first batch of effects we'll dive into are the filters and equalizers (EQ for short). These types of signal processors are used to attenuate (reduce in volume) and amplify (increase in volume) only specific frequency ranges within an audio signal. Engineers will use filters and EQs to finely craft the frequency distribution of the tracks in a song, resulting in beautiful, rich, and detailed final mixes. Of course, these tools can also be used to radically reshape sound, creating unique effects in their own right.

EQ Eight

A parametric EQ is a powerful frequency-filtering and timbre-shaping tool. While many hardware and some software mixers have some type of equalization available on every channel, you will need to add an EQ plug-in manually to a track anytime it's needed in your Live project.

The goal when using an EQ is to either boost or diminish certain audio frequencies in order to overcome problems arising from poor recordings, to reduce muddiness from overlapping frequencies in other sounds, or to emphasize certain characteristics of the sound to make it cut through the mix.

> **OVERSAMPLE:** For the highest sound quality in the high-frequency spectrum, right-click in the title bar and select Oversampling from the context menu. This feature causes EQ Eight to process at a higher sample rate internally, resulting in fewer artifacts at the cost of slightly higher CPU usage. To make Oversampling the default, right-click in the title bar after turning it on and select Save as Default Preset from the context menu.

The frequencies are often referred to as lows, mids, and highs or other subdivisions such as low-mids or high-mids. High frequencies are found in the register called *treble*, while low frequencies are referred to as *bass*. Low-mids, mids, or high-mids make up the middle section (from left to right) of the sonic spectrum. Live's EQ features a built-in spectrum analyzer to help you visualize the frequency content of your sounds, which can be a great help when your ears need a little help.

Live's EQ Eight features up to eight adjustable bands, or filters, each of which can be individually enabled or disabled (see Figure 9.1).

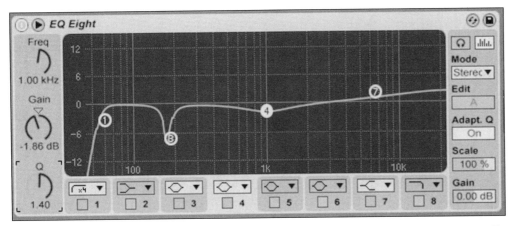

Figure 9.1 Live's powerful eight-band EQ. In this example, only bands 1–4 are in use. Turning off the bands you're not using saves CPU power.
Source: Ableton

Each filter can be used to cut or boost frequencies ranging from 30Hz to 22kHz, using one of a variety of different filter types. Each filter can be turned on or off using the eight switches running vertically across the bottom of the interface. Above each on/off switch is a menu for selecting a filter type.

The filter types, from top to bottom in the menu, are as follows:

> **Low-cut (12db & 48dB):** Also known as a high-pass filter, it aggressively removes frequencies below the specified frequency. For this filter type, Q adjusts the resonance (how much the cutoff frequency is emphasized or reduced). Gain has no effect for this filter type. The 48dB/octave version appears with "x4" next to the icon, indicating that its slope is four times as steep and reduces the frequencies below the cutoff much more dramatically. Using these to remove unnecessary low frequencies from as many tracks as possible can really clean up your mixes.

> **Low-shelf:** Reduces or boosts all frequencies below the specified frequency. With a low Q setting, the gain change will be a gentle linear slope. At high Q values, the change becomes more drastic, and you get an additional emphasis around the filter frequency. (For example, if you're cutting with a high Q, you get a boost right above the filter frequency and the greatest gain reduction directly below it.) A low-shelf is a great way to make a broad boost or cut to the low frequencies, without excessive coloration. When boosting, you may want to combine with a low-cut to keep the lowest frequencies under control.

> **Bell:** A parabolic-shaped boost or cut of a given range of frequencies. For this filter type, the Q adjusts the bandwidth of the filter—how much the adjacent frequencies are affected. This is where the most surgical adjustments in a mix occur. Use caution with high Q values in the high frequencies, as they can sound harsh. With low frequencies, however, you can get much more aggressive with the Q without concern.

> **Notch:** Like a bell curve with extremely high Q and extremely low gain, Gain has no effect for this filter type. It's especially useful for removing problems such as resonant room frequencies.

> **High-shelf:** Same as low-shelf, but acts on high frequencies. A little high-shelf boost can be a great way to add sparkle to tracks, without coloring the sound too much.

> **High-cut:** Also known as a low-pass filter, it's the same as low-cut but cuts low frequencies. High frequencies are a bit less forgiving when it comes to aggressive cutting, so unlike low-cut, this filter has more of a tendency to sound like an "effect," especially with high Q values. Try using a shelf or a bell first to see if you can accomplish the desired result.

To adjust the specific frequency that a filter acts on, you can work directly in the graphical display or use the knobs to the left. Experiment for a moment, and you'll see these are just two different ways of doing the same thing. You'll also find that when you click on the filter numbers along the bottom, the knobs refresh to show you the parameters for whatever filter you click.

Perhaps the most important power that EQ holds is its ability to preserve headroom in a mix. By reducing less important frequencies in a sound or cutting frequencies that conflict with other instruments, you end up with mixes that sound louder and clearer. For instance, if the meat of a sound is in the bass, such as a bass guitar or synth, you may want to reduce the high-frequency content of this sound to make space for your singer's voice and your drummer's hi-hat. In this case, you'd use the EQ to reduce the highs and possibly to boost the lows in the bass track.

Conversely, you can often benefit by using a high-pass filter on vocals and other instruments that don't have a lot of low-frequency content. Especially when working with voices and real instruments, there are often low frequencies, such as rumble from air conditioners and the like, doing nothing but consuming headroom and muddying up your mix. In addition to solving problems, EQs can also do a lot to sweeten certain sounds. Using a high-shelf to boost 10k can help acoustic guitars sparkle, and a bell to boost 60Hz can give a weak kick the extra power you're looking for.

> **DOUBLE STACK:** For aggressive cuts, boosts, and effects, you can stack EQs by assigning the same parameters to two or more filters. For example, you could use two 12dB low-cut filters both set to 150Hz and a Q of .75 to create a 24dB/octave filter—right in between the two built-in filter slopes.

Along the right side are a variety of useful controls. The spectrum analyzer can be turned on or off, and the headphones (Audition mode) switch can be used to listen to *only* the filter you're currently adjusting. Click and drag a filter in the graphical display to hear this feature in action. You may find it useful for zeroing in on the frequency you want to boost or cut.

Next in line is the Mode menu. Stereo is the standard mode for all stereo and mono signals. L/R differs from Stereo in that it allows you to equalize the left and right channels of a source separately (as seen in Figure 9.2). Select L in the Edit switch to EQ the left side; then press Edit again to switch over and EQ the right side. Bear in mind that L/R mode can be used to create stereo effects on mono sources by EQing left and right differently. M/S mode allows you to separately EQ the "middle" of a mix (material that is purely mono) and the "sides" of a mix (material that is purely stereo).

Adaptive Q is a feature inspired by the behavior of some classic analog EQs. It causes the Q to change automatically when adjusting the gain of bell and shelf filters. (It has no effect on the other filter types.) The theory is that the more you boost, the more desirable it is to narrow the range of frequencies you're boosting to avoid dramatic changes in the overall gain of the signal. Bear in mind that you can achieve the same results with or without this feature turned on. You may, however, find that it makes the operation of the EQ more intuitive and musical.

The Scale control is an ingenious bonus that changes the gain of all EQ bands simultaneously. So if you've created the perfect EQ curve but decide that you've laid it on a bit thick, you can scale it back a bit and apply less EQ overall. The Scale control goes all the way up to 200%, so you can use it to increase gain as well.

Finally, the Gain control should not be overlooked. Remember that boosting and cutting frequencies changes the overall gain of your signal. If you're doing a lot of boosting, then you may need to bring down the gain to avoid clipping. Conversely, cutting the frequencies you *don't* like, and then boosting the gain of a signal is often the best way to bring out the qualities you *do* like.

In the upper left-hand corner of EQ Eight, you'll find a triangular "unfold" button. Clicking on this yields dramatic results! As you'll see in Figure 9.2, this gives you a giant graphical display to work with above, and a full set of controls for each filter below.

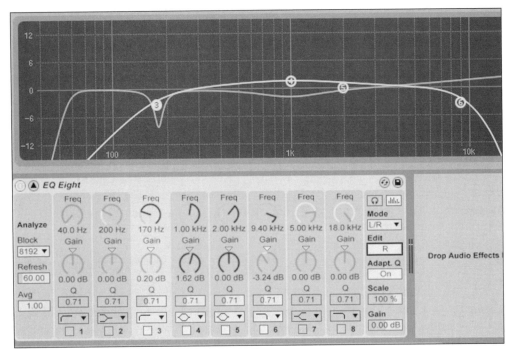

Figure 9.2 Here's EQ Eight in its expanded view. Notice that the device is now in L/R mode. While you can see both EQ curves simultaneously, you can only edit whichever band is shown in the Edit switch.
Source: Ableton

KICK ME! (PART 1): Many people will try to add bass with an EQ to get it to cut through the mix. The end result is that you end up feeling the kick more (your subwoofer will really be bumpin'), but it still sounds muddy because it is occupying the same frequency bands as other instruments in the mix.

To get that deep yet punchy tone that really cuts through, try using a bell filter with a high Q setting to cut frequencies in the 150 to 250Hz range. To find the frequency you want to cut, first boost the band and sweep it up and down while listening carefully for the drum's most resonant frequency.

By cutting this tone, the bass now occupies its own space (the low frequencies where you feel it and the high frequencies where you hear it) and cleans up the sonic image. (The range from 150Hz to 300Hz can be extremely problematic in many mixes.)

EQ Three

The DJ-style EQ Three is concerned only with three frequency bands: lows, mids, and highs. As you can see in Figure 9.3, the EQ Three has three main dials: GainLow, GainMid, and GainHi. The frequency range of these dials is determined by the FreqLow and FreqHi knobs at the bottom of the effect. The GainMid knob will boost or cut all the frequencies between FreqLow and FreqHi. The GainLow will adjust all the frequencies below FreqLow, and the GainHi knob will handle everything above FreqHi.

Figure 9.3 Lows, mids, and highs are under your complete control with EQ Three.
Source: Ableton

Because this device is modeled after a DJ mixer, you'll find that when turning the Gain knobs down, they eventually reach infinity, meaning the frequencies are completely cut. If you want, you can use the kill buttons (labeled L, M, and H) located below each Gain knob to toggle that frequency range on and off with ease.

The 24 and 48 buttons determine the slope, either 24dB/octave or 48dB/octave, at the edges of the frequency bands. This setting will be most apparent when using the kill feature of the EQ Three on a full song. For example, drag a whole song (an MP3 with lots of bass) into a clip slot and place an EQ Three on the track. Click the 48 button, place the FreqLow control at 200Hz, and kill the low band—you'll hear the bass disappear from the song. Now try clicking the 24 button. You may notice that you can hear a little more bass.

The EQ Three is a handy performance tool, but doesn't have the same sound quality as EQ Eight. And because it's modeled on mixer circuitry, it even affects the sound with all the controls at their default. If you need the particular functionality this device provides, but want the sound quality of EQ Eight, look in the Performance & DJ folder under Audio Effect Rack in the Browser. You'll find a Rack called EQ Three Rack, which provides similar functionality, but is built using EQ Eight.

> **SONIC JIGSAW PUZZLES:** Try placing three different drum loops on three different tracks, each armed with an EQ Three. Then isolate the bass in one track, the mids in another, and the highs in the remaining track. You'll now have one hybrid beat consisting of kicks, snares, and hi-hats from different loops. Try swapping or automating the kills for other rhythm combinations.

Auto Filter

One of Live's greatest live performance effects, Auto Filter (seen in Figure 9.4), is a virtual, analog-style filter with four selectable classic filter types (high-pass, low-pass, band-pass, and band-reject). Each of these can be controlled via the effect's X-Y controller and modulated by an envelope and any of seven different low-frequency oscillator (LFO) shapes. As you may have gleaned from the EQ Eight explanation, suppressing certain frequencies allows you to carve out specific problems or overcooked frequencies. The Auto Filter can do this as well, but it shines as a creative effect capable of a wide variety of sounds.

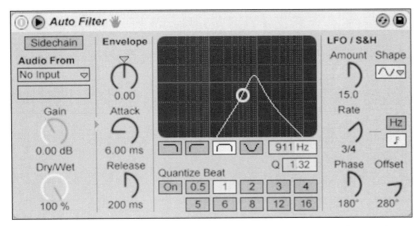

Figure 9.4 Live's Auto Filter device. If you've just been reading so far, you really need to get up and try this one. No, really.
Source: Ableton

Filter Type

Running along the bottom of the graphical display are four icons for selecting the Auto Filter's type. They are, from right to left: low-pass, high-pass, band-pass, and band-reject.

Low-pass simply means that the low frequencies pass through the filter, but nothing else does. For instance, if used on an entire song, the bass guitar and kick drums will be audible, though a little dull-sounding due to the lack of highs. Some sounds may disappear completely, such as small cymbals or shakers. Conversely, a high-pass filter will allow shimmering cymbals and sparkly guitars and synths to pass, but will suppress basses and any other instruments in the lower frequency range. How low is up to you.

Band-pass filters are basically high-pass and low-pass filters put together; thus, only frequencies falling between the two filters will pass, sounding similar to a telephone at times. Band-reject filters work opposite of band-pass—only audio lying outside of the cutoff frequency can pass.

Frequency and Resonance

To get going with Live's Auto Filter, you will want to select a filter type—Low-Pass is a good starter—then use the X-Y controller to dial in Frequency (X-axis) and Q (Y-axis). Or, if you prefer, Frequency and Q (resonance) using the numeric boxes below the display.

Increasing the Q (resonance) control will increase the intensity of the filter by adding a resonant peak around the cutoff frequency, while lowering it will cause the filter to roll off more smoothly. If you really crank up the Q, you can get some very intense effects as you move the filter frequency. This can sound great, but be sure to watch your volume!

LFO

To the right of the X-Y controller is the LFO, which can be used to modulate the filter frequency. The Amount knob controls the amplitude of the modulation, while the Rate controls its speed. Next to the Rate knob is the Shape menu. These waveshapes are fairly self-explanatory—the sine wave at the top creates smooth changes, while the square wave creates choppy ones. The best way to get a feel for the different waveshapes is to crank up the Amount, add a bit of resonance, and listen. The bottom two waveshapes are random (sample and hold), the first one being mono, while the second one generates separate random values for the left and right channels.

When the Phase control is set to 180 degrees, the LFO will generate opposite modulations for the left and right channels, creating a stereo effect. In other words, as the frequency of the left channel is increased, the frequency of the right channel is decreased. Increasing or decreasing the Phase will bring the phase relationship of the left and right LFOs closer together until eventually they become identical.

The Rate control can be adjusted in Hertz by clicking the Hz switch or synchronized to the tempo by clicking the switch with the note icon. Depending on which you select, there are different options available for the Phase control. When Rate is set to Hertz, two switches appear near the Phase knob. When the lower switch is clicked, the Spin knob appears. Spin changes the speed of the left and right LFOs relative to each other, creating a swirling effect. When Rate is set to tempo sync, the Offset knob appears. This can be used to create some interesting rhythmic effects. As you increase the Offset, you shift peaks and troughs of the LFO off the beat instead of right on it.

Envelope

The Envelope knob determines how much the input signal's volume will modulate the filter frequency. This type of modulator is commonly known as an "envelope follower" because it creates an envelope that "follows" the signal's amplitude. Positive values cause the filter frequency to be turned up, while negative values turn the frequency down as the volume increases.

The effect can be fine-tuned by using the Attack and Release controls. Attack determines how long it takes for the frequency to reach its maximum value, while Release determines how long it takes for it to return to its original value. Crank the Envelope knob to get familiar with these controls. Short Attack and Release times will tend to give you a funky, clucking effect because you'll get more of the filter sweep for each note. Longer times will tend to make the effect more subtle since it takes longer for the filter to open up, and it tends not to release all the way back to its original value before opening again.

Quantize Beat

The Quantize Beat parameter affects filter modulation (generated either by the LFO or the envelope) by forcing the filter frequency to change in tempo-synchronized steps. The steps are specified in 16ths ranging from .5 (32nd notes) to 16 (1 bar). To get a feel for what this Quantize Beat does, load it on to a track with a sustained pad and configure the Auto Filter, as shown in Figure 9.5. You may have to adjust the frequency so you hear a nice up-and-down sweep. Now try clicking the On switch a few times. As it goes on and off, you'll hear the modulation go from a smooth sweep to a choppier sound. This is the sound of the filter frequency jumping to a new value once every 16th note. Now you can experiment with other Beat values and play with the Phase as well.

Sidechain

In Figure 9.5, you may have noticed the Sidechain section of the Auto Filter to the left of the Envelope section. This section is only displayed if you click the small triangle in the title bar.

Sidechaining refers to having an audio source, other than the one you are currently processing, trigger the envelope for an effect. In other words, in the case of the Auto Filter, you can have the envelope follow the dynamics of any track in Live, instead of following the dynamics of the signal that you are processing with the Auto Filter. Let's take a look at how this works.

If you tried out the Quantize Beat example earlier, you'll want to keep working with the same sustained pad for this example, too. We'll also need another track to serve as the sidechain source. This can be an audio or a MIDI track, but it should output something percussive with strong transients. Now, in the Sidechain section, set the Source to the percussion track, as seen in Figure 9.5. Also, make sure the LFO Amount is set to 0. There's no reason you can't use the LFO at the same time, but for learning purposes it's best to keep it simple.

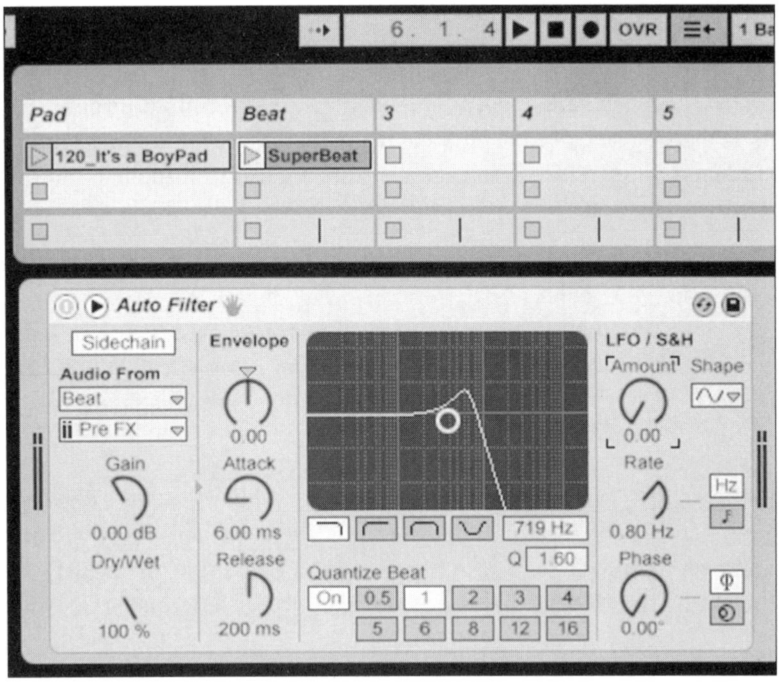

Figure 9.5 Specify a sidechain input to have the envelope of your Auto Filter follow a different audio source.
Source: Ableton

Now, play back both clips and slowly raise the Envelope control. As you do this, you'll hear the filter on the pad begin to rise and fall with the hits in the drum loop. If you're not getting enough of an effect even with the Envelope cranked, you can increase the Gain to feed more signal to the Sidechain. The Dry/Wet knob controls how much the sidechain signal is mixed with the direct signal before it is sent to the envelope. In the current example, a setting of 50% would mean that the envelope would follow the dynamics of a 50/50 blend of the drum loop and the pad. At 0%, the sidechain is bypassed completely.

> **PRE OR POST?:** In the sidechain example earlier, you may have noticed that the sidechain source is set to Pre FX (refer to Figure 9.5). This is because we want to tap the signal before it gets to the mixer. By using either the Pre or Post FX setting, you can mute the sidechain track in Live's Mixer and still have it reach the sidechain input. This way, you can get the rhythmic envelope without having to hear the drum loop. Pre FX is especially useful if you have some heavy effects on a track, but you want to use that sound unaffected to control an envelope.

Dynamic Processing

In the audio world, dynamics refers to the volume or amplitude of a sound. More specifically, it refers to the *change* in volume of a sound. The sound of a drum kit can range from quiet ghost notes on a snare drum to the thundering sound of the kick drum and toms, and it is therefore considered to have more dynamic range than a distorted guitar, which usually plays at a more consistent volume.

It therefore makes sense that dynamic processors would alter the volume of signals passing through them. But why would you want to do this? Like EQing, dynamic processing can be used to compensate for problems arising in the recording process. It can also be used to control the natural peaks that occur during live vocal performances, to exaggerate the transients in a part, or for a variety of creative effects.

Compressor

Compression can add clarity and power to your mixes if done properly. Done wrong, it can suck all life from what once was a brilliant track. For audio engineers, compression is one of the hardest things to learn to use properly and is one element that separates the big fish from the little guppies. Live 9 has a totally revamped compressor—the best sounding and most flexible one yet.

The most immediately noticeable feature of the Live 9 compressor is that it offers three unique views for visualizing the way it changes a signal's gain. Before getting into the nitty gritty of compression, let's get familiar with the interface. The three possible views are selected via the icons that run along the bottom of the device (see Figure 9.6).

Figure 9.6 Live's Compressor offers three unique views, selected with the buttons shown above.
Source: Ableton

The views are as follows:

▷ **Collapsed (default):** The most compact of all the views, showing simple meters for Threshold, Gain Reduction (GR), and Output Gain. Threshold and Output Gain are adjusted using the slider attached to the right side of the meters. In this view, the Lookahead and Envelope controls cannot be adjusted.

▷ **Transfer Curve:** This view differs from the Collapsed View only in that the Gain Reduction meter is accompanied by an X-Y grid displaying the relationship of input signal (the horizontal axis) to output signal (the vertical axis). Dragging the yellow dot horizontally adjusts the Threshold, while dragging it vertically adjusts the Ratio.

▷ **Activity:** This view is a scrolling representation of how the gain of the signal changes over time. The input signal is represented in gray as peaks and valleys along the bottom, while the gain reduction is shown as a jagged orange line across the top. Note that Threshold and Ratio are adjusted using number boxes at the top when using Activity View.

Compression Basics

In brief, a compressor is a device that will automatically turn down the volume of sound passing through it. To explain this concept, let's use a simplified example. What if you could buy something that would turn down the TV whenever something loud came on? It would keep the commercials at the same volume as the TV show, and it would also keep loud things like car explosions from blasting your neighbors awake in the middle of the night. Enter the compressor.

To get our imaginary TV compressor to work, there are a few settings you have to choose. The first one is called *Volume Trigger.* You set this one to the volume where the box should start turning down the volume. You set this to a point just slightly louder than the TV show you're watching. This guarantees that the compressor doesn't turn down your show at all. However, when a commercial comes on, it will be louder than the Volume Trigger, and the compressor will engage.

The next control you're supposed to set on this thing is the Turn-Down Amount. When the compressor engages as a result of the Volume Trigger being exceeded, the volume will be turned down by the Turn-Down Amount. Setting this to infinity makes the compressor turn down the volume to match the Volume Trigger. Thus, the commercial is turned down to the volume of the TV show.

The third setting is the Turn-Down Time. This setting sets the time that the compressor takes to turn down the volume once the commercial starts. If this value is set to a long time, like five seconds, the compressor will take five seconds to turn down the volume when the commercial comes on. The point here is to cut the volume on the commercial the moment it comes on, so you set the time to 10ms. Now, the commercial is turned down within 10ms of coming on.

The last value is Turn-Up Time. This is the opposite of the Turn-Down Time where you specify how long it should take for the compressor to turn the volume back up again after the commercials are over. You don't want to miss any of the dialogue when the show starts, so you set this to 10ms as well. But this causes an unforeseen problem: any time the announcer's voice dips below the Volume Trigger—even just trailing off at the end of a word, the volume shoots back up to its original level causing low-level sounds, such as breaths, to become unnaturally loud. Therefore, you set the Turn-Up time to one second. This way, the announcer's voice will stay down until the end of the commercial, at which point it will fade back to full volume over one second.

So that's it. You've now mastered the compressor. It turns down commercials that exceed the volume of your TV show within 10ms and then returns the volume to normal one second after the commercials are over. Nice.

If you've looked at a compressor at all, hardware or software, you know that I replaced the real names of the controls with fake names in the example above. Here's the decoder: The Volume Trigger is really the *Threshold* control. The Turn-Down Amount refers to the *Ratio*. Turn-Down Time and Turn-Up Time refer to *Attack* and *Release*, respectively. You will see all of these controls on Live's Compressor, shown in Figure 9.7.

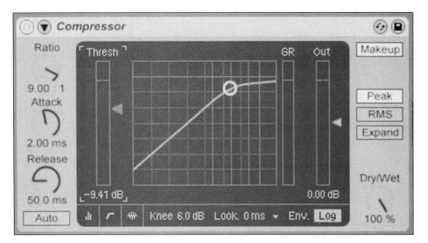

Figure 9.7 Live's Compressor, shown here in Transfer Curve view.
Source: Ableton

Many people believe that a compressor makes sounds louder. But, as you can see in the illustration above, a compressor makes loud sounds quieter. Still, engineers do employ compressors as part of a technique for making sounds louder. Compressors make the dynamic range of audio smaller, so the overall level can be higher. Imagine that you have some audio that ranges from –30dB to 0dB. If you compress the audio such that every peak over –10dB is reduced to be no greater than –10dB, you can then raise the level of the whole signal by 10dB. Now you have audio that ranges from –20dB to 0dB, resulting in a much greater perceived loudness.

Threshold, Ratio, Attack, and Release

Compression is useful in a variety of situations, but keeping peaks under control is by far one of the most common. (In electronic dance music, sidechain compression actually may be the most common of all tasks.) Some parts, such as drums and vocals, have many very short peaks, called *transients*, while others (such as a synth part with resonant filter modulation) may have peaks that occur more slowly. Knowing how to compress a sound is all about knowing what result you're trying to achieve.

How do you properly control peaks? First, you need to identify the volume at which you want to start compressing, which is done with the Threshold.

To do this, set the Ratio to the maximum, reduce the Attack to its minimum, and set the Release to 500ms. With the Threshold at its default, run the signal and watch the Gain Reduction meter to see if any compression occurs. If not, start to move the Threshold downward, until you notice the Gain Reduction meter starts to respond. This means that you've found the Threshold at which some of the transients are loud enough to trigger the Compressor. As you keep moving the Threshold slider downward, the Gain Reduction meter will begin to respond more often and will also show a greater amount of attenuation.

If you keep reducing the Threshold, there will come a point where nearly every element of the sound you're compressing, the transients and the quieter tones, will all be beyond the Threshold, thus causing the Compressor to work nonstop—always in some state of gain reduction. Back off the Threshold to a point where only the peaks are triggering the Gain Reduction meter.

The Compressor's Ratio control determines the amount of compression expressed as a ratio of the input volume to the output volume. For instance, 2-to-1 compression means that when a sound goes over the threshold by 2dB, you will hear only a 1dB increase at the output. And 4-to-1 would mean that for a 2dB increase, only a ½dB change would be audible at the output. You may also notice that for larger Ratio settings and low Thresholds, the sound may become muffled or muted as a result of the volume squashing what is going on. On the other hand, extreme gain reduction, sometimes called *overcompression*, is also useful as a special effect.

Compressor's other two controls, Attack and Release, determine how long it takes for maximum gain reduction to occur after a sound crosses the Threshold, and how long it takes for the sound to return to its original level after the sound has dropped below the Threshold. With a high Ratio and low Threshold, slowly turn up the Attack, and you'll start to hear more of the sound's natural transients passing through. Typically, a small amount of attack time (5 to 10ms) is best for retaining some sense of dynamics. When used on drums, Attack times less than 5ms can produce some interesting effects, but at the risk of squashing the natural transient in a way that makes the sound dull and lifeless. Use cautiously. Longer attacks are often used with horns, bass, and other sounds that naturally have more gentle transients. A compressor's release settings are often less noticeable when long. A long release time means that the compression continues to work for a given length of time (in milliseconds) after it has been engaged, and the signal level has dipped back below the threshold. Typically, a short release time will force the Compressor to repeatedly engage and disengage (start and stop), and a listener will be more apt to hear the repeated contrasts (sometimes referred to as pumping or breathing) and low-frequency distortion. Short release times can still be a cool-sounding effect for drums and diced-up pieces of audio (where the signal repeatedly crosses the Threshold).

The Auto switch just below the Release knob enables "program dependent" release—meaning the release time is automatically adjusted based on the material that passes through it. This setting is particularly well suited when compressing an entire mix, since there may be several different types of peaks that cause gain reduction, all of which sound better with different release times. This is also the type of release built into the famous LA-2A compressor, which is legendary for sounding great on vocals, even when applying large amounts of compression.

Knee, Lookahead, Release Envelope

The Knee control is called as such because it adjusts the point in the compression graph where the line bends—ergo, the "knee." As the Knee is increased, the bend in the line rounds out. What this represents is the Ratio and the Threshold becoming more dynamic and gradually applying gain reduction as the signal approaches the Threshold.

Especially with high ratios, the sound produced by compressors can be harsh and unnatural. This effect is partly caused by a compressor leaving a signal completely unprocessed and then slamming on the gain reduction every time the Threshold is passed—a behavior known as "hard-knee" compression. By increasing the Knee, you can specify a range of decibels below the Threshold over which gain reduction should be applied. In other words, with a Threshold of –10dB, a Ratio of 10:1, and a Knee of 10dB, a small amount of gain reduction will occur to signals hitting –20dB (the Threshold minus the Knee value). For signals between –20dB and –10dB, an increasing amount of gain reduction will be applied until the full Ratio of 10:1 is reached for signals exceeding –10dB. The result of this "soft-knee" compression is that the dynamic structure of the Compressor's output is closer to the original signal, and a more natural sound is produced.

Next to the Knee, you'll see a menu marked "Look," which sets the Lookahead. Because analog compressors respond to audio in real time, there is a limit as to how quickly they can respond to a peak. In this digital realm, this limitation can be overcome by having the gain detector "look ahead" at the audio to determine exactly when to act. By increasing the Lookahead amount, you can increase the Compressor's accuracy in responding to fast transients, and also generate some extreme compression effects impossible with analog compressors.

The Release Envelope (marked "Env") can be set to either Logarithmic or Linear. In Linear mode, the results you get are a bit more effect-oriented. Use it when you want something to sound compressed. It's great at getting a squashed, overcompressed sound, and it can really make a drum loop pop out. It should be used sparingly and deliberately—too much of it is harsh sounding. Logarithmic release is a more refined sounding mode and can be used to shape transients with a greater degree of transparency.

KICK ME! (PART 2): After you've used the EQ Eight to dial in a nice kick drum tone, place a Compressor on the track. You'll use the Compressor to shape the amplitude of the kick sound, similar to using an ADSR envelope on a synth.

The setting for the Ratio dial depends on the amount of attack already present in the kick sound. If there's already a decent amount of punch, a ratio of 4 to 1 may be all that's necessary. If the kick is flat and has no life, a 10-to-1 ratio may be in order.

You'll need a fairly short attack time, somewhere in the neighborhood of 5 to 20ms. If the attack is too short, the drum will sound short, snappy, and clipped.

Use a slightly longer setting for the Release, 25 to 50ms, depending on the bass drum's acoustics. If the drum has a long tone, a longer release will keep the tail end of the tone from popping up in volume after the loud transient of the drum has passed. If, on the other hand, the drum has a short tone, or if the drum is played quickly, a short release time will allow the Compressor to open fully before the next drum hit. If the release time is too long, only the first kick drum hit will sound right, while the others that follow shortly after will be too quiet because the Compressor is still attenuating the signal.

The Threshold should be at a point where every kick played at normal volume will trigger the Compressor. But if the Threshold is too low, the Compressor will squash the volume and never let go!

Compression Modes

On the right side of the Compressor, you'll see three different compression modes: Peak, RMS, and Expand. In Peak mode, the Compressor will respond to any signal that goes over the threshold, whereas RMS responds more slowly and will have less effect on transients. The advantage to RMS is that when applying compression to complex sources, such as an entire mix, you may not always want an overall gain reduction in response to an individual transient. However, since RMS will allow transients greater than the threshold to pass straight through, it's not well suited to anything where you need very accurate control, such as drums.

Expand is a different beast entirely. This mode exactly inverts the Compressor's behavior from reducing the gain of high-level signals to increasing them instead. Expansion is useful when working with signals that may sound lifeless due to a dynamic range that is too small, such as a signal that was initially recorded with too much compression. (There's a limited amount that this can help, though, so don't record with a lot of compression unless you really know what you're doing.) Additionally, expansion can sometimes help with recordings made in unpleasant sounding rooms. By exaggerating the volume of the peaks, it's possible to effectively turn down some of the room reflections.

Makeup, Output Gain, and Dry/Wet

If you've been experimenting with the Compressor, at this point you've probably noticed that even though you're applying all sorts of "gain reduction," the signal isn't getting softer—in fact, it may actually seem to be getting louder. This is due to the Makeup switch (in the lower-left corner) being activated. It's automatically compensating for the amount of gain reduction being applied to the peaks and bringing up the overall level of the signal. While this works nicely, there might be times where you just want to turn down errant peaks without bringing up the overall level. To do this, just turn off Makeup. Whether or not it's turned on, you can always tweak the output level using the Output control.

Dry/Wet is a handy control for blending some uncompressed signal into the Compressor's output. For everyday mix tasks where controlling the peaks in a signal is the goal, this knob should stay at 100% (no dry signal). However, when using Compressor with more extreme settings, this control has enormous potential. When using compression as an effect, you may love the squashed sound you get but find there's a big downside in terms of lost transients and natural tone. With Dry/Wet, you can dial some of the original sound back in to complete the sonic picture.

Sidechain

Expanding the Sidechain section (see Figure 9.8) reveals a powerful set of controls for shaping your sounds. When the Sidechain switch is enabled, the gain detector listens to the source specified in the Audio From menus, instead of the signal being processed. This external source can be the output of a track or any source that Live's routing system can access. For example, you could use the top menu to specify a track containing a Drum Rack and the second menu to pick the kick drum chain within the rack.

A classic use of sidechain compression is to use the kick drum to trigger gain reduction in the bass track, to solve the problem of competing frequencies in the low end of a mix. If you're not sure what this means, try it out: load Compressor onto a bass track and set its Sidechain to the kick drum. You'll immediately see the device begin responding to the kick drum signal instead of the bass.

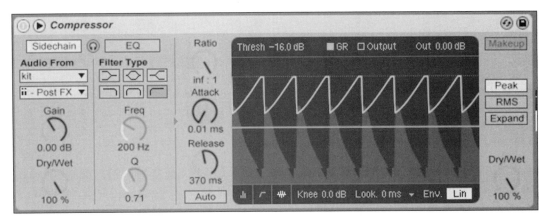

Figure 9.8 Compressor is shown here in Activity view, with its Sidechain section open. The Sidechain section features an EQ so you can trigger compression using only certain frequencies of the Sidechain source. The settings here show how you might trigger bass compression using the kick drum in a drum loop.
Source: Ableton

PUMP IT UP!: In much of contemporary electronic music, sidechaining signals to the kick drum is an essential part of the sound. You'll hear this technique used to create dramatic pulsating effects, sometimes called "pumping." Not strictly used on bass, pumping can be used to give rhythmic energy to pads, leads, percussion, and even effects like delay and reverb.

Insert Compressor onto a track and set its Sidechain source to the kick. Set Mode to Peak, Ratio to maximum, Attack to minimum, Knee to 0dB, and Env. to Linear. Now, with audio playing back, reduce the threshold until you're seeing and hearing some very intense gain reduction. The Release control is where you'll fine-tune the effect. Crank it up to somewhere between 200ms and 1s. In this range, you get an audible swelling in between each kick drum hit. The exact value you'll use depends on the tempo of the song, how busy the kick part is, and the feel you're going for. Once you've got the hang of this, you can fine-tune the other settings to taste.

But what if your kick drum is already mixed into a drum loop? We can work with that! After you've set the sidechain input to the track that your drum loop is on, enable the EQ section. Now, solo the bass track and click the headphones icon (Sidechain Listen) directly to the left of the EQ switch. Now, you're hearing the Sidechain source (the drum loop) instead of the bass track. Select the low-pass filter and bring the frequency down until most of the other drums disappear. Then you can turn off Sidechain Listen and tweak the Compressor controls until you get the desired amount of gain reduction. You can even adjust the Dry/Wet mix and boost the Sidechain Gain control so you're getting compression triggered by both the kick and the bass.

The Sidechain EQ can also be used without an external Sidechain source. In this case, a copy of the audio that you are compressing is used to feed the Sidechain. This technique is frequently used for de-essing, which is the process of softening the sharp "sss" sound that can occur in vocal parts. By filtering out all the lower frequencies or boosting the sibilant frequencies (often 8kHz and higher), you can force the Compressor to respond only when a strong "sss" escapes the vocalist's lips. Typically, this will require some careful tweaking of the Threshold and a very fast attack.

Gate

Where compressors focus on reducing volume spikes above a certain threshold, gates help turn down low-level signals beneath a certain threshold. Gates are a tool for reducing background noise, microphone bleed, and undesirable reverb decay. They are also a creative tool for chopping up audio loops and creating wild rhythmic effects by using the sidechain. Figure 9.9 shows Live's Gate effect.

A gate effect operates just like it sounds. Certain audio can make it through the gate, while other audio cannot. The minimum level to get through the gate is set by the Threshold slider. Any incoming sound quieter than the threshold will cause the gate to close, thus attenuating the signal. Once the gate opens, it remains open until the signal goes below the Threshold value *minus* the Return value. In other words, if Threshold is –10dB and Return is 5dB, the gate will open for signals above –10 and stay open until the signal goes below –15.

To get a feel for this, set Return to zero and adjust Threshold until only the highest peaks of the signal come through. At some point, you'll discover a phenomenon called "chatter" where the gate opens and closes rapidly as the signal crosses back and forth across the Threshold. Increasing Return will stop the chatter and impart a more natural sound to the gating.

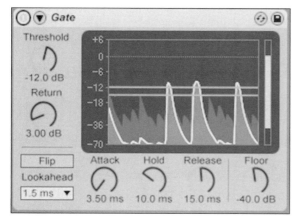

Figure 9.9 Live's Gate effect.
Source: Ableton

The Attack, Hold, and Release settings determine the rate at which the gate opens and closes. For instance, a very short attack will make the gate open quickly when the threshold is exceeded, sometimes resulting in harsh, audible clicks.

Similarly, the Hold and Release functions affect how long the gate remains open after the signal has fallen below the Threshold. Hold is a fixed minimum amount of time the gate must stay open, while Release is the speed at which it closes. The Flip switch turns the gate upside down—only signals *below* the threshold will get passed. While not often the most practical thing, the Flip switch can be used to generate some interesting glitchy effects on your beats, and can be very effective when used in conjunction with the Sidechain.

Floor is the amount of gain reduction applied when the Gate is closed. When used as a corrective tool for microphone bleed or noise reduction, you may need to experiment with less gain reduction to get natural sounding results. When Gate is being used as an effect, try turning this all the way down for the most dramatic effect.

The Sidechain opens up loads of creative possibilities for the Gate. Its settings are identical to those described in detail in the "Compressor" section in this chapter. For an interesting experiment, try the Auto Filter sidechain example (involving a sustained pad and a drum loop) with the Gate. By opening and closing the Gate using a beat, you can turn the pad into a chopped-up rhythm part.

Glue Compressor

This compressor takes its odd name from a common piece of audio engineer-speak: namely, the ability of compression to make a mix sound "glued together." This difficult-to-describe quality refers to the final result sounding like a cohesive whole, while still being composed of clear and carefully delineated elements. One of the most famous compressors for achieving this result is the master buss compressor found in SSL consoles, the compressor on which Glue is modeled (see Figure 9.10).

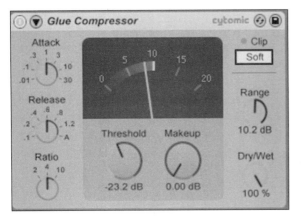

Figure 9.10   The Glue Compressor brings a bit of big console sound to Live's sound palette.
Source: Ableton

All of the basic controls found in Compressor are the same here, with the exception that the output Gain knob is called *Makeup* and the Attack, Release, and Ratio settings are limited to the same values found on the original hardware. (Make sure to read the "Compressor" section if you need a briefing on the basic functionality of this device.) The primary difference with Glue Compressor is that it is optimized for dealing with complex sources, like a drum buss or an entire mix, and it models the circuitry of the analog device on which it's based, and thus is capable of producing some sonically pleasing color. With the Soft switch enabled, the device's grit and color is maximized, as an additional waveshaping algorithm is used to limit peaks and produce subtle distortion.

One control unique to Glue Compressor is Range. This setting gives you the ability to limit the amount of compression applied to an absolute value. For example, setting range to –10dB means there will never be more than 10dB of gain reduction applied, regardless of the Threshold and Ratio settings. This is very handy when using this device on a buss or an entire mix, because in these cases it's often desirable to use very small amounts of gain reduction—sometimes a maximum of 2 or 3dB.

The unfold switch in the title bar can be used to expose the Sidechain controls. These work just like those of Compressor, so review that section of this chapter for more information on this topic.

Limiter

Ever notice that when you complete a mixdown of your music, it's still not nearly as loud as commercial tracks that you've bought? This is because after the mixdown phase, most tracks go through a separate mastering process to balance the overall frequency characteristics and also to increase the overall loudness of the track. In fact, volume has become such an obsession with many artists and labels, that it's now routinely discussed in engineering circles as the "loudness wars." The number one weapon used to fight in this war is the Limiter (see Figure 9.11).

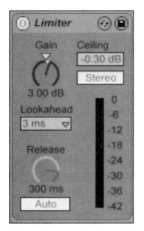

Figure 9.11 Live's Limiter is great for getting your tracks a few dB hotter.
Source: Ableton

Live's Limiter is the simplest of all of the dynamics processors. It simply prevents the signal from ever going above the volume specified by the Ceiling parameter. In traditional audio engineering terms, a Limiter is a compressor with a ratio of 10:1 or greater, although usually when you see a "brickwall limiter" device, such as this one, its ratio is generally fixed at "inf," meaning that the signal is never allowed to exceed the threshold.

The Limiter has no threshold control. That's because the Ceiling functions as the threshold. If your Ceiling is set to −1dB, and you feed it a signal that contains no peaks above −1, then the Limiter will have no effect. To apply limiting, you would simply increase the Gain control until the signal begins to exceed the Ceiling. Then you'll see the Gain Reduction meter begin to flash, and you'll hear the overall level of the signal become louder without ever clipping. As you continue to increase the gain, you'll start to get some distortion and will eventually destroy all of the dynamics in the signal, so listen carefully and go easy if in doubt.

The Release knob can be used to fine-tune the Limiter's release characteristics, but for most applications, Auto will work just fine. Lookahead functions like a simple Attack control. At lower values, it responds faster to peaks, which results in more limiting but also a potential increase in distortion. This is always the trade-off with increasing gain through limiting. The more you apply, the less dynamic and more distorted the signal becomes. To find the right amount, it's a good idea to put on some headphones and crank up the gain until you can hear distortion; then back off until you've found an acceptable level.

The switch marked Stereo should generally be left alone unless you don't mind messing with the stereo image of the material you're working with. In Stereo mode, a peak in either channel will cause gain reduction to occur on both sides, preserving the stereo image. By changing this to L/R, you can treat each side separately.

Multiband Dynamics

If you're still wrapping your head around what dynamics processors do, then you may want to spend more time with Live's basic Compressor and Gate before digging into the Multiband Dynamics device (see Figure 9.12). If you're already a seasoned engineer, then you're certainly familiar with the power of this type of processor. This section assumes that you know the basics of compression and gating, so make sure to read through the Compressor and Gate sections if you need to brush up on these concepts.

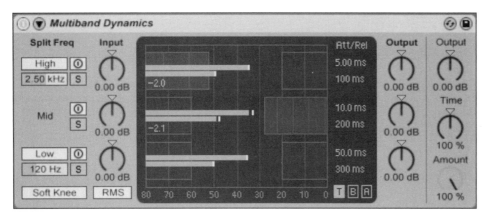

Figure 9.12 Live's Multiband Dynamics.
Source: Ableton

Essentially, a multiband compressor (the most common type of multiband dynamics processing) is what you get if you breed an EQ and a compressor. For example, in the case of the EQ Three, the signal gets split into three different bands, each of which has its own volume control—one for turning each of the bands up or down separately. In the case of a multiband compressor, each of the bands gets its own dynamics processor, capable of automatically turning the volume of that band down, depending on the volume of that band in the input signal. For the Multiband Dynamics device, Ableton has created a processor that is capable of both upward and downward compression and expansion, which means that each band can be automatically turned either down or up in response to the signal going either above or below a given threshold. There's an awful lot of functionality packed into this relatively small interface.

In the case of Live's new Multiband Compressor, the three bands are laid out from top to bottom instead of left to right. Each band has its Activator and Solo switches, while the high and low bands each have an On/Off switch, which can be used to make the device use just two bands or even one band (in which case it's not a multiband processor at all).

Below each of the On/Off switches, you'll also see a number box for specifying a frequency. These are the crossover points for the device, and they define the exact range of frequencies that each of the bands controls. So you'll see that the High frequency band includes everything above 2.5kHz by default, but by changing this value, you can easily make the High band include only frequencies above 5kHz. The Mid band then handles everything below 5kHz down to whatever frequency is specified for the Low band.

As you play a signal through this device, you'll see meters in the center display for each band, showing the volume of the signal. The clear blocks at the far left and right of the display are a graphical representation of the Threshold and Ratio settings. The left-hand block is used to display settings for either upward compression (making a signal louder when it dips below a given threshold) or standard expansion (making a signal quieter when it dips below a given threshold), which is similar to gating. The right-hand blocks make settings for upward expansion (making a signal louder when it exceeds a given threshold) or standard downward compression.

In any of these cases, the threshold is set by dragging the edges of the boxes left or right, making them longer or shorter, and the ratio is specified by dragging up or down anywhere within the boxes. You'll see that, depending on the direction you drag, the box turns either orange or blue. Blue signifies ratios of greater than 1, which means gain reduction, while orange signifies ratios of less than 1, meaning there will be a gain increase when the threshold is crossed. To view these values numerically, click the B (for Below) or A (for Above) in the lower right-hand corner of the display. *Below* shows you the settings for the left-hand block, while *Above* shows the ones on the right. The T (for Threshold) will adjust the Attack and Release times.

In practice, multiband processors are often used in mastering. For example, you might want to leave the low end of a dance track big and uncompressed, while giving the mids more of a squeeze so they don't get painful at high volumes. When you're learning to use Multiband Dynamics, don't be afraid to turn off the Activator switch for two of the bands and just focus on one. For example, if you've got a part that sounds too crisp, but EQing it makes it sound too dull, try turning the mid and low bands off and see if you can get what you want by applying a little compression to the top.

Multiband Dynamics also features a Sidechain section, which functions just like that of Compressor, except that it lacks an EQ section. Refer to the "Compressor" section in this chapter for more information.

Delay Effects

Ableton's Delay effects group may just be the company's most creative effects ever. Each effect features solid tools for both assembling new rhythmic variations and creating innovative textures with repeated long sounds. While many of the delays have some similar controls, each delay is also somewhat specialized and has some unique features. As you explore them one by one, don't be afraid to do lots of experimenting and get lost in your own creativity.

Simple Delay

While you may think we are starting simple, Live's Simple Delay is still a formidable stereo, tempo-syncable delay, with a rhythmic beat-division chooser (see in Figure 9.13).

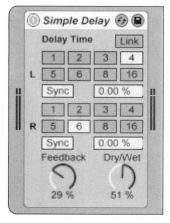

Figure 9.13 Live's Simple Delay plug-in.
Source: Ableton

Looking at the device, you can see two separate beat-division choosers—one for the left channel and one for the right. If you are in Sync mode—where the small Sync box is illuminated in green—each boxed number represents a multiple of the 1/16-note delay time. For instance, choosing a 4 would mean a four-1/16-note delay, or a full 1/4-note hold, before you would hear the delayed note sound. An 8 would be two beats, and 16 would be four beats—typically, an entire measure. In either of the beat-division choosers, you can select 1, 2, 3, 4, 5, 6, 8, or 16 for your delay multiple.

As mentioned, this beat dividing works only if the green Sync button is depressed for that channel (right or left). *Sync* means that the delay is set to synchronize with the song tempo (beats per minute). If you disengage the Sync, you can manually set delay time with precision of up to $\frac{1}{1000}$ of a second by click-dragging (up or down) on the Time field box. Note that with Sync engaged, this same box allows adjustment of the delay time by a percentage. This means that you are slowing or speeding up the delay below or above the current project tempo. In other words, you can add a little slop, or even approximate a triplet feel, if your delays are sounding too strict.

> **DOUBLE WIDE:** Any signal can be given stereo width by using an easy delay trick. Set both the left and right sides of a Simple Delay to Time mode and then set the left delay to 1ms and the right to 20ms. Next, set the effect to 100% wet. It will sound as if the center has dropped out, and the signal is coming only from the sides. To further customize this effect, experiment with different delay times and Dry/Wet settings.

The Dry/Wet knob determines how much of the effect versus original sound you hear. *Dry* is the term audio engineers use to refer to the original sound, while *wet* is the delayed or affected sound. A setting of 12 o'clock, or 50%, for Dry/Wet will create a delay signal that is at the same volume as the original. A 100% Wet setting means that you will no longer hear the original sound, only the delay effect.

Feedback controls the duration and intensity of the effect. By increasing the percentage of Feedback, you raise the effect's signal output to its own input. The circular signal created by Feedback will radically shape the delay, from slapback echo (short delay time, low feedback) to a wild echo chamber potentially spiraling out of control (with large amounts of feedback).

> **ALL WET:** When effects plug-ins are located in one of the Return tracks, set the Dry/Wet setting to 100% wet. Since the original source sound is still audible through Live's Mixer, there is no need to route any dry signal through the effect.

Ping Pong Delay

Like a game of Ping-Pong, Ableton's Ping Pong Delay (see Figure 9.14) plays a game of stereo tennis with your sound by serving it up from left to right. In looking at this device, you may notice that many of the controls are similar to the Simple Delay covered earlier. Like Simple Delay, Ping Pong Delay is a stereo delay with built-in tempo synchronizing capability, and it sports the same delay-time beat-division chooser boxes, as well as the same Dry/Wet and Feedback controls; however, Ping Pong Delay is a little more creative in terms of what frequencies actually get delayed (repeated). You will find a band-pass filter, complete with an adjustable X-Y controller axis to adjust both the cutoff frequency and the width of the frequency band (the Q). You can select between 50Hz and 18kHz and a Q from .5 to 9dB.

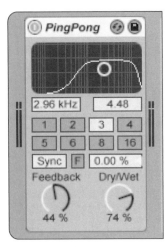

Figure 9.14 Live's Ping Pong Delay bounces a signal from left to right.
Source: Ableton

Notice that the same Sync and delay time boxes are also present in Ping Pong Delay. When Sync is activated, Ping Pong Delay will rhythmically synchronize your audio delays from left to right, according to your beat-division chooser. Once you deactivate Sync, you can set the delay time manually from 1 to 999ms.

Next to the Sync switch is a tiny little button labeled *F*. This is the Freeze button. When active, it will cause the Ping Pong Delay to repeat indefinitely without fading away and without adding new audio into the loop. Therefore, you can "freeze" what is repeating by activating this button. When you deactivate it, the delay will continue to decay and repeat as normal.

Filter Delay

Next in Live's group of delay effects is the powerful Filter Delay. This effect is actually three delays in one: one stereo delay and two mono delays—one on each stereo channel. Individual delays can be toggled on and off via the L, L+R, and R boxes on the far left, seen in Figure 9.15. Similarly, each high- and low-pass filter can also be switched on and off via the green box labeled On (default setting) in the upper left-hand corner next to the X-Y controllers.

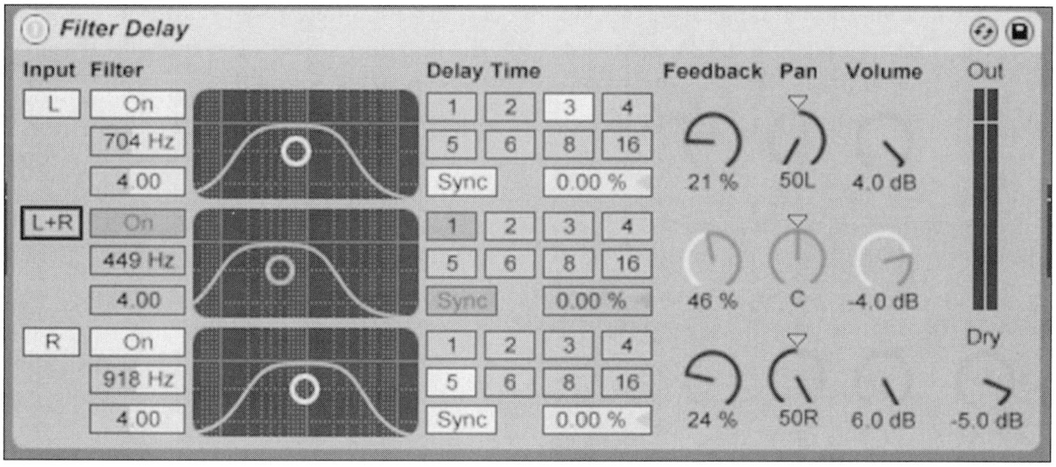

Figure 9.15 Live's very flexible Filter Delay. Notice that the L+R input is disabled in this example, causing the device to produce completely independent results for the left and right channels.
Source: Ableton

The Filter Delay device is made up of three individual delays, each with its own filter. The X-Y controllers work in the same way as the Ping Pong Delay. The Y-axis determines the bandwidth (Q), while the X-axis shifts the frequency. Each delay also features its own beat-division chooser with tempo-syncable delay times.

On the right-hand side of the plug-in, you will see Feedback, Pan, and Volume controls specific to each delay. Each feedback control will reroute the delayed signal back through that delay's input (just like all Live delays). Each delay's Pan knob can be used to override its default setting. For instance, if you pan the L delay (top delay) to the right side (with the top Pan knob), you will hear it on the right.

Instead of a Dry/Wet knob, the Filter Delay has separate Volume knobs for each delay. The unaffected signal level is controlled with the Dry knob, located in the lower right-hand corner. For a 100% wet signal, turn the Dry setting to 0.

> **IN TRANSITION:** Right-click in the title bar of the Simple, Ping Pong, or Filter delays to reveal the Transition Modes: Jump, Fade and Repitch. Select Repitch and play with the delay time while passing a signal through. As the delay time changes, you'll hear the raising and lowering of the delayed signal's pitch, just like you would with a tape delay or analog delay unit. Jump works almost identically to the default Fade mode, but it allows the production of digital artifacts created by changing delay times. Fans of a glitchy digital sound palette may like this mode.

The Input switches at the far left are used to turn the delays on and off, while the On/Off switches next to the filter can be used to enable or disable filtering of the signal. These options make the Filter Delay the most customizable of Live's delay units.

Grain Delay

Grain Delay is among Live's more complex and creative effects. The Grain Delay is the same as Live's other delays in that it has many of the same controls: Delay Time, Feedback, Dry/Wet mix, and Beat Quantize settings. While the other delays we've seen so far had a filter at the input stage, the Grain Delay has a granular resynthesizer instead. The basic concept is that Grain Delay dissects audio into tiny grains, staggers the delay timing of these grains, and then opens up a toolbox full of pitch, randomized pitch, and spray controls for some far-out sound design results. While all the common delay controls exist in this device, the lion's share of the Grain Delay interface (seen in Figure 9.16) is taken up by a large parameter-assignable X-Y controller.

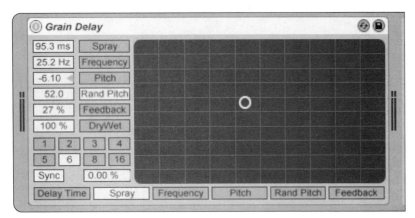

Figure 9.16 Live's Grain Delay can take audio apart, randomly altering the structure and pitch before replaying the sound.
Source: Ableton

Frequency

This is the second parameter in the delay interface, but its setting affects all the others, so I'll explain it first. In the Grain Delay, small grains of sound are quickly dispersed. The Frequency setting determines the size and duration of each grain that will be subsequently delayed and can range from 1 to 150Hz. The default setting of 60Hz means that each second of incoming audio is divided into 60 grains. This means that a low setting creates a large grain, while higher Frequency settings create smaller grains. High-frequency settings (lots of small grains) will help keep sounds with rhythmical timing, such as drum loops, intact through the resynthesis process. Low-frequency settings will sound more natural for long sounds, such as textures and pads. If you are having trouble getting a desirable setting out of the Grain Delay, set the frequency to 150 and work backward from there.

Spray

The Spray parameter roughs up the sound, adding noise and garble to the delayed signal. This setting will allow the Grain Delay to choose a random delay offset amount for each grain. If the Frequency setting above is a high value, the effect of Spray will be more pronounced, as there are more grains to randomize every second. The delay time for Spray can range from 0 to 500ms. Smaller values tend to create a fuzzy-sounding delay effect, while a larger Spray setting will completely take apart the original signal.

Pitch versus Random Pitch

Like the Spray parameter, Random Pitch tends to throw sound around. The amount of randomness can range from 0 to 161 in terms of intensity (0 being the lowest intensity). The plain old Pitch parameter ranges from 12 to −36 half steps, while allowing for two decimal-point interim values. In other words, fine-tuning a delayed signal's pitch to an actual, discernible tone would be best suited for the Pitch control; trying to eliminate, destroy, or add movement to a pitched signal is the strength of high Random Pitch values. You can use Pitch and Random Pitch in tandem for some robotic and wild pitch modifications. As with the Spray control, the higher the Frequency setting, the more pronounced the Random Pitch effect will be because there are more grains to be resynthesized.

Putting Grain Delay to Use

Now that you have some idea of just what kind of mischief the Grain Delay is up to, it's time to get familiar with using Grain Delay's X-Y interface. The parameters it controls are selected by clicking one of the boxes located along the side and bottom.

Along the X (horizontal) interface, you will see the boxes for Delay Time, Spray, Frequency, Pitch, Random Pitch, and Feedback. The vertical Y-axis can be set to control Spray, Frequency, Pitch, Random Pitch, Feedback, and Dry/Wet controls. To set feedback to be controlled by the Y-axis, simply click on the vertically aligned box labeled *Feedback* just above the Dry/Wet setting. To enable the X-axis to control the delay time, click the Delay Time box in the bottom left corner.

Now you're ready to graphically manipulate these controls. Vertical moves affect the Y-axis, while horizontal moves alter the X-axis.

> **SHIFT MY PITCH UP:** One of the more straightforward applications for the Grain Delay is to provide an echo at a pitch different from the original track. Leave the Spray and Random Pitch values at 0 and choose your delay time normally. If the Pitch value is at 0, the Grain Delay will be working like the Simple Delay in that it delays only the incoming signal. Change the Pitch setting to transpose the echo to a new note. For example, choosing a Pitch setting of 12 will cause the delayed signal to come back an octave higher than the original. This can be fun on vocal parts.

Reverb

While Ableton's Reverb device may not seem like a delay, it is certainly from the same time-based effect family. Reverberation occurs when sound bounces off a surface, usually many surfaces, many times. In the process of reflecting, the original sound dissipates, becoming diffuse and eventually disappearing altogether. Depending upon the shape and reflective qualities of the room, certain frequencies will be more pronounced than others in the reverberated sound, or *tail*.

The number of controls may seem daunting, but as we step carefully through the signal path, you will see that it all makes sense. Before we get carried away, take a quick look at Figure 9.17.

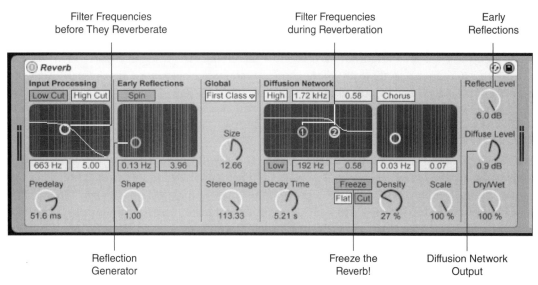

Figure 9.17 Live's feature-laden Reverb plug-in.
Source: Ableton

Input Processing

The first link in Reverb's signal chain is the Input Processing section. Here you have on/off selectable Low- and High-Cut filtering, as well as a Predelay control. The Low-Cut and High-Cut X-Y interface allows you to trim your input's frequencies before they are reverberated. Similar to Live's other delays, the X-axis shifts the frequency of the cut (50Hz to 18kHz), while the Y-axis changes the bandwidth (.50 to 9.0). You can also turn each filter off by deselecting its green illuminated box. I recommend spending some time playing with this filter each time you use this effect. Think of these filters as altering the acoustic characteristics of a room. For instance, a concrete room may not reproduce low frequencies as well as an acoustically engineered studio room. Each room will favor completely different frequencies.

Also, check out the Predelay control for adding milliseconds of time before you hear the first early reflections, or delayed sound, of the forthcoming reverberation. Predelay is very useful for preserving the definition of the sound you're adding reverb to. Even with longer decay times, you can crank up the predelay to prevent the original sound from becoming too wet or buried by the effect. While the Predelay can range from .50 to 250ms, to simulate a normal-sounding room, the Predelay works best below 25ms.

Early Reflections

Early reflections are the first reverberations heard after the initial sound bounces off the walls, floor, or ceiling of the room—yet they arrive ahead of the full reflection, or tail. At times, they sound like slapback delays or mushy portions of the whole reverberated (diffused) sound. The Reverb houses two early reflection controls: Shape and Spin. Spin's X-Y interface controls, Depth (Y-axis) and Frequency (X-axis), apply a subtle modulation to early reflections. Results may range from shimmering highs to whirligig panning flourishes. For quicker decay of early reflections, try increasing the Shape control gradually toward 1.00. Lower values will blend more smoothly with the normal reverb diffusion.

Global Settings

In Reverb's Global settings section, you can select the quality level of the reverb: Eco, Mid, or High. The three settings will demand small, moderate, and large processor power, respectively. You may also determine the size of the imaginary room via the Size control, which ranges from .22 (small/quiet) to 500 (large/loud). A Stereo Image control selects from 0 to 120 degrees of stereo spread in the reverberation. Higher values will be more spread out, while lower ones approach a mono sound.

Diffusion Network

The Diffusion Network is by far the most complex-looking area of the Reverb effect. These controls help put the final touches on the actual reverberation that follows closely behind the early reflections. From here, you will be able to decorate and control the finer points of the reverberated sound. To begin with, High and Low shelving filters can further define your imaginary room's sound. By shaving off the highs, for instance, your room may sound more like a concert hall or large auditorium, while brightening up the diffusion (raising the high shelf) will approximate a "bathroom" reverb. Similar to X-Y interface-controlled filters, each filter's X-axis determines frequency, while the Y-axis controls bandwidth. Turning these filters off will conserve some system resources.

Beneath the High and Low shelving controls, you will find the Reverb's Decay Time settings, which range from an extremely short 200ms to a cavernous 60-second-long tail. Long reverbs are mesmerizing but can make audio sound muddy and jumbled if used profusely.

To test the coloring and sonic quality of your Reverb, you can use the Freeze control. Any time you press Freeze, Reverb will indefinitely hold and reproduce the diffusion tail. When Flat is activated, the low- and high-pass filters will be ignored. In other words, your frozen Reverb tail will contain all frequencies. An active Cut command prevents further audio from being frozen, even if it is passing through the Reverb. The second X-Y interface in the Diffusion Network, labeled Chorus, can add subtle motion or wobbly effect to the overall Reverb tail diffusion. When not in use, deactivate the Chorus button to save system resources.

The final section in Diffusion Network controls the density (thickness) and scale (coarseness) of the diffusion's echo. The Density control ranges from .1% (a lighter-sounding reverb) to a 96% rich and chewy reverb, while Scale can run from 5 to 100%, gradually adding a darker and murkier quality to the diffusion. A high Density setting will diminish the amount of audible change made by Scale controls.

Output

The Output section is the final link in the Reverb signal chain. At this stage, just three knobs, Dry/Wet, Reflect Level, and Diffuse Level, put the finishing touches on your masterpiece. Dry/Wet controls the ratio of original, unaffected sound to affected, reverberated sound that you hear coming from the effect's output. The Reflect Level control knob adjusts the amplitude (level) of the early reflections specified in the Early Reflections box, from −30 to +6 dB. The louder you make the early reflections, the more you will hear an echo of the true sound (which will sound even more like a slapback delay as opposed to a reverb).

In similar fashion, the Diffuse Level controls the amount of Diffusion Network level in the final Reverb output. A low diffusion level will diminish the reverb tail, while a high amplitude of Diffusion Network will increase the overall presence of the effect.

Modulation Effects

The term "modulate" simply means "to change," so by itself, it doesn't really tell us much about what these effects do. Generally speaking, when we speak about modulation effects, we are talking about ones that are driven by an LFO, such that an inherent part of the effect is the sound of it changing over time. Make sure that you're clear on the role of the LFO in the Auto Filter and Auto Pan effects, and you'll have a much easier time understanding the ones in this section. That said, some of these effects also produce quite useful results without using the LFO section at all. As usual, carve out some time to explore each one fully.

Chorus

When you listen to a group of people singing a chorus, each member of the group has slightly different timing and intonation, even if they're singing the same words with the same melody. The result is a large and lush vocal sound achieved by the variations in all of the voices.

The Chorus effect attempts to re-create this phenomenon by taking the input signal, delaying it by varying amounts, adding a touch of random Pitch Shift, and then blending the results with the original. In other words, Chorus effects assume that two sounds are better than one. It is common to run synthesizers, guitars, vocals, and strings through a chorus. The doubling, or even tripling, effect of a chorus makes solo voices sound more powerful, takes up more space in a mix, and therefore sounds more "present."

Live's Chorus (see Figure 9.18) features two parallel delays that can be set for .01 to 20ms or linked by activating a tiny equal sign (=).

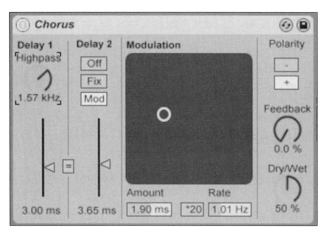

Figure 9.18   Live's Chorus effect. Note the tiny equal sign (=) between the delays. This button syncs the two.
Source: Ableton

Delays 1 and 2

The effect's first delay will always be active when the Chorus is on. To adjust the delay's timing, slide the fader. The adjustable Highpass filter knob bypasses chorusing low frequencies, which can often become muddier and less defined when doubled. The definable range is 20Hz to 15kHz. Delay 1 can be used on its own or in parallel with Delay 2.

Chorus's Delay 2 can add even more thickness and intensity to your sounds. Delay 2 can run in two separate modes, Fix and Mod, and can be bypassed by selecting the top visible button labeled Off. Fix mode will force Delay 2 to the timing specified by its slider. Mod mode will allow the delay time to be modulated by the effect's Mod source.

Modulation

The Chorus's Modulation section is where the effect gets its movement. This section controls a sine wave oscillator (an LFO), which can be used to change the timing of the two delays. Whether you are going for completely unrecognizable new sounds or just looking for a little more stereo spread, you will want to spend some time fiddling (click-dragging) with the Modulation X-Y controller. Horizontal moves change the modulation rate from .03 to 10Hz, while the vertical axis increases the amount of modulation from 0 to 6.5ms. So if Delay 1 is set to 1ms, and you have a modulation amount of 1ms, the LFO will continually change the delay time between 0 and 2ms. The modulation rate changes the speed of the LFO from subtle movements to bubbly vibrations. You also have the option of typing in values by simply clicking on the box, typing a number within the allotted range, and pressing the Enter key.

The LFO will modulate both delays in stereo. This means that the delay times used for the right and left channels will be different, which increases the stereo intensity of the effect. This also means that if both delays are being modulated, there will be four different delay times at any given moment. How's that for fattening up a sound?

If you are looking for radical sonic redesign, the *20 button multiplies the Chorus' LFO rate by 20. While this may not sound great all of the time, the *20 multiplier will push the envelope of the dullest of sounds.

Feedback, Polarity, and Dry/Wet

For increased intensity, the Feedback control will send part of the output signal back through the delays. The more feedback you elect to add, the more robotic and metallic your sounds will become. The positive and negative polarity switch determines whether the signal being fed back to the delays is added to or subtracted from the new input signal. To hear the greatest contrast between the two polarities, you should use short delay times and increase the Chorus Feedback. The results are often frequency and pitch related. For example, a low-frequency sound becomes a high-frequency sound, a pitch may shift by as much as an octave, and so forth. Finally, the Dry/Wet control determines the amount of original versus chorused signal going to output.

Phaser

The Phaser (see Figure 9.19) introduces phase shifts in the frequencies of a sound. When this effect is in motion, it has a sort of whooshing sound that can give your sounds a smooth sense of warmth and motion. It can also cut into your sounds if cranked up too far, thanks to some unorthodox controls.

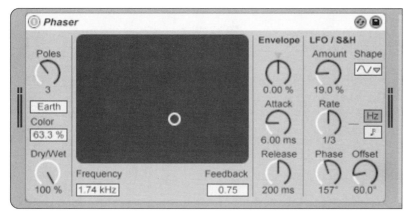

Figure 9.19 Star Fleet requires that you be equipped with a Phaser at all times.
Source: Ableton

Poles, Color, and Mode

The Phaser uses a series of filters to create the phase shifts you hear in the sound. The Poles control sets the number of filters, or notches, that are used in the Phaser. If you use a lower number of poles, the Phaser effect will not be as pronounced as when you use a larger number of poles.

The button below the Poles knob sets the mode for the Phaser. The button toggles between Earth and Space. This switch adjusts the spacing of the notch filters, but that's not important. What you need to know is that when *Earth* doesn't provide an intense enough effect for you, it's time to move to *Space*. The Color control will further change the overall tone when Earth mode is active.

Frequency and Feedback

The large X-Y area in the middle of the Phaser is for adjusting the center frequency and the feedback amount. Move the dot on the screen left and right to adjust frequency (or use the number box in the lower-left corner). Vertical movement will adjust the feedback (whose number box is in the lower-right corner). You normally won't find a feedback control on a typical Phaser, but it's a control that Ableton added to its Phaser to help emphasize the Phase effect.

LFO and Envelope

Phaser's LFO section is used to automatically modulate the Frequency parameter. This section is a duplicate of the LFO found in the Auto Filter. You'll use the Speed controls to set the LFO rate either in relation to the current tempo or freely in Hertz. The relation of the left and right LFOs is set with the Phase/Spin controls. Finally, the LFO's overall influence on the Phaser frequency is set with the Amount knob.

Like the LFO, the Envelope is identical to the envelope follower you'll find in the Auto Filter device. It works by using the volume of the incoming signal as a means to modulate the frequency of the Phaser. The speed at which the envelope follower responds to changes in input volume is governed by the Attack and Release knobs. Use the top knob (Envelope Amount) to increase the envelope's influence on the Phaser frequency.

Flanger

The Flanger bears an extremely close resemblance to the Phaser, both in design and use (see Figure 9.20). A flanger works by taking a sound, delaying it by a continuously changing amount, and blending it back with the original sound. This introduces constructive and destructive interference between various frequencies in the sound, producing a characteristic comb filter effect. The Flanger has a much more metallic edge than the Phaser. Its sound can become quite abrasive with high feedback settings, as you'll see in a moment.

Figure 9.20 In the old days, flanging involved playing two identical recordings on tape machines and then touching the flanges of one of the tape reels to subtly shift the timing of the two recordings. Live's Flanger makes the same effect easier and cheaper to achieve.

Source: Ableton

Hi Pass Filter

As mentioned previously, the Flanger will make a copy of the input signal and mix it back in with the original after a brief delay. Often, this can product inharmonic (unpitched) results, which can make melodic parts "muddy." To alleviate this effect, you can pass the input signal through a Hi Pass filter. When the delayed signal is mixed back in with the original, the flanging will take effect only on the higher frequencies, leaving the lower frequencies intact.

Delay and Feedback

This looks quite similar to the X-Y control in the Phaser, doesn't it? Functionally, it's the same—horizontal movements adjust the delay time, while vertical movements increase the Feedback. Because the Flanger uses a delay, there will be a pitch to the effect, which is related to the Delay Time parameter. As the delay time is shortened, the pitch will seem to rise. When you crank up the Feedback, the pitch will become even more pronounced.

Envelope and LFO

These two sections are identical in functionality to those of the Phaser and Auto Filter, except they modulate the delay time of the Flanger. To push things to the max, switch the Feedback polarity of the Flangers by clicking the small + button next to the Feedback number box in the bottom-right corner of the X-Y control. By default, the LFO is set to 100% to create the classic "swoosh" that flangers are known for.

Distortions

This brings us to the third group of Ableton's devices: the Distortion effects. While each of these effects can quickly and drastically alter your audio content, taking time to learn the ins and outs of these babies can take your mixes to a whole new level. Note that both Saturator and Dynamic Tube have a Hi Quality mode to reduce aliasing artifacts in high-frequency sounds. This mode is turned on by right-clicking in the device's title bar and selecting Hi Quality from the context menu. There's only a small CPU hit for using this feature, so it's generally recommended to turn it on.

Overdrive

Overdrive is the simplest of Live's distortion effects. Instead of trying to be the most flexible effect, Overdrive models the behavior of some popular effect boxes for guitar. As the term is usually used to signify, Overdrive (see Figure 9.21) produces a warm, harmonically rich effect that is useful on a wide variety of sources. Even at high settings, it does not produce the harsh clipping that Saturator is capable of.

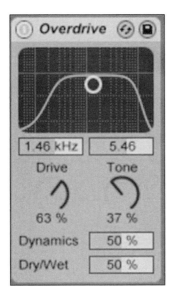

Figure 9.21 Overdrive: Live's "stomp-box" distortion.
Source: Ableton

The heart of Overdrive is the Drive knob: turn it up to get more distortion. There are two different EQ adjustments as well: the bandpass filter above, which is applied to the signal before the drive circuit, and the Tone knob, which adjusts the tone post-drive. This gives you a lot of flexibility. For example, cutting some lows with the bandpass filter may clean up the mud that you might get from distorting a bass, while the Tone knob can be used to control any harsh-sounding artifacts that the Drive circuit adds to the signal.

To further customize the sound, use the Dynamics and Dry/Wet controls. Dynamics is a simple compressor—high values preserve the original dynamics of the sound, while low values increase the compression. Don't underestimate the importance of the Dry/Wet control. In the previous example, you would use this control to make sure that you added in enough of the dry signal to compensate for the low end that you've removed from the overdriven one.

Saturator

If you like the sort of effect produced by Overdrive, but you need something more programmable, Saturator is where you'll turn next, as shown in Figure 9.22. This effect not only has a variety of analog distortion models, but it is also capable of producing digital clipping and has a flexible waveshaper.

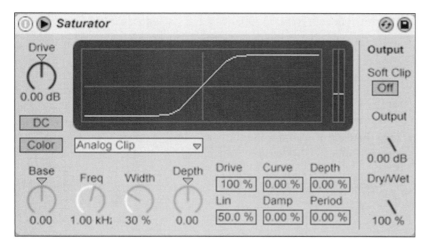

Figure 9.22 The Saturator: Subtle edge or gateway to destruction.
Source: Ableton

Waveform Display

The top of the Saturator interface is dominated by the large waveform display. Manipulating the controls below the display will give you insight into how the effect modifies your signal by looking at the resulting curve.

You can choose six different modes of signal shaping using the drop-down menu below the display: Analog Clip, Soft Sine, Medium Curve, Hard Curve, Sinoid Fold, and Digital Clip, each with its own distinct characteristics. The Waveshaper mode allows flexible control of the waveform through the six adjustable parameters listed just below the drop-down menu:

 ▷ **Drive:** Not to be confused with the Drive knob (see below), determines the amount of influence of the wave-shaping effect.
 ▷ **Curve:** Adds harmonics to the signal.
 ▷ **Depth:** Controls the amplitude of a sine wave superimposed over the distortion curve.
 ▷ **Lin:** Alters the linear portion of the shaping curve.
 ▷ **Damp:** Flattens the signal, acting as a sort of super-fast noise gate.
 ▷ **Period:** Determines the density of the ripples in the sine wave.

These controls are specific to the Waveshaper and are not available in other modes.

Drive

On a dynamic distortion unit such as this, the Drive knob is where you'll demolish your sound; you'll find this to the left of the waveform display. The higher the Drive amount, the more the input signal is amplified. This forces more of the signal into the distortion range, slaughtering the sound at high levels. If you're getting too much distortion, you can reduce the Drive into negative amounts so that only a slight portion of the signal is distorted.

Below the Drive, you'll see the DC offset switch, which removes extremely low frequencies that can't be heard. But it does consume headroom in your mix, especially when processed with an effect that increases gain, such as the Saturator.

Color

When the Color toggle switch is on, the four controls below it also become active. These controls are similar to the tone controls on a guitar amp. The Base knob will increase or decrease the amount of bass distorted by the effect. The last three knobs set a high-frequency EQ with specs for frequency, width, and depth (gain).

Output

As you increase the Drive amount, you will increase the volume of the distortion, often to the point of overpowering other instruments in your mix. Pull the Output down a bit to bring the sound back where it should be. A Dry/Wet control here sets the amount of effect being heard. When the Soft Clip button is activated, an additional instance of the Analog Clip curve will be applied to the final output.

> **HI-QUALITY:** Saturator, Flanger, and Dynamic Tube all have a "Hi-Quality" mode that can be turned on by right-clicking in the title bar and selecting "Hi-Quality" from the context menu. This mode reduces aliasing and produces a sweeter tone in the high frequencies, but uses a little more CPU power.

Dynamic Tube

The Dynamic Tube effect models the distinct effect that vacuum tubes can have on audio (see Figure 9.23). It doesn't really sound like most distortion effects. It can provide some extremely subtle effects, somewhere between compression and distortion, while its more aggressive settings sound like equipment malfunctioning!

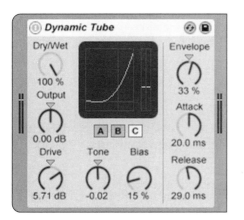

Figure 9.23 The Dynamic Tube saturation effect.
Source: Ableton

This effect allows you to choose between three different tube models: A, B, and C, with C being the most distortion-prone tube and A being the cleanest of the bunch. With Bias set at 0, tube A won't produce any distortion at all. It can, however, produce some very "hot" sounding compression.

To get familiar with Dynamic Tube, try it out on a drum loop. Sweep the Tone knob to both of its extremes, and then listen to what happens when you bring Envelope down to –300%. With a negative Envelope value, less distortion is produced for louder sounds, bringing back more of the loop's original punch.

The Tone control determines what frequencies (higher or lower) are most affected by the tube-distortion effect, while Drive sets how much of the incoming signal is routed through the tube. Setting the Drive control higher will result in a dirtier output.

The Bias control works in conjunction with the Drive control. It determines how much distortion the tube is capable of producing. As you turn this up to the top, the signal will really start to break apart into dirty, fuzzed-out noise. You can modulate the Bias control with the Envelope controls at right. The higher the setting of the Envelope knob, the more the Bias setting will be influenced by the level of the input signal. You can use the Attack and Release knobs to adjust how quickly the envelope reacts to the input.

Erosion

Erosion uses an unusual method for sonic degradation. By rapidly modulating a very short delay time, strange distortion artifacts are created. The modulator can be Noise, Wide Noise, or Sine, as seen beneath the X-Y interface (pictured in Figure 9.24).

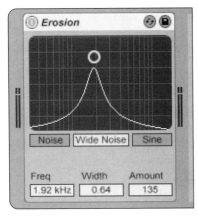

Figure 9.24 Live's Erosion device window, primarily taken up by its unusual X-Y field.
Source: Ableton

Depending upon which mode you currently have active, Erosion will use either a sine wave or a noise generator to modulate a very short delay. The only difference between the two noise modes is that Wide Noise uses a separate noise generator for each channel, resulting in a stereo effect.

To control the degree of Erosion's effect on a sound, move along the Y-axis to change the level of the modulation signal and the X-axis to control the frequency. For Wide Noise, the Width can be adjusted by holding Alt (Option) while dragging vertically. In my experience, the most consistently pleasing results are achieved using the Sine modulator. Try cranking up Amount and automating Frequency for some glitchy goodness.

Redux

While you're digging into tools for sonic decimation, you will definitely want to check out Live's Redux device. Redux is a bit-depth and sample-rate reducer that can make even the prettiest of guitars, or anything else for that matter, saw your head off (see Figure 9.25). Of course, results need not be this drastic if you are capable of restraint. In fact, reducing the fidelity of a sample is like a tip of the hat to old Roland, Emu, and Akai 8- and 12-bit samplers—or even old 2- and 4-bit computer-based samples. (Commodore 64, anyone?)

Figure 9.25 Live's Redux is a talented bit-depth and sample-rate reducer.
Source: Ableton

The controls for Redux are split into two tidy sections, with a Bit Reduction knob and On/Off switch on top, and a Downsample knob and Hard/Soft switch on the bottom. The default position for Bit Reduction is 16-bit (off). As you reduce the bits, you will hear an increasing amount of noisy grit infect the sample. Anything below 4 bits causes a dramatic increase in gain, so use caution. The numerical setting will indicate the bit depth (for example, 8 = 8-bit, 4 = 4-bit). Extremists can try trimming it down to 1-bit, but be warned: this gets LOUD!

When it comes to sample-rate reduction, the settings are a little more inexact. In Hard mode, downsampling will stick with whole integers such as 1, 2, and 3 (up to 200) for dividing the sample rate, while in Soft mode you can adjust from 1 to 20 to the nearest hundredth of a point (1.00 or 19.99). A setting of 1 means you are not hearing any sample-rate reduction—oddly, the higher the number, the lower the resulting sample rate.

For a quick course, spend a minute perusing the Ableton factory presets, such as Old Sampler and Mirage. This will give you a basic template to work from. Also, while you are in Playback mode, try toggling between Hard and Soft Downsampling with different settings for a cool effect.

Vinyl Distortion

The imperfections of vinyl have actually become quite lovable these days. Whether you are missing the dust pops and crackles of an old record or the warped vinyl sound of a record left out in the sun, vinyl has a certain retro charm. Though CDs and digital recordings are great, they are hopelessly clean and free of these impurities. Of course, Ableton thought about this, too, and as a result, we have Vinyl Distortion (see Figure 9.26).

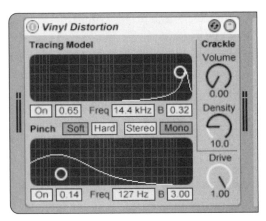

Figure 9.26 Live's Vinyl Distortion effect hopes to make you miss your turntable just a little bit less.
Source: Ableton

Vinyl Distortion is divided into three separate sections: Tracing Model, Crackle, and Pinch. While the controls for Tracing Model and Pinch look identical, each section generates a totally different sound. Also note that the Soft/Hard and Stereo/Mono switches are also a part of the Pinch effect. If Pinch is off, these controls will remain grayed out (inactive).

Tracing Model adds a subtle amount of harmonic distortion to your audio as a means of simulating wear and tear on vinyl or an old stylus. To adjust the intensity of the distortion, increase the Drive by moving the yellow circle along the Y-axis (which ranges from 0.00 to 1.00). Adjust the frequency of the harmonic on the X-axis (which ranges from 50Hz to 18kHz) or input a value manually by typing in the box. To adjust the size of the bandwidth you are affecting, hold down Alt (Option) and click-drag forward or backward on the yellow circle.

The Pinch section of Vinyl Distortion is a more drastic and wild-sounding distortion at the input level. The resulting richer stereo image is from Pinch's 180 degrees out-of-phase harmonic distortions. Like the Tracing Model, you can increase the intensity of the distortion through the Y-axis. The X-axis will configure the frequency range. You will want to pay special attention to the Soft/Hard boxes to the right of the X-Y interface in the Pinch section. Soft mode is engineered to sound like an actual dub plate (acetate), while Hard mode will sound more like a standard vinyl record. Also, the Stereo/Mono switch applies to the Pinch effect only.

No vinyl simulator would be complete without a vinyl pop and crackle effect. Crackle provides two simple controls: Volume and Density. Volume is obviously the level of the hiss and crackle in the mix. Density adds a thicker amount of noise to the output. Note that you will hear the crackle and hiss whether Live is in playback mode or not.

Miscellaneous

This last section of devices covers Live's more esoteric and hard-to-classify plug-ins. Some of these could have been squeezed into other sections of this chapter, but they are all unique enough that it made sense to give them their own section.

Amp and Cabinet

Amp and Cabinet are two completely independent effects designed by the modeling wizards at Softube. While they can certainly be used separately, they are designed to go hand in hand. Amp models the signal path of several classic guitar and bass amplifiers, while Cabinet reproduces the sound of a variety of speaker cabinet and microphone combinations. These two effects are included with Live Suite only.

Guitar amplifiers and speaker cabinets (both real and virtual) have long been part of many engineers' sound shaping toolkits. While Amp and Cabinet are certainly useful for processing direct-recorded guitars and basses, they are also great for applying distortion and unusual EQ characteristics to a wide variety of sources. When you're having trouble getting a sound to find its unique place in a mix, sometimes these devices provide just the color and edge you need.

Amp

The most important control in this device is the Amp Type selector, which offers the following modes: Clean, Boost, Blues, Rock, Lead, Heavy, and Bass (see Figure 9.27). As you'll discover quickly, each of these modes sounds radically different from one another. Run a signal through Amp and try them out. You'll know pretty quickly which of these works for the sound you're trying to process, if any. As you move from left to right, the models tend to produce more distortion until you get to Bass, which is a clean model optimized for bass guitar, but may produce good results on a variety of sources.

Figure 9.27 Are you ready to Rock?
Source: Ableton

Once you've picked a model, experiment with the Gain control. Decrease it if you want a bit less distortion and crank it up to hear the amp model at its most aggressive. Adjusting Gain will change the overall volume of the signal; use the Volume control to compensate for this. The Bass, Middle, and Treble controls adjust the lows, mids, and highs respectively, with Presence acting as an additional high-end adjustment for adjusting the sparkle. The Presence knob varies quite a bit in the various amp models, so make sure to experiment.

Cabinet

In the real world, the signal coming out of a guitar amplifier is almost always passed into a speaker cabinet, where its output is then captured by a microphone. In the virtual world of Live, you can achieve this same effect by placing the Cabinet effect after Amp.

When Amp is run on its own without Cabinet (see Figure 9.28), you'll notice that it produces some very intense treble frequencies (just like a real guitar amp would). One of the first things you'll notice when adding Cabinet to the signal path is the taming of these intense high frequencies and the imparting of a mellower characteristic to the sound.

Figure 9.28 Amp's best buddy, Cabinet.
Source: Ableton

The first parameter for adjusting the sound is the Speaker menu. The configurations in this menu follow the convention <number of speakers> × <speaker size>. So, for example, 4 × 10 means a cabinet with four 10-inch speakers in it. Selecting a speaker configuration is much more art than science, although you may notice that the 12" speakers reproduce a bit more low end than the 10" ones. The 4 × 10 Bass cabinet reproduces the most high-end sound of the bunch, as it models a style of bass cabinet that contains tweeters for delivering crisp highs.

The next adjustment is the microphone type and placement. Condenser microphones tend to capture more high-end sounds and a more balanced sound overall, while Dynamic mics are known for their focus and punch when used on speaker cabinets. Placement has a big impact on sound as well. Off-Axis placement tends to capture more low-end sounds, while Far placement emulates recording the speaker from across the room, capturing room reflections and a sense of space.

Output

Finally, both Amp and Cabinet allow stereo or mono operation via an Output switch and have a Dry/Wet knob for blending unprocessed signal with the output. Be aware that both devices are relatively CPU-hungry, and running them in stereo doubles the required resources.

Auto Pan

Auto Pan is a conceptually simple but surprisingly powerful device. It will automatically pan the position of the track from left to right in cycles. It does this by alternately turning down the volumes of the left and right sides of the channel. When the left side is turned down, the sound will be heard from the right, thus making it sound as if the track were panned to the left. The mixer's Pan control is not affected at all.

The Auto Pan interface is split into two sections. The top section contains a graphical representation of the volume pattern being applied—for display purposes only. The Auto Pan is adjusted by using the knobs and buttons on the lower half of the interface.

Amount and Rate

When the device is first loaded, it will have a flat line through the middle of its display, and you will hear no effect. The reason you hear nothing is because the Amount knob is set to 0%. As you turn this knob up, you'll hear the sound begin moving left and right. The higher you set the Amount knob, the "wider" the left-to-right movement will be.

As you increase the Amount knob, you'll also see the graphic begin to change on the Auto Pan interface. When the Amount reaches 100%, you'll see two sine curves representing the left and right channels. What these curves tell you is that when the left channel is at full volume, the right channel will be at its lowest volume (see Figure 9.29). As the left channel drops in volume, the right channel will rise and vice versa. The button below the Amount knob will switch the left and right Pan assignments (Normal vs. Invert).

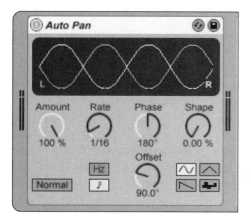

Figure 9.29 By looking at the picture in the Auto Pan window, you can see the relationship of the left and right channels over time.
Source: Ableton

The Rate will change the speed of the left-right motion created by the Auto Pan. You'll see that as you turn up this knob, not only does the left-right speed increase, but you'll also see the graphic waveform change in kind. The rate can be set in either cycles per second (Hz) or divisions of the beat (the musical note button).

Phase and Shape

Next on the list of Auto Pan controls is the Phase knob. If you move this knob while watching the waveform graphic, you'll see that this knob adjusts the phase relationship of the left and right curves, or the position where the waveforms start. When set to 180 degrees, the two curves are out of phase, meaning one channel is at full volume while the other is silent. If you twist this knob down to 0 degrees, the two curves will now be in sync (you'll see only one curve), resulting in the left and right channels changing volume in sync. The Auto Pan will no longer pan the signal from left to right—it will simply turn the volume of the whole signal up and down. This is where the Auto Pan device begins to function beyond what its name implies, and it becomes a "chopper" or rhythmic volume control.

Below the Phase knob, you'll find either the Phase and Spin buttons (when in Hz mode) or the Offset knob (when in Beats mode). These controls work identically to their counterparts in the Auto Filter, so review that section if you need the details on how they work.

The last knob on the Auto Pan is the Shape knob. As this knob is turned clockwise, the waveform will slowly morph into a square wave. When set to 100%, this will cause the Auto Pan to flip-flop the audio between the left and right channels—there will be no motion through the center. Of course, setting this knob at an amount less than 100% will allow you to hear some of the left-right transition.

In real terms, we use this knob to make the pan "stall" at the left and right extremes. Sometimes, even though the Amount knob is set to 100%, it doesn't sound like the sound is fully panning from left to right, especially when being mixed in with the other parts of the song. This is because the sound is panned fully left and right for only an instant before the Auto Pan begins to pan it back again. Turning up the Shape knob results in flat lines at the top and bottom of the waveform, causing the pan motion to sit at these extremes for a moment before panning back to the other side. The result is a more pronounced panning motion that can be heard best over an entire mix.

The final controls of the Auto Pan are the Waveform Selection buttons that control the shape of the modulation, just like in other LFOs you've encountered in Live. The last button in the lower right is for a random waveform where the volumes of the left and right channels are changed at random. When this mode is selected, the Phase knob adjusts the left-right deviation of the randomness. When set to 0%, the random pattern will influence the left and right volumes identically, resulting in random changes to the sound's volume. When set to 100%, the difference between the left and right volumes will increase, resulting in random panning patterns.

CHOP IT UP: When Phase is set to 0 degrees, the Auto Pan will simply turn the volume of the sound up and down. Try this out: load an entire song onto a track and use Auto Pan. Set its Rate to 1/8, shape to 100%, Phase to 0 degrees, Offset to 270 degrees, and Waveform to sine. As you increase the Amount knob, you'll begin to hear the track volume jump up and down in 1/8-note steps in sync with the song. Turn up Amount to 100%, and you'll have chopped the song into tiny slices!

For a really crazy effect, try slightly altering the Phase knob. When the two waveforms are just slightly out of phase, you'll hear each strobe zip across your speakers as one side is turned on just slightly before the other.

Beat Repeat

Glitch-heads, rejoice! Ableton brings you the Beat Repeat device (see Figure 9.30). Now you can produce the classic beat-stutter with the push of a button, or even cause repeats to happen randomly.

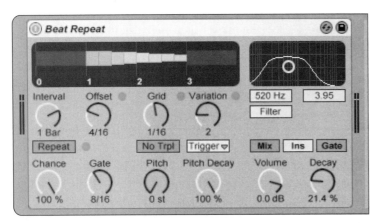

Figure 9.30 Th-Th-Th-This dev-v-v-v-ice is sw-ee-ee-ee-ee-t!
Source: Ableton

Grid and Variation

You set the size, or length, of the repeated segment with the Grid knob. Turn on Repeat and try tweaking this knob. You'll hear the Repeat size change in real time—an awesome effect for remixing. The No Trpl button will remove the triplet values when scrolling through the grid sizes, which is handy if you want to keep all the rhythmic repeats in sync.

The Variation knob just to the right of the Grid knob introduces randomness to the grid size. When set to 0%, the grid will always be what you've set with the Grid knob. As this value increases, Live automatically changes the grid, based on the mode selected in the pop-up menu below the knob. When you select Trigger in that menu, Live gives you a new grid size anytime you start the Repeat function. It will hold the grid size until you stop or retrigger the Repeat. The 1/4, 1/8, and 1/16 settings will change the Grid setting at the specified time interval. The Auto setting will change the grid size after every repeat. This can get really hairy, as you can have a single repeat of 1/64 followed by a repeat of 1/6, followed by 1/16, followed by 1/2, and so on. The results are truly unpredictable!

Offset and Gate

These two knobs determine when an automatic repeat will start and how long it will last. When Offset is set to 0, the repeat will start the instant it is called by the Interval and Chance knobs. If you turn this knob clockwise, you'll see it count up in 1/16 notes—with the knob turned up halfway, the value will be 8/16. This means that the Beat Repeat won't start until the third beat of the bar. You'll also see the Repeat markers move in the display as a visual aid.

The Gate knob sets how long the repeats will last once triggered. If set to 4/16, the repeat will last for a quarter note. If set to 8/16, the repeats will last for half a bar. Therefore, using Offset and Grid, you can specify any location in the audio to repeat, as well as how long to do it.

To hear all these properties at work, launch the Automatic Scene. This will play the same drumbeat, but through a Beat Repeat on another channel.

Chance, Interval, and Repeat

In its default state, Beat Repeat's Chance parameter is set to 100%, which means that repeats will be generated every interval. With interval set to 1 Bar, you'll hear repeats once per bar. If you set Chance to 50%, there will only be a 1-in-2 chance that the Beat Repeat will trigger.

It's also possible to set the Chance knob to 0% and trigger the repeat effect manually using the Repeat button. Try this out. As soon as you click Repeat, you're off to the races. Click the Repeat button again to turn it off, and the regular beat will resume. Obviously, this button is named well.

Mix, Insert, and Gate

These three buttons control the output mode of the Beat Repeat. So far, you've been using the Insert mode. In Insert mode the original drumbeat is silenced whenever repeats are occurring. Click the Mix button and try using the Repeat button. In Mix mode, you'll hear the original drum beat while the repeats occur—the two are being mixed together. The final mode, Gate, always silences the original signal and only outputs the repeats. This mode is useful when you've placed the Beat Repeat on a return track, especially if you've chained additional effects after the Beat Repeat.

Volume and Decay

The Volume knob sets the volume of the repeated sounds. Note that the first repeat is always at the original volume. I like to decrease the volume a little bit so that the music comes back in heavier after the repeat. It's almost necessary to turn this down when you're using small grid sizes because the repeats become so fast that they start to make a tone of their own.

The Decay knob will cause the volume of each consecutive repeat to be quieter than the first. This means that your repeats will slowly (or quickly) fade away to silence each time you trigger Repeat.

Pitch

The Pitch controls can be used to introduce pitch shifts into your repeats. The Pitch knob will simply transpose the repeated sound down by the specified number of semitones. The Pitch Decay knob works similarly to the Volume Decay knob, except that it makes the pitch drop further and further with each consecutive repeat. It's possible to make the repeated sound drop so low in pitch that it becomes inaudible. This is a neat tool to use in conjunction with the Volume Decay because you can make your repeats drop in pitch and fade away at the same time.

Filter

This filter functions in the same way as the filter in the Ping Pong Delay, except that the repeated sounds are not fed back through this filter. When Repeat is on, you can engage the filter and choose a specific frequency range for the repeats. This can give your repeats a lo-fi sound in comparison to the normal part. You can even change the filter frequency and width while Repeat is running for even more animation.

Corpus

Corpus is the effect version of Collision (see Figure 9.31). It's included when you buy Collision (or the Live Suite), making it the only audio effect that doesn't come with the basic version of Live. The majority of the effect is nearly identical to Collision, so we'll be focusing on the aspects that differentiate it here. Like Collision, this effect is only included with Live Suite.

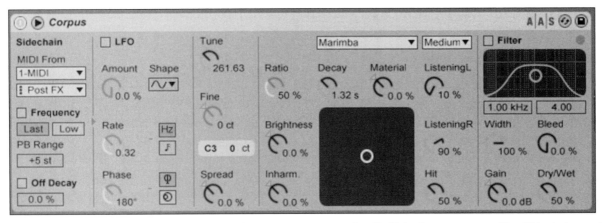

Figure 9.31 Corpus processes any sound source you want using Collision's resonators. The Sidechain section at the left allows you to control the pitch of the resonators via MIDI.
Source: Ableton

The main difference between Collision and Corpus is that there is no Excitator section. This is because the effect uses the input signal to get the virtual resonator vibrating. The area that would be used for the Excitator is instead filled by an LFO, which controls the pitch of the resonator. For more information on how Ableton's LFOs work, please consult the "Auto Filter" and "Auto Pan" sections of this chapter.

What makes Corpus really interesting is its Sidechain section, which is displayed by clicking the triangular unfold switch in the title bar. Unlike the other Sidechain sections we've looked at, this one uses a MIDI track as its source, because Corpus can receive MIDI notes to control the pitch of the resonators. So, for example, I could use Collision to produce some unusual resonance on a synthesizer sound and use the synth's MIDI part to make sure that the resonance is perfectly tuned to every note played by the synth. To get this working, pick a MIDI track from the menu in the Sidechain section and then click the Frequency switch to enable it.

Since the Sidechain makes this device behave like a hybrid effect unit/synthesizer, the other controls in the Sidechain section are very synth-like. Last and Low determine how Corpus responds to multiple MIDI notes being input simultaneously, with Last tuning the resonator to the pitch of the last played note or Low choosing the lowest note. Pitch Bend determines how much the resonance can be controlled by pitch bend messages.

At the bottom of the Sidechain section is the Off Decay switch, which causes the resonators to stop resonating when Note Off messages are received via MIDI. When turned on, the speed with which the resonators are silenced is controlled by the percentage box below. When off, the Decay controls the resonator decay, without regard to the length of the incoming MIDI notes.

Looking to the right past the LFO controls, you'll notice that the pitch controls are slightly different than Collision. If you're using the Sidechain, you'll see Transpose and Fine controls, which can be used to change the resonator pitch relative to the Sidechain input. Otherwise, there's just a Tune control. In either case, you can use Spread to detune the left and right channels.

Frequency Shifter

The Frequency Shifter is a powerful effect capable of creating subtle modulation or massive sonic deconstruction. This device, shown in Figure 9.32, can do ring modulation and frequency shifting, so it's like two effects in one.

Figure 9.32 The Frequency Shifter—not for the faint of heart!
Source: Ableton

Frequency shifting adds a fixed amount in Hertz to the incoming signal, producing strange inharmonic sounds. Start out by adjusting the Fine knob (leave Frequency alone). Try creating a shift of about 3Hz and pull the Dry/Wet down to 50% to hear some really cool phasing effects. Clicking the Wide switch will give the effect stereo depth, as it raises the pitch in the left channel while lowering it in the right. (You'll also notice that it changes the label of the Fine switch to Spread.) Now move on to the Frequency control. This one requires very little explanation—it's not a subtle effect!

Switching into Ring mode changes the effect to ring modulation, which involves both adding and subtracting a fixed amount, resulting in a slightly different but still bizarre-sounding effect. In Ring mode, the Drive control can be enabled to add distortion to the signal. Use the numeric box to dial in the right amount. The LFO is used to modulate Frequency automatically. It is nearly identical to the LFO in the Auto Filter, with the exception that the Amount knob is labeled in Hz so you know exactly how much the LFO will vary the frequency.

Since this effect can change pitch so dramatically, it often works well on sources where it is not important to retain a specific tonality. Make sure to give it a workout on drums and percussion.

Resonators

Similar to Corpus, when a sound is fed through the Resonators, it causes a set of virtual resonators to start vibrating, or creating a tone at their set pitches and volumes (see Figure 9.33). Even though this effect has quite a few controls, it's conceptually much simpler than Corpus.

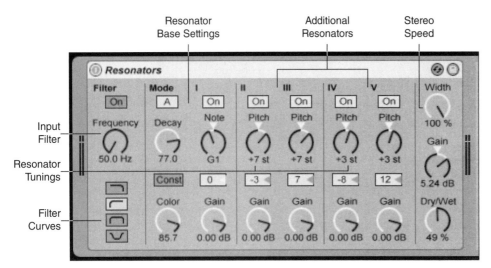

Figure 9.33 The Resonators device will start generating pitches based on an input signal.
Source: Ableton

To begin, crank the Dry/Wet mix knob fully clockwise to isolate the sound of the resonators. Turn off the Input filter so a full-range sound is feeding the device. Adjust the settings for Resonator I first, since the other four resonators base their tones and pitches on the first. You'll see that you have control of the decay of the resonators (best heard on sparse percussion tracks), as well as the color and pitch. Once the first resonator is set, engage the other resonators and use the Pitch knobs to set their frequencies relative to the first. This makes it simple to create chords using multiple resonators; then transpose them all using the first resonator's Pitch knob.

Resonators II and III and Resonators IV and V can be panned apart from each other by increasing the Width knob. This can help create a lush tonal pad that blends well with a mix. You can also use the input filter to remove frequencies that may be overpowering or saturating the resonator banks. The Gain knobs are used to achieve a blend between the various resonators, allowing you to emphasize certain pitches over others.

Spectrum

Spectrum isn't an audio effect, but it does process audio (see Figure 9.34). Instead of changing the sound that passes through it, Spectrum generates a real-time display of the audio's frequency content. This can be very useful for isolating problematic frequencies or for helping you learn more about the important frequencies in various sounds, thus improving your mixing skills. As of Live 9, the EQ Eight includes a built-in spectrum analyzer, so this device may get a bit less use. Nevertheless, it provides some additional flexibility the EQ version doesn't have, so it's worth knowing a bit about.

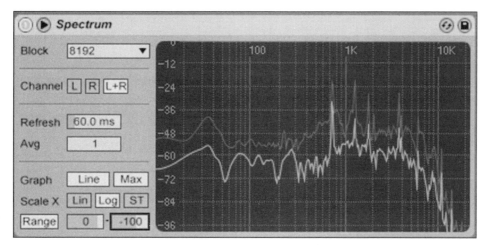

Figure 9.34 Spectrum is here to help you visualize your sounds.
Source: Ableton

The display represents frequencies horizontally from low to high and amplitudes vertically. By default, the amplitude range is set to Auto, which can be a little confusing. In Auto mode, the decibel range shown automatically adjusts to the overall volume of the material being monitored, so the display may jump around a bit. If you're new to the Spectrum device, I recommend turning off the Auto switch (in the lower right) and instead specifying a range of 0 to –100 dB. Once you get a feel for this, you can adjust the range to your liking.

The Graph setting can be used to switch the display between Bins (a series of vertical lines) or Line, which traces the overall frequency curve. The Bins look awfully pretty but can be quite distracting, so you may prefer Line instead. Max causes the display to maintain a constant line representing the peak value for every frequency. This is a very useful feature and generally recommended.

For most uses, the rest of the controls never need to be adjusted. The Refresh value can be increased to decrease CPU load, and the Avg value can be turned up if you're less interested in monitoring individual peaks and want to focus on the average spectral content of a signal. In the upper-left corner of Spectrum, you'll find an unfold switch that will super-size the display.

Utility

The humble Utility, shown in Figure 9.35, never generates much excitement, but it is a very handy device with a variety of audio tools. Some of the features seem so simple that you may not realize how they'll be useful until the day you stumble into a circumstance where you need just that thing.

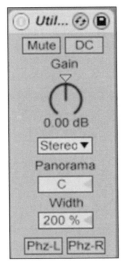

Figure 9.35 Utility is a nifty little problem solver.
Source: Ableton

Mute, DC, and Gain

Mute and Gain are just what they sound like: a button for silencing the signal and a simple volume control. They are useful to have in device format because they allow you to place these functions anywhere in any signal path. For example, many producers avoid using automation on the Mixer's volume control and automate the Gain knob on a Utility device instead. This leaves the Mixer volume as a final stage where overall volume adjustments can be made without disturbing the automation. DC is a high-pass filter for removing extremely low frequencies below the audible range.

Channel Mode, Panorama, and Width

Channel mode gives you complete flexibility over which portion of a stereo signal is utilized and the option of swapping the left and right channels as well. Let's say you have a stereo file and you want to use only the left channel. Setting this menu to Left outputs the left channel on both sides, as if it were a mono signal. Panorama is a simple pan control.

Width is useful because it allows you to change the balance of the "middle" (purely mono information) to the "sides" (information that is unique to the left and right channels). At 200%, all mono information is eliminated, leaving only the purely stereo. At 0%, the inverse is true. This control is useful for checking mono compatibility, adjusting the stereo width of a signal, or for building custom Mid/Side processors using Audio Effect Racks.

Phase

The bottom switches allow you to separately invert the phase of both the left and right channels. This comes in handy to correct phase problems when combining multiple recordings of the same source (such as when multiple microphones are used).

Vocoder

Vocoders have a long and storied history. Originally popularized in the 1970s by artists from Kraftwerk to ELO, the vocoder is famous for its ability to create talking synthesizers and singing robots by applying the complex envelope of a human voice to any sound source. Throughout the years, many other applications have been discovered for Vocoders, and Ableton has used these developments to create a very useful, modern implementation of this classic effect (see Figure 9.36).

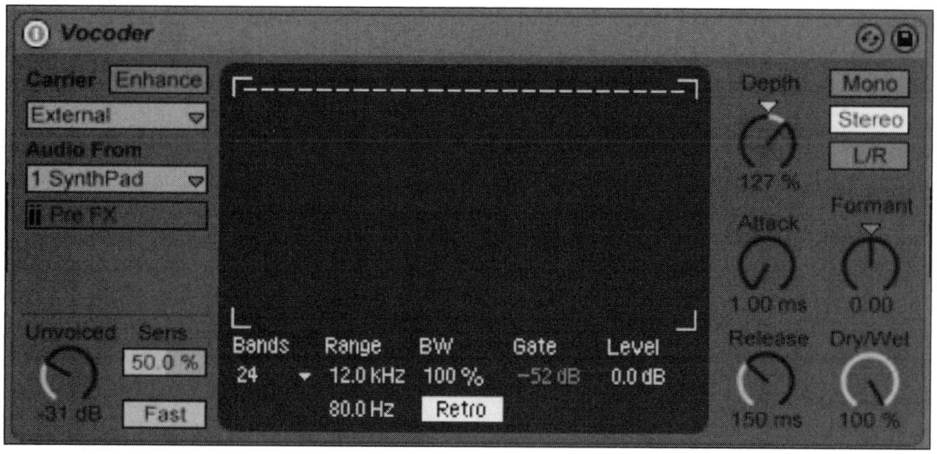

Figure 9.36 Live's amazing Vocoder.

Source: Ableton

A vocoder deals with two different signals: the Modulator and the Carrier. The effect is created by splitting the Modulator (a vocal, or any other signal you choose to run through it) into an array of narrow frequency bands and then analyzing the amplitude of the individual bands in real time to produce an envelope that can be applied to another sound, known as the *Carrier*.

In Live's Vocoder, the Modulator is the signal being produced by the track into which the Vocoder is inserted. So, if you were to drop a Vocoder into a vocal track, the clip playing on that track would be the Modulator. The Carrier is selected from the menu in the upper-right corner of the effect. The options are as follows:

▷ **Noise:** This setting uses a built-in noise oscillator to generate the output signal. The X-Y controller below modifies the sample rate and density of the noise to produce different colors. This setting is particularly good for producing percussive sound effects.

▷ **External:** This is the setting you use for classic Vocoder effects. Specify another track to use as the source, such as a synth pad, and the vocal on the carrier track will appear to be "singing" the synthesizer sound.

▷ **Modulator:** The most unusual of the bunch, this setting uses the modulator signal as the carrier. This allows you to create some very unusual effects by manipulating the other controls such as Depth, Range, and Release. Or you can use this mode to use Vocoder as a powerful EQ.

▷ **Pitch Tracking:** In this mode, a monophonic oscillator tunes itself to the pitch of the carrier signal and produces a wave chosen by the switches below. The accuracy of the tracking will vary greatly, depending on the source material, with polyphonic material producing some very unpredictable results.

At the top of this section is the Enhance switch, which can be used to restore high frequencies that get lost during the vocoding process. At the bottom section of the interface are the Unvoiced controls, which help the Vocoder handle unpitched aspects of the sound, such as consonants. To deal with the fact that these sorts of sounds may not produce an audible result in the Vocoder's output, a noise signal is synthesized to compensate for this. To activate this feature, turn up the Unvoiced knob to the desired level and adjust the Sensitivity until it responds to the Modulator properly. When it's all the way up, the Unvoiced synthesizer no longer responds to these sounds and produces a signal continuously.

The center display is where you can really get into the nitty gritty aspect of manipulating the filter bank. The mouse becomes a pencil when it's held over the graphical display and can be used to partially or fully suppress a particular band. When Carrier is set to Modulator, you can use this technique to use the Vocoder as a powerful filter.

The first control along the bottom of the display is Bands, which controls the number of bands used to analyze the Modulator. More bands means more accurate analysis and a more natural-sounding output, which may or may not be what you want. (What's "natural" about a singing synthesizer anyway?) Range specifies the upper and lower limits of the bands and can be used to remove any excess frequencies at the extremes. BW stands for bandwidth and controls the width of each filter. At values other than 100%, the filters either have gaps between them or overlap each other, producing a variety of interesting effects. Use your ears.

The Gate control can be used to clean up the Modulator signal by suppressing any bands below the threshold. By default, no gating occurs, as its setting is –inf. Level is a volume control for the effect output. Use this in conjunction with Dry/Wet to get the perfect blend.

Depth determines how dynamic the resulting effect is. By default, the volume envelope of the modulator is applied to the carrier. This control can be turned down to reduce the dynamic range of the output signal or increased to exaggerate it. The Attack and Release controls can be used to further shape the Volume Envelope. Note that the Release control goes up to a whopping 30 seconds and can be used in conjunction with the Noise carrier to create some really intense builds.

Finally, the Formant knob can be used to alter the frequencies of the filters that get applied to the carrier signal. This can be used to create some unusual frequency shifting effects, or can be used to change the perceived gender of the modulator when voice is used.

This effect has so many uses, it's well worth spending some time with. Try using the Noise carrier to add some extra snap and depth to a snare drum sound, use a drum part as the modulator to create a rhythmic synth part by using a pad as the carrier, or try that same drum loop Pitch Tracking mode to generate some unusual melodic material. The possibilities are literally endless.

External Audio Effect

External Effect is in a class by itself. Instead of processing audio, it provides a flexible insert point for interfacing with external hardware.

Using effect boxes in your Live productions has never been easier. Insert an external effect device in a track and select the inputs and outputs your processor is connected to, as seen in Figure 9.37. Audio from the track will now be routed through your external device. Then you can use the Gain knobs to adjust levels to and from the device. What's really cool, though, is that there is a Dry/Wet knob for blending the send and return signals. This means that you don't have to mess with the Mix control on an external effect. You can just leave your effects set up with direct signal at 0% and make fully recallable adjustments of the Dry/Wet balance from within Live.

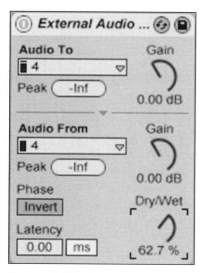

Figure 9.37 The External Audio Effect shown above will route audio through whatever hardware is connected to input and output #4 on your audio interface.

Source: Ableton

The remainder of the controls in the External Audio Effect device deal with timing issues. The Phase switch inverts the phase of the returned signal to correct phase cancellation problems that could occur when blending dry and processed signals. The Latency control compensates for delay incurred by routing the audio to and from the hardware device.

The benefits here become obvious quickly. If you have enough I/O on your audio interface, you can keep external processors connected and create presets for them. Not only can you quickly access your hardware in this fashion, but you can also insert your hardware devices anywhere in a device chain or a Rack.

Looper

Ableton creating an effect called *Looper* may sound like a strange and redundant thing. After all, isn't Live already known for being a looping monster? Well, Looper was designed to deal with the fact that folks who record loops on the fly using instruments or voice have some very specific needs that haven't always been addressed by Live. Lots of people have used Live in this way over the past few years, but it's often required various hacks and work-arounds to get it to behave more like some of the popular hardware loopers. Rather than exhaustively documenting every single feature of Looper (the Looper section in Live's manual is outstanding), I'm going to focus here on taking you through a few practical experiments so you can really understand what this device is all about.

To get started with Looper quickly, drop it into an empty audio track and focus on the extra large button called the *Multi-Purpose Transport* (see Figure 9.38). It starts by displaying a Record icon. Arm the track for recording (or set Monitor to In) and spend a moment picking a tempo in your head. Do not start playback in Live; just click the large button while simultaneously starting to count your tempo into a microphone ("1,2,3,4..."). After a bar or two, click the button again. Once you've done this, you should notice a few very interesting things. First, Live's sequencer is now running, and you should hear the loop of your counting. Take a look at Live's master tempo and turn on the metronome. Live has set its tempo by the length of the loop you just recorded. Pretty cool!

Figure 9.38 If you're a fan of hardware loopers such as the Boomerang or Loop Station, you're going to have a lot of fun with Looper.
Source: Ableton

Now, take a look at the big Multi-Purpose Transport button and the small row of icons just above it. The small icons will always tell you what mode you are currently in. Right now, you'll see a highlighted plus sign letting you know you're in Overdub mode. Any additional sounds you make will get added to the loop. The big button is displaying a Play icon. Clicking it will take you into Play mode and stop the overdubbing. Clicking it repeatedly will toggle you back and forth between Play and Overdub, allowing you to either add additional layers to your recording or just listen to playback. Finally, double-click the large button, and Looper will stop playback without stopping Live's sequencer.

So, without digging too deeply into this device's options, you should get a pretty good idea of how powerful this baby is right out of the box. If you haven't already guessed, the big reason for putting so much functionality into one button is to make it really easy for instrumentalists to control it via MIDI. Just map a single footswitch control, and you're ready to begin recording improvised loop odysseys with no further configuration. If you make a mistake as you go, just hold down the footswitch for two seconds to Undo (or Redo). When stopped, holding the button for two seconds will clear out Looper completely.

The configuration options are many. Before these next experiments, stop the sequencer and click the Clear button to empty out Looper. Now, let's say that you want the second press of the MultiFunction Transport to take you into Play mode, instead of directly into Overdub. Scan your eyes over to the right where you'll see "Record <x bars> Then <+>". Click the plus sign. You'll see it change into a Play icon, and you're done. Or try changing "x bars" to "2 bars." Now you can start up Live playing back a click or a drum loop, and a single-click of the big button will record for two bars and jump automatically into the next mode.

Just below, you'll see a menu labeled *Song Control.* Imagine that you want a double-click to stop not just the Looper but also all clips playing back in Live. Change this menu to Start & Stop Song, and you're all set. With one footswitch, you can begin recording a loop, automatically have Live start playing back prerecorded loops in time with your loop, overdub additional layers, and then stop the entire song!

By now, you may have also realized that some of Looper's functions are quantized just like clips. That's what the Quantize menu below the Multi Function Transport is for. This is very useful because it can be used to make sure that loop recording or playback starts at the beginning of the bar. The Quantization menu also affects the behavior of the Double and Half Speed buttons.

Next to the Speed knob, you'll notice up and down arrow buttons. These are used to double or halve the speed of your loop, a very common feature on looping pedals. Like these hardware devices, changing the speed of a loop also changes the pitch (just like a clip in Repitch mode). You'll see this reflected by the Speed knob—its value is displayed in semitones. It's possible to make all sorts of crazy loop textures by recording elements at different speeds. Record a guitar loop, drop it by an octave, and overdub a new layer over that. Now raise them both by two octaves and press the Reverse switch. Add additional material before returning to the original speed and pressing the Reverse switch again. Rinse and repeat.

If you want to change the length of your loop without changing the speed, use the ÷2 and ×2 buttons above. Since there are a couple of "gotchas" with these, back up the loop you've created first. Just click and drag from the Drag Me area of Looper and drop into a clip slot. Now, while your loop is playing back in Looper, use ×2 to double the length of the loop, which duplicates the loop and allows you to overdub new phrases twice the length of the original loop. Using ÷2 cuts the loop length in half and throws away the rest of it. Bear in mind that using ×2 now will not restore the loop. It just duplicates the newly truncated loop. Also be aware that Live's Undo command cannot be used to back out of these commands. You have to use the Looper's Undo instead, which only has one level of undo. Fortunately, you can drag the clip you made from the loop back into Looper and get right back to where you started.

I'm pretty confident that there are many uses for Looper that have yet to be discovered. Spend some time experimenting and see what you come up with.

Live's MIDI Effects

MIDI EFFECTS, LIKE AUDIO EFFECTS, allow you to alter MIDI data before it reaches its destination. A MIDI effect can be used by itself on a MIDI track whose output is some external MIDI sound device, or before a virtual instrument in the Track View.

MIDI data passes through the MIDI effect, which then passes the altered MIDI on. Note that MIDI effects do not change the sound that comes *out* of an instrument the way audio effects do. Instead, MIDI effects change the notes coming *in* to those instruments.

Arpeggiator

Since we are discussing the MIDI effects in alphabetical order, we get to start with the coolest MIDI device of them all, the Arpeggiator. Arpeggiators came into existence in the early days of monophonic synthesizers. *Monophonic* means "only able to play one note at a time." When synthesizer technology was in its infancy, that's all you could hope to get out of a synth—just one note at a time. This isn't much of a problem if you're playing a lead or melody part. The trouble arises when you try to play a chord, which a monophonic synth is incapable of. The solution devised was an Arpeggiator that would quickly play all the notes you held on the keyboard in series or other repetitive patterns. As a result, even though the notes don't play simultaneously, you can "hear" the chord being played because the notes are played in such quick succession.

After the Set loads, press a key on your MIDI keyboard, or just use the computer keyboard to play a note. What is this? You hold down a note, and a steady stream of eighth notes comes out. Now try holding down two notes. Instead of hearing both notes playing eighth notes, Live will play each of the notes alternately. Now try holding three notes. Live will play each of the three notes in series and repeat. That's the Arpeggiator at work (see Figure 10.1), intercepting your played notes and turning them into a sequence of notes before handing them over to the instrument loaded in the track.

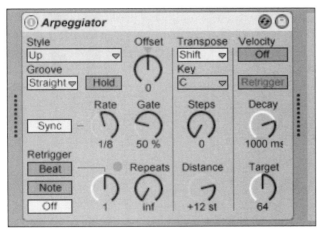

Figure 10.1 The Arpeggiator on this track is creating instant sequences from the MIDI notes it receives.
Source: Ableton

There are many ways to tweak the performance of the Arpeggiator. You can change the note order employed by the Arpeggiator, the speed at which the notes are played, the length of each note, and the quantization in relation to the grid of the current Set.

Style

The Style drop-down menu is used to select the note-order pattern employed by the Arpeggiator. The default setting is Up, which means that the Arpeggiator plays each of the held notes in sequence starting from the lowest note and working up to the highest before repeating. The Down option is the exact opposite—the Arpeggiator starts with the highest note and works down before repeating. The UpDown and DownUp patterns are simply hybrid patterns made from the individual Up and Down patterns. The UpDown style will make the Arpeggiator play up the note sequence and then back down again before repeating. The DownUp style does the opposite. The Up & Down and Down & Up modes are the same as the UpDown and DownUp modes, except that the top and bottom notes of the scale are repeated as the Arpeggiator changes direction.

The Converge style works by playing the lowest note followed by the highest note. It will then play the second lowest note followed by the second highest. The pattern will continue by playing the third lowest note followed by the third highest note, and so on, until all the notes in the scale are exhausted. The pattern will then repeat. The Diverge style is the opposite of Converge, and Con & Diverge places the two patterns end to end.

The Pinky and Thumb styles are interesting in that they alternate the note order with the highest and lowest note played, respectively. For example, when using the PinkyUp mode, the Arpeggiator will play the lowest note followed by the highest note (the "pinky note"). It will then play the second lowest note followed by the highest note again. The Arpeggiator will continue to work up the scale of held notes, alternating each with the high "pinky note" until the pattern repeats. The ThumbUp mode works in the same way, except that the lowest held note (the "thumb note") gets inserted between each step of the scale.

The Play Order style is nice in that the Arpeggiator works through the scale of held notes in the exact order as you played them. For example, if you play the notes C, E, G, and A, the resulting pattern will be "C E G A C E G A C E G A…." If you play the notes in a different order, like E, C, G, then A, the pattern will be "E C G A E C G A E C G A…."

The Chord Trigger style breaks away from the traditional arpeggiator methodology in that it plays more than one note at a time. In fact, it repeatedly triggers every one of the notes you held down. The result is a stuttered chord.

The final style options are random modes that will generate unpredictable patterns from your held notes. The Random mode simply chooses a note at random from your held notes for each step it plays. In this mode, it's possible for Live to choose the same note repeatedly—it's truly random. The Random Other pattern is a little more controlled. It will create a random pattern from your held notes, play it, and then create another random pattern and play it. The result is that you have fewer repeated notes because Live will play all the notes at least once before it creates a new pattern. The Random Once pattern is like Random Other, except that it builds only one random pattern. After the Arpeggiator plays the random pattern once, it will play it again identically. The result is a new random pattern every time you play new notes, but a pattern that repeats while you hold the notes. Pretty cool, huh?

Groove

The Groove menu is used to add a swing feel to the Arpeggiator's patterns. The intensity of the swing is determined by the Global Groove Amount value, which is displayed at the bottom of the Groove Pool.

Hold

The Hold button will automatically latch, or sustain, the notes you play so that you don't have to continually hold notes while a pattern plays. Switch this on and try playing a chord. When you release the notes on your keyboard, the Arpeggiator will continue to play. Now, play another chord. The Arpeggiator will stop the old pattern and will start the new one when it receives your new notes.

Offset

This dial is used to offset the start point of the Arpeggiator pattern by the specified number of steps. For example, if the style is set to Up and you play a C-major triad, the resulting pattern from the Arpeggiator will be "C E G C E G…." If you set Offset to 1, the pattern will be "E G C E G C…." The starting point of the pattern has been shifted to the right by one step; therefore, the pattern begins on the second note of the chord (E) as it plays.

Rate and Sync

The next two parameters, Rate and Sync, are related to one another. The Rate knob is used to set the speed at which the Arpeggiator plays each step of its pattern. The default selection is 1/8 notes. When the neighboring Sync button is on, the Rate will be constrained to note values. If you turn Sync off, the Rate will now be running free of the current project tempo and will play at the exact rate specified here in Hertz. You'll find that you can get the Arpeggiator running quite fast when you turn Sync off, even to a point where the individual notes in the scale are blurred. This is a neat special effect and is also reminiscent of SID-based synth music, like that of the Commodore 64 of yore.

Gate

This dial is used to set the length or duration of each note played by the Arpeggiator. By default, this value is 50%, which means that the notes are only half as long as the rate at which they are played. Therefore, with Rate set to 1/8, the notes are only 1/16-note long. If you set this to 25%, each note will only be 1/32-note long. This is a great parameter to tweak while the Arpeggiator is running.

Retrigger

The Retrigger parameters can be used to cause the Arpeggiator to restart its pattern when triggered with a new note or in rhythm with your song. The default Retrigger mode is Off, which means that the Arpeggiator will never restart its pattern, even if you play new notes while the Arpeggiator is running. The pattern will only restart when you stop all notes and play new ones. If you set this to Note, the pattern will restart any time a new note is played. Therefore, if you're holding three notes and play a fourth note, the Arpeggiator will immediately restart, now including the fourth note in its pattern. The last mode, Beat, will cause the Arpeggiator to restart automatically at the rate you specify with the neighboring knob. By default, this value is set to one bar. If you hold a three-note chord while this is on, you'll hear the Arpeggiator pattern start over on every downbeat of a bar.

Repeats

By default, Live will arpeggiate the notes you play for as long as you hold them. This is because the Repeats amount is set to Infinity by default. If you change this knob to a numerical value, the Arpeggiator will only run its pattern the specified number of times before stopping. Setting this to a low value, such as one or two repeats, and choosing a quick setting for the rate will cause the Arpeggiator to "strum" the notes of your chord. That is, they'll play quickly and then stop. This little burst of arpeggiation is reminiscent of old video game soundtracks.

Transposition Controls

Grouped together into a column near the center of the Arpeggiator are the Transpose controls. These parameters will allow the Arpeggiator to shift the pattern in pitch as it repeats. Start by turning the Steps knob to 1. Now play a single note. You'll no longer hear a single note being repeated. Instead, you'll hear two notes: the note you're holding, plus a note one octave higher. This is because the Distance knob is set to +12 semitones, which is an octave. By turning Steps to 1, you've instructed the Arpeggiator to shift its pitch by the Distance amount, once for each repetition of the pattern. Turn Steps up to 2 and listen to what happens. Now the Arpeggiator plays three notes for each key you press. This also works when holding multiple notes—the Arpeggiator will play the pattern once and then play it again for each step indicated, transposing by the Distance amount each time.

Now try this. Set Steps to 8 and Distance to +1 semitones. Now when you hold a single note, the Arpeggiator plays nine notes chromatically. If you hold C, the Arpeggiator will play C C# D D# E F F# G G# and then repeat. This is because the Arpeggiator is shifting the pattern (which is only the one note you're holding) eight times after it has played the original pitch, transposing it one semitone each time. Change the Distance amount to +2 and listen to what happens.

Obviously, you can create some transposition patterns that will fall outside of the key you're working in. To remedy this, there are two menus that can be used to constrain the notes to those of a selected key and mode. With the top Transpose menu, choose Major or Minor. After you make your selection, you can choose a root note with the Key menu below it. For example, set the Transpose menu to Minor and change the Key menu to D. Now press and hold D. All the notes in the resulting pattern will be transposed to the nearest note within a D-minor scale.

Velocity

The final controls in the Arpeggiator are for modifying the velocity of notes as they play. Normally, these functions are off, which makes each note of the arpeggiation pattern sound at its played velocity. That is, if you press C lightly while striking G hard, the resulting pattern will have quiet C notes and loud G notes.

The purpose of the Velocity controls here is to create a pseudo-envelope for the volume of the arpeggiation. Of course, this can be used to modify not just volume but whatever parameter velocity is mapped to in the instrument you're using. When you turn Velocity on with the top button, the Arpeggiator will modify the velocities of the notes as they repeat. The bottom dial sets the Target velocity, and the Decay knob above it determines how long the Arpeggiator takes to modulate from the original velocities to the Target. For example, if you set Target to 10 and Decay to 1,000ms and play a note with full velocity, the Arpeggiator will reduce the velocity of each consecutive note it plays to 10 over one second. You can invert this by setting a high Target velocity and playing quiet notes—the velocity will increase to the Target over the specified Decay time.

The Retrigger button will cause the velocity scaling to restart with each new note that is added to the chord. Otherwise, new notes will be constrained to the current values of the decaying velocities.

Chord

The Chord device (see Figure 10.2) will generate new MIDI notes at pitch intervals relative to an incoming MIDI note. This will allow one MIDI note to trigger a chord on the receiving instrument.

Figure 10.2 The Chord device builds a multinote (up to six notes) MIDI chord from one input note.
Source: Ableton

When the Chord device is first loaded, it will have no effect on incoming MIDI notes—they will pass straight through. As soon as you move one of the Shift knobs, it will become active. The knob sets the interval in semitones for the new MIDI note. For example, setting Shift 1 to +4 and playing a C will cause both a C and E note to be sent from the plug-in. Setting Shift 2 to +7 will create a C-major chord when you play just the C note. Playing G will result in a G-major chord (G, B, and D). You can define up to six notes to be added to the incoming note using the dials. Just below each dial is a value that determines the velocity of the new note relative to the velocity of the incoming note. You can use this if you don't want all of the notes in the chord to be the same volume. If Shift 1 is set to .50 (50%), the E in the resulting chord will only have a velocity of 64 when the incoming C has a velocity of 127. Try slowly changing this value while playing repeated notes to hear how the additional note fades in and out of the chord.

DANCE CHORDS: Chord stabs and pads are a staple of electronic music. Originally, these fixed chords were created by detuning some of the oscillators in a synthesizer so that they sounded at musical intervals (usually +7—a perfect fifth) against the base oscillators.

The Chord effect can be used to easily create the same effect. There are a number of chords already built for your use in the presets.

Note Length

The Note Length MIDI effect (see Figure 10.3) can be used to change the duration of incoming MIDI note messages. This can be used to make a MIDI part sound more rhythmically consistent, or creatively automate note durations. It can also be used to trigger your MIDI instruments with Note Off messages instead of Note On messages.

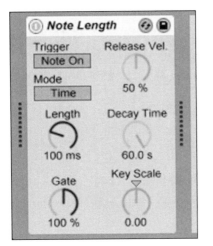

Figure 10.3 The Note Length MIDI device.

Source: Ableton

The Note Length MIDI effect has two trigger modes, which you can toggle to Note On or Note Off. In Note On mode, only the timing controls are active: Mode, Length, and Gate. You can use the Mode toggle button to sync the durations to the song Master tempo, or not, as you like. The Length knob selects the base length of the MIDI notes that the effect will output, and the Gate modifies this base by the percentage you select. For example, as in Figure 10.3, if Mode is set to Sync, Length set to 1/4, and Gate set to 50%, the Note Length effect will output eighth notes (half a quarter note).

In Note Off mode, this MIDI device will output MIDI note messages when you release your fingers from your MIDI keyboard. This will cause the notes to play through your MIDI instruments, and the length of the notes produced can be set using the timing controls below. You can also use three other controls in Note Off mode. The Release Velocity control determines the velocity of the output note (relative to the velocities of the notes you played on your controller), and Decay Time sets the length of time it will take for an incoming note's velocity to decay to zero. The Key Scale control can be used to alter the length of the output MIDI note messages, according to the pitch of the notes you play on your controller, from low to high. Set positive or negative values here to invert the relationship of pitch to note length.

Pitch

The Pitch device transposes the MIDI notes sent to an instrument, resulting in a higher or lower part (see Figure 10.4). This can be very handy in a variety of situations, such as finding the best key for a singer. Let's say you have a MIDI track playing a piano accompaniment. Just drop a Pitch effect onto the track and dial in the new key.

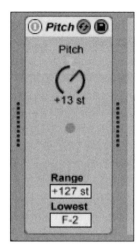

Figure 10.4 Twist the Pitch knob to transpose the MIDI data passing through the effect. Easy, huh?
Source: Ableton

The two values at the bottom of the Pitch device set the range of notes that can be used with the effect. If the bottom value, labeled Lowest, is set to C3, only MIDI notes C3 and higher will be allowed to enter the effect. The range value determines, by interval, the highest note that can enter the effect. So if the range is set to +12, notes C3 through C4 will enter the effect. Only after the incoming notes have passed the range test will they be transposed up or down.

This situation may also arise when using patches on synthesizers that have splits. If you try to transpose the MIDI information out of the appropriate key zone, the synth will start playing the notes with the patch assigned to the other zone.

> **TRANSPOSING DRUMS:** There is a situation in which the Pitch effect will have unusual results—when transposing drum parts. Because Impulse and Drum Racks assign drum sounds to individual notes, you'll end up changing which drums play, rather than transposing the pitch of the drums. For example, if a kick drum is loaded into the first cell of Impulse and a snare is loaded into the second, MIDI note C3 will trigger the kick, and D3 will trigger the snare. If you use the Pitch effect with the Pitch knob set to +2, playing C3 will result in triggering the snare drum rather than the kick.

Random

As the name suggests, the Random device will randomize the incoming MIDI notes. We can determine how liberal Live is with its randomization using the controls shown in Figure 10.5.

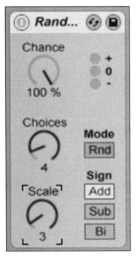

Figure 10.5 The Random MIDI device will shift the pitch of incoming notes a different amount every time.
Source: Ableton

The first control in this effect is the Chance value. This knob sets the odds that an incoming MIDI note will be transposed. At 0%, the effect is essentially bypassed because there is no chance a note will be transposed. At 100%, every MIDI note will be subject to randomization. At 50%, roughly every other note will be randomized. Once a note is chosen by the effect to be transposed, it will be shifted using the rules set up with the three remaining controls. The three parameters make up part of a sort of formula that determines the transposition.

The Choices parameter determines the number of random values that can occur. If the value is set to 3, a random number with a value of 1, 2, or 3 will be generated. This number is multiplied by the value of the Scale knob. The result is the number of semitones the MIDI note will be shifted. So if the Scale knob is set to 2, the resulting random transpositions will be 2, 4, or 6 semitones. The final variables in the formula are the Sign buttons. If Add is selected, the resulting random value will be added to the MIDI note, causing it to move up in pitch. Sub will subtract the random value from the current note. The Bi setting will randomly choose between adding or subtracting the value. The indicator lights on the plug-in panel will show when the note is being transposed up or down.

Let's run some quick examples to make sure you understand the math behind the plug-in.

1. If the Choices knob is set to 1 and the Chance knob is set to 50%, about half the time a transpose value of 1 will be generated by the Choices knob. If Scale is set to 12 and the Sign mode is set to Add, the incoming notes will be transposed up one octave half of the time.
2. If the Choices knob is set to 4 and the Chance knob is set to 100%, a transpose value of 1 to 4 will be generated for every MIDI note. You can then set the Scale knob to 3 and leave the Sign mode on Add. In this situation, every note will be transposed (Chance at 100%) by one of the following semitone amounts: 3, 6, 9, or 12 ($1[\text{Choices}] \times 3[\text{Scale}]=3$, $2 \times 3=6$, $3 \times 3=9$, and $4 \times 3=12$).
3. If the Choices knob is set to 2, the Scale knob is set to 12, and the Sign mode is set to Sub, the resulting transposition will be either 1 or 2 octaves down ($1 \times 12=12$ and $2 \times 12=24$).

Above the direction switches is an additional switch for selecting Alternate mode instead of Random mode. In Alternate mode, the effect will cycle through all of the possible values in order. So, in example 2 above, the output will be transpositions of 3, 6, 9, 12 in order, repeatedly.

Scale

Scale allows an incoming MIDI note to be mapped to another one. You can tell the plug-in that you want every incoming D# transposed up to E. You can also tell it that you want incoming Es to be taken down to Cs. Remapping pitches like this could be a great practical joke on a keyboard player, but it also has some very practical uses as well.

Don't play keyboards well? Don't know your scales? The Scale device will transpose all the wrong notes you play to the proper pitches for the appropriate key. This mapping is achieved with a 12×13 grid of gray squares that are laid out as piano keyboards. The columns in the grid refer to the *input* notes, while the rows refer to *output* notes.

If you look at Figure 10.6, you'll see that the bottom-left grid square is on. This means that when a C note enters the far left column, it runs into the orange indicator in the last row, which is the C output row. So, in this case, all entering C notes will still exit as C notes. The next column over is the input column for C# notes. As you look down the column, you run into the indicator light on the third row from the bottom, which is the output row for D notes. This means that when a C# note enters the Scale effect, it leaves as a D note.

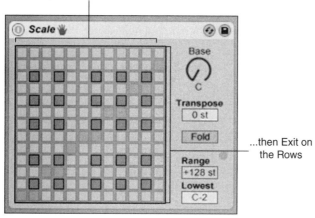

Figure 10.6 The Scale effect lets you remap MIDI notes using a unique grid interface.
Source: Ableton

The Scale effect can be a bit confusing and takes a while to get used to. Here's another way to get familiar with how it works. Play the note C, and notice the lower left-hand corner light up. Now, click a different box in the leftmost column and play the note C again. What note is being output now? Just count up in semitones from the bottommost box (or turn your head sideways and imagine that you are looking at the grid as a vertical piano keyboard!). If you've clicked four boxes up from the bottom, you'll now be hearing the note E flat.

You can use the grid to create musical scales. The pattern of indicators on the grid in Figure 10.6 is that of a major scale. Any attempt to play a black key on the keyboard will result in the MIDI note being transposed up to its nearest neighbor in the scale, since no black keys are used in C major.

> **NO SCALE?:** So you're just starting out and don't know all your musical scales? No problem. Ableton has included common scales in the presets of the Scale effect. You can load one, and then use the Base knob to adapt it to your working key.

The Base control can be used to change the starting point of the grid. In the previous example, hanging the Base control to G will change the scale to a G major. Every key played on the keyboard will now be forced to one of the pitches in the G-major scale. Notice that changing Base also moves the piano keys so the bottom row and first column are G instead of C.

The Transpose and Range boxes do what the Pitch effect does, transposing any incoming MIDI data by a fixed value and limiting the notes that will be accepted.

> **IN SCALE:** The Scale effect can keep you in key, and it can also keep the results of a Random effect in key, too. If the Random plug-in is generating too many notes that are out of key, load up a Scale effect and set it to the appropriate scale. Any stray note from the Random effect will be knocked into key by the Scale plug-in.
>
> By combining a Random and a Scale plug-in, you can make a random arpeggiator that arpeggiates the pattern of notes entering the chain.

The Fold switch will prevent Scale from outputting any notes more than six semitones higher than the input note. However, it doesn't just make these notes disappear. Instead, it drops these notes down an octave. In other words, if you've mapped an incoming D3 such that a B3 would be output, enabling the Fold switch would cause B2 to be output instead.

Velocity

The previous four MIDI effects in Live are concerned with controlling MIDI pitch information. Velocity, on the other hand, deals with (can you guess?) velocity data. It's very much like a Compressor or Scale plug-in for velocities. The grid display is like the display used in the Scale device (see Figure 10.7). Input velocities are mapped across the X-axis (the bottom of the grid), while output velocities are on the Y-axis (the right edge of the grid).

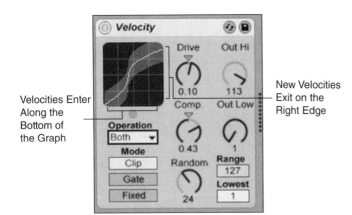

Figure 10.7 The grid of the Velocity effect shows the effect of adjusting the various parameters in real time.
Source: Ableton

In its default setting, there is a straight line from the bottom-left corner of the grid to the upper-right corner of the grid. This means that every input velocity maps to the same output velocity.

Increasing the Drive knob will cause the line in the grid to begin to curve. This new shape shows that low input velocities (near the left edge of the grid) are mapped to higher output velocities. This will raise the volume of notes played quietly, while leaving the loud notes basically unchanged. Decreasing the Drive knob below zero has the opposite effect, causing loud input velocities to be mapped to lower output velocities. Only the loudest input notes will still leave the plug-in with high velocities.

The Comp ("Compand"—meaning Compression/Expansion) knob is like the Drive knob, except that it creates two curves instead of one. Turning this knob up past zero exaggerates the velocity curve by making quiet notes quieter and loud ones louder. Lowering the Comp knob below zero has the opposite effect, forcing more of the values to the middle of the range. Be aware that, like the Pitch effect, the Velocity effect is changing the notes fed into an instrument. Because of this, increasing the Comp knob will not make the part sound compressed as it would if you placed a Compressor after the instrument. It will merely limit the velocities sent to the instrument while the instrument continues to output an uncompressed sound.

The Random knob defines a range of randomness that can be applied to the incoming velocities. As this knob is increased, a gray area will form on the grid, showing all the possible velocities that may result from the random factor.

The Out Hi and Out Low knobs determine the highest and lowest velocities that will be output from the effect. The Range and Lowest values work like their counterparts in the Pitch and Scale effects. The Clip, Gate, and Fixed buttons determine the action taken when an input velocity is outside of the operation range set by the Range and Lowest values. In Clip mode, any velocity outside of the range will be bumped into range. The Gate mode will only allow notes with velocities within range to pass. Fixed mode will force every incoming velocity to be set to the value determined by the Out Hi knob. Finally, the Operation menu can be used to specify whether the effect should process the incoming note's velocity, release velocity, or both.

BREATH OF LIFE: Velocity randomization can be used to add subtle variation to a programmed part. Humans can't play with the consistency of a machine, so randomizing the velocity of certain parts a small amount can make a beat sound more alive. This is especially effective on hi-hats and shakers.

Remote Control

A S BRIEFLY EXPLAINED IN CHAPTER 3, "Live Interface Basics," nearly everything in Live can be controlled via MIDI or your computer keyboard. This is referred to as *remote control*. Most of this chapter will focus on MIDI control since it's deeper and more flexible than computer keyboard control.

Because the computer keyboard can only transmit key presses, it's best suited to simple tasks like launching clips or controlling on/off switches. MIDI controllers, on the other hand, can have buttons, keys, knobs, joysticks, sliders, and X-Y pads. This can make them seem awfully complicated, but in fact most MIDI control is fairly simple. Regardless of the physical design of your hardware, most MIDI remote control is communicated with two types of data: note messages and control change (or continuous controller) messages, also referred to as CCs.

There are also numerous controllers on the market that can act as control surfaces for Live, which means there is no configuration required for them to work. These include devices designed for Live, such as the Akai APC40 and Novation LaunchPad, as well as numerous other devices from a variety of manufacturers. However, even if you're working with a control surface, there are going to be cases where a little customization is required and knowledge of Live's remote control system will really come in handy.

At the end of this chapter, you'll find an extended section on Ableton's own Push. This is a controller for Live that incorporates all of the functionality of a control surface, but includes Browser integration, a custom drum-programming interface, and a variety of other features that go beyond the typical controller.

Enabling Remote Control

In order to use a MIDI controller as a remote, it must be enabled in the MIDI tab of Live's Preferences (see Chapter 2, "Getting Live Up and Running," for more information). Some supported devices can be enabled in the menus at the top, while others must be configured using the switches below. There are even cases where you may set up a single device in both areas. Let's take a closer look.

Control Surface Setup

When a MIDI controller is natively supported by Live, it appears in the Control Surface menu, shown in Figure 11.1. When you select your controller in this menu, it can automatically implement certain behaviors in Live known as *instant mappings*. Many control surfaces can be automatically detected by Live, so they will work from the moment you plug them in, and you won't even need to take this step. Live allows you to use up to six control surfaces simultaneously.

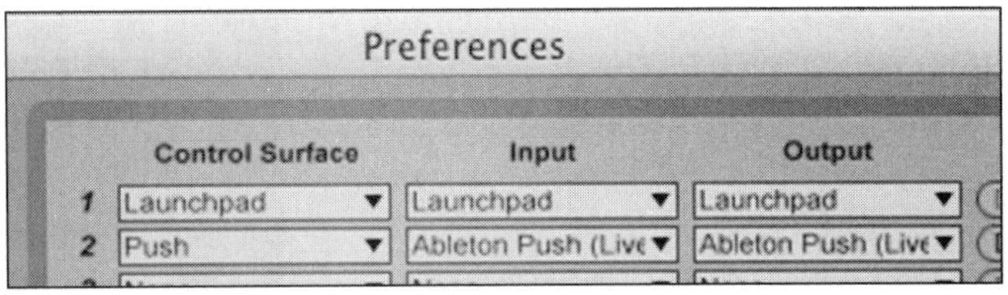

Preferences

	Control Surface	Input	Output
1	Launchpad ▼	Launchpad ▼	Launchpad ▼
2	Push ▼	Ableton Push (Live ▼	Ableton Push (Live ▼

Figure 11.1 Select your controller in the Control Surface menu to enable instant mappings. The controller's Ports are usually identical (or very similar) to the controller name.
Source: Ableton

If your controller doesn't appear in this menu, it means it's not natively supported by Live. However, this doesn't necessarily mean it can't be used as a control surface. Some devices require additional software installation, after which the device will appear as an available control surface. Check with the hardware manufacturer for more information.

Manual Controller Setup

Below the Control Surface menus is list of the MIDI devices connected to your system. Any device that you want to use for remote control must have its Remote switch turned on. Figure 11.2 shows two controllers enabled for different purposes. The first controller can only be used for remote control. The second device can only be used to record MIDI clips and play virtual instruments.

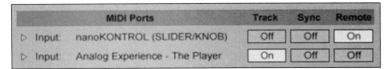

		MIDI Ports	Track	Sync	Remote
▷	Input:	nanoKONTROL (SLIDER/KNOB)	Off	Off	On
▷	Input:	Analog Experience - The Player	On	Off	Off

Figure 11.2 Turn Remote on to enable remote control. Turn Track on to enable a controller for standard MIDI recording.
Source: Ableton

It's also possible to turn both Track and Remote on for a single device. If you've got a keyboard controller that also has knobs and sliders, you may do exactly that. As long as you avoid doing any remote mapping of piano keys and other controls that you're going to use for Track input, you'll be just fine.

You'll also find that Live allows you to select a MIDI controller in the Control Surface menu, *and* enable it as a remote below. This is handy because it enables instant mappings and manual mappings on the same controller.

For example, let's say you're using an APC40, but you find that you never want to use the Arm buttons during performance. By enabling the Remote switch for its input port, you can map these buttons to whatever you want, and the instant mapping behavior will be disabled only for those buttons. If you delete the manual mapping, the instant mapping comes back—*instantly.*

KEYBOARD CONFLICTS: Unlike MIDI remote control, computer keyboard remote control is automatically enabled. However, you need to be aware that the Computer MIDI Keyboard setting (the piano keys icon in the Control Bar) turns most of your computer keyboard into a MIDI keyboard and may disable your mappings.

Turn this switch off to avoid problems with computer keyboard remote control. If you keep it on, you'll be limited to using keys not implemented as part of the computer MIDI keyboard. If there's a conflict, the keyboard will flash when you press the conflicting key.

Instant Mapping

Instant mappings vary quite a bit depending on the type of controller you're using, but they fall into a few categories. Many control surfaces have basic mixer control. For example, the APC40 contains eight faders that control volume, and several rows of buttons that control the Arm, Solo, and Track Activator switches. It's also very common for control surfaces to have a bank of eight knobs that will automatically map themselves to the currently selected device. This topic will be discussed in detail next.

Control surfaces with a bank of 16 drum pads can be used to automatically control Drum Racks. This is particularly handy when using large kits which use more than 16 pads, because the control surface's drum pads will stay mapped to whichever of the Drum Rack's 16 pads are currently selected in the Pad Overview. To enable the drum pads on this type of control surface, you must enable the Track switch for the control surface's input port.

Device Controls

Instant mapping is especially useful when it comes to working with devices. Assuming that you already have a supported control surface selected in your MIDI preferences, click on the title bar of any device (see Figure 11.3). You will see a small hand appear, indicating that it has been mapped to the controller.

Turning your controller's eight device control knobs will manipulate the first eight parameters of the device you've selected, or the eight macro knobs if you've selected a Rack. Your control surface will also have a button that allows you to get to additional banks of eight parameters of the device, should it have more. Many control surfaces have left/right buttons for navigating to other devices in the track. If not, you can select devices using the mouse or the left/right arrow keys on your computer keyboard. As soon as a new device is selected, the hand appears, and the device controls map to it.

Figure 11.3 The blue hand indicates that the Auto Filter has been mapped to the device controls of a control surface.
Source: Ableton

If you right-click in the title bar of the device, you will see a context menu including the option Lock to Control Surface for each of the designated control surfaces you have connected. This enables you to always control a specific device, no matter where your immediate focus is in Live.

If you want to see the details of how Ableton has mapped the controls of your particular control surface into Live, there is a Control Surface Reference in the Help View, which contains a list of all currently supported hardware devices and the details of their instant mappings.

BE THERE NOW: While in the MIDI map, notice that the title bar of a device can be mapped just like any device parameter. This enables you to map a button on your controller that will select the device, mapping it instantly to your control surface.

Clip Launchers

The easiest way to launch clips is to use a control surface with a clip-launching matrix, such as the LaunchPad, APC40, or Push. When a grid controller is connected and configured, a rectangle appears around the area of the session view that is being controlled. The rectangle can only be moved from the controller, not from within Live.

The clip-launching matrix will give you visual feedback to show you the status of the clips in the Session. For example, the LaunchPad's buttons will glow yellow to indicate that a clip is loaded, green to indicate that a clip is playing back, and red to show that a clip is recording. Some controllers have different color schemes.

If multiple grid controllers are connected, Live will display multiple rectangles in different colors. Whether you want them side-by-side to control different tracks, or above one another controlling different clips in the same tracks is up to you. It's a very flexible system (see Figure 11.4).

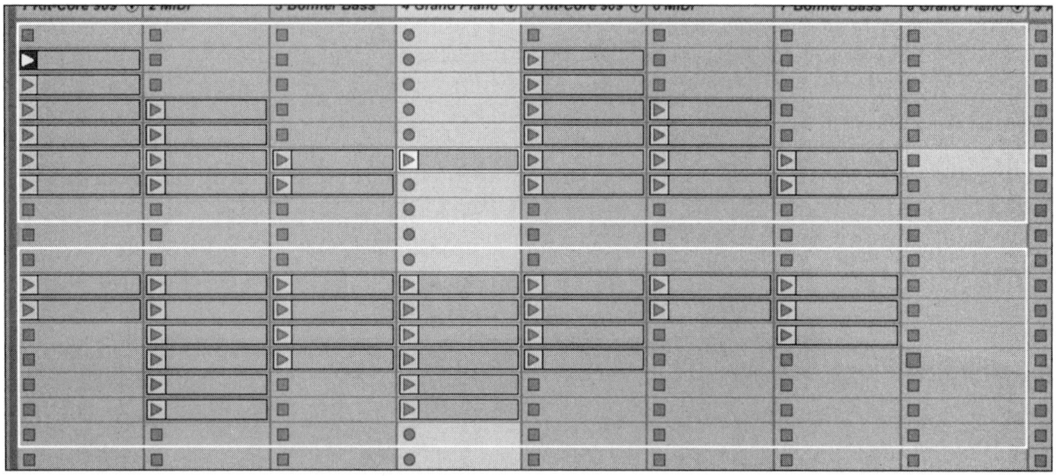

Figure 11.4 This is how the Session View might look with two different clip-launching control surfaces connected. The colored rectangles can be freely adjusted in any direction.
Source: Ableton

Clip launchers will *only* work if the device is enabled as a control surface. If the controller is only enabled as a remote, you'll still be able to send messages from the buttons in the matrix, but they won't automatically control clips.

Remote Mapping

As explained in Chapter 3, the basic process of mapping is easy. First, enter Map mode (see Figure 11.5), click the control you want to map, and then press the key or move the MIDI control you want to assign control to.

Figure 11.5 Click Key to map your computer keyboard or MIDI to map MIDI remote controllers.
Source: Ableton

> **MULTI MIDI:** In most cases, Live will allow you to map a single physical control to multiple on-screen controls simultaneously. In cases where this would cause a conflict, Live will warn you and automatically remove the old mapping before implementing the new one.

When a control is mapped to a computer key, it's labeled as seen in Figure 11.6. Live recognizes both lowercase and capital letters, most special characters, and the numbers on the numeric keypad. The only computer keys you can't map are those reserved for special purposes, such as the spacebar, Return, and Tab keys. To remove a manual mapping, enter Map mode, click on the control, and press Delete.

Figure 11.6 The letters q and w have been mapped to the Track Activators of tracks 1 and 2.
Source: Ableton

Let's take a closer look at what happens when you map MIDI controllers. After the control is mapped, Live displays a small box showing the MIDI channel and message that have been mapped (see Figure 11.7). When notes are mapped, Live tells you the note name. If you send a CC, you'll see the CC number after the MIDI channel.

Figure 11.7 The Track Activator has been mapped to note A1 on MIDI channel 1. The volume slider is mapped to CC 22, also on channel 1.
Source: Ableton

When it comes to CCs, there are two types: absolute and relative. Faders and knobs are typically absolute controllers. They send values from 0 to 127 and can move any control from the bottom of their range up to the top, with a resolution of 128 steps. If you're manually mapping absolute controllers, it's a good idea to make sure you understand the takeover modes on the MIDI/Sync tab of Live's Preferences (as explained in Chapter 2).

Relative CCs are typical of endless knobs called *encoders*. A relative control message is one that tells Live "move this value up" or "move this value down," in other words, there's no direct correlation between the value of the controller and the value in Live. It just takes the control from its current position and moves it in one direction or another.

Remote messages come in a number of different flavors, but typically Live can automatically detect which type is being used. Whenever you map a control, the menu seen in Figure 11.8 is displayed in the lower left-hand corner of the screen. Take your time when mapping a CC—move it slowly, and Live will detect its type. If a type is incorrectly detected, you'll see the control jump around or other bizarre behavior when you try to use it. If this happens, check the controller's documentation and manually enter it in the menu.

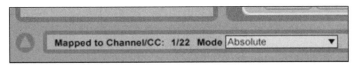

Figure 11.8 This menu shows you the type of CC your controller is sending.
Source: Ableton

> **MIDI MESS:** Bear in mind that manual mappings are not bound to a specific controller. For example, if you map the note C3 on channel 1, Live will respond to this note regardless of the MIDI controller that sends it. This is why you have to be careful when you have a lot of controllers connected. Make sure not to enable remote control for devices that you don't mean to use for this purpose. For the most complex MIDI setups, the easiest way to avoid conflicts is to have each device transmit on a different channel.

The Mapping Browser

Whenever you enter the Key or MIDI Map mode, the Browser transforms to show you all of the current mappings. Not only does this give you a useful reference of every mapped control, but it also allows you to specify control ranges, using the Min and Max parameters. For example, in Figure 11.9, you'll see a track volume configured so it can't go above 0dB (as opposed to its default of +6dB)—a very handy technique to avoid clipping during performance.

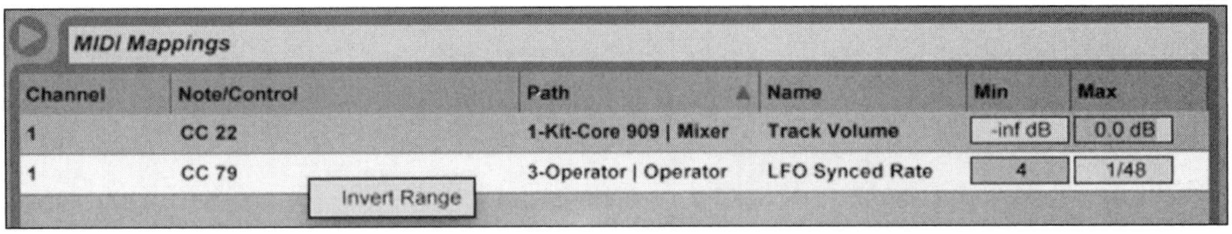

Channel	Note/Control	Path		Name	Min	Max
1	CC 22	1-Kit-Core 909	Mixer		Track Volume	-inf dB	0.0 dB
1	CC 79	3-Operator	Operator		LFO Synced Rate	4	1/48

Invert Range

Figure 11.9 The top mapping shows a volume control limited to a maximum of 0dB. In the second mapping, the Invert Range context menu is being used to flip the Min and Max levels.
Source: Ableton

You can also set Max *below* Min in order to invert the behavior of a control. You may be wondering why you'd want to do this, but there are actually a few common cases. Let's say you've got a tempo-synced LFO mapped to a knob. By default, turning the knob up will make the LFO slower because its value is getting *higher*—you're moving from 1/32 to 1/16 and eventually all the way up to 4 bars. To a lot of folks, it makes more sense to have the LFO get faster as you turn up the knob.

Special Mappings

There are quite a few ways that Live can be mapped that may not be apparent at first glance. For example, the Tempo control has two segments when in Map mode. The left segment is for coarse adjustments, while the right adjusts in fractions of a BPM.

Figure 11.10 shows a few areas of interest when it comes to mapping. The title bar of a track can be mapped in order to show its Track View. The clip status area can be mapped to show the Clip View for the currently playing clip in that track. If no clip is playing, this mapping won't do anything.

Relative clip launchers allow you to launch a clip based on the currently selected scene, but notice that these only appear in Map mode. In the Master track, you'll see some additional controls in the same row as the relative clip launchers. These are used for navigating through the scenes. The up/down arrows can be mapped to move up or down one row at a time, while the numeric box can be mapped to an encoder for scrolling through scenes.

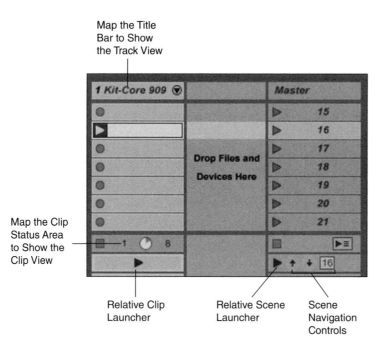

Figure 11.10 A few hidden goodies in Map mode.
Source: Ableton

> **TWEAK THAT CLIP:** You can assign MIDI and key controls to many parameters in the Clip View. Be aware, however, that mappings in the Clip View do not stay stuck to a particular clip. Instead, the assignments work on whatever clip is currently being displayed in the Clip View. Therefore, if you use a MIDI knob to transpose a clip, you can click on another clip and the same MIDI knob will now transpose the new clip.

The crossfader is another control that offers additional options when in Map mode. In Figure 11.11, you will see that the crossfader has three sections. Mapping the center section to a MIDI controller will give you access to the entire range of the fader, while the outer edges let you map the absolute left and right positions for fast cuts. This way, you can have a crossfader that is controlled by a single MIDI fader, three individual keys, or any combination thereof. Welcome to the future!

Figure 11.11 The crossfader is different than most of Live's controls in that it has three separate areas that can be mapped to MIDI controllers or the computer keyboard.
Source: Ableton

Remote Controlling Plug-In Devices

Controlling the parameters of a plug-in device, such as a VST audio effect, is a little more difficult, due to the fact that each plug-in has its own unique graphical interface. Because of this, Live cannot superimpose the mapping overlay on the plug-in controls while in Map mode. To solve this problem, Ableton has included an unfold switch at the upper-left corner of a plug-in's title bar. Unfold the plug-in, as seen in Figure 11.12, to reveal a generic display of the plug-ins parameters.

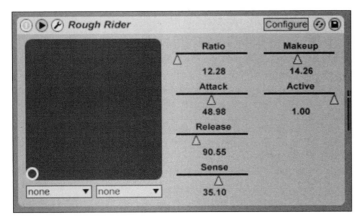

Figure 11.12 Pressing the small triangle in the corner of the plug-in reveals a generic display of the plug-in's parameters.
Source: Ableton

If the device has more than 32 parameters, no parameters will be shown, and you'll have to configure it to display the ones you want to map. To add a parameter, click the Configure switch in the title bar and move any control in the plug-in window. A horizontal slider will appear for every control you move. These sliders can be mapped like any other control.

About MIDI Controllers

To remotely control Live, literally any MIDI controller can be used. MIDI devices come in different varieties best suited to different tasks, but it doesn't matter whether you've got an old MIDI synthesizer, or the latest LED-encrusted behemoth; they're all compatible. What varies is the physical controls they offer and how much configuration they require.

While there's quite a bit of configuration that can be done within Live, it's important to understand that the specific MIDI messages sent by your controller can impact the results you get. Some controllers allow you to program every knob and button to send specific messages, while other controllers do not. Typically, you can expect piano keys and drum pads to send note messages while knobs and sliders (and anything that can be moved through a range) transmit control change messages.

Whether or not you need a programmable controller depends on the complexity of your MIDI setup and what you need to do with it. For example, there may be cases where you want to use several controllers and have each one transmit on a different MIDI channel to avoid conflicts. There might be a case where you want a button to be *momentary* (sends one message when the button is pushed and another when it is released) as opposed to *toggle* (sends one message when pushed, and a second message when pushed again).

These are settings that are set within the controller and cannot be changed from within Live. Sometimes this is done with lots of menu diving on the hardware (read the manual carefully!), and sometimes this is done with a software editor (generally a much easier task). So, if creating a highly customized performance setup is a task you need to accomplish, you should consider buying at least one controller with a good software editor, such as a Korg Nano, or any of the controllers from KMI or Livid.

Some controllers require that you install separate software before you can use them with Live. Some, such as the Novation LaunchPad, won't work at all until a driver is installed, while others will work as generic MIDI controllers right out of the box, but require additional software installation to allow control surface support with Live. Just make sure to the check the manufacturer's website for the latest downloads and you'll be all set.

Push

Push is Ableton's own dedicated hardware controller for Live. Conceived of as an "instrument" rather than simply a MIDI controller, Push focuses heavily on the initial compositional phase: programming drums, creating parts with virtual instruments, and tweaking devices.

Therefore, it's important to understand that this focus is very MIDI-centric and comes with some limitations. For example, at the time of this writing, there is no way to arm an audio track from Push.

However, it's safe to assume that Push will evolve a great deal. The Live user manual has a very good step-by-step guide for getting up and running with Push, and you should definitely consult it to make sure you have the most up-to-date information. What's presented here is meant to accompany that information rather than replace it. Select "Read the Live Manual" from the Help menu rather than consulting the printed manual for information on Push; the digital version is much more up-to-date.

One very important thing to know about Push right out of the gate is that many of the command buttons are designed to do one thing when pushed and another when held down. For many of the buttons on the right (Scales, Repeat, Accent, Note, Session), a single push switches Push into a new mode, while holding the button down enables the mode temporarily and returns Push to its previous state when you release it.

In the case of the buttons on the left, it's a bit different. For example, a single push of Quantize immediately performs quantization. Holding it down presents quantization options, including the option to turn record quantization on or off. Similarly, holding down Fixed Length allows you to select a predetermined length for all newly recorded clips, while a single push is used to turn this mode on or off.

Another word of advice: When learning Push, keep an eye on your computer screen as well. Even though the ultimate goal may be to make music on Push and avoid gazing at Live, you'll get a more solid understanding of what's going on if you watch what happens to your clips and devices on-screen while working with the hardware.

> **THE BRIGHT SIDE:** Push is fully bus powered and does not require that you use the power supply that comes included. When the power supply is used, the buttons, pads, and display all glow brighter.

Getting Started

Here are a few things about Push that you'll need to know right away (see Figure 11.13).

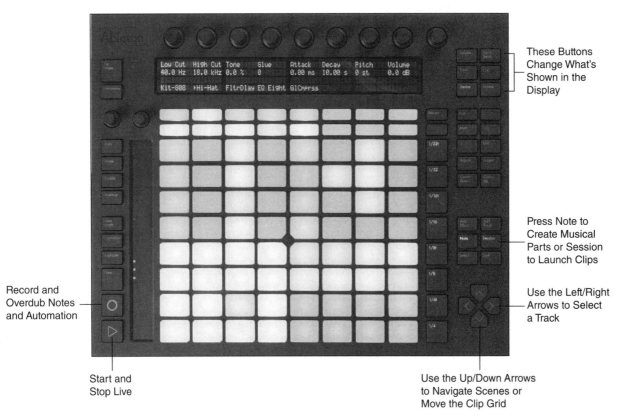

These Buttons Change What's Shown in the Display

Low Cut High Cut Tone   Glue   Attack   Decay   Pitch   Volume
40.0 Hz 18.0 kHz 0.0 %   0   0.00 ms 10.00 s 0 st   0.0 dB

Kit-808 ►Hi-Hat FltrDlay EQ Eight GlCmprss

Press Note to Create Musical Parts or Session to Launch Clips

Use the Left/Right Arrows to Select a Track

Record and Overdub Notes and Automation

Start and Stop Live

Use the Up/Down Arrows to Navigate Scenes or Move the Clip Grid

Figure 11.13 Most of Push's functions are clearly labeled and easy to find. All of the buttons are backlit. When a button goes dark, that means that it has no functionality in the current mode.
Source: Ableton

▷ **Tracks:** Navigate from track to track using the left and right arrows in the lower right corner. Alternately, tracks can be selected using the buttons beneath the display (when Volume, Pan & Sends, Track, or Clip are shown). When a track is selected, it is automatically armed for recording. New tracks are created by pushing Add Track. By default, a MIDI track is created, and the display switches to Browse mode. Hold down Add Track to create different types of tracks.

▷ **Clips:** Press Note when you want to create new MIDI clips. (Push is in Note mode by default, so you may be able to skip this step.) New clips are created by pressing Record, or by entering a note in the step sequencer (as explained later). Press Record a second time to stop recording and begin looping. When Fixed Length is turned on, pressing Record creates a clip of a specified length and begins looping automatically. Pressing New does not create a new clip, but instead moves you to an empty clip slot, so you're ready to make a brand new clip. To edit a clip's loop properties, press Clip.

▷ **Mixer:** Press Volume or Pan & Send to see an overview of these settings for eight tracks at a time. Which eight tracks are shown is determined by the position of the colored rectangle in the clip grid in Live. Press Session and use the left/right arrows to move the grid. Hold down Shift to move left/right in banks of eight. Press Track to see detailed information for an individual track. The second row of buttons is used to mute or solo tracks, depending on the status of the Mute and Solo buttons.

▷ **Browsing:** Press Browse to select instruments or press Add Effect to browse effects. To add MIDI Effects, hold down Shift and press Add Effect. Instrument presets are organized by device and then by a predefined set of categories. If you save your own presets into folders that match the Ableton categories, they will automatically be aggregated into that category when browsing. Presets saved into folders with different names will be shown in a category called Others.

▷ **Launching:** Press Session for the clip-launching matrix. The Scene/Grid buttons to the right of the pads are used to launch scenes. When Note is selected, the up and down arrows launch scenes, but not in the conventional way. Global quantization is ignored, and the clips all behave as if they're in Legato mode. This means that you can navigate from scene to scene in an extremely fluid way without ever interrupting the flow.

Drum Programming

When a track containing a Drum Rack is selected, Push automatically switches into Drum Programming mode. Programming drums on the Push is a lot of fun. While many controllers focus on performing drum parts using pads or step-sequencing using a grid, Push does both simultaneously.

The top half of the pads is the step sequencer. By default, it represents two bars with 16 steps in each bar. (Each row constitutes one half of a bar.) This can be changed by selecting a different note division (using the 1/4 to 1/32t Grid buttons at the right), but I'd suggest starting out by mastering the 16-step grid and then venture into the other divisions later. To add drum hits to the sequence, first push one of the Drum Rack pads in the lower left to select a drum. Then push buttons in the step sequencer to add the selected drum to a given step.

Hold down a step to reveal additional controls in the display. You can adjust velocity and note length, and move the note forward or backward a small amount by twisting the Nudge encoder.

> **DOUBLE VS. DUPLICATE:** Once you've created a part, you can make it twice as long by pressing Double. Duplicate, on the other hand, makes a copy of the currently playing clip and places it in the clip slot below.

To record drums live, just press Record and bang away on the pads. Whether or not your performance is quantized as you record is up to you. Hold down Quantize to display the settings for turning Record Quantization on or off. My preference is to leave quantization off while recording, and then quantize after the fact if necessary. When perfectly quantized parts are necessary, I use the step sequencer. This is a great advantage offered by having both programming approaches handy.

When you play Push using the pads, the steps will appear in the grid even when they haven't been quantized. This is a cool feature that allows you to see how your pattern looks on the grid, even though it may not be strictly aligned with it. This creates an interesting opportunity and a potential problem. After playing a part, you can quickly quantize an individual hit by pushing the step twice. The first push deletes the hit, and the second re-creates it, perfectly aligned to the grid. Just be aware that if you've played a note really late or early, it may appear on the step before or after the one you intended.

Using the step sequencer to edit parts you performed, however, can be tricky. What if you want to experiment with turning certain hits off, but don't want to lose the timing when you turn them back on again? Instead of deleting notes, hold down the Mute button while pushing the notes you want to remove. The notes will be deactivated, and they will switch to a dim yellow color. Hold Mute and press them again to reactivate them. (Fortunately, Push also has an Undo button so you can easily step backward if you forget this workflow.)

> **QUANTIZE:** A single push of Quantize will quantize the entire clip. To quantize a single drum, hold down Quantize and then press a drum pad. Voila! Only that drum gets quantized.

The loop length controls occupy the lower right set of pads. At first, these may appear to be the most uninteresting part of the drum programming controls, but they are actually a brilliant solution to a basic problem. When programming longer drum parts, you're often faced with the need to focus on an individual bar while working on its details, and then jump back out to listen to the bar in context. Repeating this process over and over can be a hassle, but with the loop length grid it's a piece of cake.

Each pad in the loop length section represents one of 16 possible bars. Pushing any of these buttons causes the clip to jump immediately to this bar. To specify a range of bars, hold one pad and then press a second. For example, pressing pad 1 (the one in the upper left of the loop area) causes bar 1 of the clip to loop. Holding down pad five and then pressing pad 8 creates a four-bar loop including bars 5 through 8.

> **THE (DON'T) TOUCH STRIP:** The touch strip is used to navigate the Drum Rack's Pad Overview. Be careful not to lean on it while you're playing the drum pads, or you could end up playing an empty set of (dull yellow) pads! If this happens, run your finger along the strip until the drum pads glow bright yellow again, and you'll be back in business.

Replacing Individual Drums

Push makes it easy to load sounds into the pads of a Drum Rack one at a time. The trick to doing this is to make sure that the pad is selected *before* pressing Browse (otherwise, you'll end up browsing for entire kits). First, press Device and then press one of the drum pads. At the far left of the display, you'll see the name of the kit, followed by the name of the pad. Press the button directly below the pad to select it. Now, when you press Browse, you'll be taken to individual drum hits, rather than entire kits. Sweet!

Notes Mode

When you select a track containing any instrument other than a Drum Rack, Push switches into its unique "keyboard" mode. This is Ableton's take on how to program melody or harmony using a grid instead of a piano keyboard. If you're an experienced keyboardist, this may be a mere curiosity, or it may be a fun new way to experiment. After all, you're sure to come up with some different ideas when playing a totally new instrument!

> **OLD SCHOOL:** Consider plugging a sustain pedal into one of the input jacks on the back of Push. You may find that it makes the pads much more expressive and playable for melodic instruments. Also, remember that if you prefer a traditional keyboard controller, there's no reason you can't hook one up to your computer and use it alongside Push.

By default, this mode presents you with only the notes in a given scale (C major by default). Each blue pad marks the tonic (root) note of the scale. Therefore, anyone who knows a little music theory will expect to see a blue pad, followed by seven white pads, and then another blue note. And, indeed on the bottom row, that's exactly what you do see, but beyond that the pattern doesn't continue, because Ableton has taken advantage of the fact that a grid is two-dimensional, unlike a piano keyboard, which is strictly linear.

By default, notes are organized in fourths along the vertical axis and steps along the horizontal axis. This is similar to the arrangement of notes on a string instrument such as a guitar or bass. And just like those instruments, this means that the same chord or scale can be played in a variety of locations in the grid. Play the lower four pads of the grid in order from left to right. When you get to the fourth pad, notice that the far left pad in the second row lights up as well. This means they are the same pitch.

The note layout can be changed by pressing Scales once and then holding down Shift. The first two options in the display(4th^ and 4th>) allow you to choose between the fourths being vertical or horizontal, while the second two options allow you to switch to horizontal or vertical thirds. The last two options are Sequential. These abandon the scheme of having a vertical vs. horizontal interval and simply organize the notes in steps along either axis.

> **SENSITIVE SOUNDS:** Push's default pad sensitivity may work just fine while banging out drum parts, but when playing melodies and chords it's a bit too stiff for most people. Hold down User to reveal the Pad Sensitivity setting in the display. Even turning it up one notch makes a big difference. If sensitivity is not what you're after, press Accent. This will cause all pads to play at maximum velocity, regardless of how hard you play.

The Scales button reveals controls for selecting the key and scale of the note grid. For example, to play in Bb Lydian mode, you would scroll in the first menu to Lydian and then select Bb in the row of keys shown. If you're not experienced with music theory, you can study to make sense of this, or take it as a purely experimental endeavor. If you find a scale you like, you'll be able to use this scale across any other parts you create and every other part will be in key.

Bear in mind that, at the time of this writing, the scale settings are *not* saved with the Live Set, so if you're experimenting, you'll need to make a note of your scale settings if you want to be able to return to your set another time and play in the same key.

For some types of music, you'll be able to select a single scale and make an entire song. However, much great music moves across keys, and uses notes outside of a single key center to create harmonic and melodic interest. Fortunately, the scale display also allows you to switch from In Key to Chromatic mode, which provides a layout in which every note is included, but only the notes from the selected scale are lit. This provides an interesting perspective on scales and allows you to move outside them when necessary.

The scale display also lets you turn Fixed mode on or off. In Fixed mode, the pads always keep their original orientation, which means that the lower right corner is always C. When you switch keys, the available notes change, but the overall range of the pads is unaffected. With Fixed mode turned off, the grid reorients itself around whatever root note you select. For example, if you select the key of G the entire range of the pads changes, and the blue notes all become G instead of C.

One interesting way to generate chord patterns using Push is to repeatedly press the same pads while changing the key in Scale mode. If you do this in Fixed mode, you'll get subtler changes, with individual notes moving a half step as necessary to stay in key. With Fixed mode turned off, you'll get very clear movement from chord to chord as you change key. For example, if you play a C-major triad (C-E-G) with scale set to C and change the key to G, the whole chord will move up a perfect fifth (G-B-D).

Device Mode

Push the Device button to edit device parameters in the selected track (see Figure 11.14). Device view is very easy to use, as long as you understand how to navigate devices and Racks. Tracks can contain multiple devices, each with many parameters, all of which are edited using Push's eight encoders. Navigation is done using both the buttons underneath the display and the In and Out buttons.

There are two types of navigation you'll be doing: navigating from device to device, and navigating within Racks with multiple chains. Navigating from device to device is a simple matter. When a track contains multiple devices, they're shown along the bottom of the display. Use the top row of buttons to select a device and the bottom row to activate or deactivate. When a device is selected, the encoders will instantly map to whatever eight parameters Ableton has deemed the "favorites." If you've selected a Rack, these will be the eight macro knobs (if they've been assigned).

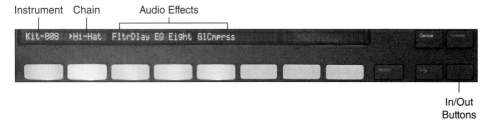

Figure 11.14   In Device mode, all of the available chains and devices are shown along the bottom, while the encoders control the device parameters.
Source: Ableton

To dig deeper, you'll need to push the In button. This takes you to a new page where the device's controls are organized into banks (a maximum of eight). Along the bottom, you'll see the names of the banks, which can be selected with the top row of buttons.

> **BANK JOB:** Be aware that with some devices you won't be able to get to every single parameter, no matter how many banks you navigate through. The workaround here is to create a Rack. For example, when programming Operator, I like to be able to access the oscillator's waveform, which isn't a part of any of the banks. To solve this, I've saved a Rack containing Operator and mapped the waveform control to a macro knob.

When a Rack containing multiple chains is selected, pushing the In button causes the display to show each chain. Use top row of buttons to select the chain you want to edit; then push In again to display the devices within. Select a device and continue as described previously.

Because Live allows nested Racks, device chains can be very deep, and the navigation can take some getting used to. This is an area where I strongly suggest you play with the controller while keeping a close eye on your screen. Follow the little blue hand that appears in the title bar of the devices! It's the key to knowing what Push is controlling at any given moment.

> **AUTOMATE IT!:** To automate device controls, press Automate (this enables the Automation Arm switch in Live) and then press Record. Automation is written from the moment you move an encoder until the moment you stop touching it. (Push's encoders are touch-sensitive.)

Working with Plug-Ins

At the time of this writing, Push only allows you to browse built-in devices. To work around this, create Racks for your plug-ins. For example, if you want to use Native Instruments Massive, create an Instrument Rack containing Massive and save it as a preset. When you browse devices using Push, the new Rack will appear in the Instrument Rack category.

If you want to use Push's device controls with plug-ins, you'll have to set them up using the Configure switch, as explained in "Remote Controlling Plug-in Devices" earlier. You may also want to assign your favorite controls to the Rack's Macro knobs, but strictly speaking this is not necessary. The controls you add by configuring the plug-in will all become available to Push either way. They'll be distributed into eight banks according to the order in which the generic sliders are displayed in Live. When configuring, drag them into the order you want. For example, if you want all of your filter controls to be in the first bank, make sure they are the first eight parameters listed.

Playing Live...Live

MOST BOOKS WRITTEN ABOUT MUSIC-PRODUCTION SOFTWARE WOULD NOT INCLUDE A CHAPTER LIKE THE ONE YOU'RE ABOUT TO READ. As you will discover, it's a real treat to use the same software to create your music *and* perform it. Because of its flexible control methods and instant response to user input, Live is the perfect companion for a gigging musician. Live performs wonders in all types of scenarios, ranging from DJ gigs to improvisational music and theater. Regardless of what type of musician you consider yourself to be, I recommend reading all the information presented in this chapter. Any technique relating to the use of Live is pertinent—innovations can come from taking ideas from one musician's style and applying them to your own style.

The Hybrid DJ and Remixer

Whether or not DJing and remixing is your thing, it's worth studying this section. You already know that Live can sync loops together with Warping. DJs use this powerful mechanism to sync entire songs together. They also use an array of clips to manufacture new arrangements of the songs, literally creating their own remixes right in front of the dancing masses. By learning the techniques employed here, you'll achieve a firmer grasp on manipulating the tempo of any piece of audio.

The reason this section is called the "Hybrid DJ" is that whether you perform original songs, tracks you download, improvised multitrack loop jams, or mashups, the techniques and concepts of DJing hold some relevance for all of them, and they are the conceptual "glue" that can be used to look at these varied approaches in a unified way.

Preparing Your Audio Files

The process of DJing with Live is twofold: First comes the work of downloading, ripping, and warping songs, followed by the joy of putting it all together in a performance. Live supports multiple compressed and uncompressed file formats. You can use WAV, AIFF, SD2, MP3, AAC, Ogg Vorbis, Ogg FLAC, and regular FLAC, which means you can use most audio files you'll ever encounter.

While 320kbps MP3 files are of high enough quality for most applications, bear in mind that Live will decompress any compressed file into the Decoding Cache when you add it to a Set. Therefore, not only are you potentially compromising sound quality when using compressed audio, but you also end up using *more* disk space because you're storing both a compressed *and* an uncompressed version of the file.

Once you have your songs pulled together, you're ready to begin the second step of prepping a file for DJing. In order for Live to keep the song in time with any others that you may be playing, you'll need to place Warp Markers in the file to indicate the location of beats in the track. Warping an entire song sounds like quite an undertaking, but with practice you'll find yourself doing it faster and faster. In fact, while I wouldn't ever recommend this, there have been a few times I've ended up warping songs on stage during a gig!

This section assumes that you're already familiar with the basics of warping covered in Chapter 6, "Tracks and Signal Routing," so refer back to it if necessary. Also, one final note before we begin: *Don't forget to press the Save button after you've gotten your song warped.* Otherwise, the next time you drag the song into a set, your properly placed Warp Markers won't be there.

Analyzing and Auto-Warping

Every time you bring a new audio file into Live for the first time, it gets analyzed. At the very least, this means that the waveform display gets generated and stored in a file with an .ASD extension. When this file is generated, Live makes guesses about the length and original tempo of the file. For short, evenly timed, properly cut loops, this is a very simple process. For entire songs, it's somewhat more complicated. This is why Live has a special preference for dealing with entire songs (Auto-Warp Long Samples, located in the Record/Warp/Launch tab of the Preferences dialog).

> **ANALYZE THIS:** You may have noticed by now that the first time you drop a song into Live, it takes some time to analyze it. Here's a trick for those of you who have a big collection of tracks and want to save some time. Navigate to a folder full of tracks in the Browser. Then right-click the folder and select Analyze Audio from the context menu. Go grab a beer or do some laundry, and when you return, the tracks will be ready to go!

If you let Live automatically use Auto-Warp on your songs, and the material you're working with is straightforward, it will often do most of the work for you. Don't ever assume that it will do *all* of the work for you. Always check the tracks and look out for some of the common problems discussed next.

One common problem in Live is that the first downbeat of the song is wrong. This means that it gets the tempo right, but the song will be offset from the metronome and other clips. In other cases, the introduction to a song sometimes confuses Auto Warp enough that it gets the tempo wrong as well.

In Figure 12.1, you'll see a dance track where Live has made a few errors. The introduction has no kick drum, and the syncopation of the rhythms has confused Auto Warp as to the location of the first downbeat and the tempo. To help Live out, we're going to place 1.1.1 where the kick drum comes in instead of at the beginning of the song. This is done by a combination of ears and eyes. Listen for the area where the kick comes in and then zoom in on that section. Use the Scrub tool to launch the song from this section and visually locate the first kick drum. This takes a little practice, but pay attention, and you'll get it.

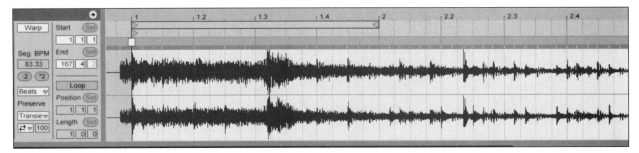

Figure 12.1 Even though this song's first downbeat is at the very beginning, Auto-Warp has placed 1.1.1 a bit further in. Also, look at the Seg BPM box, and you'll see that Live has guessed the tempo to be 83.33, even though it's actually 125.
Source: Ableton

After you've located this first clear downbeat, right-click the transient marker above it and select Set 1.1.1 Here, as seen in Figure 12.2a. Then right-click the Warp Marker that gets created and select Warp From Here. (There are several different versions of this command, so refer to Chapter 5, "Clips," if you need more information.) Finally, move the start marker to the left, as seen in Figure 12.2b so the clip plays back from the introduction. *Make sure that you move it back an even number of bars.* For example, if the intro is 16 bars, the start marker should be at –16.1.1.

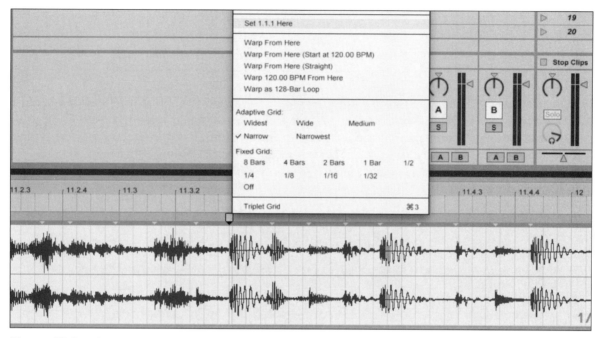

Figure 12.2a Once you've identified the first clear downbeat, right-click and select Set 1.1.1 Here. Then right-click again and select Warp from Here.
Source: Ableton

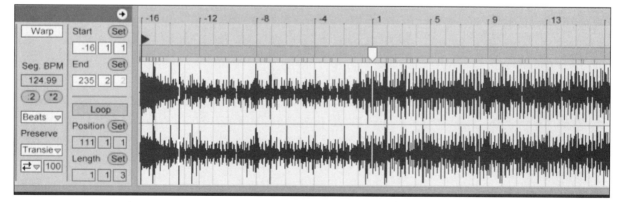

Figure 12.2b After helping Auto-Warp figure things out, you can pull the start marker back to –16.1.1 so the song plays back from the beginning of the intro.
Source: Ableton

Another common mistake that Auto-Warp makes is getting the tempo wrong by a tiny fraction. Very often, it's really easy to see this mistake just by looking at the Seg. BPM box. For example, a track may be identified as 124.99 when it's really 125 BPM. However, this is a judgment call you must make by ear. What I do is turn on the metronome and then float my mouse just above the waveform display so it turns into the Scrub tool (the speaker). Then I spot-check the track by launching it from various points in the track. In the case of a minute discrepancy, you won't be able to hear it drift from the metronome until several minutes in. To correct an error like this, just type the corrected value into the Seg. BPM box and check it again.

> **PAINT BY NUMBERS:** Sometimes when you type a tempo into the Seg. BPM box, you'll find that it's grayed out. This is because this Segment BPM can only be edited after you've clicked on a Warp Marker, even if there's only one in the clip. For clips with multiple Warp Markers, the Seg. BPM box displays the tempo for the segment between the Warp Marker you click on and the next Warp Marker in the clip.

In Figure 12.3, we're looking at a Talking Heads track that's been Auto-Warped. Notice that there's a number of Warp Markers due to the natural fluctuations in the tempo. In this case, Live has done a good job with the tempo, but it's placed the downbeat an entire beat off. If you pull the start marker back to –1.4, everything syncs up pretty well. However, you'll still want to execute the Set 1.1.1 Here command by right-clicking the start marker, so the timeline above the waveform makes sense in relationship to the rest of your clips.

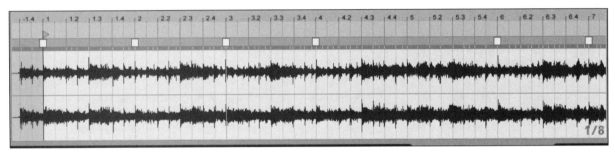

Figure 12.3 With this song, the tempo is correct, but the song starts exactly one beat late.
Source: Ableton

Just like everything else, becoming a warping master takes practice. Different tracks require different tweaks to get them just right. The techniques described previously will work for the majority of music you will encounter; however, there will be cases where you need to warp your audio from scratch. Let's take a look at that next.

Manual Warping

The best way to begin warping a song manually is by tapping to figure out the tempo as closely as possible. Start by turning off the Warp button in the Clip View. This will make the clip play at its original speed, regardless of the tempo of your Live Set. Launch the clip and begin tapping along with the song using the Tap Tempo button. (For better accuracy, map this button instead of clicking with the mouse.) Since Live's Tempo display is accurate to two decimal places, you'll probably get tempos like 125.82 BPM or 98.14 BPM instead of round numbers like 110 BPM or 85 BPM.

After you've got the rough tempo, zoom in and move the Start flag to the first clear downbeat of the song. Then right-click on Start and select Set 1.1.1 Here. If you're working with material that you're sure has a completely steady tempo, then you're almost done. Scroll over and find the next clear downbeat. If you're working with rhythmically complex music, this might not be until the beginning of bar 3 or 5. If you've tapped the tempo fairly accurately, the downbeat should already be pretty close to the beginning of the bar. Just drag it into place, spot-check the track against the metronome, and you're probably done.

If the song drifts a few minutes in, check the Seg. BPM box as mentioned earlier and try rounding the tempo up or down to the next whole number. Otherwise, adjust a downbeat later in the track to line it up with the beginning of the bar. If doing this throws off the timing earlier in the track, then your material is not completely steady, and you'll have to use multiple Warp Markers as described next. Remember to experiment freely: the Undo command is your friend!

If you're working with material with rhythmic fluctuations, you'll need a Warp Marker every so often. For some material, every 32 bars may be enough, and for others, you may need one every bar (or more!). Sometimes this is as simple as zooming in at the beginning of every four bars, double-clicking to create a Warp Marker at the downbeat, and dragging it over to the beginning of the bar. In problem cases, you might have to use the loop technique (see Figure 12.4).

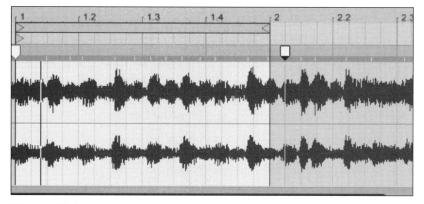

Figure 12.4 This loop doesn't play back smoothly. Notice that I've created a Warp Marker at the actual downbeat of the next bar. Once I drag it left to line up with end of the loop, it sounds great.
Source: Ableton

The loop technique works like this: After tapping the tempo, adjust the loop brace around the first one or two bars of the clip and begin playback. Chances are, the loop won't play back smoothly. Look to the right of the loop brace and see if you can identify the downbeat of the next bar in the waveform display. Create a Warp Marker for it and drag it so that it lines up with the right-hand edge of the loop brace. Depending on whether your tapped tempo was too fast or too slow, you may have to drag it to the left or right. Use your ears and zoom in as far as necessary to tweak things until the loop sounds correct. Then move the loop brace ahead so it begins on the downbeat you just adjusted (click on the brace and press the up arrow) and repeat the process.

Every now and then, you can get great results using a combination of manual and automatic warping. Sometimes Auto Warp can get a few bars of material right and then makes a mistake. In this case, try dropping a Warp Marker at the downbeat every time the warping drifts off; then right-click it and use the Warp From Here command. For some material, this can be a real time-saver.

While there is no silver bullet to make sure you always get everything warped properly, this section arms you with a very powerful set of techniques that can be adapted to almost any material you will encounter.

Selecting the Right Warp Mode

This is a topic on which there are many different opinions and no overarching consensus. Theoretically, Complex Pro mode provides the best quality for warping entire songs, but in practice, this isn't always the case. Factors that affect the sound quality of warped audio include the original spectral characteristics of the song, the amount you are speeding up or slowing down the song, and whether or not you are transposing the song or playing it back at its original pitch.

If you know you're not going to change the tempo or pitch of a song during a performance, you should use any mode other than the Complex modes. At the original tempo/pitch, the other Warp modes have no effect on the sound quality, while the Complex modes always do. For heavily percussive dance tracks, Beats mode can work very well. I will generally select No Loop (the forward arrow) from the Transient Loop Mode menu (see Chapter 5) when using Beats mode. This can give the track a slightly choppy sound when slowing tracks down, but I happen to like that for some material. The downside of Beats mode for entire songs is that it can create an unpleasant warbling in the bass sometimes.

You may feel that your songs don't work well in either Complex or Beats mode. There are many musicians who feel that Texture mode provides the best overall balance of sound quality and preservation of transients. There are others who only use Repitch mode, which sounds excellent but limits your ability to match songs by key. My personal approach is to take each song on a case-by-case basis and listen closely before making a decision. As with so many things musical, the last and best advice is to use your ears and experiment.

Performance Techniques

Now that you've got your Warp-Marked files ready, we are going to discuss a variety of techniques used by artists on stage. Let's start by looking at traditional DJs, their equipment, and their performance methods, but again this information is relevant to just about everyone performing with Live. For DJs, learning these techniques and expanding on them will move you into a new and constantly evolving world that blurs the line between DJing and live performance.

The DJ Mixer

In Figure 12.5, I have set up Live's Session View like a standard two-channel DJ mixer. There are two audio tracks, each assigned to different sides of the crossfader. There are EQs loaded onto each of the audio tracks, and a few DJ Audio Effect Racks on the Master track.

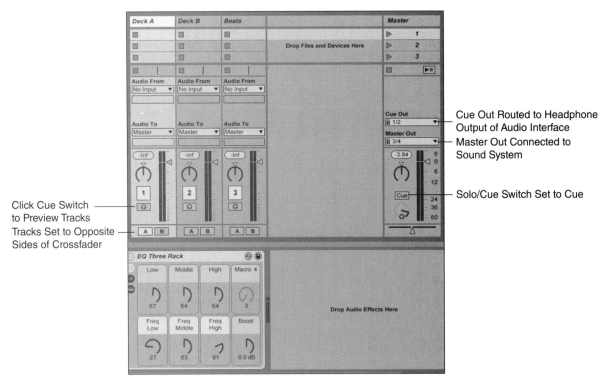

Figure 12.5 A simple Live Set ready for DJing, with a bonus third track for extra beats.

Source: Ableton

In order to cue or preview tracks, you'll need an audio interface with four outputs—two outs for the main mix and two others to feed your headphones. Many audio interfaces have assignable headphone outputs, while others have the headphone out hard-wired to a specific pair of outputs. In this case, we're assuming that outputs 1/2 will feed the headphones. Therefore, in the Master track outs, 1/2 are specified for Cue and 3/4 for Master. Connect outputs 3/4 to the sound system.

Now you're ready to cue tracks through the headphones as shown previously. Please note that enabling Cue on a track does not remove it from the Master. You'll need to turn off the Track Activator button or turn down the volume to keep it only in the headphones. Once the track is properly cued, you can bring up the volume and send it out to the mains.

Figure 12.6 shows another approach. A Cue track is used to hold tracks before you play them. It has its Cue switch on and Track Activator off, so any audio clip in this track will be heard only in the headphones. Tracks like these can be used as virtual "record crates." Load all the songs you think you might want to play. Then, after you're done previewing it, drag the clip from the cue track over to Deck A or Deck B.

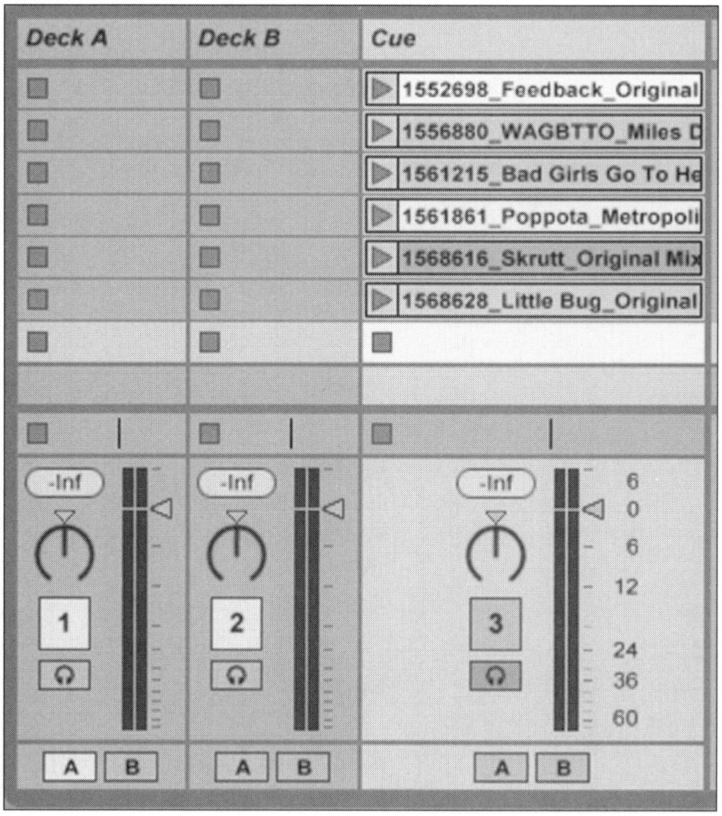

Figure 12.6 This setup features an additional "cue track." You launch clips on this track for private headphone listening before dragging it onto one of the "live" tracks.
Source: Ableton

Finally, it's also possible to simply use Live as a replacement for CD players or turntables and do all of your mixing on a standard DJ mixer. All of the previous examples have you sending a single stereo pair out of the computer into the sound system (or a single channel on a DJ mixer, as is often the case). When you do this, you'll need a MIDI controller to handle your volumes and EQs. Using the routing shown in Figure 12.7, you can send different tracks directly out of different outputs on your interface and handle volume, crossfade, EQ, and cuing on the DJ mixer.

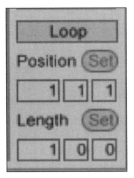

Figure 12.7 These two tracks are routed to separate outputs and can be sent into two different channels on a mixer.
Source: Ableton

Looping

Live lets you define loop points on the fly by using the Set buttons for the Position and Length parameters in the Clip View (see Figure 12.8). While a clip is playing, you can press Set Position to set the point where the loop begins and Set Length to set the loop's end point *and* turn the Loop switch on in one step. When you turn the Loop switch off, the clip will continue to play to the end. If you turn it back on again, the clip will jump back to playing the loop.

As you'd expect, the Set switches can be mapped to a controller, but remember: since these buttons are in the Clip View, the controller will only set the loop points for the clip that's currently being displayed. To jump to the currently playing clip from your controller, you'll have to map the Clip Status indicator, as explained in Chapter 11, "Remote Control."

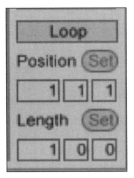

Figure 12.8 Map the Set buttons shown above for on-the-fly looping. Map the Loop switch, too, for enabling or disabling the loop.
Source: Ableton

Beats, Bass, and Beyond

Thanks to the fact that you've warped all of your audio files and they are playing on a temporal grid, you can easily add loops to enhance your Set. An extra beat can be used to smooth the transition between songs, or you can segue into an improvised loop jam before playing the next track. Or load up a virtual instrument track and perform parts live. If you want, you can record new MIDI clips during the gig and create loops on the fly.

A word of caution here: Since the possibilities here are literally endless, start simple and expand as you get more comfortable performing with Live. What you're able to pull off during practice is often a bit beyond what you can during the gig. Having 10 extra tracks may theoretically afford you much more leeway to improvise during a show, but having so much to keep track of can also turn seriously stressful if things don't go as planned.

Live Arranging

It can be really handy to make multiple clips from a single song, each having different starting points and loops (see Figure 12.9a). Having these on hand will allow you to launch the clips in any order you want, remixing the arrangement of the song right in front of your audience.

Once you've created these clips, you can highlight them all and drag them into the Browser to create a new Set (see Figure 12.9b). You could drag them into the User Library or create a folder on your hard drive just for this purpose and add it to Places, as explained in Chapter 3, "Live Interface Basics." The next time you want to play this song, drag the Set from the Browser into your DJ Set and your stack of clips will be ready to go.

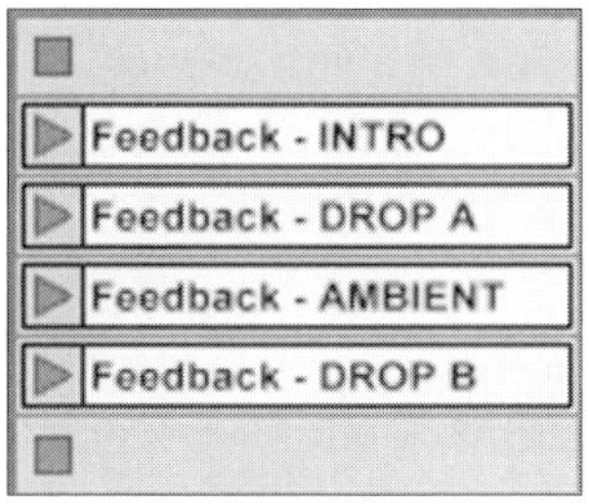

Figure 12.9a These four clips are all made from the same song. This approach makes it easy to jump around within a song, and extend or shorten sections during performance.

Source: Ableton

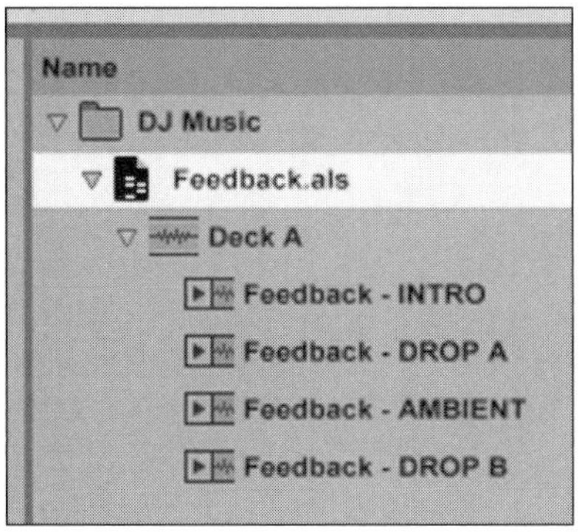

Figure 12.9b This Set was created by dragging the four clips from Figure 12.9a into the Browser. It's completely unfolded here so you can see the clips contained within.

Source: Ableton

Master Effects

Don't forget that in addition to all of the sonic mayhem you can create with Insert and Send effects, you can also put effects in the Master track. Experiment with using a Beat Repeat, Auto Pan, or a Redux (just to name a few) on the entire mix. This can work wonders for emphasizing breakdowns or smoothing over transitions.

It can also be helpful to place a Limiter in your Master track to make sure that you don't clip your outputs. That said, it's important to make sure that you're not hitting the Limiter unnecessarily and crushing your dynamics. For this reason, dial in negative gain on the Limiter (try –3dB for starters), which will give you some extra headroom to mix tracks and loops together. This way, limiting only occurs if something extreme happens.

Live Bands and Other Performance Concepts

Many gigging bands are using some form of accompaniment, either prerecorded tracks or beat boxes, to embellish their sound. Many times, the bands feature multi-instrumentalists who write more parts for a song than can be played at once. When you have the multitracking capabilities of Live at your disposal, you can easily compile the parts you need for accompaniment and break them into scenes. As you perform, you can move through the scenes, or you can record an arrangement to play again during a gig.

> **MAKING THE SCENE:** To quickly get a chunk of your Arrangement into the Session View, select a range of time in the Arrangement View; then right-click and choose Consolidate Time to New Scene from the context menu. When you return to the Session, you'll have a brand new scene with the material you selected. This can provide a great starting point for preparing a multitrack performance Set.

Click Track

In order to stay synchronized with Live, one or more members of the band may want to listen to a Click track, which is a metronome sound synchronized with the parts in your song. Usually, this amounts to nothing more than turning on Live's metronome and setting the Cue output to a pair of headphones (like we did in the DJ example earlier). The drummer will usually be the one who needs the click. He'll play along with the metronome in the headphones, and the band will play along with him. As a result, you all play together with Live.

Of course, since everything is tempo synced in Live, you could use a regular drum loop as the click track. Instead of turning on the metronome, load a drum loop onto a track and send it to the headphones. Some musicians will find it easier to play against a drum loop, as opposed to the generic metronome sound.

Tap Tempo

Along with playing to Live's click track, you can make Live play to *your* click track. Assign a MIDI button or key to Live's Tap Tempo button. As your band plays, you can tap in your tempo, and Live will follow it. A drummer can assign an electronic trigger to the Tap Tempo and then tap a few beats here and there to keep Live in sync.

> **COUNT OFF:** Give Live four taps as you count off the beginning of your song. Live will start on the downbeat along with the rest of your band, and it will continue playing at the tempo you tapped.

Live Effects

Besides being a flexible backup player for your band, Live can also act as a flexible effects box. There are more and more acts these days where Live is functioning both to play beats and to process acoustic instruments (or vocals) to blend them better into an electronic context. For example, to add an effect to a live source, run the mic or line into an input on your computer's audio interface and select it as an input on an audio track. Switch the track's monitoring to In and place the effect of your choice on the track (see Figure 12.10). The effect can now be controlled by a mapped controller or by automation, which causes changes to happen in sync with the song.

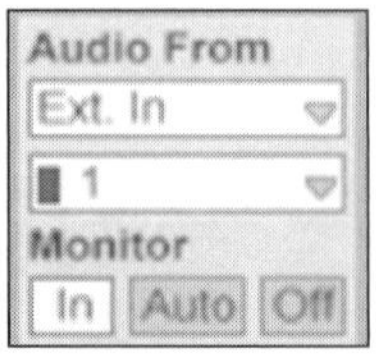

Figure 12.10 With a valid input selected and Monitor set to In, you can pass audio through a track for effects processing.
Source: Ableton

Real-Time Loop Layering

Using Live's Looper (see Chapter 9, "Live's Audio Effects") or the recording functions within the Session View (see Chapter 5), you can record new clips easily and layer them on the fly. For example, you can play a simple bass line, loop it, and then layer a rhythm part on top of it. You can then improvise on top of these new loop creations, making a song right before the audience's eyes (and ears).

The method for achieving these layers is accomplished best with a MIDI foot controller, such as the KMI SoftStep, so you can control Live with your feet, leaving your hands free to play your instrument. There are many ways to configure a live looping setup, so it's best to start simple. You can map Arm switches to enable or disable recording, and scene navigators (see Chapter 11) to move up or down in the Session View. The Session Record and New buttons can also be mapped for jumping to an empty clip slot and starting a new recording with a minimum of footwork.

Theater

Sound cues are one of the most important elements for adding realism to a stage production. Sound effects, such as wind, rain, thunder, city traffic, church bells, and crying babies, are played through the house system, and sometimes music cues play a role as well. In order to play a sound instantly when using Live, you'll need to turn off Launch Quantization either in Live's Control bar or individually in your clips. You'll also commonly switch off Warp so the sample will play at its original pitch and speed.

Live 9 Power!

I N THIS FINAL CHAPTER, we'll be looking at an assortment of more advanced techniques, along with a few things that just don't fit anywhere else, such as the File Manager and Max For Live.

Getting Your Groove On

The power of loop-based music is also its biggest problem: repetition. While repetition can be magic for keeping a dance floor moving, the "feel" can become stagnant, ultimately making music monotonous and uninspired. To combat this, it is important to understand the three heavy hitters of groove: dynamics, timing, and variation. What you'll find in this chapter are suggestions that can be used in addition to, rather than in place of, Live's built-in Groove feature.

Be aware that some of this is very subtle stuff, and it is not always immediately apparent to the untrained ear. For example, when I'm talking about dynamics here, I'm not talking about a song having a quiet section and a loud section. Rather, I'm talking about the variations in the volume of the hi-hat part over the course of a bar.

▷ **Dynamics:** Whether you're working with audio or MIDI, it's worth exploring the effect of subtle volume changes on your parts. Altering the velocity of a few MIDI notes or adding a volume envelope to tweak a couple of hits in an audio loop is one of the simplest ways to breathe life into your sound. Dynamic variations can be built in to shorter loops with envelopes while working in the Session View, and then more can be added in the Arrangement View using Automation. For example, you might decide to make one hit slightly louder every eight bars.

▷ **Timing:** It's not uncommon to hear drummers and bass players talk about being "ahead of the beat" or "behind the beat." For example, the bass player may play right on the beat, while the drummer plays the 2 and 4 snare hits slightly behind. Or perhaps the drummer plays ahead of the beat, ever so slightly, rushing the snare and hi-hats while the bass player lays back. These subtleties are often what make music rhythmically compelling. It's not that you should avoid perfectly quantized rhythms, it's just that they often sound more exciting when contrasted against something that's pushing or pulling against them a little bit.

For some people, this subtlety is achieved by performing parts live to get the natural timing variation that comes with performance. For others, it's a process of surgically adjusting MIDI notes or Warp Markers ahead or behind. You can hold down Ctrl (Cmd) to disable the grid temporarily while dragging or just zoom in until the grid is 1/256 or smaller. It's also possible to make entire tracks rush or drag by using the Track Delay. Try starting out with values of +/− 10ms if you want to experiment with this.

▷ **Variation:** Some people like to make tons of variations in the Session View while composing, while others build an arrangement first, and then create variations in the Arrangement View, by using Split and then making modifications to the separated clips. It doesn't have to be anything fancy—taking the kick drum out for a beat or two, altering a note in the bass part, or inserting a dramatic pause are just a few of the many ways you can keep things interesting. To really get busy with variation, get into the Clip Cuttin' Clinic that follows.

Clip Cuttin' Clinic

No matter how good your programmed parts are, you'll still find ways to enhance them through creative editing in the Arrangement View. And the better an editor you are, the more fun you can also have with prerecorded loops, using them as raw material instead of just prefabricated musical ideas. While the techniques shown here are for all sorts of material, I find they are often easiest to learn with drum beats. But that said, the only goal here is experimentation and discovery, so dig in with any material you like!

Most of these techniques will be demonstrated with audio, but you'll find that many apply to MIDI as well. For techniques that are audio only, you can still try it out on your MIDI parts as long as you Freeze and Flatten them first. Sometimes the simplicity of audio and the power of Live's Warping tools beats the flexibility of MIDI.

Before getting started with the following experiments, turn on the Loop switch in the Arrangement so you can hear what you do while you edit. Figure 13.1 shows a drum loop that's been cut into multiple slices using Split—Ctrl (Cmd)+E. After doing this, it's easy to rearrange the order of the slices. Use Duplicate to copy certain ones, and Delete to remove others. Even if you do this randomly, many a happy accident will occur. If you need to bring your mashed up beats back into the Session View, use Consolidate to make a new clip out of the slices.

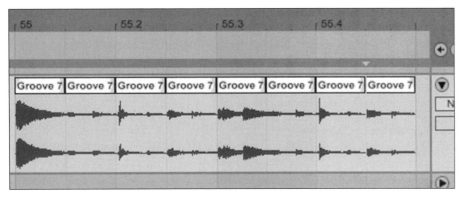

Figure 13.1 Repeatedly split any clip. Then go crazy.
Source: Ableton

Once you've sliced up a clip, there's lots of other fun to be had. Try using the :2 and *2 buttons in the Clip View to double or halve the original tempo of a slice. Add crazy Warp Markers or change the transposition, and then experiment with the Warp modes to generate different artifacts. Don't forget the Rev button, which can be used to reverse clips as well. After reversing a slice, you may find that you have to slide the clip in the timeline to correct any unpleasant timing variations this creates. Zoom in until the grid is super fine, or hold down Ctrl (Cmd) to temporarily disable the grid.

You can also generate variations by moving the Start marker within individual slices. To do this, select the clip and then make sure the Loop switch is turned on in the Clip View. (If it's not, moving Start and End will simply move the boundaries of the clip in the timeline). Now, move Start or even move around the loop brace, and you'll see that the clip remains in the same place in the timeline, but you're moving the audio within it. You may find that this technique is more interesting when used on slightly longer slices, since you'll get bigger chunks of the original material offset in interesting ways.

Occasionally, when working with audio clips, you may realize that it would be easier (or more fun) to manipulate the audio from a MIDI device. No problem! Just drag the clip into a Drum Rack, Impulse, Simpler, or Sampler. You can even drop the clip directly into the Track View of an empty MIDI track and cause a Simpler to be created. The clip's Start position will be used within these devices automatically.

> **HOVER:** While dragging an object in Live, you can hover the mouse over the title bar of any track and cause its Track View to be displayed. In the previous example, this means you could drag a clip to the title bar of a MIDI track, wait for the Track View to appear, and then drop the clip into the device.

Harnessing Follow Actions

Follow Actions are some serious stuff. The carefully thought-out rules governing Follow Actions will allow you to do innumerable things, limited only by your imagination. Not only can they be used to enhance live performances, but they are also a wonderful compositional aid, helping you create variations you might never have thought of on your own. Check out the "Follow Actions" section in Chapter 5, "Clips," for a refresher on how all of this works.

Here are a few ideas for using Follow Actions:

▷ **Loop variations:** Here's another technique that's useful when you want a part to be very steady, but want to keep it from becoming stale. Create two (or more) loops that are nearly identical, but have subtle variations, such as an extra hi-hat or kick-drum hit. Set the first clip to randomly trigger the second clip from time to time. You'll set the second clip to retrigger the first. The result is that you get a constant beat with an additional snare hit thrown in occasionally, mimicking the way a real drummer would modify his beat on the fly.

▷ **Fills:** Follow Actions can be used to make sure the main beat always comes back after you trigger a drum fill. Figure 13.2 shows a stack of drum parts. The top clip is the main beat. Every clip below it is a drum fill. Each of these variations has Follow Actions A set to First, as shown in the figure. By having all of the fill clips trigger the main beat right after they start, you've guaranteed that the main beat will start on the next bar. (The main beat clip is set to Bar Quantization.) In this example, each of the fill clips has a Launch Quantization of 1/16, so you can launch multiple clips one after the other and piece the fill together in real time.

Figure 13.2 The top clip is set to Bar Quantization, while the others are set to 1/16. Each fill clip launches the first, so the beat will always kick in after the fills.
Source: Ableton

Don't just try this with beats; try it with other types of parts, too. Create multiple clips and treat them with different effects and parameter tweaks. Set them to Legato mode so that the playback position is traded off as you switch clips. It will sound like you're performing crazy processing on the part as you switch between the clips.

▷ **Legato madness:** Make a dozen or more variant clips. Set them all to Legato with a Follow Action of Any. Set the Follow Action times to something pretty short (1/8 or 1/16) and let it rip. Live will start jumping randomly between all your variations. Use Arrangement Record to capture the results and then edit together your favorite bits in the Arrangement View.

Minimizing Performance Strain

No matter how fast and new my computer is, I always seem to find a way to tax it beyond its capabilities. While most of Live's built-in devices are pretty CPU efficient, you can bring your system to its knees by using a lot of them in Sets with loads of tracks. Third-party plug-ins are harder to generalize about. Some are very lightweight, while others can cripple your system with just one or two instances. Here are a few tips for staying on top of your CPU load.

▷ **Freeze tracks:** This feature will render everything on the track into an audio file, so effects and virtual instruments can be disabled. Simply right-click on the track's name and choose Freeze track from the Context menu. If your computer is really struggling, select every track you're not currently editing and freeze them all at once. If you need to edit anything that's been disabled by Freeze, you can unfreeze the track, make your edits, and then refreeze it. If you can't Freeze something due to a routing issue, you can always record from track to track (see Chapter 6, "Tracks and Signal Routing") or use Export Audio/Video to export a single track.

▷ **Eliminate clips using Complex mode:** Unless it's absolutely necessary to use Complex or Complex Pro, use a different Warp mode. For clips where you need it for sound quality reasons, right-click on any clip or group of clips that use Complex and select Consolidate. A new clip will be written to disk. It will sound identical (as long as you don't change the tempo), but will no longer use Complex mode.

▷ **Delete unused elements:** If you have unused tracks that have been silenced with the Track Activator, remember that those tracks may still be wasting resources. Delete them. If you're finished working in the Session view and only need the Arrangement, delete *everything* from the Session. Not just the clips. Delete the scenes as well until you're down to the minimum of one empty scene. Use Save As to save a new version of your Set before deleting, in case you need to get anything back.

▷ **Increase your buffer:** Be aware of the impact of your Buffer Size (in the Audio tab of Live's Preferences) on CPU usage. The smaller your buffer, the higher the drain on your computer's resources will be. It's not uncommon during a final mixdown to set the Buffer Size to its maximum value to help your computer keep up with numerous instruments and effects. You can reduce it back to a small size later if you need low latency.

▷ **Lower the edit density:** Sometimes simply having a large number of clips close together in the Arrangement will make it difficult for your hard drive to keep up. This can happen as a result of extensive vocal editing, or from using the techniques described in the "Clip Cuttin' Clinic" earlier. Select groups of clips and use Consolidate to turn them into a single clip.

Templates

In the File/Folder tab of Live's Preferences, you're allowed to save a default Set that's loaded whenever you start Live or select File > New Live Set. However, with all the different uses for Live, chances are that you won't be able to create a "one-size-fits-all" template to handle every situation. In this section, we'll look at a few approaches to working with reusable Sets.

One easy way to manage a collection of templates is by using the Templates folder. In your User Library, create a folder called *Templates* (if there isn't one already) and save your template Sets into it (see Figure 13.3). When you double-click to open a Set from this folder, Live will automatically open a copy of the Set and name it "Untitled." This way, you don't have to worry about accidentally editing your template.

Figure 13.3 Use this folder to store your reusable Sets. Double-click to open a copy, or just drag one into the currently open Set.

Source: Ableton

Drag-and-Drop Import and Export

Also bear in mind that Sets can be imported into other Sets by dragging them from the Browser. Conversely, you can export Sets by dragging one or more tracks, or a group of clips, into the User Library or another folder in the Places area of the Browser. (See "Live Arranging" in Chapter 12, "Playing Live...Live," for a practical example.) Using this technique, you can create a highly modular setup where useful tracks and clips can be imported at will.

Even if you don't specifically create templates in this fashion, bear in mind that any Set can be unfolded in the Browser, revealing its tracks and clips. This means you can grab musical elements from any Set, at any time. Be aware that unfolding large Sets is a rather resource-intensive process and may move quite slowly. If your computer stalls as you drag from the Browser, be patient. Hold the mouse button down and wait until Live shows that the imported elements are ready to be dropped.

When importing templates that contain clips, you'll discover that you have the option of dropping the clips into existing tracks or dropping them into the Drop Area to create new tracks. Because templates can also contain devices, it's important to know that should you choose to drop the clips into tracks, the devices will only be imported if the existing tracks contain *absolutely no devices*. Also note that when importing Sets containing *no clips* into the Session View, you'll have to drag the Set to the title bar area, and you won't be allowed to drop it in the clip grid.

If you export a Set containing audio clips, there is a file management issue to consider. Remember that Sets only *reference* audio files, they don't contain them. Therefore, you need to consider whether you want Live to copy the audio files along with the exported Set. This is handled by the Preferences screen shown in Figure 13.4.

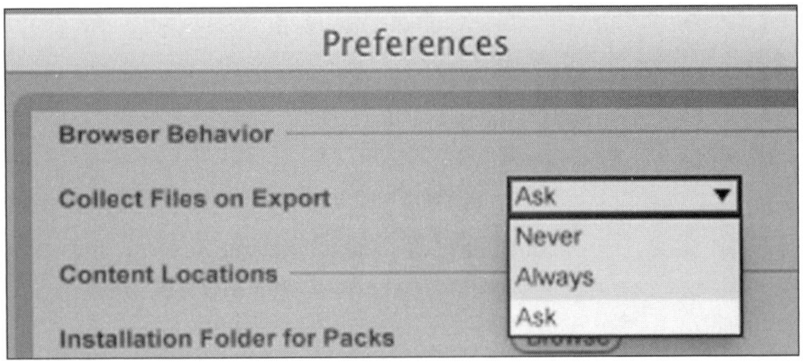

Figure 13.4 When exporting Sets and presets, Live gives you full control over whether or not all the referenced files are exported as well.
Source: Ableton

You will discover that when exporting to locations other than the User Library, Live automatically creates a Project folder for the exported Set (unless you export it into an existing Project folder). If you choose to export the audio files as well, they will be placed inside this new Project. In the User Library, this is handled behind the scenes.

CLIP TIP: If you drag a single clip into the Browser, a Live Clip is created. A Live Clip is sort of like a Set containing only one clip. It contains not only audio or MIDI but also the devices from the track the clip was originally on.

Defaults

In your User Library, you'll see a folder called *Defaults*. Live uses the contents in this folder as templates for a variety of objects. When you right-click in the title bar of a device and select "Save as Default Preset," a device preset or .als file is created in this folder.

There are a few other behaviors you can customize here as well. For example, inside the Dropping Samples folder, you'll find a folder called On Drum Rack. Configure a Simpler or Sampler any way you like and then drag it into this folder. The next time you drop a sample on to a Drum Rack, your custom configuration will be used.

The Audio to MIDI folders are used to customize the MIDI tracks that are created when the Convert to New MIDI Track commands are used. Drag instruments from the Track View into these folders, and the next time you convert audio to MIDI, the instruments you've chosen will be used in the new MIDI tracks.

> **TRACK TIP:** If you find that you're regularly setting the same routings or adding the same devices when you create new tracks, you can create default track settings. In the context menu of a track's title bar, select Save as Default Audio Track or Save as Default MIDI Track. The track settings are saved in the Defaults folder as an .als file.

Scoring to Video

They say timing is everything. Nowhere is this more evident than in scoring music for the moving image. Whether you are adding sound effects, mood music, or creating a complete soundtrack, Live's ability to easily manipulate the timing of audio makes it a great tool for fitting sound to picture.

Importing Video

Getting video into Live is simple: Just locate the video file you want to import in the File Browser and drag it into your Live Set. The audio will be loaded on an audio track in Live, and the video will appear in a special floating video window. Only video files in QuickTime format (.mov, .mp4, or any other format playable by QuickTime) are supported.

You can only work with video in the Arrangement View. If you drop a movie into the Session View, the clip will load as audio only. Once loaded, the video clip will look like any other audio clip in Live, except that you will see virtual "sprocket holes" in its title bar.

Video clips in the Arrangement View behave more or less just like audio clips. Thus, by dragging a video clip into the arrangement and aligning it with the beginning of the first measure, you can quickly start scoring to picture and creating a soundtrack. You can use Live's FX and audio editing tools to edit the video clip's associated audio in the Arrangement View, just like any other audio clip. (You will find that Consolidate, Crop, and Reverse operations will cause your video clip to be replaced by an audio clip.)

The Video Window

The Video window opens automatically when you add video to the Arrangement. Start Live, and the video will follow playback. You can drag the video window around wherever you want. You can resize it by clicking on the lower-right corner, or expand it to full-screen mode by double-clicking on the video itself. If you close the Video window, it can be reopened from the View menu.

Keeping Sound and Video in Sync

The most common application for video in Live will probably be for creating a new soundtrack for a video clip of a given length. In this application, the most important thing is not to disturb the timing of the video inside Live. To maintain sync, simply drag your video clip to the beginning of the Arrangement View and make sure that you have the video clip's Master/Slave switch set to Master. This makes the video Live's tempo master, meaning that any changes to the Warp Markers in the video will change Live's master tempo—not the playback speed of the video. Setting the video as the tempo master enables you to define hit points in the video, which will affect the playback speed of the other clips in your session. Changing the speed of the video to match your music will not make you a very popular film composer!

Saving/Exporting

After you have finished your new soundtrack, you will want to save your work either as a new movie or as an audio file to be turned over to a film editor. If you're just exporting audio, there are a few things to bear in mind. First, the safest bet for turning in your soundtrack to an editor is to make an audio file the exact length of the video you were given, so the start points line up exactly, and there won't be any confusion about where your sound cues go. Second, if you're exporting audio only, don't forget to mute the audio on the video track; otherwise, you'll get a file containing both the dialogue and the music. The standard sample rate for digital video is 48 kHz, but for Internet streaming, 44.1 kHz is just fine. That said, when creating audio for someone else's film or video project, the best policy is simply to ask them the format they want.

To create a video, select File > Export Audio/Video and turn on Create Video File in the bottom section of the dialog. The menu below allows you to choose the type of video encoding you desire. If you need to customize the video settings in any way (to optimize it for Internet streaming, for example), use the Edit button next to Encoder Settings.

As you will probably notice once you start working with video clips, any audio editing commands that you apply to the audio track hosting your video clip will affect the video playback as well. In other words, you can use all of Live's warping and editing functions to create video and audio edits. So get busy taking advantage of Live 9's video export capabilities to create some warped video mashups—YouTube awaits!

Managing Files

No matter how careful you are, it's going to happen—files will get lost or misplaced, or you're going to occasionally get confused about where all those great sounds from last year's project came from. The good news is that Live's File Manager is here to help you get a handle on what's going on.

Select Manage Files from the File menu to open the File Manager. When it opens, you'll be given the option to manage either the current Set, the current project, or the Live Library.

> ▷ **Manage Set:** This will present you with options and information pertaining only to the current Set. You can locate missing samples, collect external sample files into the project folder, or simply view all of the samples in your Set.
> ▷ **Manage Project:** Remember what we just said about saving multiple versions? When you've done this, using the Manage Project feature is very useful. For example, it can tell you how many external samples you have for every version of your Set and collect them into the project folder, so you can make sure that your project is self-contained for each and every version of your Set that you have saved.
> ▷ **Manage User Library:** This feature will give you information about all of the presets and samples stored in your User Library. It can be used to get things back into shape if files have gotten moved or lost.

Manage Set

Let's take a look at what happens when you choose Manage Set. Figure 13.5 shows the window entitled Current Live Set that opens when you choose this option. Like all of the File Manager's windows, it's broken into several sections, each with a small triangle to the left that can be used to hide or show the section. The first section is View and Replace Files. Clicking the View Files button will reveal a list of all of the samples used in the Set (see Figure 13.6). The Location column next to the sample name will tell you if the file is located within the project folder, in an external location, or is missing. Clicking the Edit button to the left of the sample name will open the file in the audio editor you have specified in the File/Folder tab of the Preferences screen.

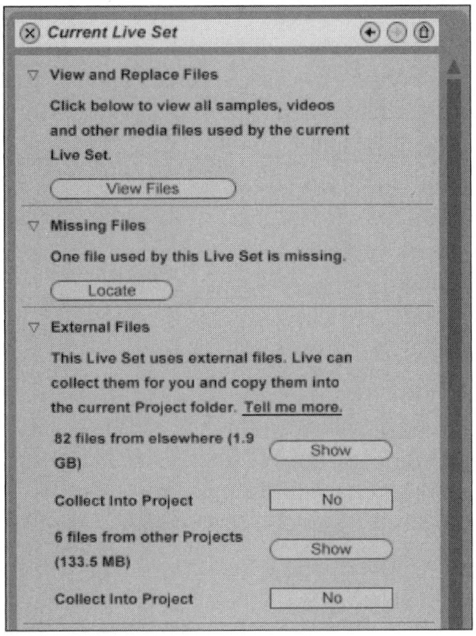

Figure 13.5 Manage Set reveals a window with information about the locations of the files in your set.
Source: Ableton

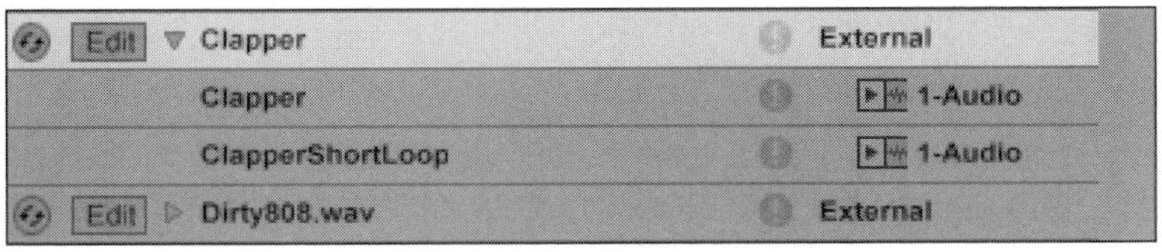

Figure 13.6 You can unfold a sample to reveal all of the clips that contain it.
Source: Ableton

View Samples reveals the sample list, which shows you all of the samples in your Set, and all of the clips that contain them. You can replace samples or open your audio editor from here.

Clicking the Hot-Swap button to the left of the sample name will reveal the file's location in the File Browser. While the Hot-Swap button is highlighted, any file you double-click in the File Browser will be used to globally replace that sample in your Set. That means that any clip that is based on this sample will be updated to use the new sample. All of the other properties (such as loop points and transposition) of the clip will be retained. Another way to globally replace samples in your set is simply to drag a file out of the File Browser and drop it into the File Manager—directly onto the sample you want to replace.

Looking at the title bar of the File Manager, you'll notice a set of three Web Browser style buttons in the upper right-hand corner. You can use the Back button (the left-pointing arrow) to return to the Set Management overview. If at any point you want to return to the main File Manager window, you can use the Home button on the far right.

Finding Lost Files

Below the View and Replace Files section of the Manage Set window is the Missing Files section (see Figure 13.7). Clicking the Locate button in this section will bring up a list of missing samples in the Set. Instead of having a Hot-Swap button next to these samples, there is a Search button, which can be used to execute a search for the file in the Browser.

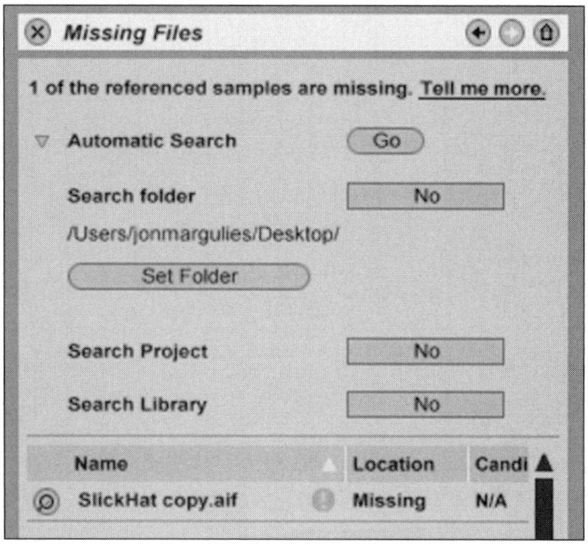

Figure 13.7 The Missing Files window can be used to identify and replace individual samples or automatically search for all lost audio files.
Source: Ableton

The other way to replace missing samples is to use the Automatic Search feature in the Missing Files window (see Figure 13.7). What's nice about this feature is that it lets you search for all of your missing samples in one shot, instead of one at a time. Here's how it's done:

1. Expand Automatic Search to reveal the search options and set the Search Folder switch to Yes, unless you only want to search your project folder and the Live Library, in which case you can skip to Step 3.
2. Click the Set Folder button and navigate to the folder you want to search. Any subfolders in this location will be searched as well.
3. Set the Search Project and Search Library switches to Yes if you believe your files may be in the current project folder or the Live Library.
4. Click the Go button at the top of the window.

When the search is completed, Live will tell you how many "Candidates" (how many potentially correct files) were found and how many samples it was able to automatically replace with the candidates it found. The missing samples list will now be updated to show the replaced files, changing their location status to either Project or External. There will be two main reasons a file does not get replaced automatically. Either the missing file cannot be found at all, or more than one file has been found that matches the name of the missing file. In this case, the location will read Candidates, and the number of possible replacement files found will be listed in the Candidates field (see Figure 13.8).

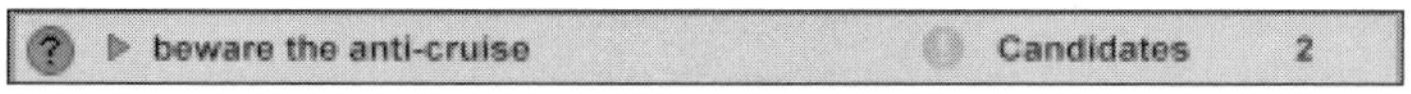

Figure 13.8 When more than one file with a matching name is found, Live needs you to intervene and pick the right one.
Source: Ableton

Clicking on the ? button will reveal a list of all the matching files in the File Browser. You have a few choices to determine which is the right one. First, you could simply enable the Preview button and decide by ear. Another option is to right-click in the Browser's header and show the Path (Place) or Date Modified columns in the Browser. Once you've found the right file, you can double-click or drag-and-drop as described earlier.

External Samples

The final area of the Current Set window is the External Files section (refer to Figure 13.5). If all of your samples are already within the current project folder, this section will be empty. If not, the first Show button will allow you to view all samples that exist outside of the current project folder but that are within the main folder of other projects. The other Show button will reveal samples in other locations. Note that Live considers the Library to be a "project," so any files from the Live Library are considered to be contained in another project.

Below the two Show buttons are switches that will allow you to collect (copy) these external samples into your project folder. These differ from the Collect All and Save command, in that they allow you to specify what samples should be copied into the project. You can differentiate between files that are in other project folders and files elsewhere. To actually copy the samples and save the current Set, use the Collect and Save button at the bottom of the File Manager.

Manage Project

Manage Project contains several features that are identical to Manage Set (except that they act on all Sets in the project), so I'll just focus on the features that are different here.

The first area of the Manage Project window is the project location—it just shows you the path of the current project. After that is the Project Contents section, which tells you the number of Sets, Live Clips, Preset Files, and Samples in the project. Clicking any of the Show buttons will reveal the referenced files in the File Browser (see Figure 13.9).

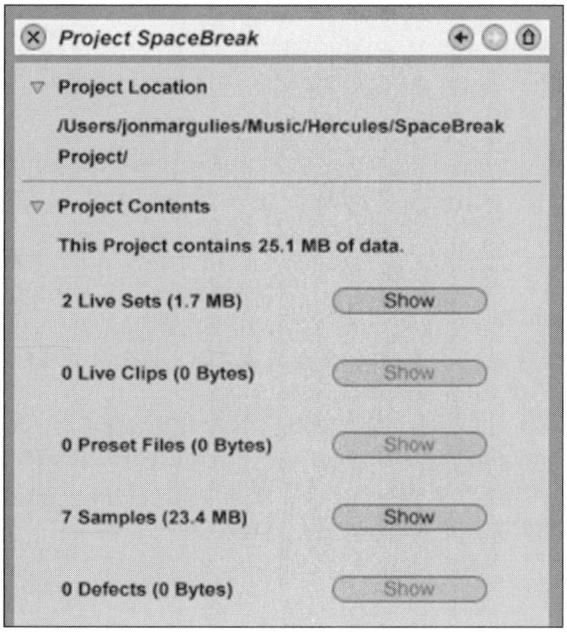

Figure 13.9 Project Contents tells you about all sorts of different files that exist within your project.
Source: Ableton

> **UPPER MANAGEMENT:** What if you want to manage files for a project or Set other than the one you have open? Fear not. Even though the Manage Files command opens the current Set/project by default, there's a way to get to others without closing your current Set. Simply navigate to a Live Set in the File Browser and right-click it. Select the Manage File option that appears in the context menu, and it will open in the File Manager. If you want to manage a project instead, right-click the project folder and choose Manage Project from the context menu.
>
> Here's another trick that may save you some time. The next time you want to replace a sample, right-click the waveform in the Clip View and choose Manage Sample File from the context menu. The File Manager will open with that sample highlighted in the samples list.

The next area of interest is the Unused Files section (see Figure 13.10). When working on a project, it's possible to generate many extra audio files that don't end up getting used. These could be multiple takes of a live performance or earlier versions of a loop before you effected and resampled it to perfection. This section differentiates between files that were recorded into the Set, created with the Freeze command, created with the Consolidate command, and files not created by the current project. Clicking the Show button will reveal these unused files in the File Browser, where you can choose what you want to do with them. While I heartily recommend getting rid of unnecessary files to recover disk space, I also strongly recommend backing up the entire project first, extra files and all, before deleting anything. Bad things can happen. Like a lot of what I have to say, this recommendation is based on a true story!

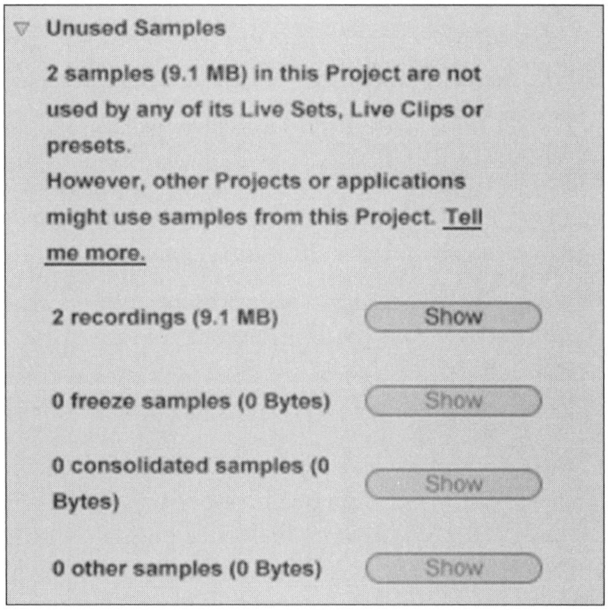

Figure 13.10 Getting rid of unnecessary audio files can reclaim a lot of disk space.
Source: Ableton

The final section of the Project Manager is the Packing section. This section lets you create a Pack from your project. A Pack is simply a compressed archive file (much like a zip file) containing everything in the project folder. If your project uses external files, there will be a warning message to remind you that the Pack will be missing some necessary files. If your plan is to transport this Pack to a different machine, it's important to use Collect All and Save first.

Max for Live

For many years now, Max/MSP (or just Max for short) has been a favorite of those who need to create customized audio and MIDI tools, whether they are simple MIDI patchers, software instruments, or the brains behind complex interactive multimedia installations using sound and video. In fact, before Ableton Live came along, most of the laptop performers I knew were using software built in Max/MSP! Now, this graphical programming environment integrates directly with Live. It is included with Live Suite and available as an add-on for Live Standard users.

The integration of Max with Ableton Live is one of the most innovative things to happen in music software for quite some time because it integrates a completely open-ended programming tool into a stable sequencer with a familiar workflow. With Max for Live, you'll get a powerful set of instruments and effects, plus the ability to download many additional devices from the ever-growing community of Max programmers.

If you're the programming type, you'll also be able to create devices that act just like Live's built-in devices and make tools that interact with the Live API (application programming interface). This means that you have access to the guts of Live itself, and can programmatically access things such as Live's tempo, a clip's groove properties, a current Set's track names, or nearly anything you can think of.

If all this talk of programming and APIs makes your head spin, don't worry. There are plenty of devices that come ready to use as-is, and many more that can be downloaded separately. In this next section, we'll take a look at some of the devices that come included with Max for Live and at the process of adding on devices. The programming itself is a very deep topic that goes well beyond the scope of this book, so there will just be a very brief look at this side of things.

To get started with Max for Live, you'll have to install it first, because it's not part of the basic Live installation. Just visit the Software page of your account at ableton.com, and you'll find it there. If you've installed Max and it's still not working, visit the File/Folder tab of the Preferences screen and check the Max Application Preference, which should point to the location where Max is installed.

All of the devices discussed next are found in the Max for Live view of the Browser. If the devices are missing, you'll need to download the Max for Live Essentials pack from the Your Packs page of your ableton.com account.

Drum Synths

Drum samples are great. With a working knowledge of how to program Simpler, Sampler, and Drum Racks, you can get a great deal of variety out of a modest number of samples. However, there are still good reasons to work with purely synthesized drums. There is something about being able to freely shape a drum sound while pushing against the natural limitations of a particular synthesis engine that yields all sorts of satisfying results. Synthetic sounds can also be automated, and velocity can be mapped to create variations and movement that would be hard to get with sampled drums.

The latest version of Max for Live comes with a brilliant tool kit for synthesizing drums—a series of modules designed to be used in the pads of Drum Racks, each one specialized for producing a different type of sound. You'll find these modules under Max Instrument, or if you want to get up and running quickly, check out the pre-built Drum Racks. (Go to the Drums view in the Browser and look for the Racks with "DrumSynth" in the name.)

Just drop one of these devices into a MIDI track or into a pad of a Drum Rack, and you're ready to go. There are too many of them to discuss all of the parameters in detail, but since they are all customized to produce one particular kind of sound, it's hard to go wrong. Twist some knobs and experiment. As shown in Figure 13.11, unfolding the device reveals a matrix for mapping note velocity. Use the switch to the left of a parameter to map velocity to it. The default scale of 0 to 100 works for most applications. 100 equals whatever you have manually set the parameter's value to. When a parameter has been mapped to velocity, its knob turns from blue to yellow.

Unfold to Reveal Velocity Mapping

Figure 13.11 The DrumSynth Kick loaded into a Drum Rack.
Source: Ableton

You'll also find a switch marked Keyboard in this area. When used directly in a track, rather than in a Drum Rack, you can turn this on to allow the synth to be pitched across the keyboard. Otherwise, its pitch will be fixed, and it won't track the keyboard's pitch at all.

You may find that because these devices all produce a particular sort of synthetic sound, they aren't suited to all your needs. They can still be quite useful, however. For example, you may want to use a sampled kick and snare to form the backbone of your song but use synthetic hats and claps. It also works well to layer synthetic and sampled drums. Just drop a Max for Live drum synthesizer module into a pad that already contains a sampled drum while holding down Alt (Cmd) to create a layered pad containing both the sample and the drum synth.

Modulators

Max for Live includes several devices that are totally unlike any of Live's built-in devices. These devices, which I've decided to call *modulators,* are strictly in the business of controlling the parameters of other devices. The other devices could be effects or instruments, or even Live's Mixer. By getting clever with these modulation devices, you can essentially turn Live into one big modular synthesizer.

Instead of comprehensively covering every modulator, I'll be diving deep on a couple of devices and covering all of the core concepts that you need in order to figure out how they all work.

LFO

This device is a great example of how Max for Live can change your world. Want to do rhythmic modulation of a reverb's decay time, or randomly change the waveform in Operator? Piece of cake.

LFO comes in both an audio effect and a MIDI effect version, and both of them have identical basic functionality. Either one can be used to control any type of device. The only difference is that the MIDI version can respond to MIDI input as well. (More on this in a moment.)

After dropping LFO into a track, click on the Map switch, and it will start blinking (see Figure 13.12). Now, move the control to which you want to assign the LFO. This can be a device or mixer parameter in the same track or on another track. If you want to assign it to a plug-in device parameter, you'll have to first make sure that the parameter is visible to Live, as explained in the "Remote Controlling Plug-In Devices" section of Chapter 11, "Remote Control."

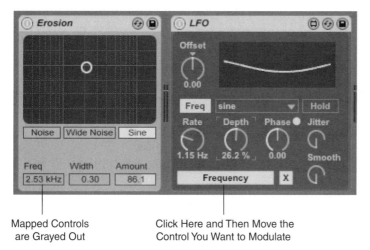

Mapped Controls
are Grayed Out

Click Here and Then Move the
Control You Want to Modulate

Figure 13.12 The LFO modulating the Frequency parameter of Erosion.
Source: Ableton

As soon as the control is mapped, it will become grayed out (it can't be adjusted manually while the LFO has control), and it will bounce back and forth to show the LFO's modulation. Adjusting the LFO itself is very similar to adjusting the LFO on Live's built-in devices, but the parameters have different names.

Depth changes the amount of modulation, while Rate adjusts the speed. Above Rate is a switch that can be switched between Freq and Sync to allow modulation in hertz or tempo synchronized divisions of the beat. Offset determines the LFO's center point. To get a clearer understanding of this, set Depth to 0% so no modulation occurs. Then move Offset to adjust the mapped parameter to whatever sounds like a good starting point. As you increase the Depth, you'll hear the LFO modulate the value farther away from this point.

There's a menu for selecting the shape of the LFO. Jitter is used to introduce some randomness into the LFO shape, while Smooth rounds off the edges. Small amounts of jitter can be very effective for introducing some subtle irregularities, while higher values are downright chaotic. Smooth doesn't have a big effect if you've selected Sine in the Shape menu, but when combined with harder-edged shapes like rectangle, it can produce some interesting results.

The LFO available under Max MIDI Effect (LFO MIDI) looks just like the audio version, until you unfold it (see Figure 13.13). This one looks identical except for the unfold switch at the right, which reveals controls that allow you to control the LFO from various MIDI parameters just like you would be able to do on an instrument. For example, you can map the LFO speed to velocity or key input, and you can set note input to retrigger the LFO if you choose.

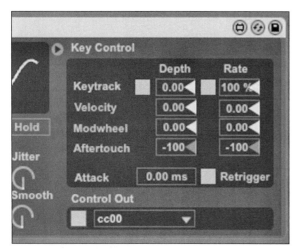

Figure 13.13 MIDI LFO allows your performance to dynamically change the modulation.
Source: Ableton

Envelope Follower

Envelope Follower is a Max Audio Effect, which, like LFO, does not actually process the audio directly. Instead, it measures the gain of the incoming signal and generates a modulation curve, which can be mapped to a device parameter. For example, if you place Envelope Follower in a snare drum track, it will measure the volume of the snare drum. Use the Map button to assign the modulation to a device parameter. Envelope Follower will then measure the snare drum's volume and modulate the mapped parameter in response.

To change the range of the modulation, adjust the Min and Max boxes next to the Map button. If you set Max *below* Min, negative modulation will be generated. This means that the mapped parameter will get turned *down* as the volume of the source increases.

For example, if you place the Envelope Follower in a snare drum track, but map it to the volume of a synthesizer part, you could cause the synth part to swell after every snare drum hit by leaving Max and Min at their default values and adjusting Rise and Delay to taste. Or you could make the synth part duck on every snare drum hit (just like you would with sidechain compression) by setting the Max value *below* Min.

Device Randomizer

Randomization can provide a great starting point when doing sound design. This device provides you with an easy way to scramble the parameters of any device as part of your sonic explorations. Just like LFO and Envelope Follower, Device Randomizer must be mapped before it will do anything. First, click on the Map button and then on the title bar of the device you want to randomize. The device will offer two different modes of randomizing: Auto, which applies continuous random modulations, and Trigger, which generates random values when the Randomize button is pushed.

A word of caution when using Device Randomizer with complex devices such as synthesizers. You'll quickly discover that randomizing these sorts of devices produces a lot of unusable results. It's not that you should expect randomization to ever produce consistently great results, but the more complex the device you're randomizing, the greater the chance that you'll get results that produce no sound or a terrible sound. To get this under control, click the Edit tab and press the unfold switch. Here you'll be presented with all of the parameters of the mapped device next to an On/Off switch. Any parameters set to Off will be excluded from the randomness.

Envelope

Envelope is a Max MIDI Effect that generates freely assignable ADSR modulation in response to note input. It works just like the built-in envelope on an instrument, but you can assign it to anything you like. This opens up not just the possibility of adding additional ADSR envelopes to instruments, but also to have effect devices controlled by an envelope.

The envelope is triggered as soon as MIDI note input is received, after which it modulates the mapped parameter through a range of values, according to the ADSR settings and the Min and Max boxes. Be aware that even though this device displays a graphical representation of the envelope, you'll have to make the adjustments with the knobs below. The Envelope's overall speed is set by the box to the left of the Map button.

Sequencers

The next two devices are very different, but since they're both based on a similar step-sequencing concept, I've decided to call them *sequencers*. The first is a MIDI sequencer in a more conventional sense—it generates a series of notes at varying pitches. The second is in the business of chopping up an incoming audio and sending it out transformed in a variety of ways.

Mono Sequencer

The Mono Sequencer offers a different approach to MIDI sequencing. Instead of using MIDI clips to sequence devices, the Mono Sequencer allows you to use an approach based on the step sequencers from the early days of analog. While this might seem like a limited way to program parts at first, what you may find is that its limited tool set and approach sends you off into unexpected areas and gets you making parts you might not have otherwise come up with.

The Mono Sequencer (see Figure 13.14) is organized around a main window that displays the steps of the sequencer (16 by default). At the bottom of the window is the step-enable area, which is used to determine whether or not a note will be sent at that step. Above is an area for editing five parameters of each step: pitch, velocity, octave, duration, and repeat. Repeat determines how many rapid-fire repeats of the note occur in the step. Even at the lowest value, the repeats are *really* fast and generate buzzing, machine-gun type effects.

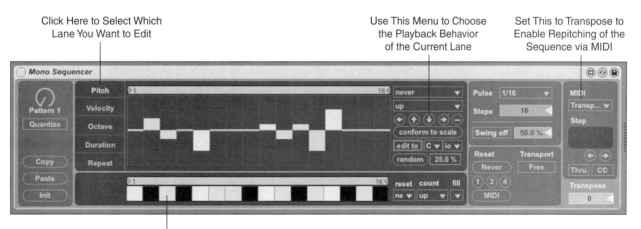

Figure 13.14 Try creating MIDI sequences using Mono Sequencer instead of MIDI clips. Then create MIDI clips to transpose the sequences as they play!
Source: Ableton

One of the very cool and unusual things about this sort of step sequencing is that you can decide to play the sequence forward, backward, or even randomly. Each parameter can have its own behavior, so you could have the octave sequence play in random order, while the pitch plays backward and forward. It's true that 16 steps may not sound like much, but techniques like this allow you to generate quite a lot of variety from a small amount of programming.

Also of particular interest is the way that Mono Sequencer handles MIDI input. By default, it is set to Transpose, which re-pitches the entire sequence based on note input. This makes the mono sequencer into a very powerful tool, a sort of arpeggiator on steroids. You can experiment to create cool patterns and then grab your MIDI keyboard and turn these patterns into bass lines or leads. In the Transpose and Gate setting, the sequencer will only run as long as a note is held down, as opposed to standard Transpose mode, which keeps the steps running all the time.

Also be aware of the Pattern knob at the upper-left corner. Turn this, and you'll discover that this device can hold up to 12 totally unique sequences. The Pattern knob is an enormously powerful performance control. Not only do you have transposable, randomizable sequences, but you can also switch between them with the turn of a knob. My one piece of advice when you start playing with this device is to make sure that your loved ones can reach you, as you may disappear for several weeks.

Buffer Shuffler

The Buffer Shuffler is an experimental, glitchy beast that may not make a lot of sense at first. If you find that to be the case, first get your head around Mono Sequencer, and you'll have an easier time with it. Instead of generating a sequence of MIDI notes, this device takes incoming audio, divides it into slices, and then transforms each slice using a step-sequencing paradigm.

The centerpiece of Buffer Shuffler is a grid that displays a user-adjustable number of steps (see Figure 13.15). These steps represent how many slices the incoming audio will be divided into. The individual steps can then be modified in a variety of ways. The default view is used to rearrange the slices. (This view is labeled Left, which refers to the left channel of the stereo signal. By default, the left and right channels are linked, but you can unlink them if you want to rearrange the two channels independently.)

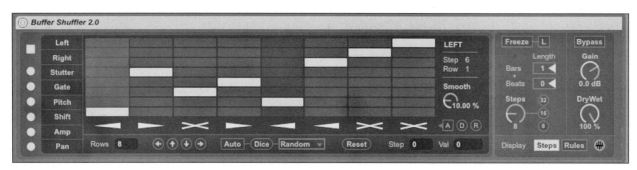

Figure 13.15 Buffer Shuffler: gateway to glitched-out mayhem.
Source: Ableton

Move the blocks up or down to determine which slice gets played on which step. The default diagonal pattern plays the slices in order; move them up or down to trigger earlier or later slices on a given step. Below each step is an arrow or an X, which determines the direction of a particular slice and whether or not it is muted. Click to cycle between forward, backward, and mute.

Along the left of the grid are the other parameters that can be sequenced. These are basic parameters, such as Amp (volume), and special effects, such as Shift and Stutter. Click on one to reveal a sequencer for this parameter. Along the bottom of each view, you'll see a Min and Max value for specifying the range across which the parameter can be sequenced.

For example, when Gate is selected, you can move a block upward to allow more of the slice to play, while moving it to the bottom mutes it completely. With Shift selected, you can move a block upward to increase the amount of frequency shift that is applied, or move it to the bottom to bypass the effect on that step. Get a feel for how these parameters work, and the others will be easy to figure out.

Below the grid is a button marked Dice, which is used to transform the sequence for the currently displayed parameter. Select Random in the adjacent menu and click Dice to generate a random pattern, or Permute to apply limited randomization to an existing pattern. You'll also find options to shift the pattern in a variety of other ways (left, right, invert, and so on). Click Auto to automatically Dice the parameters every time the sequence cycles around.

Convolution Reverb

For some, this device alone may be worth the upgrade to Max for Live. Convolution is a technology that allows the ambience of a space to be re-created from an audio sample called an *impulse response* (or IR). Not limited to real spaces, impulse responses can be created from hardware effects units or synthesized to generate wild, new Reverb and Delay effects.

Convolution Reverb is the basic version of this effect, while Convolution Reverb Pro offers more comprehensive tweaking at the cost of greater CPU usage (see Figure 13.16). To get started with Convolution Reverb, press Hot-Swap, and the Browser will present you with a long list of presets, based on many different IRs. In the Pro version, presets can be loaded using the two menus at the bottom of the display.

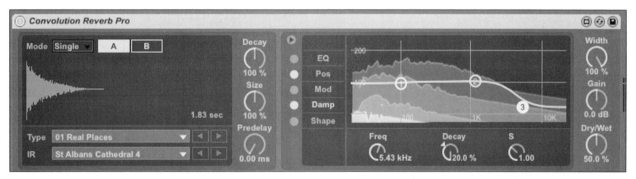

Figure 13.16 A much more powerful alternative to Live's built-in Reverb device.
Source: Ableton

Convolution Reverb Pro also lets you go one step further by selecting Split in the Mode menu above. This allows you to load two different impulses simultaneously—one for the early reflections and one for the reverb tail. The right side of the Pro version can be unfolded to expose several different editors for further tweaking. Damping lets you change the characteristics of the reverb by adjusting which frequencies are absorbed or reflected by the space, while Modulation can be used to apply subtle pitch effects or full-on chorus. Shape gives you control over the level of the early reflections and allows you to tweak the length of the impulse response with fades.

All of these options make for some very interesting sound design possibilities, but be aware that convolution uses some serious processing power, and each of these modules adds more to the burden. Disable any modules you're not using to save power. Even using the standard version of this effect, you'll find it to be a bit heavy on the CPU. Consider using it on a return track and share the reverb between multiple tracks. Alternately, use it as an insert, and then Freeze and Flatten the track. Doing so opens up all sorts of fun editing possibilities. (Try it!)

Adding More Devices

A quick Internet search for "Max for Live devices" will reveal numerous sites where additional devices can be downloaded, many of them for free. Max for Live devices are files with an extension of .axmd. Strictly speaking, they can be dragged from anywhere on your hard drive and dropped into a Set. Realistically, however, you'll be much better off if you keep them all located in one place. Making a folder in your User Library is the easiest bet.

When moving a Set to a different computer, any Max devices used in the Set must be included with the project. The Collect All and Save command handles this for you, so as long as you execute this command before moving the Project folder, you'll be all set.

Parting Thoughts

As you can imagine, there are many more tricks and tips still waiting for you to discover. There are as many different ways of working with Live as there are different kinds of music. The more time you spend experimenting, the more you will discover what works for you. And that's really all that matters. There's no "right" way to work with Live, just different methods, some of which you will find more efficient and inspirational.

Also, check out Ableton's user forum, which will teach you that no matter what you've learned, someone else is doing things totally differently. Sometimes, you'll pick up tricks that will greatly enhance your workflow, and sometimes you'll just be reminded that finding your own way is the most important thing of all. Either way, you're invited to share your ideas and interact with other Live users. It's a great community to be a part of.

Please visit me at hobo-tech.com for my latest Live tips and musical releases. Feel free to drop a note and let me know about the music you've made with Live. Thanks for reading!

Index